VAN DORN

Department of Archives and History
State of Mississippi

VAN DORN

The Life and Times of a Confederate General

Robert G. Hartje

VANDERBILT UNIVERSITY PRESS

Copyright © 1967 by

VANDERBILT UNIVERSITY PRESS

Library of Congress Catalogue Card Number 67-16280

First Paperback Edition 1994

94 95 96 97   4 3 2 1

ISBN 0-8265-1254-2

Printed in the United States of America

To Martha

Who gave Patience, Encouragement, and Love

Contents

Introduction

*I*N May 1863 death removed from the Confederate command system two of its highest ranking officers. Ironically, death intruded on two careers just as each had reached his pinnacle of success. In Virginia, tragedy overshadowed the Chancellorsville victory as General "Stonewall" Jackson succumbed to wounds accidentally inflicted by his own troops. At Spring Hill, Tennessee, General Earl Van Dorn met death more ignominiously at the hands of an irate physician who claimed that the diminutive Confederate officer had violated his home. Thus departed from the scenes of action two important Confederate commanders—West Pointers, Mexican War heroes, Civil War generals—one a quiet, taciturn, unyielding Virginian; the other a dashing, demonstrative, headstrong Mississippian. The South would honor the one and lament his passing. The other would be lost in the shadow and confusion that surrounded his hectic career and his tragic death.

The American Civil War period suggests many problems that we readily associate with modern war. As challenging as any of these problems in this complex struggle was that of leadership. Unlike twentieth-century wars, this was still a war of personalities, the last in which so many achieved individual distinction, and much of the search in both armies was for men to lead military units, large and small. Men cloaked in obscurity rose rapidly to positions of high command by displaying courage and leadership capabilities in the thick of battle or at the planning table. Others, offered these same opportunities, failed at crucial moments and were relegated to assignments of diminished responsibility. It was not a lack of courage, patriotism, or desire that kept this lesser breed of men from success. Instead, some leadership deficiency, usually too subtle to be distinguished until it was too late, prevented them from earning the glory and honor for which they longed. In the Union army William Rosecrans, Joseph Hooker, Ambrose Burnside, and John Pope never rose to the expectations of their superior officers. John Pemberton, Leonidas Polk, John Hood, and Earl Van Dorn were prominent Southern generals who failed to fulfill the hopes of their fellow countrymen. All of these men earned small niches in the much-written history of the great war, but none ranks among the war's greatest leaders.

Despite their failures, these individuals and others like them often played as conspicuous roles in moments of decision as their more illustrious and successful comrades in arms. Readers of Confederate military history may typify the Southern general as a Lee, a Jackson, or a Stuart; yet much of the outcome of the war was determined by the men who moved the pawns in obscure theaters of operations unaffected in great measure by the grander strategy set forth by the War Department, the President, or the ranking general. Strategic planning is certainly important in war, but as Professor T. Harry Williams said recently, "Tactics is often a more decisive factor than strategy." (*Military Leadership: North and South*, p. 2.) Failing in their tactical assignments, this lesser breed often brought defeat and confusion to well-conceived plans. It was not that they did not try; they just seemed to lack the ability to win. The Civil War was a war of frustrated hopes, and more commanders belong to this group than to that elite few who continually rode and fought to fame and victory.

From no officer was more expected at the outset of hostilities in 1861 than from Earl Van Dorn. Few men of his age had more military experience and prestige. His record of service in the Mexican War and on the Indian border indicated that he possessed courage and definite leadership possibilities. He could almost write his own ticket. He loved the army and was never as happy as when engaged in battle. Handsome, courageous, an excellent horseman, and a personal friend of President Jefferson Davis, he seemed destined for the military glory he so ardently coveted. His early service in the war embellished his record, and in late 1861 he was transferred to the Virginia theater of operations where so many officers were to enshrine their names in the military annals of their country.

But Earl Van Dorn lacked some vital quality as a man and as a general that kept him from achieving the success that his country expected. He and others like him became victims of a too-rapidly expanding army. Because of a shortage of qualified leaders, the Confederacy often bestowed high command upon men who had shown promise only in minor roles of leadership. Often these men, with limited knowledge and abilities, were not able to cope with new and complicated assignments. Responsibilities of high command frustrated them and brought disaster on the battlefield. Confederate history is replete with tragic figures who commanded too many too soon.

Van Dorn failed on both occasions when he was given command of a sizeable army. In both situations he seemed unable to grasp the full dimensions of the larger battlefields. He split his forces and then lost control of his men. Speed, so vital in small unit operations, became his obsession. It worked well when he could survey his entire command, but in larger-scale tactics he seems to have failed to realize that speed had to be coupled with intensive planning to bring success.

Relegated to the secondary role of cavalry commander in Mississippi and Tennessee, he showed courage, energy, and vision as he achieved some success in a type of operation for which he was better adapted. Cavalry came into its own in the West in late 1862, and Earl Van Dorn was one of its most successful commanders. Enemy outposts, railroad lines, bridges, roads, and supply depots were his targets as he continually harassed the armies of Generals U. S. Grant and William Rosecrans and helped hold off their final push. But even in these campaigns, his weaknesses sometimes shone through. Although his battle plans were well conceived and his overall objectives were well chosen, he never seemed to master all the details necessary to bring great success. Van Dorn was a good officer, but he could not adjust well enough to changing situations to be called a great leader.

This book was conceived in the belief that a study of military figures of secondary importance will shed considerable light on the scenes of action in which they participated. A study of Earl Van Dorn reveals certain shortcomings and weaknesses of character that were strong factors in determining the final outcome of the war in the West. Although war records and personal reminiscences of many of the military heroes abound, much of the detail of Van Dorn's personal life remains in obscurity. His somewhat unsavory personal life caused his sister systematically to destroy much of his correspondence that might otherwise have given important insights into his checkered career. Mr.

I. H. F. Claiborne of Port Gibson, Mississippi, Van Dorn's home town, collected many of the remaining personal effects of the general after the war only to have them destroyed in a fire in 1866. The absence of this sort of data often leaves the biographer of the general with important gaps in his narrative.

From the remaining records and correspondence, it is impossible to determine accurately the important childhood developments that shaped his career and personality—such things as his education, his friendships, and the intimate intra-relationships of his immediate family. His courtship, his philosophy of life, his relations with his children, even the true story behind his assassination remain obscure because of lack of source material. Despite the mystery enshrouding these important periods of his life, Van Dorn still stands out as a personality of the war deserving some consideration. He is one of the most prominent figures in the story of the war in the West from 1861 to 1863. More important, though, he represents a counterpart to the Lees, the Johnstons, and the Jacksons as an officer, and on several occasions his presence on the battlefield was as important negatively as theirs was positively.

The material presented has been meticulously researched and carefully studied. The Bibliography supplies the sources for that material which is not indicated by footnotes. In the best interest of the reader, only the direct quotation and questionable issues have footnotes in the book. If the reader has further need of source information, he is encouraged to write the author.

This work was begun under the direction of the late Frank L. Owsley, whose inspiring teaching on the Civil War is well remembered by those fortunate enough to have been in his classes. Professors Herbert Weaver and Henry Lee Swint of Vanderbilt University made valuable contributions to the manuscript and were patient counselors of the author during much of the early research. Mr. John R. Peacock of High Point, North Carolina, contributed much important information, and Professor William Coyle of Wittenberg University corrected many errors in grammar and syntax. I am also indebted to Professor Bell I. Wiley of Emory University, Professor Nat C. Hughes of Memphis, and Professors Charles Chatfield and Albert Hayden of Wittenberg for facts and suggestions that improved the narrative. I wish also to thank the staffs of the Vanderbilt, Wittenberg, and Yale libraries; Mrs. Morton Parsley and Peter Brannon of the Tennessee and Alabama State Libraries, respectively.

and the staff of The Infantry School Library at Fort Benning, Georgia. To the Danforth Foundation I owe thanks for time to put words and thoughts together, and to my family I offer my deepest appreciation for enduring and offering encouragement in the darkest moments of research and writing. Thanks, also, to the Vanderbilt University Press, especially to Miss Elizabeth Chase, for editorial assistance and encouragement.

Robert G. Hartje
Wittenberg University

VAN DORN

CHAPTER ONE

The Mississippian

*A*BOUT halfway from Vicksburg to Natchez, the North Fork of Bayou Pierre joins the less conspicuous South Fork and then meanders off through marshes and swamps until it finally empties into the Mississippi River about twelve miles away. Nearly a mile south of the point of confluence sits a picturesque and historic little town, Port Gibson, Mississippi. Named for the man who donated the town site, the community flourished early in the nineteenth century in the midst of the lucrative Mississippi cotton culture. Though not a river port in its own right, Port Gibson achieved distinction as a trading center by being joined to the Mississippi River commerce by bayou, road, and isolated trail. Thus the little town prospered by its nearness to the lifeline of early Western transportation and trade while avoiding the bustle and confusion so often associated with true river communities. A well-planned little town of that day, Port Gibson contained ornamental shade trees along broad streets, churches, a splendid courthouse, several academies, and many handsome residences. In those beautiful colonial homes, wealth and luxury abounded, and Negro servants toiled in a world of ante-bellum planter aristocracy.

Today on a knoll of a plateau just outside the town, there stands a spacious, square, double-brick mansion, commanding an excellent sweep of the valley off toward the river. Still a prominent landmark of the sleepy little Southern community, it is now very much in need of complete renovation. Such was not the case in 1820. Then it was a prominent and admired structure known locally as "The Hill." Its occupants were well-known citizens of the community, the Peter Van Dorns.

The Van Dorns always took great pride in their home. Inside the house were specially selected elaborate furnishings and decorations in harmony with the times but somewhat unusual for the frontier. The

3

new blended beautifully with the old. Venetian slats above the tops of all the first-floor windows controlling the flow of air into the rooms added an arrangement well advanced for its day. Other furnishings were less modern but in good taste.[1]

Outside the house, paved walks lined with jonquils and towering trees and a spacious well-kept garden of fruit trees and vegetables added to the rustic beauty of the entire estate. To the rear of the mansion a carriage lane ran through a grove of poplars where neighbors often observed the family carriage, driven by a well-dressed Negro slave, wending its way laboriously around its twisting curves toward the village down below.

The Van Dorns of "The Hill" were not only prominent residents of Port Gibson; they were a family with a history. They traced their ancestral background to prominent European forebears. One of them, a Baron Van Doorn, was an important sixteenth-century Dutch landowner who served for a time as Lord High Chancellor to the King of Holland. Descendants of the baron immigrated to America in the seventeenth century where they became land owners and community leaders in New Jersey. In the middle of the eighteenth century one of their number, Jacob Van Dorn, might have become the family's first Westerner but for the circumstances of his only frontier experience. Caught up by the restless spirit of adventure which possessed so many of the male members of his family, he purchased a thousand acres of land near what is now Cincinnati, Ohio. Bidding farewell to his family he traveled to the site of his purchase with hopes of settling there, but upon his arrival at his prospective home he was so shocked by the wildness of the area that he promptly changed his mind. It was with no regret that he sold his tract of land hastily for five dollars and a silver watch and departed abruptly for New Jersey. It was a long walk to the East coast, and it was on the East coast that he would remain. He would leave it to his son, Peter, to conquer the West. For his own part Jacob settled permanently in New Jersey, became a successful business man, and lived to a ripe old age as the patriarch of a large clan.

Peter A. Van Dorn was born in New Jersey on September 12, 1773,

1. Much of the background information on the Van Dorn family can be found in His Comrades, *A Soldier's Honor: With Reminiscences of Major-General Earl Van Dorn*, hereinafter cited as *A Soldier's Honor*. This is a published defense of Earl Van Dorn which contains excerpts from letters, papers, and conversations concerning the late general as compiled by his sister, Emily Van Dorn Miller.

the firstborn of Jacob's children. Even in his youth he too displayed the distinctive family restlessness. As a student at Princeton he studied for the ministry, but he never felt a call to the parish; instead, he looked to the West but with more permanent results than his father. After his graduation from college he packed his bags and departed for the lower Mississippi Valley. He is seen first at Natchez, but for unknown reasons he soon moved up the river to Port Gibson. At Port Gibson he did well, quickly establishing himself as a successful merchant and self-made lawyer. An excellent scholar, a prominent Mason, described as a man of unswerving courage Peter was soon much esteemed by his contemporaries. By 1820 Port Gibson and southern Mississippi hailed him as one of the region's brightest leaders. Politicians searched him out for counsel; his friends sought his favor. Meanwhile his own political career had advanced modestly; first, he received a life appointment as Judge of the Orphans' Court for the Southern District of Mississippi and then was elected a member of the state House of Representatives. In 1817 he became Clerk of the House. Four years later the Mississippi Legislature selected him to work with William Lattimore and General Thomas Hines in laying out Jackson as the state's capital city.[2]

While at Natchez, Peter Van Dorn married Sophie Donelson Caffery, a native of North Carolina, a recent immigrant to Mississippi. Sophie, too, had a prominent family background; her father was Captain John Caffery, a daring frontiersman who entered Tennessee with Colonel John Donelson in 1780. The most famous member of her family was her aunt, Rachel, who made her mark in history as the wife of Andrew Jackson. Local tradition around Port Gibson was that General Jackson always had a warm affection for his wife's niece, possibly because of the striking resemblance of the two women.[3]

2. *Mississippi*, American Guide Series, p. 122. In 1829 when the legislature gave the governor the authority to appoint an educational committee "to inquire into all the means and resources of this state which may or can be applied to the purposes of establishing a general system of education suited to the various local interests of the citizens," the governor chose Judge Van Dorn as one of three appointees. Dunbar Rowland, *The Official and Statistical Register of the State of Mississippi*, p. 137.

3. One of Miss Caffery's sisters was also the mother of a Confederate major general, John George Walker, who later served as a United States consul. Emily Van Dorn said that her mother was a niece of Mrs. Jackson. *A Soldier's Honor*, p. 16. *See also* William W. Clayton, *History of Davidson County, Tennessee*, p. 396; letter of Mr. Edward Caffery of Biloxi, Mississippi, to Mr. John R. Peacock of High Point, North Carolina, July 9, 1954, copy in the possession of this writer. (Mr. Caffery's grandfather was a brother to Earl Van Dorn's mother.)

Earl Van Dorn was born at "The Hill" on September 20, 1820, the fourth child and the first son of Peter and Sophie. He was a handsome child and had a striking personality even as a youth. His sisters welcomed him with enthusiasm, quickly bestowing upon him their affection. From his crib to his youth they mothered him and looked to his every wish. Earl became the center of the family's attention. Somewhat spoiled by this experience, he sought the center of the stage for the remainder of his comparatively short, but full, life.

Of Earl's youth in thriving Port Gibson, little is known except that his was an exciting life in an ever-increasing family. It seemed a secure world there on the Mississippi frontier as planters throughout the valley prospered on cotton, sugar, and slavery. It was a Protestant world, a White world, "a genteel and well-regulated society." As one authority recorded it, "They live profusely; drink costly Port, Madeira, and sherry, after the English fashion, and are exceedingly hospitable."[4] The Van Dorns moved in these circles among the Vertners, the Stamps, the Parkes, the Bertrams—all prominent names. They claimed membership in the Episcopal Church. Like their neighbors they owned well-dressed servants, they rode fine horses, and they entertained lavishly.

In this world Earl Van Dorn spent his childhood. He hunted in the nearby woods and canebreaks; he fished and swam in the nearby streams with the other boys of his own age; a natural horseman, he dashed across the Mississippi countryside astride one of his father's thoroughbreds. Ahead, his future pointed to the gracious life and security of the Mississippi Valley. Or did it? What were the thoughts on the mind of the young rider who rested his mount in the cool shade of the flowering trees after a hot chase across the Mississippi lowlands? Did he dream of the life of the planter? Or did he smell the smoke of battle and dream of man and horse against an unseen enemy? Earl Van Dorn may have dreamed, but it is doubtful if his dreams were of a quiet life in Port Gibson.

In 1829 Sophie Van Dorn died; her end was hastened by excessive childbirth and frontier surgical practices. Of the nine children, six were born in the last nine years. She had been a good wife and mother to her family, always showing greater understanding and compassion than the father whose professional and social affairs often interfered

4. Katherine M. Jones, *The Plantation South*, p. 236.

with his home life. But it was young Earl who demanded and received so much of his mother's attention—Earl of the light flaxen hair and bright steel-blue eyes, so like his father in looks and ambition but so like his mother in temperament, a proud and sensitive youth.

After Mrs. Van Dorn's death great changes came to "The Hill." From father to youngest child they missed the tenderness, the gentleness, the great understanding so much a part of Sophie Van Dorn's world. Responsibility for the welfare of the children now shifted to the less capable hands of the father and his three oldest daughters, Octavia, Mary, and Jane. Octavia, the eldest, took charge. Possessing a high degree of organizational ability, this young lady managed affairs with remarkable efficiency for several years. She could not, however, replace her mother in the affections of her brothers and sisters, especially with sensitive young Earl. Certainly the loss of his mother was a great blow to a youngster not yet ten years old, and it is not difficult to surmise that this loss was a contributing factor to his later erratic and vacillating nature. Though there is no record of an open rift between him and Octavia, his great companion and confidante then as well as in the turbulent years that followed was another sister, Emily.[5]

Octavia continued her dual role as mother and sister until her own marriage, when she left her Mississippi home and moved to Maryland. This was another harsh blow for the Judge, whose health was already failing. Unable to manage his family and his own work, he decided to send his youngest child to live with Octavia, to keep the older girls at home, and to put Earl and Aaron in an academy at Baltimore not too far from sister Octavia. For the first time Earl left his native state.

The loss of his wife and the sorrow of his broken home weighed heavily upon Judge Van Dorn. His health soon broke completely under the strain of sorrow, age, and overwork, and he died at Port Gibson on February 12, 1837. To the end he cared for his children. All of them he remembered in his will. He took special cognizance of the needs of his sons, Earl and Aaron, toward an advanced education by making special provision in his will for them to enter the National College at Washington, D. C., after their graduation from the Baltimore academy.

5. Emily seems to have been very close to Earl. She was his most constant correspondent, and she saved much of his writings as well as that of others who concerned themselves with him.

If Earl respected his father's intentions he left no record of it. His desires were of another sort and for a different type of education, so he remained at the Baltimore school only until he could make another opportunity. To him as to many other Southern boys, the thought of an education at the United States Military Academy held strong appeal. In the world of Southern aristocracy in which he had been raised, the church and the army were the noble professions, and it was to the latter that Earl turned his attention. Under his mother's watchful eye he had begun his formal education, probably at a Port Gibson academy. But outside the classroom he had played at war in the warm Mississippi sun and dreamed his dreams of glory. When he decided definitely upon a military career is not recorded. To his sisters he early confided his hopes for a "profession of arms."[6] This enthusiasm for the military life never waned as he approached young manhood, and West Point became his ideal and hope. By the time he was sixteen he no longer played at war, but he took definite steps toward the realization of his fondest dream. Even before his father's death, he had boldly written to President Andrew Jackson about his military aspirations and requested the President's influence in obtaining an appointment to the United States Military Academy.

At first he received no reply from "Uncle Andrew," and the dreams of the youth clouded in months of frenzied waiting. Shaken by the death of his father, young Earl, sensitive lad that he was, suffered prolonged periods of melancholy as he awaited word from his application. Then it came! At the moment that the letter of appointment reached him, the dejected young man sat under a tree on the Baltimore academy playground lamenting his fate.

If Earl dreaded the grimness of life behind the long gray walls at West Point, he gave no indications of such fears. In late June 1838, he packed his bags for his departure. There would be stresses and strains as he adapted to the new life on the Hudson River, but one suspects that the boy who boarded the stagecoach for New York embarked upon this new life eagerly. On July 1, 1838, he became a soldier and enthusiastically embraced the military profession for the rest of his life.

The young Mississippian presented a fine appearance as he entered the military academy. Although he was less than five feet eight inches

6. *A Soldier's Honor*, p. 17.

tall, his short stature was compensated by his striking features and near-perfect physique. Piercing blue eyes set off his handsome face and wavy blond hair. He carried himself well—his head back, a slight swagger in his walk. Even at the threshold of his military career, he looked every part the soldier.

Earl Van Dorn could hardly have picked a more appropriate time to enter West Point. The academy had just passed through one of the most painful ordeals in its early history—an unsuccessful Congressional move to wipe it out of existence. Although its merits as an educational institution were perennially questioned by Congress, its permanency was assured after this encounter. West Point was coming of age, and would-be generals sat in her drab classrooms and learned the mysteries of the art of war. Together the cadets listened to the finest professional staff the academy had thus far assembled: men who attempted with some degree of success to incorporate into their instruction both the needs of the American frontier and the Napoleonic influences of the European military schools.

Foremost among the professors from whom Earl learned the arts of war was Dennis H. Mahan, an 1824 West Point graduate, a first-rate engineer whose European training had led him to the study of the great continental engineers: Napoleon, Jomini, Vauban, and Cormontaigne. Other professors of note who taught the young cadet during his four years on the Hudson included William H. C. Bartlett, a nineteenth-century scientist of note; Albert C. Church, a mathematician who published many important works during his long period of West Point service; Jacob W. Bailey, professor of chemistry, inventor, and pioneer in microscopic investigation; and Robert W. Weir, artist of note and professor of drawing at the academy from 1837 to 1879. The influence of these teachers upon young men destined to fight two major wars is incalculable. American and foreign observers expressed open admiration for West Point's "quality of education," but the greatest testimony for the academy came from the actions of its graduates. It was not by chance that her graduates commanded in every major engagement of the Civil War and most of the time, in both armies.

Despite its strengths, West Point had one glaring deficiency—one that became evident only under the stress of a greater war than any imagined by teacher or pupil in those training days—one that affected many a young officer too hastily placed in command of a large military unit in the field of battle. Because of the peculiar military needs of the new nation, the United States Military Academy before the Civil War offered little training to prepare young men for high command in the broader aspects of leadership required in a war of greater dimensions than isolated frontier engagements. Generally, its instruction in strategy and tactics stressed small-unit operations. For the most part the curriculum neglected the science of war involving administration, logistics, and grand strategy. Walter L. Millis described the training in terms of "the military fundamentals: honor, initiative, physical courage, the ability to obey orders, to take care of one's men and to get up the ammunition and the rations."[7] This lack of training in the theory of command sorely handicapped graduates, especially those like young Earl Van Dorn who had little inclination to pursue such studies on their own initiative.

This weakness was more the fault of the academy than of the individual student, however. Unfortunately for the cadets, they faced little direct contact with the writings of the leading European military authorities of their day that offered substantial theories on the study of war. Cadets could read the early works of Baron Antoine Henri Jomini, Karl von Clausewitz, and others in the academy library, but little effort was made to incorporate these works into the requirements for graduation, and insufficient attention was given to them in class recitation. It is not that these European thinkers had the final answers in tactics or strategy for budding young American officers-to-be, but these men had studied war on a grander scale and had participated in and analyzed some of the greatest actions of the century. Because the cadets daily encountered heavy assignments and long drill periods, only the most diligent found time to spend on those ponderous untranslated sources.

Naturally some of the European influence rubbed off on the chief American military training institution. In recent scholarship on the American Civil War, much has been made of the influence of those European theorists, especially of Baron Jomini, on commanders in both the Union and Confederate armies. Professor T. Harry Williams considers Jomini's influence "profound," one which "must be taken into account in any evaluation of Civil War generalship."[8] Professor David

7. *Arms and Men*, p. 95.
8. Quoted in Donald, *Why the North Won the Civil War*, p. 28.

Donald is even more emphatic: "[T]he military history of the first two years of the war reads like little more than exegesis of Jomini's theories."[9] Even some of the participants in the war recognized the importance of the Swiss officer's influence. In an official order issued from his headquarters in Memphis, Tennessee in July 1862, General William T. Sherman gave testimony to this influence: "Should any officer, high or low," he wrote, "after the opportunity and experience we have had, be ignorant of his [Jomini's] tactics, regulations, or even the principles of the Art of War, it would be a lasting disgrace."[10]

Chief interpreter of Jomini's theories at West Point during Van Dorn's cadet days and for many years afterward was Professor Dennis H. Mahan, whose own writings smack heavily of the influence of the Swiss military expert. Before Van Dorn's time the cadets had studied Jomini's writings, but these important works were dropped from academy requirements because of their difficulty except for abridgements and Mahan's lectures. Professor T. Harry Williams says that Mahan did little more than just reproduce Jomini's ideas.[11]

But the question remains: were Mahan's interpretations of the complex Napoleonic strategy and tactics an adequate substitute for the originals? Were the cadets not shortchanged in the Academy's emphasis on small units and on what amounted to a limited interpretation of larger-scale actions by Professor Mahan? Jomini's was an anatomical analysis, more "a post-mortem analysis rather than a creative work for the future." If studied without the later developments that stemmed from them, even later writings of the same officer, these theories tended to fix upon the commander the "geometrical aspects of military operations, in lulling them [the commanders] into ignoring the effects of technological developments and the psychological aspects of the art of war."[12] Professor Williams has gone so far as to suggest that Professor Mahan was a poor substitute for studying Jomini because he presented too narrow an interpretation of his complex program of action. Mahan, possibly concentrating on the small unit wars which were anticipated

9. Donald, *Lincoln Reconsidered*, p. 90.

10. United States War Department, *The War of the Rebellion: A Compilation of the Official Records of the Union and Confederate Armies*, Ser. I, Vol. XVII, Part 2, p. 119; hereinafter cited as *Official Records Army* (Unless otherwise indicated, all citations are to Series I.)

11. *Military Leadership: North and South*, p. 9.

12. R. Ernest Dupuy, *The Story of West Point*, pp. 195–196.

for West Point graduates, stressed too much "celerity of movement." Embracing Jomini's "rapidity of movement" and concentration of force caused neglect of other principles that in the long run may have been more important. The Swiss general also spoke of taking care of your own supply and communications lines even while menacing the enemy's. In the hands of a rash young commander with a one-dimensional mind, too much emphasis on speed could be disastrous. This was exactly the case of Earl Van Dorn and many, many others in the American Civil War.

Whether a more intensive and comprehensive study of the theories of war would have changed Van Dorn's military career for the better cannot be determined. Certainly later he suffered in the field as much from his own inability to comprehend and effectively apply the lessons he had received as he did from the limitations of the education. He was no military genius; this is now obvious. Few American commanders in that war were. Van Dorn was one of those officers German Field Marshall Maurice de Saxe once categorized when he said: "Unless a man is born with a talent for war, he will never be other than a mediocre general."[13]

But neither was Van Dorn a complete failure. As an officer leading small units, his leadership in three wars was commendable—sometimes exceptional. When his training was adequate, he was fairly successful. Well versed in military engineering and indoctrinated by Mahan's *Treatise on Field Fortifications*, he did an excellent job in defending Vicksburg during the summer of 1862. Mahan had written: "[P]lace the militia soldier on his natural field of battle, behind a breastwork, and an equilibrium between him and his more disciplined enemy is immediately established."[14] At Vicksburg Van Dorn followed his teacher's advice by properly employing partisan rangers in the city's defense. Well trained at the academy in small unit cavalry tactics and a superb horseman in his own right, the Mississippian also proved himself a capable commander in mounted infantry or cavalry actions.

But confronted with large-scale planning or with troops maneuvering from several positions, Van Dorn seemed to lack that fine edge that makes great generals. At the battles of Pea Ridge, Arkansas, and Corinth, Mississippi, he split his large attacking forces before the enemy,

13. Quoted in Donald, *Why the North*, p. 25.
14. Dennis H. Mahan, *A Treatise on Field Fortifications*, p. vi.

and in each instance he eventually lost proper control of his army. Had he known and properly applied Jomini's guiding principle of concentration of forces upon the decisive point of battle more effectively in each case, he might have recorded significant victories. Some knowledge of Clausewitz might have been even more helpful. Would he have fought these battles with part of his troops uncommitted if he had been on intimate terms with the German's concept of economy of forces? "Whoever has part of his forces . . . [unused] while the enemy's are fighting, is a bad manager of his forces."[15]

But even when familiar with tactical lessons, Van Dorn often erred. He attacked at Pea Ridge, taking the battle to a well-entrenched enemy with an undisciplined army. Why did he not heed Mahan's warning? "To suppose irregular forces capable of coping on equal terms with disciplined troops is to reason, not only against all probability, but against a vast weight of testimony to the contrary."[16]

In Van Dorn's failures in these two battles, there is evidence of both personal weakness and shallowness of academic training. Certainly he had been taught to scout his field of attack, yet in each case he had not reconnoitered properly. Was it his own deficiency or was it poor teaching that failed to impress upon him a more intimate knowledge of the arts of war? Did he not know, or was he just unable to apply the three basic principles stressed in all of Jomini's writings? These principles were that battles could be won only when men were in proper position to fight, when outposts were established to keep constant contact with the enemy, and when communications lines were free and open at all times. Whether success would have been guaranteed in Van Dorn's case with proper application of these principles it is impossible to say, but failure came when they were violated. Van Dorn, like too many other Civil War generals, had been trained for command of the small unit. The exigencies of large-scale war brought these men too quickly into situations that demanded more than their capabilities. These failures were the failures of men and of their educational system. Their failures color the history of the Civil War as much as the glorious victories of their more illustrious comrades in arms.

As can be suspected by now, Earl Van Dorn's record as a cadet was

15. Dallas D. Irvine, "The French Discovery of Clausewitz and Napoleon," *Studies on War*, p. 20.

16. Mahan, *A Treatise*, p. v.

spotty. It was his own lack of incentive that prevented him from digging deep into the military classics as did Robert E. Lee, P. G. T. Beauregard, and Henry W. Halleck when they were students at the Academy. West Point men of his day remembered young Earl well but not as a student. To them he was a small, handsome, hot-headed youth, "literally at the foot of his class."[17] Although he was a member of one of the most distinguished classes to be graduated from the Academy, his own record as a cadet was not impressive. In fact, he and James Longstreet seemed to vie for the lowest rank in the class. At the end of Earl's first year his only achievement of note was his rank near the top of his class in drawing, one of the comparatively new subjects in the school's curriculum.

Behind classroom doors West Point lost some of its luster for the young man. He wrote to his sister in his first year that he felt it impossible after exercising, studying hard, and drilling extensively "to sit down and write with fresh spirit to anyone." "Life is monotonous here," he said, adding that he needed "something to dissipate a heavy cloud of melancholy." It was not that his dreams of glory had been stifled. It was only that to the active, ambitious lad West Point had for the time become a prison, an obstacle to realizing his hopes and dreams. If only he could get into active service, he lamented, then he might write of "hairbreadth escapes in the deadly breach."[18]

Dressed in the uncomfortable uniform of the cadet, strait-jacketed in a program of rigidity, constantly inspected and harassed by officers and upperclassmen, stifled by regulations, the breaking of which added demerits to the cadet's record, the young cadet found life difficult indeed. For young Earl, accustomed as he was to the freedom of his Mississippi home, the ordeal was at times almost unbearable. His dissatisfactions, coupled with his natural fiery disposition, led to many disciplinary disturbances, so many in fact that during his third year he accumulated 193 demerits. Accumulating 200 demerits in a single year meant immediate dismissal.

What young Earl did to rate so many demerits is impossible to say, but at least one possibility looms large. About a mile from the Academy, infamous Benny Havens ran a pub which, though officially off-limits to

17. Henry Coppee, *Grant and His Comrades*, p. 133.
18. *A Soldier's Honor*, p. 15.

cadets, was a spot frequented by them. There is no definite record of Earl's visiting the "House by the River," but since nearly all the cadets, including Grant and his close friend, Longstreet, were at least occasional visitors, it can be suspected that Earl also knew the famous sport of "running it to Havens." Frequent visitors to Buttermilk Falls, the location of the tavern, were the members of the Independent Roysterers Club, a score of cadets secretly organized "to promote social intercourse."[19] The only member of this club ever officially identified was one of Earl's classmates, Richard W. Johnson, but it is suspected that most of the other members were also of the Class of 1842. Earl's membership cannot be definitely established, but the events of his later life and the excessive number of demerits he received at the academy make him a likely candidate for membership.

Although he accumulated 183 demerits in his senior year, Earl improved his grades slightly and finished fifty-second in the class of fifty-six, ahead of Longstreet who had to settle for last place. Earl's best grades in his graduating year were in infantry tactics for small units and in drawing; outside the classroom he excelled in horsemanship and field soldiering. As a skilled horseman he must have shared moments with Cadet Sam Grant, also a horseman of note who often distinguished himself with spectacular efforts on an Academy mount.

It was an interesting class that assembled at West Point on July 1, 1842, to receive their diplomas. Handsomely dressed in their gray cadet uniforms with the brass buttons shining and their boots blackened, these young men marched through the graduating line to become one of the most distinguished classes in the history of that institution. Fourteen members of the group eventually became generals. One of them, William S. Rosecrans, reaching that rank in the Union army, later opposed Van Dorn, by then a general in the Confederate army, in a bloody Mississippi engagement. John Pope, number seventeen in the class, was Earl's opponent at Farmington, Mississippi. Another member, Gustavus W. Smith, as a Confederate general, competed with him for an assignment in Virginia in 1861. Van Dorn relieved Mansfield Lovell and Martin Luther Smith as commanders at Vicksburg in the summer of 1862. Other outstanding members of the class included four Union major-generals: Abner Doubleday, John Newton, George Sykes, and

19. Dupuy, *West Point*, pp. 187–193.

Seth Williams; three Confederate lieutenant-generals: Richard H. Anderson, Daniel H. Hill, and James Longstreet; and Confederate Major-General Lafayette McLaws. Two members of the class were killed in Mexico: George Mason near Fort Brown and Calvin Benjamin while fighting near Van Dorn in the American attack on Mexico City.

Earl's low grades left him no choice in his branch of the service. His first assignment was as an infantry lieutenant in the Seventh Infantry Regiment at Fort Pike, Louisiana, on the Gulf of Mexico. Reporting there in September after a graduation leave, the young man got his first taste of active service. From the beginning it appears that he enjoyed field duty. The West Point melancholy disappeared, but his longings were still for the feel of battle. Nevertheless, his future was with the army; many of his contemporaries served only their required time in the armed forces and then departed to more lucrative positions in civilian life. Earl Van Dorn took his career seriously like many young Southerners who came to West Point in proportionately larger numbers than their Northern colleagues; a greater percentage also remained on active duty after graduation.

In December the War Department transferred the Seventh Infantry to Alabama, where Van Dorn alternated his service for the next two years between Fort Morgan and the Mount Vernon Arsenal. The young lieutenant was described at the time as being handsome and having regular features, fine blue eyes, and wavy blond hair. He had kept his fine physique and poise and was still an excellent horseman, well liked by fellow officers for his conviviality.

Earl's status as a lady's man, for which he later acquired considerable renown, is unknown at this time, although he apparently possessed most of the natural attributes. While stationed at Mount Vernon Arsenal, he met and courted the young daughter of a prominent resident of the area, Colonel James D. Godbold. The courtship seems to have taken a whirlwind turn and resulted in a sudden marriage only a few months after their first meeting. Caroline, or Carrie, as the young lady was called, was only sixteen years old at the time, and apparently there was considerable parental objection to the union. When Lieutenant Van Dorn's next assignment took him away from the Alabama area, the parents insisted on Carrie's staying on the home plantation. Consequently, Earl and his wife were apart during the first years of their marriage. They renewed these periods of separation often during the later years of Van Dorn's lifetime, finally to the extent that the two were seldom together. Theirs was a strange relationship, clouded for the biographer by the complexity of Earl's later life and the dearth of their remaining correspondence.

At twenty-three the turmoil that was to mark so much of Earl's restless life had begun. The problem of living outside West Point was proving as difficult as living within the Academy's walls. But young Earl had achieved his first goal: he was an officer in the United States Army, assigned to a crack infantry regiment. He now had only to make his mark.

CHAPTER TWO

The Mexican War

*T*HE Mexican War was the first major conflict in which graduates of the United States Military Academy put their training to the test of the battlefield. In this strange interlude of imperialistic conquest, West Point established its reputation as an important military training center. Its trainees earned the respect of America's highest ranking officers, few of whom were themselves academy trained. During this war the young men of a new generation made their "marks." Commanders in every major engagement of the war recorded their achievements with enthusiasm—their courage before the enemy, their intelligence in planning and reconnoitering, their effectiveness as small-unit commanders. A roster of the successful young officers of the Mexican War reads like a "Who's Who" of the generals from both North and South who directed operations in a greater American war a little over a decade later. It was almost as though the war south of the border was a preliminary for the Civil War. In the actions before determined Mexican armies, the old leaders passed their genius of command to bright young leaders. The new generation responded to the challenge. Motivated by the compulsions of a new age, they began their climbs toward the fame and the glory they coveted.

Among those names cited for gallantry, few stood out above that of Earl Van Dorn. Robert E. Lee, Braxton Bragg, P. G. T. Beauregard, and U. S. Grant rendered more valuable service to the invading Americans, but Jefferson Davis's evaluation was that Van Dorn was "more frequently noticed in the official reports of the battles for gallantry in action . . . than any other officer in that army."[1] Dabney Maury, a

---

1. *The Rise and Fall of the Confederate Government*, II, 388.

close associate of Earl's throughout his army career, spoke the thoughts of many who knew him when he wrote that "no young officer came out of the Mexican War with a reputation more enviable than his."[2]

Despite the frequent appearances of his name in the official reports of his battle commanders, little remains of the personal record of Van Dorn's participation in the Mexican War. Too often one must see him through the actions of his contemporaries, in the movements of his unit and the officers with whom he served, in the scant correspondence from his own pen. Earl Van Dorn was a hero in this war, an active participant in nearly all of its major engagements, but the effect of that war upon his personality and military growth is obscured by this dearth of material. His commanding officers did single him out for praise on many occasions, but our appetites are whetted for more intimate details of the actions that merited such praise.

One combs the many diaries, memoirs, record books, and voluminous correspondence of those trying days, hopeful of some reference to his service, his feelings about the war, and his leadership growth—but too often in vain. Although many of the young officers knew Van Dorn personally then and later, none recorded his intimate actions. Lieutenant Beauregard noted him once in his own diary but in error, referring to him as the "aide" of General John Quitman instead of General P. F. Smith.[3] Important personal narratives that are literally filled with the minutiae of the campaigns seldom, if ever, make reference to him at any time. To the student of the Mexican War, Earl Van Dorn appears only as a shadow in that conflict.

Despite the shallowness of source material on this stage of his development, the fact remains that the Mexican War was an important factor in Van Dorn's growth just as it was in the lives of so many who were destined for greater deeds, and it must be so-considered. In Mexico Earl had his first opportunity to test his courage and his initiative on the battlefield. Here he first tasted glory and earned promotion, honors for which he had probably longed since those lonely hillside rides back in Mississippi. In war the young man knew capable generalship, and he must have recalled many of the actions of those officers when he, too, faced the rigors of high command. In the scant record

2. "Recollections of General Earl Van Dorn," *Southern Historical Society Papers,* XIX, 192.

3. T. Harry Williams (ed.), *With Beauregard in Mexico,* p. 98.

of his achievements and actions in Mexico, something of that war's
influence upon the young man appears. Through these records one
discerns the emerging person, the maturing soldier, if but in shadow.

Van Dorn, like many of his contemporaries, probably had very little
understanding of the true meaning of the Mexican conflict, particularly
in reference to its implications for future United States—Mexican relations. To him war was always personal. As a Southerner he probably
greeted with enthusiasm the chance to add territory that would benefit
his region. As a seeker of fame and glory, he certainly welcomed the
war for the opportunities it offered him to advance his own career.
From his meager correspondence there is the ring of a kindred spirit
to that of ambitious George B. McClellan, also a member of the American expeditionary force. "I came down here," wrote McClellan, "with
high hopes, with pleasing anticipation of distinction, of being in hard
fought battles, and acquiring a name and reputation as a stepping stone
to a still greater eminence in some future and greater war."[4]

Van Dorn echoed these sentiments in a letter to his sister in 1846.
Writing from a barrel top in desolate Camargo he spoke with boyish
enthusiasm:

> Don't you poor helpless female population wish you were men that you
> might snatch a sword and join in the game for glory? What does the gambler
> know of excitement who has millions at stake on a card? He loses but mil-
> lions. . . . But here *life* is to lose—glory to win. Who can know what the bosom
> feels, how the heart swells with burning emotions, hopes, proud longings for
> distinction.[5]

If Van Dorn did not understand the true meaning of the Mexican
War, he should not be judged harshly for this fact. This war began in
a flurry of excitement and confusion, and it ran its course under similar
circumstances. Tension between the United States and Mexico had increased during the closing days of President John Tyler's administration over Texas's wish to join the Union. The lame duck Congress of
1844, accepting the election of James K. Polk to the Presidency as a
mandate from the American people to bring fruition to Texas's hopes,
passed a joint resolution offering statehood to that beleaguered territory. This action shocked the Mexican Government, and her minister

4. William S. Meyers (ed.), *The Mexican War Diary of George B. McClellan,*
p. 17.
5. Earl Van Dorn to Octavia, July 20, 1846, *A Soldier's Honor,* p. 23.

departed abruptly from Washington in protest. Anticipating that Texas would accept the offer of the joint resolution and become a state "entitled to defense and protection from foreign invasion," the United States War Department ordered the transfer to Texas of an American "task force" which had recently been organized at Fort Jesup, Louisiana. This force, commanded by rugged old Zachary Taylor, contained some of the finest "regulars" in the American Army. In July 1845, these troops moved by boat from New Orleans to St. Joseph Island off the coast of Texas. Here they remained two weeks. Then on July 31, to protect the Texas border against the unlikely event of a Mexican attack, General Taylor crossed the Nueces River and bivouacked his army at the little village known as Corpus Christi.

Mexican officials, looking at the Nueces River as the furthermost United States boundary, lashed out verbally at this "protective occupation," warning loudly that further advance toward the Rio Grande would be *casus belli*. Taylor watched and waited, seemingly unconcerned about the enemy so close to his own camp, all the while gathering more and more troops into his command.

Lieutenant Van Dorn arrived at Corpus Christi on August 30 as a member of the Seventh Infantry Regiment. He had spent a two-month leave with his wife in her Alabama home early in the year before joining his regiment at Fort Pickens, Florida. Then from Pickens he had journeyed to Corpus Christi via Fort Jesup. As with the other young officers, Van Dorn welcomed these moves, always hopeful that they were leading toward a quick and decisive showdown with the Mexicans.

General Taylor's prolonged stay at Corpus Christi denied immediate action to his "task force" members. Cautioned against rashness and urged to treat any Mexican advance across the Nueces with "punctilious courtesy," the old general initiated no offensive whatsoever, awaiting action from the diplomatic front.[6] As he delayed, impatient troops chafed in Texas heat and rain and prepared for the ordeals of a long campaign. Weary, toilsome hours on the drill field, dismal nights in their damp blankets, dangerous missions through rattlesnake-infested thickets—these were the duties of the soldiers. Their battles were against insects, illness, and raspy-voiced commanders who ever urged them through the monotonous routines of field duty. They ate fish and pork and beans; they complained about their food, their mail, the shortage

6. Justin H. Smith, *The War with Mexico*, I, 124.

of women; but they shaped up into a formidable force. Discipline was necessarily harsh, for this was the largest body of regulars that had been assembled since the Revolutionary War, and the inexperienced officers found commanding large numbers of ill-disciplined troops a most difficult undertaking.

Most exasperating of all to both officers and enlisted men were the long periods of inactivity. "Nothing is seen or heard [here]," wrote Lieutenant George G. Meade, "but the regular sounds of the drum, sending the men to bed, and the shouts of drunken men in the little town . . ."[7] A few horse races enlivened the dreariness of the Texas winter, and on one occasion a company of strolling actors entertained an appreciative soldier audience. But in their tents, with the northern wind whistling about them, the men talked of war. Would Mexico fight? When?

1845 ended, and still General Taylor awaited word from Washington as to his next move. Meanwhile, negotiations for a peaceful settlement between the two antagonists was coming to an end. Early in 1846 military action took priority over diplomacy when Secretary of War William L. Marcy directed Taylor to move his army south to the Rio Grande River as soon as it could be done conveniently with reference to the season and the routes by which this movement would proceed. Soldiers cheered this news lustily, and on March 8, 1846, they eagerly began the 150-mile march, the first phase of an American campaign that would lead all the way to the capital city of Mexico.

General Taylor made his first contact with the Mexican Army on March 20 at Arroyo Colorado where General Francisco Mejia, commanding the Mexican forces, placed his army across the path of the advancing Americans and threatened their progress. Mejia wanted to attack Taylor at this point and probably would have if he had not received orders to the contrary. His alternative action was to bluff the invaders by threatening to fire on them if they advanced beyond their Corpus Christi base. Taylor was not deceived by the bluff and proceeded unmolested to Point Isabel where he ordered the immediate construction of a temporary supply depot. Leaving a few troops to guard this new base, the old general marched his other troops to the Rio Grande, arriving opposite Matamoros on March 28, "with colors

7. *Life and Letters*, pp. 40–41.

flying and music playing," causing much excitement among the populace across the river.[8]

Convinced by the Mexicans' actions that they would soon attack his small army, Taylor ordered his engineers to build a fort on the Rio Grande, "a large bastioned field work opposite the lower end of the city."[9] This redoubt, first named Fort Texas, was a pentagon with bastioned fronts, large enough to take care of an entire army. It was built on a triangular point of land with the river on two sides of it, a poor defensive spot about which Taylor had been warned. It was within the walls of this fort that Lieutenant Van Dorn first tasted combat with an enemy.

Across the river from the new fort the Mexicans were not idle. They had issued their warning, but the Americans had paid them no heed. Under a new and more aggressive commander, General Mariano Arista, they awaited an opportunity to strike at the unwelcome invader. Such an opportunity presented itself on April 24 when Taylor dispatched a party of dragoons to watch enemy proceedings up the river. Mexican troops waited in ambush for the scouting party and then attacked them, killing or wounding sixteen of them and capturing the rest, including Captain William Hardee. This was the signal for which the restless troops in both camps had been waiting. Both armies prepared for action.

The Mexicans moved first. Striking out in what he hoped to be a surprise move, General Arista took the initiative by marching most of his army north around the American position. He designed the operation with the specific intention of cutting off Taylor's supply and communications lines. Taylor responded to this threat with a decision to split his own force before the enemy. Most of his army he led directly toward Arista's army. The Seventh Infantry Regiment he left to garrison his river fort. Then while he maneuvered to keep his lines to his supply base open, veteran campaigner, Major Jacob Brown, took charge of the Fort Texas defenses, preparing hastily for an attack from across the river.

Brown's garrison of fewer than 500, including the sick and the lame of the army, cheered their departing comrades and then turned to their

8. George A. McCall, *Letters from the Frontiers*, p. 438.
9. Smith, *The War with Mexico*, I, 148.

more serious task of preparing their half-completed fort for defense. Lieutenants Braxton Bragg and George Thomas brought the four eighteen-pounders into position, and infantrymen built fortifications for protection. Even the tents were cut up and made into sandbags.

The Mexicans at Matamoros opened their attack at daybreak on May 3. Their artillery pieces, which they had cradled behind crude parapets, opened fire, and their deafening peals echoed along the windings of the Rio Grande as they poured shot and shell against the walls of Fort Texas. Quickly Bragg and Thomas returned their fire. Firing continued heavy but ineffective on both sides for the remainder of the day, and the Americans dug in, almost hoping for a direct assault. The Mexicans had no plans for crossing the river, however, and they contented themselves with their wild and inaccurate firing.

For six days the Mexicans continued their long-range bombardment with no better results than those of the first day. More effective were the continuous insults they hurled across the narrow stream, barbs which prompted greater efforts from the fort's defenders. The Americans held on doggedly, their morale high, their casualty rate low.

Despite this good fortune, life was not easy within the walls of the poorly constructed fort. For all the defenders it was sleepless nights and smoke-filled days. And though there were only two battle casualties, they were important ones. During the first day's action a Mexican ball decapitated a sergeant at his post. Then on the third day of the siege, another ball took off the leg of Major Brown; he died on May 9.

Though not mentioned for honors in any of the official reports of this siege nor included among the five officers who were given brevets after the attack, Lieutenant Van Dorn had a small taste of glory during the engagement. Captain Hawkins, acting commander of the fort after the death of Major Brown, mentioned no name when he reported the incident, but all evidence points to Van Dorn as the man involved. Hawkins's statement is in part:

During the . . . night the halyards of the flag on the outside had become unrigged, and, as the firing had become too intense to re-establish them, a temporary staff was erected on the inside, and the national flag of the Seventh Infantry raised as a substitute. . . . [The following day] an officer of the Seventh succeeded in lowering the topmast and rigging the halyards, but found he could not raise it again without great labor and exposure; he therefore lashed it in position, and raised the national flag, after having stood a succession of round shot, canister, and shells from the enemy's batteries for fifteen or twenty minutes.[10]

Another version of the event was more profuse in its praise and more specific in its reference to Van Dorn. According to this version, recorded later by Earl's sister, the flag fell in front of the fort during the night. When volunteers were called for to rescue it, Van Dorn led the way. Then

amid a storm of shot and shell, tearing up the ground at his feet, he triumphantly raised the flag, flung it to the breeze, and returned to the fort unharmed, amidst shouts of applause from his comrades."[11]

Van Dorn's own version of the flag rescue supports the evidence that this was indeed an exciting experience:

During the bombardment of Fort Brown, I had the honor to be shot at several times *outside* of the fort, when I went out to hoist the stars and stripes, which were some hundred yards or more off. I dodged several bombshells which threatened to fall on my head. I skipped out of the way of a rolling howitzer ball . . . musket balls flew around me at one time like a thousand humming-birds—so I had the sound of all kinds of music.[12]

The engagement at Fort Brown later lost much of its luster in the wake of the more important battles fought by General Taylor at Palo Alto and Resaca de la Palma, victories which accounted for the lifting of the siege on the Rio Grande. But the Fort Brown affair was an important one for Earl Van Dorn; it was his initiation into a new and exciting fraternity, one to which he paid homage for the remainder of his days.

General Taylor returned to Fort Brown after his two important victories, elated at the results of his first encounters with the Mexicans. On May 18 he pushed his new advantage and sent part of his army across the Rio Grande, occupying Matamoros without firing a shot. This objective in hand, he again procrastinated. The Mexican army evaporated before him, its troops retreated to fight again deeper in the interior, and Taylor watched them leave. New heroes sweated in the Matamoras sun; their days dragged ever slower as they recalled

10. Captain Hawkins to General Taylor, May 10, 1846, *Senate Documents,* 29 Cong., 1 Sess., Doc. 388, p. 34.
11. *A Soldier's Honor,* p. 21.
12. Earl Van Dorn to Octavia, July 20, 1846, *ibid.,* pp. 22–23.

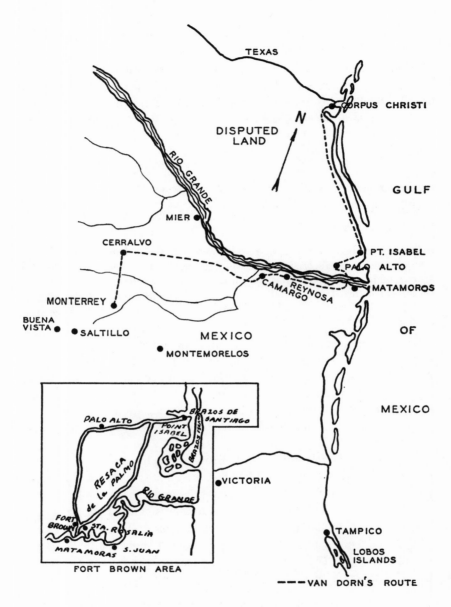

NORTHERN MEXICO

the excitement of the recent engagements and hoped for more action. To Van Dorn the prolonged stay on the Rio Grande was "a great worry," for his unit maintained its battered fortress, a garrison against an enemy flown.[13]

It was not until July 6 that Taylor resumed his march into Mexico, and this time it was the Seventh Infantry that led the way. Their route was to Camargo via Reynosa; their purpose was to serve as the advance detail for the entrance of the entire American army into Mexican territory. Marching was difficult. First it was the intense heat and deadly pestilence that struck the troops; then it was rain and flooding rivers which delayed their advance. Finally when large flooded areas completely blocked their way, steamboats picked them up and transported them on to Camargo where they arrived on July 15. It was the Seventh Infantry and Bragg's artillery that occupied that dismal little town.

If the new arrivals had expected something better than Matamoros, they were sorely disappointed. Earlier Camargo had been a well-organized town of about 4000 inhabitants, a center of north Mexican business. When the Americans arrived there, the floods and recent civil disturbances had taken their tolls. The streets were covered with mud, the stores had been sacked, and only frames of many of the dwelling places remained. The only place of business left was an old druggist shop.

Van Dorn's group camped in the plaza in the center of town. During the daylight hours they lounged in the surrounding buildings, seeking protection from the intense heat. Again there was no action other than dull training routine and preparation for encounters which they could only imagine. In Camargo they were even more isolated than at other posts. Their only outside contact was restricted to occasional excursions to nearby towns to replenish their commissary's whiskey supplies.

In the midst of such dullness, Van Dorn and other officers took a special interest in the returning village life. "The people are very strange in their customs, especially the ladies," he remarked to his sister. "They do some things and leave undone other things, which would make one of you faint, yet to them it is natural—they are so *naive*."[14] Dress and undress habits of the women of an invaded country intrigued American soldiers then as always. Ben McCulloch spoke en-

13. *Ibid.*
14. *Ibid.*, p. 23.

thusiastically of the "unveiled charm" of Camargo girls.[15] Van Dorn
was more descriptive, revealing again an interest which appears to
have diminished little as he grew older: "The only part of dress which
they are at all particular about is the skirt," he wrote, "but a bodice
they scorn to wear." He also took occasion to record a bathing custom
of these young women, swimming in the river at twilight *"al fresco,"*
usually under the close surveillance of many of the American invaders.[16]

These colorful episodes were only temporary interludes in the soldiers' daily routines. Life was harsh at Camargo, and Van Dorn, like
many of his comrades, spoke critically of the difficulties they faced—
long monotonous drills, sleeping on the cold ground, sickness, and
those prolonged periods of inactivity. Earl also struck an occasional
note of homesickness for wife, family, and friends. "How do you think
I stand the separation from my dear wife?" he wrote to Emily, "I
wonder if she can still love me when I married her only to leave her
in distress at my absence." But there was something strange in this
relationship, something that cannot be completely deciphered from
their remaining correspondence. What did the young, over-protected
girl expect of her young officer? How faithful was he to his marriage
vows? "But she [his wife] encourages me to great deeds," he added,
almost as an afterthought. "And if Heaven wills it, I will win a smile for
my return."[17]

Camargo was a world apart for American doughboys intent upon end-
ing the war and returning home, but to General Taylor it was an important interval between battles. After drill and maneuver had put
his troops into fine condition for action, he reorganized his command
into two divisions and made final preparations for an attack against
Monterrey. The new First Division, consisting of the Third and Fourth
Brigades, he assigned to salty old Major General David E. Twiggs. In
the Second Division, commanded by William J. Worth, he placed the
First and Second Brigades. The Seventh Infantry Regiment was part
of the Second Brigade in this new arrangement.

The shuffle in unit assignments brought new opportunity to many
younger officers including Lieutenant Van Dorn. General Persifor F.
Smith, the commander of the Second Brigade chose him as the ad-

---

15. Samuel C. Reid, Jr., *The Scouting Expeditions of McCulloch's Texas Rangers,*
p. 73.
16. *A Soldier's Honor,* p. 23.
17. *Ibid.,* p. 24.

jutant for his brigade; young Earl held this job three months, a period covering the entire Monterrey campaign. This was an important assignment for such an inexperienced officer, for General Smith was one of the finest American generals in Mexico. Described as "a fine specimen of a soldier," and noted as a man of courage and sound judgment, Smith was the kind of teacher that a future general needed. From the beginning of the new association, Smith seems to have had a special interest in his adjutant, and Van Dorn in turn held the general in high esteem. Undoubtedly this was a good arrangement for both men. Van Dorn served General Smith well in his new assignment; the general provided him with stable leadership and important military training.

Meanwhile, at Camargo the American army sweated and wished for action. In Washington civilian and military brass looked over the war situation and made plans of their own for action. Chief designers for a new strategy included Secretary of War Marcy and General Winfield Scott. Taylor was too slow. Something had to be done to supplement his actions. Marcy and Scott also felt that another army should be in the field, one that would strike directly at the enemy capital city. Their new plan included a landing at Vera Cruz and a march inland by a large American force somewhat in the manner of the operation of Cortez and his ancient conquistadors. To prepare the way for this new offensive, the War Department then directed General Taylor to "press forward your operations vigorously to the extent of your means, so as to occupy the important points within your reach on the Rio Grande and in the interior."[18]

These new plans hardly pleased the self-made old soldier commanding near Camargo, but he responded to his orders immediately upon receipt. First he sent General Worth and part of the Second Division across the San Juan River to establish another depot at Cerralvo. Then he dispatched General Smith's contingent to join them, so by early September he was in an excellent position to advance upon Monterrey and attack its formidable defenses.

If Taylor was a bit peeved at Washington's pressures for faster action, not so his men in the field. Said one of their officers: "The men are in high spirits and ready for any service . . . required of them."[19] Van Dorn wrote in the same spirit. Though he admitted it was "unmilitary"

18. Secretary Marcy to Taylor, *Senate Executive Document*, No. 60, p. 335.
19. Francis Baylies, *A Narrative of Major General Wool's Campaign in Mexico*, p. 17.

BATTLE OF MONTERREY

to speak of troop movements, he could not resist announcing to his sister that "a big battle" was brewing near Monterrey, and he was very enthusiastic about it.[20]

At Monterrey, seven thousand Mexican soldiers awaited Taylor's army of about six thousand. In and around the city they had constructed a vast system of field fortifications in anticipation of the attack. Taylor's spies brought him this information at Marin, a little town sixty miles distant from Monterrey, and there he made his final dispositions of troops for the last leg of his march against the city. Then as his army approached Monterrey, he expressed the hope that he could take the city "pretty much with the bayonet."[21] Other officers were not so optimistic, and there was some consternation among them as they neared their objective.

A heavy canopy of overhanging clouds blocked the "gringos'" view of the city when they arrived at its outskirts on the morning of September 19, 1846. It was not until near midday that the clouds lifted, and then they beheld before them "the rich and lovely valley of Monterrey, a beautiful undulating plain."[22] General Taylor lingered a while before his objective and then ordered an afternoon reconnaissance.

After the reconnaissance had brought information of Mexican dispositions, the officers all agreed that Monterrey would be no easy objective. A river, a mountain, roads, passes, and buildings combined to offer near-ideal conditions for a besieged army. Taylor knew that a direct assault would be too costly for his own army, so after a conference with his generals he decided on a two-pronged attack plan. One prong would strike directly at the outer edge of the city, the other would flank the city to the north and cut across the Mexican supply line, the Saltillo Road. Without their supply route the city's defenders would be just another Mexican army defending an isolated city. Taylor chose General Worth's Second Division to flank the city; he would lead the frontal attack himself.

General Worth made his move on September 20. In his ranks, Lieutenant Van Dorn, celebrating his twenty-sixth birthday, rode close to General Smith. Ahead of him the Texas Rangers, under Ben McCulloch, led the way, anxious to make first contact with the Mexicans.

20. *A Soldier's Honor*, p. 24.
21. Quoted in Singletary, *The Mexican War*, p. 34.
22. Reid, *The Scouting Expeditions*, p. 142.

Cheering ranged through Worth's long column late in the day when they had nearly flanked the city; the Rangers had been fired upon— the battle was on. For the remainder of the day, however, there was only skirmishing; Worth finally halted his entire force just short of the Saltillo Road at dusk. To his men he promised a dawn attack.

It rained torrents at Monterrey that September night. Troops were wet to the skin, and some of their powder and artillery pieces suffered from the exposure. By early morning of September 21, Worth's unit was in a dangerous position. He was separated from Taylor's supply depot with provisions enough to last only four days. All about his position, heavily armed Mexicans awaited his advance; their big guns and sharpshooters were well hidden in gorges and passes of the threatening mountains. Worth's hopes for victory lay with his determined men and in his own genius as a commander. Ever optimistic, even in the face of the heavy odds against him, he moved his troops toward the enemy in the darkness and drizzling rain before dawn, and when daylight appeared, his army was ready to take the initiative in a new attack.

The Texas Rangers again engaged the enemy first, and they fought as though possessed of demons as they cut their way through the Mexican defenders. Van Dorn could only watch this action from the distance and await his own chance to be thus engaged. His time came near the end of the Rangers' attack. Fire from Mexican batteries atop two imposing heights on either side of the Saltillo Road cut off the Rangers' drive and temporarily halted Worth's offensive. Seeing these obstacles, Worth turned to General Smith's command. He pointed dramatically toward Federation Hill, a proclivity south of the Saltillo Road, the obvious source of much of his discomfort, and said calmly: "Men, you are to take the hill. I know you will do it."

"We will," the troops shouted in chorus.[23]

Van Dorn was in the lead unit that began the ascent of the steep and rocky cliff that led up to Fort Soldado on top of Federation Hill. The going was rough all the way as the Mexicans poured grape steadily into their hard-pressed ranks. On they went, determined for conquest, finally arriving at the rim of the hill after an hour and a half of furious climbing. At the rim officers and men engaged the Mexicans in hand-to-hand fighting, and American bayonets accounted for many casualties. "Gringo" fury won out. Fort Soldado fell, and the victorious

23. *Ibid.*

troops streamed down the hill to await their next bloody assignment. General Worth did not keep them waiting long. Across the road was Independence Hill, another Mexican stronghold, and from its guns also poured a galling, enfilading fire into the attackers' unprotected flanks. The new objective was set. Worth anounced an attack on the hill to begin just before dawn on September 22.

Rain again failed to dampen the spirits of the determined Americans, though the downpour continued well into the next day. Taking advantage of the cover offered by the elements, Worth attacked on schedule. For the second time in two days, Van Dorn was in the thickest of the action as the troops pushed their way through Mexican small-arms fire. Again he was engaged in hand-to-hand combat as the men converged upon the Bishop's Palace, the key fortification atop the hill. Again Yankee determination and power won out as the Mexican defenses collapsed before their onslaught.

The collapse of the Mexican positions along the Saltillo Road sealed the fate of Monterrey's western defenses. After the fall of the Bishop's Palace, resistance in that sector of the city collapsed completely. Meanwhile, Taylor had also forged a successful offensive against strong fortifications in the eastern part of the city. The end of the battle of Monterrey on September 23 marked another great victory.

Though Lieutenant Van Dorn cannot always be clearly distinguished in the smoke of battle, the three-day engagement was an important one to him. This battle was a milestone in his career, one of his severest engagements. He had crossed muddy fields under heavy enemy fire. He had personally engaged the enemy. He had faced death and the prospects of death on the battlefield with the calmness of a veteran. More important he had been a close observer of the unfolding strategy of a successful operation, a strategy strikingly similar to his own at Pea Ridge, Arkansas, nearly sixteen years later. And there was glory at Monterrey for the young lieutenant! General Smith took special notice of his service, praising him highly for his conduct both as an officer and as his own adjutant.[24] General Worth also singled him out

24. Successful service as an adjutant was an accomplishment of some note in the American Army of the early 19th century. Of Jefferson Davis's appointment as a regimental adjutant early in his own career, one of his leading biographers wrote that it "indicates better than anything else what manner of man he was." This office, wrote William E. Dodd, "is generally filled by one who is proud of the service, punctilious as to the performance of the details of military duty, and careful of his own appearance. . . ." *Jefferson Davis*, p. 39.

SOUTHERN MEXICO

GULF OF MEXICO

VERDE
SACRIFICIOS
ANTON
LIZARDO
CERRO GORDO
PLANO DEL RIO
MANGA DE CLAVO
VERA CRUZ
MEDELLIN
CORDOVA
ORIZABA
JALAPA
PEROTE
N

RIO FRIO
PUEBLA
TEXCOCO
MEXICO
TACUBAYA
COYOACAN
AYOTLA
LAKE CHALCO
CHALCO
XOCHIMILCO
PADIERNA
GUADALUPE
HIDALGO
CHAPULTEPEC
MOLINO DEL
REY

for commendation from his own "personal observation."[25] Lieutenant Van Dorn had made his first mark as a soldier to be closely observed for the future.

If the victorious troops expected a respite from marching and fighting after Monterrey, they were sorely disappointed at the next action. Scott and Marcy had their way, and they set an offensive against Vera Cruz to begin early in 1847. General Scott immediately began assembling his new army at Tampico, a force which was to be reinforced with many of Taylor's "gallant officers and men," including the Seventh Infantry Regiment and Earl Van Dorn. Taylor, with his own reduced force, was ordered to hold a line of defense across northern Mexico.

Van Dorn arrived in Victoria, en route to Scott's army, in early January after a long march across some of Mexico's most desolate countryside. He was sustained in his enthusiasm for war by the prospects of new action ahead and by a special assignment he received in a reorganization of Scott's army. In a new arrangement General Smith again paid him honor by selecting him as his personal aide-de-camp, an assignment he held for the duration of the war.

Scott did not tarry long at Tampico. His men were on board ship in the Vera Cruz harbor on March 5 ready for a landing. Sickness had taken a heavy toll from their ranks, but the troops watched the first bombardment of the Mexican port with great enthusiasm, hopeful for a quick landing. Finally on March 9, after several days of heavy shelling, the first wave of troops landed at a point a few miles below the city proper. Van Dorn watched this and another wave of troops land before his own unit went ashore.

Meeting little enemy resistance on this sector of the beach, the American force moved up the beach to besiege the city. Unlike the large offensive that had marked the action at Monterrey, the action around Vera Cruz was marked by isolated guerrilla-like clashes between small units. Van Dorn was involved in one of these clashes on March 24 over the occupation of an important bridge just outside the main gate; his unit drove the Mexicans from their position in a "handsome affair."[26] Again the lieutenant was in the thickest of the fight, and again General Smith singled him out for his gallantry.

25. Report of General Worth, September 28, 1846, *Senate Executive Documents,* 29 Cong., 2 Sess., Doc. 1, p. 107.
26. Raphael Semmes, *The Campaign of General Scott in the Valley of Mexico,* p. 46.

Mexican resistance at Vera Cruz ended in late March; the city was occupied by the Americans on March 29. "Bien, c'est une affaire! The crisis is past!" enthusiastically wrote Captain George A. McCall.[27] Van Dorn did not share his fellow officer's enthusiasm despite his new commendation and his recent promotion to first lieutenant. To his father-in-law he complained that the soldiers had just been "spectators" in the battle. The "cannon did the business," he lamented.[28] Of the strategic significance of the city, he seemed to care little. To him it was just "rubbish and dirt."[29] His was a concern for personal recognition.

For General Scott, however, Vera Cruz was the beginning. His next move came quickly. By April 8 he had General Twiggs's division on the National Road en route to Jalapa to push the war closer to the Mexican capital city. With his back to the wall, General Santa Anna, again in command of the Mexican forces, made desperate preparations to block Twiggs by concentrating his army across his path at Cerro Gordo in a group of irregular hills about halfway between the coast and Jalapa. These hills flanked the National Road and commanded its approach into the interior. Just north of the highway two cone-shaped peaks dominating the short range of hills gave Santa Anna the focus for his defense arrangement. On Telegraph Hill, the taller of the two peaks, the wily Mexican commander placed six hundred of his best troops, and from its heights he pointed five of his long-range guns directly at the highway. La Atalaya, the other hill, he garrisoned with only a few men as a token defense against what he considered an improbable flanking attack. To impede the progress of enemy troops attacking these hills, the Mexicans piled trees and brush amidst heavy natural undergrowth.

On April 11 General Twiggs's advance unit arrived at Plan del Rio, a small village four miles from the Mexican position. Impetuous Twiggs was all for making an immediate attack on Telegraph Hill, but cooler heads, including Robert E. Lee and U. S. Grant, prevailed to restrain this enthusiasm until the arrival of General Scott. Scott surveyed the situation critically and then, influenced by the brilliant reconnaissance of Captain Lee and Lieutenant Beauregard, decided upon a less desperate plan of action. Cut off by a river south of the highway, he would

27. McCall, *Letters from the Frontiers*, p. 483.
28. *A Soldier's Honor*, p. 24.
29. *Ibid.*, p. 25.

strike at Santa Anna's left flank by sending part of his army through the lower hills north of the highway over a newly discovered trail. In a simultaneous action in the center of the Mexican line he would engage Santa Anna's main body. The difficult flanking operation Scott assigned to Colonel William S. Harney, serving in place of General Persifor Smith who was at that moment in sick bay. Harney was ordered to seize La Atalaya and then attack Telegraph Hill on its flank.

Early on the morning of April 17, after work crews had removed much of the debris on the trail, Harney's troops began their march. As at Monterrey Lieutenant Van Dorn was again in the flanking force, this time as Harney's aide. He was at his commander's side as they advanced slowly through a narrow valley over the rugged terrain among oaks, mesquite, chaparral, and cactus. About noon they reached the vicinity of La Atalaya where Harney detached the Seventh Infantry from his command to take the hill. The Seventh moved quickly, but it encountered a stronger enemy position than had been expected. Action was sharp with Harney and Santa Anna both sending up reinforcements. Despite the persistent efforts of the defenders, Harney's men pressed on, finally pushing the Mexicans to the crest of the hill where the bloodiest fighting of the day ensued. Despite Santa Anna's resolution to hold on, Harney was not to be denied. Personally leading his reinforcements into the fray, he ended the first day's operation by occupying the summit of La Atalaya. That night Van Dorn and his comrades slept on their arms atop the hill while additional guns and troops were brought into the valley below in preparation for the main battle at Telegraph Hill on the morrow.

Sunday morning, April 18, was ushered in by an artillery duel. From his position on La Atalaya, Harney looked across the valley to the heights of the larger hill and prepared to attack. About 7:00 A.M. he gave the signal, and his men again charged into the valley and then "up that terrible hill." The colonel, with his aide beside him all the way, led the attack. When he was threatened by a sizable Mexican unit at his rear, he yelled out above the roar of battle: "Let them attack; we will carry the hill, then the whole force can't budge us a foot."[30]

His troops then swept on "under a plunging fire in their front and

30. John Sedgwick, *Correspondence*, p. 40.

a rolling fire in their flank."[31] Although they suffered heavy casualties, they continued to work their way through the obstacles up the hill. With little protection but with utmost steadiness, they approached the palisade breastworks where the contact was close and the fighting was intense. Colonel Harney and his aide continued at the head of the troops; Harney waved his sword and shouted encouragement to his hard-pressed troops. Fighting in the midst of the Mexican line at the rim of the hill, Lieutenant Van Dorn killed two Mexican defenders. Gradually the defenders retreated before this determined onslaught. Soon the Stars and Stripes flew over Telegraph Hill, and the enemy reluctantly retreated toward Jalapa. The Seventh moved onto the National Highway to cut off the retreat of a few of the stragglers, but heat and exhaustion prevented a full-scale pursuit. Scott had hoped to destroy the entire Mexican army, but he had won a great victory nevertheless. He was ready to move deeper into the interior, and his army continued its move westward to Jalapa, Perote, and finally to Puebla.

Again the events of war had dealt kindly with Van Dorn. Not only had he gone through the thickest fighting unscathed, but he had also won citations from his commanders again. Colonel Harney gave "especial thanks" to him for the "efficient aid" and the "individual gallantry" which he displayed.[32] General Scott singled him out in his official report of the battle and commended him for his service. There was also another brevet, this time for gallant and meritorious service in battle. Brevet Captain Van Dorn was older and probably some wiser than the rash second lieutenant who saved the battered flag at Fort Brown, but he was still as impetuous as ever and just as hungry for glory.

To trace Scott's march across Mexico is a narrative in itself. Too often it is a story of frustration and antagonizing delay brought on by intense heat, sickness, delayed supplies and reinforcements, and enlistments run out as Scott and his men sweated in Mexico's hottest season from late April to early August. What of Van Dorn during the lengthy period between battles, a time he usually deplored anyway?

31. L. U. Reavis, *The Life and Military Services of General William Selby Harney*, p. 199.
32. Harney's Report, April 21, 1847, *Senate Executive Document 1*, 30 Cong., 1 Sess., p. 282.

In records, reports, and correspondence now available, not a word appears of his personal activities during these trying days. He returned to his post as aide-de-camp for General Smith when that officer recovered his health, and he remained close to General Smith until the end of the war. Otherwise his face is again lost in a sea of American faces, his life probably running a similar course in central Mexico to that of others in the army about whom more was written. Although he is lost in the crowd, one can suspect him "as anxious to be moving toward the Halls of the Montezumas" covetous of another brevet, occasionally solacing himself with the others in the dullness of Puebla with *aguardiente*, a liquor as comforting as "newly distilled whiskey."[33] Was he not sometimes in the streets of the city arrayed in his best uniform, in his tent amidst the wild and jagged hills near the city, or climbing the lava-covered hills to a castle or a cathedral with other curious officers? He probably pursued Mexican lancers across the hot countryside when they harassed the American outposts, watered his horse at a hacienda, and maybe even flirted with a dark-eyed señorita.

There must have been the lighter moments for the hot-blooded, impetuous young Mississippian! Did he, with Raphael Semmes, gaze at one of the nymphs in "glorous des habelle," a sight that might well have quickened "the lazy current of life in the veins of even an old bishop?"[34] Did he sample the sherbet and receive the attentions of a young lady the French call *la grisette* while in Perote? Did he help swell the pews of the crowded churches in Puebla thus bringing the retort from the natives: "Beware, Mexicans! These Yankees, when in Jalapa, where there were plenty of pretty women, and where gallantry was the order of the day, were obsequious and attentive *beaux*, but now that they have arrived in *Puebla of the Angels*, where religion is in vogue, they have suddenly become *saints!*"[35]

Whatever his actions, he can only be seen in shadow, but one readily suspects that he tired quickly of life in the interior and that he was overjoyed when General Scott issued new orders on August 6 for his troops to take up the line of march toward Mexico City again. Van Dorn took his place beside General Smith in Twiggs's division as the troops moved out from Puebla on August 7. There were 10,000 officers

33. Semmes, *Campaign of General Scott*, pp. 165, 178.
34. *Ibid.*, p. 147.
35. *Ibid.*, pp. 151-152.

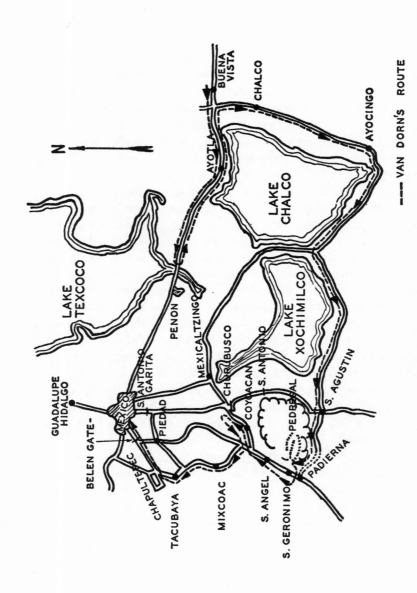

MEXICO CITY AREA

and men in Scott's command, and there were high hopes throughout the ranks that a conclusive victory was about to be fashioned.

To attack Mexico City was a perilous undertaking under any conditions, but it was made more so by the vigilance of the Mexicans in their defense against the hated "gringos." Mountains and lakes acted as natural barriers to invaders, and walls around the city also limited access into its streets and helped its defenders to concentrate their strength and guns at strategic points near the gates. This defensive arrangement prompted new decisions in Scott's command on the eve of the attack. After a careful survey of the countryside, the American commanding officer and his military council decided upon a change of course; they would move southward around Lakes Chalco and Xochimilco and onto another road, one which led from the south into the capital.

Scott's new advance toward Mexico City resulted in intense fighting and heavy casualties on both sides, and through most of the action the figure of a gallant Mississippian shines forth with amazing consistency. Through the wooded Padierna, erroneously called Contreras by the Americans, went Scott's men, to Churubusco and on to Chapultepec, contested at every point by determined Mexicans until gradually they faded before the advance. Van Dorn was in the thickest of all these actions except Churubusco.

In the blinding rain he ascended the heights of the Padierna with General Smith, wading knee-deep in mud and water, arriving behind enemy lines at dawn. General Smith praised him lavishly for his personal participation in the furious fighting that routed the Mexicans in less than half an hour. Smith wrote:

The events of Fort Brown, Monterey, Vera Cruz, and Cerro Gordo had afforded to my aide-de-camp, Lt. Earl Van Dorn [pay rank; brevet rank was major], opportunities of calling forth the commendations of his commanding officers. He has not let pass the present one; but though his gallantry was again shown in personal conflict with the enemy, it is far from being the highest quality of a soldier that he possesses.[36]

Van Dorn continued to win the hearts of his commanders by his soldierly bearing. In addition to Smith's official citation of praise, the

36. General Smith's Report, August 23, 1847, *Senate Executive Document 1*, 30 Cong., 1 Sess., p. 329.

brevet captain was promoted to brevet major as a reward for marked distinction in the hills before the enemy's position at Padierna.

At Chapultepec and in the final charge into Mexico City, the new major was as usual in the center of the hottest action. In the first engagement he took his customary place among the lead troops who stormed the Mexican stronghold in the military college located atop a narrow ridge of volcanic rock. It was in the pattern of Monterrey, Cerro Gordo, and Padierna, and it was just as deadly.

With the ascent of Chapultepec a success, the way was clear to attack the Belén Gate where the Mexicans guarded final entrance into their capital. General Smith's troops again led the way, coming under heavy artillery fire from the Mexican batteries as they moved toward the gate. Then a canister barrage from the Americans cut deep into their ranks and weakened their resistance so that the infantry accelerated his charge. Additional fire power pouring from inside the city failed to slow the progress of these yelling, firing demons. Van Dorn's enthusiasm is typical of the advancing veterans. Though wounded in the foot as he entered the Belén Gate, he continued the charge and personally cut his way into the citadel inside the city.

Fighting ended on this last spectacular note. The war was over. Officers had only to write their reports; the enlisted men had only to await shipment home. It was up to the diplomats to take the stage and try to negotiate a lasting peace from the shambles of war.

While officers recorded their observations of battle achievements and awarded kudos to the deserving, again Major Van Dorn's name was prominent. General Smith continued to praise his aide, recording "the gallant bearing of my aide-de-camp . . . who was everywhere engaged in his duty, under the hottest fire, and even after receiving a severe contusion in the foot from a musket ball." His name was again in General Scott's report, this time on his "list of individuals of conspicuous merit."[37] Earl Van Dorn was indeed one of the most decorated officers in the war. Certainly he could expect some choice assignments in the months ahead!

The American troops reluctantly settled down to the dreary tasks of occupation duty; their thoughts turned to home or a transfer. Like other soldiers who return to the dull pursuits of garrison life after

37. Scott's Report, September 18, 1847, *Senate Executive Document* 1, 30 Cong. 1, Sess., p. 380.

stirring action in the field, many expressed dissatisfaction with their officers and fellow soldiers. Van Dorn put something of this feeling in a letter to his sister in January 1848, in reply to her question concerning his thoughts on the possible identity of the next President of the United States: "I care so little about it," he wrote, "that I never have turned a thought to the subject. I know General Taylor to be honest now, but whose honesty, whose principles can stand the test of *Power*—of high places?"[38]

Van Dorn also expressed his doubts at the prospects of any permanent peace with Mexico, centering his criticism against the War Department for wanting to break up the American expeditionary force. Everything was in a state of chaos as he saw it. Things were so uncertain, he explained to his sister, that he knew not if the morrow would find him on his way to California or beginning the long return to Mississippi. Despite the state of flux he found himself in at the Mexican capital, Major Van Dorn never once ceased being the professional soldier. In the same letter to his sister he emphasized that he could never be happy in anything but an army career. "The minds of civilians and ours run in different directions," he wrote.[39] In these words he probably struck a very important truth, maybe a terrible truth.

The brightest spot for Van Dorn in Mexico was his continuing role as General Smith's aide, especially when the former New Orleans lawyer was made military governor of the occupied capital. This new office provided both men an exciting change from the regular routines of occupation duty and gave them an entrée into the higher social life of the city. Since there was much activity in Mexican society during those days of reconstruction, this proved to be a coveted post.

Major Van Dorn remained in Mexico until May 1848, when he finally departed for the United States on a three-month leave of absence. Everywhere he went he received a hero's welcome, but it all culminated in an affair in Port Gibson where he was presented with a citation and two costly swords for his war achievements. The gift was given by the Mississippi legislature and the citizens of his home town.

Major Van Dorn's next duty assignment was to report to General Zachary Taylor in Baton Rouge in the early fall. This came as a surprise to him since he had been expecting to rejoin his old regiment at

38. Van Dorn to Octavia, January 13, 1848, A *Soldier's Honor*, pp. 25–26.
39. *Ibid.*

Jefferson Barracks, Missouri. In November he and Mrs. Van Dorn moved into a quadrangle of army barracks in the city and settled down for their first lengthy domicile together. Their new home was made livable by neat furnishings and a lovely court in the open center. Here life was pleasant, at least for a time. Earl was able to engage in his favorite hobbies, drawing and painting, and during the winter months he took up portrait copying with some degree of success. There was also social life in abundance, an aspect of this assignment that appealed especially to Carrie. Not only were the young couple able to entertain guests from among their circles of friends in Baton Rouge, Port Gibson, and Mobile, but they were often in the company of General and Mrs. Taylor. To be near the Taylors when the old general was so prominently in the national spotlight was indeed an honor for the couple.

The peace and serenity of home life went well for some months, but gradually Earl tired of the monotony. He said that he found it difficult to become "settled and satisfied with calmer pursuits."[40] Sharing a home with his wife seemed finally to amplify the restless nature so apparent in his emotional make-up. He expressed his growing feelings of frustration almost bitterly in a letter to his sister from their Baton Rouge home:

Carry and myself now sit down to our meals opposite each other and alone and present a perfect picture of domestic felicity . . . and we have nobody to strike our elbows when carving our ducks or pouring out our tea and coffee . . . everything is so silent. I feel too much the passing wing of time— almost hear it.[41]

For seven months the Van Dorns lived in Baton Rouge before Earl returned to field duty. After Baton Rouge he rejoined the Seventh Infantry Regiment at Jefferson Barracks for training preparatory for a trip to Florida and the first of his many actions against the Indians. He stopped at New Orleans briefly en route to Florida, spending the night of September 7, 1849, with a good friend in that city. What of his wife during this period? At Earl's request the friend wrote to Carrie and explained her husband's reasons for not writing. "He was very busy," the friend explained, "having his company to attend to,"

40. *Ibid.*, pp. 27–29.
41. *Ibid.*, p. 28.

and then as though that was not convincing enough he added, "besides attending to a lot of commissary stores."[42]

At Palatka, Florida, the major served as depot commissary during the operations against a small band of Seminole Indians who for some time had been in a state of open rebellion. The Seventh Infantry had little difficulty putting down this revolt though the Seminoles never gracefully accepted their transfer to the reservations in the West. Again there is little of Earl's personal participation on record. The action was so limited that only the field leaders were mentioned by name in the official reports of the operation.

When this tour of duty in Florida ended in February 1850, Van Dorn was again removed from the field. His next assignment was recruiting duty with headquarters at Newport Barracks, Kentucky. Recruiting duty called for much travel, and in 1851 he was reported as far west as Forth Smith, Arkansas, where he had recruited one hundred men and was awaiting arms for them.[43]

Meanwhile, something was happening in Washington that would bring him a completely different sort of assignment. In 1851 Congress introduced a bill providing for the establishment of a "Military Asylum for the relief and support of invalid and disabled soldiers of the Army of the United States."[44] After the passage of this bill that same year, institutions of this sort were set up in Washington, D.C. and New Orleans, Louisiana. Each branch of the asylum was to be staffed with a governor, a deputy-governor, a secretary, and a treasurer, all to be selected from the officers of the regular army by a Board of Commissioners of that particular institution. On November 11, 1851, the New Orleans Board selected Van Dorn to serve as both secretary and treasurer, to be stationed at the temporary place of reception of the new asylum in New Orleans. Thus began one of the most unusual phases of his varied career.

Again Earl and Caroline lived together for a time until a yellow fever epidemic struck in and around the city. Caroline returned to

42. Lt. N. H. McLean to Mrs. Van Dorn, September 10, 1849, in Van Dorn Collection, Montgomery, Alabama.

43. Mary Russell to Mrs. Clinton W. Lear, November 15, 1851, in George H. Shirk, "Mail Call at Fort Washita," *Chronicles of Oklahoma*, XXXIII, 25.

44. General Scott to Secretary Conrad, December 31, 1851, *Senate Executive Documents*, 32 Cong., 1 Sess., Doc. 27, p. 2.

Mount Vernon where she could be with her parents when the baby arrived. The baby, a girl, was born on April 1, 1852. The proud parents caller her Olivia. The dashing father loved his beautiful little daughter very much, and he testified to this love in many passages in his personal letters from this date on. But Livy, like her mother, soon took a back seat to military duty. He would think of them from his distant post, he would write of his love, but he took more seriously the army life to which he was wholly dedicated. Another child, Earl, Jr., was also born while the major was assigned to the Louisiana asylum.

In 1853 the asylum was moved to a 110-acre site at East Pascagoula, Mississippi. Temporary accommodations were provided for all the inmates, and Van Dorn was made acting governor. He remained at the asylum for nearly four years but was responsible for very few improvements. The Government was more interested in the branch in Washington, and officials paid little attention to the New Orleans branch. A few inmates, never over eight after 1852, continued to reside in the temporary buildings, and Earl Van Dorn impatiently served out an unwanted assignment.

CHAPTER THREE

Frontier Life

*T*HE quiet years at his desk passed slowly for the Asylum's restless
governor. The methodical duties at Pascagoula were too much a
contrast to earlier, more exciting days. Too often the dramas of far-
flung battlefields, past and future, flashed through his mind. What of
the old Seventh Infantry? What were they doing? What troops were
fighting the Indians? How did they merit such an assignment while
he stagnated in a hot office? His Anglo-Saxon sentiments cried out his
desires. Certainly one could fight Indians with more fruitful results
than he was having. Would not a man of action serve better in the field
than in a Louisiana retreat so far removed from reality? The old soldiers
passed back and forth before his window, their lives spent, their hopes
rooted only in the present. Inside Major Van Dorn watched their slow
promenades and fretted for the field.

Again it was Congress that intervened and changed the course of
his life, this time in a direction more to his liking. In 1855 Congress
created two new cavalry units, the First and Second Cavalry Regiments, and Van Dorn's assignment to one of them initiated a new and
exciting phase of his career.

After the conclusion of the Mexican War, the focus in America
turned abruptly to Southwestern Indians. The Government had encountered Indian difficulties on every frontier, but its problems that
arose out of the terms of the treaty of Guadalupe Hidalgo were of a
special order. By the terms of that treaty the United States agreed to
prevent marauding Indians from entering Mexico from the American
side. Two main courses of action were open to fulfill this obligation.
The first was the traditional military way. The War Department would
push them by violence from the coveted lands. The other way was to

negotiate with the Indian leaders and attempt to pacify their restless people. Indian agents would offer treaties, reservation lands, and educational opportunities, hopeful of bringing about a rapprochement between White settler and Indian.

After the hostilities with Mexico, the United States Government attempted both of these methods in the Southwest. Forts were built along the Mexican border, troop strength was increased, and two large reservations were established—all to little avail. To the frontiersman it was the military policy that offered the most appeal. Obsessed by the thought that a good Indian was a dead Indian, the immigrants to Texas felt their greatest security when blue-coated soldiers rode near their settlements. Lengthy negotiations led only to a policy where half-civilized savages passed in and out of reservations at will, always a threat to peace and order.

Friction between the settlers and the Indians increased in the early 1850s as the settlers took over more land, killed the buffalo, and polluted the streams. Resenting these intrusions of the Whites as well as the limited space of their reservations, the Indians often slipped out of their new homes and joined other bands of marauders in pilfering and robbing the settlers. The Whites, anxious to get on with the process of community building, struck back with a vengeance. When the Indians exhibited strength and numbers too great for their limited resources, they again turned to Washington and cried aloud for more help.

In 1853 General Scott spoke at length in his annual report of the Indian problems on the frontier. Stressing the military solution, he urged the creation by Congress of two new regiments of dragoons and two of infantry. Secretary of War Jefferson Davis suggested doubling the forces on the frontier to face the Indian menace. Congress discussed the matter and did nothing.

In his annual report for 1854, Secretary Davis reopened the matter of more troop units, this time pushing Scott's proposal over his own. General Scott reaffirmed his own position to the House Military Committee. "In Texas," the old general stressed, "the Indian hostilities have been more destructive than at other points principally on account of the small force stationed in that country." He spoke of a need for more troops dictated by both "policy and humanity."[1]

1. Price, *Across the Continent*, pp. 13–15.

Congress debated the issue of increased troop strength with much feeling. In the Senate Sam Houston and Thomas H. Benton led the opposition to such action. They were concerned about two aspects of the new bill. In the first place, they felt that the army was ill prepared by education or training to handle the Indian problem. They preferred local Rangers. In the second place, they seem to have distrusted the Secretary of War. The creation of these new regiments would provide him an unusual opportunity to make special assignments to his favorites at the expense of the other officers in the service.

Opposition faltered, however, and on March 2, 1855, Congress passed a bill that created two regiments of cavalry and two of infantry. Secretary Davis promptly recognized the cavalry units as a separate branch of the army. Excluding many prominent regular army officers, as had been predicted, Davis then filled these regiments with men of his own choosing, many of them Southerners who had won their spurs in Mexico. This does not suggest duplicity; choice assignments always go to choice troops, and the Mexican veterans were the army's finest. The impressive list of officers of the two regiments included such names as Robert E. Lee, Joseph E. and Albert S. Johnston, John B. Hood, Kirby Smith, George H. Thomas, Fitzhugh Lee, J. E. B. Stuart, and Earl Van Dorn, all Southerners, and all, with the exception of Thomas, to become Confederate generals. In the history of the American army there have been few military units with such illustrious personnel. These were proud, ambitious, eager young men, destined for great deeds. Kirby Smith expressed all their enthusiasm when he remarked casually that his unit, the Second Cavalry, would soon be *the* regiment of the Army."[2]

One wonders about the role of Jefferson Davis in the appointment of this select list of officers. Did he fill the regiments "with his creatures" to the exclusion of other officers "whom he disliked?"[3] Why were there so many Southerners?

Answers to these questions can be found in the complications of the times. Southerners were prominent in the regular army at that time because more of them had remained on duty after the Mexican War. Also, the South and the Democratic Party had taken leading roles in fighting that war, and it was often sectional favor rather than merit

2. Parks, *Kirby Smith*, p. 87.
3. Lee, *General Lee*, p. 53.

which had brought choice assignments and promotions to the Southern officers on duty. Therefore, by the end of the war, many of them were in prominent places in the military forces and were likely candidates for choice assignments. Of course many of them, including Van Dorn, had earned their spurs in combat.

Then one must also consider the importance that the South gave to the expansion of the Southwest frontier. Texas was much more important to the agrarian South than to the industrial North, or at least so it seemed, and Jefferson Davis did represent the strong pro-Southern feeling that existed in America. That he had larger plans for the officers of the First and Second Cavalry Regiments hardly seems possible, though in the end his appointments in these units did work to his personal advantage when as President of the Confederacy he began the challenging task of putting together an army. Richard W. Johnson, a member of the original cadre of the Second Cavalry—a Kentuckian who remained loyal to the Union during the Civil War—later evaluated Davis's actions, "This was six years before the beginning of the war and a little too early for one to predict with any degree of certainty the supreme folly of a war between the sections."[4] Johnson's personal opinion seems to be a fair historical judgment.

At the Pascagoula asylum, Van Dorn received notice in April 1855, of his appointment to the Second Cavalry as commander of Company A. He was ordered to Louisville, Kentucky, and promoted to captain in the regular army to date from March 3. This made him the highest ranking officer of that grade in the two cavalry regiments. Though a brevet-major already, the promotion did carry with it a welcome increment to a very low salary. Never a wizard in money matters, the young officer was usually plagued with financial difficulties.

Organization was the big task ahead for the officers of the new cavalry units. The First Cavalry was first in the field. Commanded by Mexican War veterans Colonel E. V. Summer and Lieutenant Colonel Joseph E. Johnston, the new dragoons were patrolling Sioux country west of Fort Leavenworth by late summer of 1855. Meanwhile, the Second Cavalry, commanded by Colonel Albert S. Johnston, held its first muster in Louisville in late spring under its assistant commandant, Lieutenant Colonel Robert E. Lee. Manpower needs was the first order

4. Richard W. Johnson, *A Soldier's Reminiscences in Peace and War*, p. 97.

of business among the newly assigned officers. For frontier duty the Army needed men who could ride and shoot and hold up physically under the rigorous life in the West. Each company commander faced the task of recruiting his own men from especially selected areas. Van Dorn went to Mobile, Alabama, near his wife's home. He quickly raised his quota of recruits and departed with them for Jefferson Barracks, Missouri, for a general assembly of the entire Second Cavalry Regiment. When they arrived at the Missouri fort, Van Dorn's company received expensive gray horses as their official mounts; thus they were called the "Mobile Grays," a designation which stuck with them throughout the Indian campaigns.[5]

During the summer Jefferson Barracks was a beehive of activity. Under the able leadership of Major William J. Hardee, drill began in earnest and continued daily despite the terrible heat. Hardee was a stern taskmaster, and reports of increasing Indian activity in Texas spurred him on. Officers of the Second Cavalry faced even heavier assignments than did the enlisted men. Lieutenant Richard Johnson complained about the new activity, "Between drilling their companies, reciting tactical lessons, or being drilled in the manual of the sabre and carbine, there was no leisure time for any one from reveille to tattoo."[6]

The summer in Missouri was indeed a difficult one for the new cavalry unit. Sickness struck down many and impeded training progress. Cholera made a brief appearance and greatly alarmed the men. Ague and desertion took heavy tolls. Because of slowness in the shipping of requisitions the troops also suffered from lack of proper and sufficient clothing. But these were good men, "among the best riders in the world," and they were anxious for duty in Texas.[7] As autumn approached, Texas waited impatiently for them to move. Autumn in Texas was a bad time, "the season of trouble," and the Comanches pressed hard. The War Department issued the following order in late October:

The Second Regiment of cavalry at Jefferson Barracks will proceed, by easy marches across the country, to Fort Belknap, Texas, to be there dis-

5. The average cost of each horse was about $150, a high price at that time. These were the best horses the Army could buy, and many of them came from famous lineage.

6. *A Soldier's Reminiscences*, p. 98.

7. Albert G. Brackett, *History of the United States Cavalry*, p. 197.

posed of by the Commanding General of the Department of Texas, who will make timely arrangements for stationing the regiment on its arrival within his command.[8]

What the War Department understood by "easy marches" through the Southwest with winter approaching is difficult to see, but despite the cold wind in their faces the 750 men and 800 horses of the Second Cavalry departed from Jefferson Barracks on October 27 in a happy frame of mind. It was a colorful procession that took up the march that morning. The grays, roans, bays, sorrels, and browns pranced ahead, feeling the enthusiasm of their riders. Soldiers raised their black felt "cowboy hats" for a final salute, and the troops were on their way.

Their line of march toward the Southwest was through Missouri, over the Ozark Mountains, across northwestern Arkansas, through the Indian Territory, and finally to Fort Belknap, Texas. From its beginning it was a difficult march. During the first month it rained nearly every day. The weather grew cold, the winds were fierce, the roads became a quagmire. Sickness was commonplace among the troops, and the ambulance and wagons carried too many human burdens. Those too ill to travel were left at frontier towns and outposts.

Meanwhile the troops made their way laboriously through Missouri and Arkansas into Indian Territory. They paused briefly at Tahlequah, the capital of the Cherokee Nation, and then at nearby Fort Gibson. After battling a severe storm, they finally crossed the Canadian River on December 5, 1855.

The first bright spot of the trip came a week later at Fort Washita, an outpost about 30 miles south of the river, where they were received with a thirteen-gun salute. Here Mr. Samuel Hanes, the post sutler, and the army officers of the fort provided generous hospitality for the weather-beaten guests. Most of the Second Cavalry's officers took part in the gala activities, and one of them later wrote that "when the champagne began to flow, a more jolly set of fellows I do not remember to have ever seen." Life in the new frontier command could have its lighter moments, and as Lieutenant Johnson said, ". . . sparkling wine always develops wit and good humor among gentlemen."[9]

The welcome respite ended all too soon, and the troops again mounted to continue their trip. The next two weeks were the hard ones. The prairies in the Southwest were desolate after a year of grasshopper in-

8. Johnson, *A Soldier's Reminiscences*, p. 99.
9. *Ibid.*, p. 103.

festation. The cold winds blew strong and drove the men to what little shelter they could find. A severe norther with winds up to sixty miles per hour caught them on December 22; and hail, snow, sleet, and continuing freezing cold faced them for the remainder of their journey. "In the whole course of my military experience," wrote Kirby Smith, "I have never seen men suffer more."[10] Cold, tired, and hungry, they arrived at Fort Belknap in sub-zero weather on December 27. If they expected relief at the Fort, they were greatly disappointed. Most of them had to camp in the brush without sufficient fuel until adequate arrangements could be made to care for them.

Fort Belknap was only the distribution point for the Second Cavalry. There, orders from the Headquarters of the Department of Texas dispatched them by units to pivotal points throughout central Texas. Within a few days they were again in the saddle, enroute to new destinations far from civilization. Major Hardee with four companies, commanded by Captains Van Dorn, George Stoneman, Theodore O'Hara, and Charles J. Whiting, established Camp Cooper on the Clear Fork of the Brazos River near an Indian reservation not far from the Fort Belknap-San Antonio Road. The troops arrived at their new post on January 3, 1856, and pitched tents which they used for shelter until they could construct stone buildings later in the spring.

Winter's blasts raged intermittently in early 1856, often pinning the troops close to their quarters. Men and horses suffered together before the elements. Then spring came, almost in the midst of winter. Van Dorn and his men quickly discovered that rigors of frontier service were not restricted to winter months. Cold weather had been bad, but spring and summer offered new problems. Patrols across the hot dry plains with bacon and hard bread in their saddle bags, sweltering rides during the day under a hot Texas sun, cold nights under a saddle blanket—these and other hardships tested the courage of man and horse with consistent regularity. Van Dorn viewed the countryside through which he rode and called it "a pristine contiguity of saddest wilderness."[11] Lieutenant Johnson added similar sentiments: ". . . it is not unusual to see rattlesnakes, prairie owls and prairie dogs occupy the same hole in the ground," he wrote.[12]

On April 9, 1856, Camp Cooper greeted a new commander, Lieuten-

10. Quoted in Parks, *Kirby Smith*, p. 88.
11. Earl Van Dorn to his wife, April 27, 1856, *A Soldier's Honor*, p. 337.
12. Johnson, *A Soldier's Reminiscences*, p. 115.

ant Colonel Robert E. Lee, just returned from court martial duty. Lee replaced Major Hardee who moved to Fort Mason. Van Dorn welcomed the new commander, and at least one of Lee's letters written in July 1860 indicates that the men were more than just casual acquaintances.[13]

Upon his arrival at Camp Cooper Colonel Lee, hoping for an opportunity to "humanize" the Indians, began a series of talks with the chief of the Comanches in the Camp Cooper area. From this chief, Catumseh, he learned that over 1000 hostile Comanches lived to the north of the camp and were in no mood to be "humanized."

"It will be uphill work, I fear," wrote Lee of the job ahead of him. "Catumseh has been to see me," he continued, "and we have had a talk, very tedious on his part, and very sententious on mine."[14] Meanwhile, he took every precaution to keep the Indians away from the settlers by maintaining a constant vigil over the area with his cavalry. One long patrol after another gave Lee a good idea of the topography of the land and the activities of the Comanches. What he saw of these Indians did not please him. The Comanches, he wrote in a moment of disgust, "give a world of trouble to man and horse, and, poor creatures, they are not worth it."[15]

The long hot rides on the Texas plains, the inactivity within the camp, the harsh living conditions, and other hardships of the frontier had their effect upon Earl Van Dorn. From time to time the loneliness of this region overwhelmed him. Bits and pieces of his correspondence of this period reveal a rekindling of a youthful love for his wife. Whether it was because of the depressing atmosphere of his surroundings, his great love for his daughter, or just the absence of social life at Camp Cooper, his letters from Texas take on a new sentimentality. He began writing his wife once a week, and in these letters he was the lover, expressing his love to her in more poignant expressions than appear in most of his other letters. An impassioned outburst to Carrie in 1856 included the following:

Your disinterested love breathed even through the faint medium of a letter, comes to me like the babbling of some pure fountain to the ear of a

13. Robert E. Lee to Earl Van Dorn, July 3, 1860, Miscellaneous Manuscript Collection, Library of Congress. During the summer of 1857 Van Dorn often "chatted with Lee" while the two were on court-martial duty at Camp Cooper. Rister, *Robert E. Lee in Texas*, p. 84.

14. Crimmins, "Robert E. Lee in Texas," *West Texas Historical Association Yearbook*, VIII, 5.

15. William J. Jones, *Life and Letters of Robert Edward Lee*, p. 80.

weary traveler of the desert. 'How weary, stale, flat, and unprofitable' would this miserable, monotonous life seems to me, here in this exile, were it not for the love that quickens the blood in the heart when I think of you and my dear little prattlers. . . . Hope, like the sustaining hand of an angel, buoys me up, and I meet you once more—even fancy lends its bubbles to float me to your door, where I meet you—embrace you—kiss you—love you and press your throbbing bosom to my own.[16]

To Earl Van Dorn life on the desert was a "stern, sad reality." He missed his wife and children, and even his dreams of glory faded for the moment. Maybe the melancholy of those hot rides did bring the Van Dorns closer together as he suggested:

Here in this solitude, where memory alone gives you to me, where love keeps you ever present, I have more fully learned your worth, and know more appreciatively that you are necessary to my happiness. I long to be with you and look forward with hopeful happiness to our reunion—it shall be soon.[17]

In what must have been a moment of unusual anguish, Earl even promised to send for Carrie when he reached a permanent station. This promise he never kept even though other officers did bring their wives to Texas. Actually, one could hardly blame him for this, however, for drought, flies, ants, choking dust, heat, and loneliness took a heavy toll even from the strongest.

By May 1856 Lee was desperate for some sort of action against the Comanches. Word from Headquarters pointed up new and more severe depredations, but the hideout of the Indians remained unknown. Early in June, Brigadier General Persifor F. Smith, Van Dorn's old Mexican War commander now commanding the Department of Texas, directed Colonel Lee to organize an expedition to move deep into Texas and ferret out a hostile band of Comanches that were led by a notorious chief; Sanaco. General Smith advised Lee to take four companies on the expedition, two each from Camp Cooper and Fort Mason.

Officers and men in both camps received this news enthusiastically and eagerly volunteered their services. This was the kind of action that "made life at a border post tolerable."[18] To Van Dorn's delight, Lee chose his and Captain O'Hara's companies to join the two companies from Fort Mason on the expedition. The four companies rendezvoused

16. Earl Van Dorn to his wife, April 27, 1856, A Soldier's Honor, p. 337.
17. Van Dorn to his wife, May [?], 1856, ibid., p. 339.
18. W. S. Nye, Carbine and Lance, p. 40.

at Fort Chadbourne on June 18 where Colonel Lee consulted with Major Robert S. Neighbors and the other Indian agents there about the possible location of the hostile bands. Neighbors gave what information he had and then offered the services of the celebrated scout, Jim Shaw, and his Delaware Indians as special guides for the expedition.

At Shaw's suggestion Lee's little force headed westward toward some mysterious smoke signals which kept reappearing over the horizon. The troops rode quickly toward the headwaters of the Brazos and Colorado Rivers as if they expected the Indians to meet them there. The weather was hot, the road was dry and filled with holes. The going was rough, and they were four days out from Fort Chadbourne before they found any positive clues. Without warning they stumbled upon several Indian camp sites and lots of fresh trails—but no Indians. Increasing the pace their search continued westward for several more days as they explored canyons, valleys, and draws throughout the immediate vicinity of their discovery. Then illness and heat took their tolls, and Lee called a halt in the field. Quickly he dispatched the invalids back to Fort Chadbourne and called for reinforcements to continue his search.

On June 17 the companies of Captains Kirby Smith and W. R. Bradfute joined Lee, and the search began again. Before leaving the headwaters of the Brazos and the Colorado Rivers, Lee divided his command into three groups to fan out more and cover a greater area in a shorter time. Lee himself took one group; Van Dorn and O'Hara took the others. Van Dorn's group received the choice assignment of investigating fresh Indian trails and smoke newly discovered by the scouts.

Van Dorn's forces, accompanied by Jim Shaw, left the main command early on June 29 eager to get on the trail of "such miserable devils." All that day they moved rapidly in the direction suggested by the scouts. About ten miles behind them, Captain O'Hara followed a line parallel to their own; each unit was hopeful of spotting the Indians first. Toward evening Van Dorn again observed the smoke signals. Shaw warned that they were set by Comanches. This was too good to be true—Van Dorn had discovered the Indians before the others. Figuring a strong force ahead of him, he encamped for the night but not before dispatching a messenger to Captain O'Hara informing him of the situation. The messenger failed in his mission and returned shortly with information that he could not locate O'Hara's command. Provoked by this indolence, Van Dorn decided to move against the Indians without help from the other troops. This was a bit foolhardy, but all the troops were overanxious for contact with the elusive Comanches.

Early on June 30 Van Dorn began his new movement toward the smoke, screening his troops by following draws and ravines. Some excitement spread through the ranks as the smoke came closer. Suddenly they were upon the Indian camp. Yelling loudly the troops charged into the ravine which sheltered the fire and the Indians, but within the camp was little of what they had expected. There before them were three Comanche warriors and an Indian woman. Surprised by the sudden intrusion, two of the warriors put up a fight while the third succeeded in mounting his horse and racing quickly down the canyon. The troops killed the first two Indians with a spray of gunfire and then captured the woman and twelve horses. While the scouts interrogated the captive woman, O'Hara and his men appeared on the scene. They had heard the shots and also had been hopeful of some action. Fearing the presence of a larger Indian force nearby, Van Dorn spread the troops out to search a wide radius while the questioning continued. Nothing was found by any of the patrols, and little was learned from the squaw. She and a band of twelve Yamparika warriors had just recently returned from a successful plundering expedition in Mexico. They had hardly crossed the Mexican border when white men attacked them and killed eight of the warriors. The survivors had continued on through Texas, raiding along their way, stealing cattle and horses, and plundering isolated settlers. When discovered by Van Dorn's party, they had just stopped to eat, rest and jerk some beef. One member of the group had departed just before the arrival of the troops.

This was disappointing news, so Van Dorn called in his troops and returned to his rendezvous point. Colonel Lee was much disappointed to have missed even this small fray, but the little skirmish was a tonic to the weather-beaten dragoons. Enthusiastically the officers organized new scouting missions and searched the area for miles around in hopes of some action with a more substantial force. Their searches were in vain. All Indian trails led to Mexico, so on July 23, after over a month in the field covering over 1100 miles, Lee's troops returned to Camp Cooper. On the return Van Dorn, scouting one of the flanks, found a large empty Indian camp in the Concho River valley, but alas, the camp had been vacated earlier in the spring.

Camp Cooper looked good to the tired troopers, but their respite

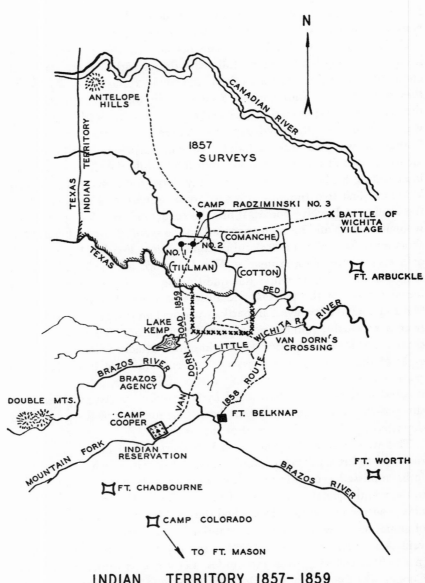

N

ANTELOPE
HILLS

CANADIAN RIVER

1857
SURVEYS

TEXAS

INDIAN TERRITORY

TEXAS

CAMP RADZIMINSKI NO. 3

X BATTLE OF
WICHITA
VILLAGE

(COMANCHE)

NO. 2

NO. 1

(TILLMAN)

(COTTON)

RED

FT. ARBUCKLE

VAN DORN ROAD 1859

LAKE
KEMP

WICHITA R. RIVER

LITTLE

VAN DORN'S
CROSSING

BRAZOS RIVER

BRAZOS
AGENCY

1858 ROUTE

DOUBLE MTS.

CAMP
COOPER

FT. BELKNAP

MOUNTAIN FORK

INDIAN
RESERVATION

FT. WORTH

BRAZOS RIVER

FT. CHADBOURNE

CAMP COLORADO

TO FT. MASON

INDIAN   TERRITORY 1857- 1859

from field service was short lived. At San Antonio Colonel Albert S. Johnston had replaced General Smith as commander of the Department of Texas; Colonel Johnston had once commanded the Army of the Republic of Texas. One of Johnston's first actions was to reorganize the Second Cavalry into squadrons of about one hundred men each and redistribute them to more strategic spots in Texas. Under this new arrangement Van Dorn became commander of the First Squadron with orders to organize and supervise a military station near the crossing of the Colorado River and the Fort Mason–Fort Belknap Road.

Van Dorn departed from Camp Cooper on July 28, 1856, and by the end of August he had set up a new camp at the location designated. He called the new post Camp Colorado. Again the first quarters were tents set up along the line of the river. The flooding river caused the commander to move his camp to nearby Jim Ned Creek early in the fall, and there the troops erected adobe buildings which served cavalry troops for many years.[19] Camp Colorado and the other outposts strengthened the defense line in Texas, and little Indian trouble was noted for nearly a year. Except for a partial concentration at Fort Belknap in 1858, the entire Second Cavalry was not again reunited until 1860.

For the next year cavalry troops in Texas spent their days on scouting missions and patrolling. At Camp Colorado Van Dorn was especially effective in his patrols, and by 1858 he was one of the most respected officers in the regiment. He was well liked by his officers and men, and he seemed to take special interest in them and their activities. He never sent out a patrol without first making an elaborate map of all the surrounding area, and these maps helped to increase the effectiveness of the patrols. The First Squadron fought no major battles, but one of Van Dorn's scouting parties engaged a small Comanche band on the North Concho River in late December 1856. The squadron leader was not present at the short skirmish in which the troopers decisively defeated the Indians.

Except for a month of service in the field and an occasional court martial trial at Camp Cooper, Van Dorn was at or near Camp Colorado for over a year. Again he was lonely and longed for family and home.

19. During the Civil War these buildings became a gathering post for deserters and desperados. Crimmins, "The Military History of Camp Colorado," *West Texas Historical Association Yearbook*, XXVIII, 72.

Most of his spare time he spent in reading, writing, or painting, a favorite hobby. Mrs. Albert Sidney Johnston was also a painter, and it
pleased him very much when she gave him some paints. With them he
painted landscapes, camp scenes, and portraits. On one occasion he
copied a picture of the Johnstons' daughter for the Colonel and his wife.

It was horse racing always, though, that commanded the most attention among the officers and men of the Second Cavalry. Their horses
were of the finest stock, and they raced as thoroughbreds. Van Dorn
was an excellent horseman; he owned a fine mount and won both
money and "baskets of Champagne" in the tense races that highlighted
camp activity.

On the Texas frontier Earl Van Dorn came into his own. Not only
was he popular among the soldiers but his striking personality also made
him a great favorite among the citizens of the state. His dashing exploits
both on and off the field provided topics of conversation around many
a dinner table or camp fire. He had changed little from his Mexican
War days. He was still impulsive, shortsighted, and a bit arrogant. But
definite leadership qualities were emerging, and his indomitable courage was the pride of the regiment. Lieutenant Fitzhugh Lee, a member
of his squadron, admired him very much, describing him as "thoroughly
a soldier in all that constitutes a brave conscientious officer . . . easily
the most conspicuous officer of his grade."[20] About medium height, he
was strongly built with a small waist and broad shoulders. At this time
he began to show signs of a natural ability to handle small cavalry
commands.

Although Colonel Johnston's forces established tranquil relations between the settlers and the Indians, peace on the frontier was short lived.
On May 18, 1857, the War Department called Johnston from Texas to
head an expedition against the Mormons in Utah. Johnston's replace-
ment in Texas was erratic Brigadier General David C. Twiggs. Johnston
had been unusually effective in holding the Indians in check, and his
departure was a signal for a sudden marked increase in Comanche
raids throughout the state. Another factor combined with this change
in command also helped intensify Indian activities. Earlier in 1857,
many surveys had been made in the Indian lands north of Texas, and
new proprietary interests had cut further into territory occupied by the
nomadic Comanches. In retaliation the Indians began to move into

20. Quoted in *A Soldier's Honor*, pp. 261–263.

Texas to plunder the whites. By January 1858, the white settlers in Texas were up in arms, and they flooded the office of the Secretary of the Interior with petitions demanding that something be done to protect the rights of the settlers in this new area.

General Twiggs pondered his dilemma. What could he do? His troops had engaged the Comanches and Kiowas in twelve separate engagements during the year past, and although none had been of great significance, each had followed the same pattern. There had been a lively skirmish, a few casualties, and then the Indians had disappeared into the hills and valleys north of the Texas border. Technically General Twiggs's hands were tied. War Department orders limited the activities of the Second Cavalry to a policy of pursuing Indians only after they had committed depredations. This defensive policy kept them from carrying the war to the villages of the Indians, and the savages exploited this policy to their own advantages.

Van Dorn was among those officers of Twiggs's command who found these restrictions most annoying. In January 1858, he and his command chased a band of Comanches and Kiowas who had stolen a large number of horses from Texas citizens. The pursuit took them to the Canadian River where they watched the Indians disappear beyond their range of operation. Van Dorn complained vigorously of Army "red tape," hopeful that he would be given greater leeway in future actions.[21]

Spring came, and the Indians increased their raids. Negotiations continued in other quarters but to little avail. Meanwhile, soldiers in dirty blue uniforms rode endless patrols in blistering Texas sun and choking dust on the trails of Indian bands, only to be frustrated time and again by the War Department restrictions and Indian elusiveness.

In May the War Department suddenly changed its tactics in Texas but, in a most unexpected manner. In Utah Territory Colonel Johnston's troubles with the Mormons had increased beyond expectations. He needed troop reinforcements to meet new threats. The War Department turned to the Second Cavalry, his old command. Orders to Texas directed General Twiggs to concentrate his troops at Fort Belknap in preparation for their new assignment. In May and June the companies of the Second Cavalry assembled at Fort Belknap as ordered. This was the first time since 1855 that the frontier had been left so wide open. It was a signal for the Comanches to increase their raids.

21. Clara Lena Koch, "The Federal Indian Policy in Texas, 1845–1860," *Southwestern Historical Quarterly*, XXIX, 116.

Texans complained loudly at this turn of affairs. If their Government would not protect their property, they would do it themselves. In May a group of prominent citizens decided to take matters into their own hands by taking up arms against the Indians. Led by Rangers Shapley R. Ross and John S. Ford, a citizens' force attacked and destroyed a Comanche camp just north of the Canadian River.

At Fort Arbuckle the news of this attack was received with dismay. Lieutenant J. E. Powell, working under the Office of Indian Affairs of the Department of Interior, was even then in the process of peace negotiations with a group of Comanches when he heard of the attack. Upset at this action, the lieutenant vented his feelings to Washington in no uncertain terms. His comments were to little avail. Two conflicting policies were still in effect on the frontier; the "carrot and the stick" were being employed simultaneously by two different departments. Military authorities encouraged violence while Department of Interior officials counseled negotiations and a strong reservation policy.

At Fort Arbuckle, Lieutenant Powell continued his discussions with the Indians, and before the summer ended he had convinced some of them that if they really wanted peace they had to prove their sincerity by returning all the goods they had stolen, mainly horses, to the proper owners. Existing evidence indicates that the War Department and the citizens of Texas were not informed of this action, but if they were informed they chose to disregard it. The citizens' force struck a second blow, this time against the very Indians with whom Lieutenant Powell had been negotiating. This assault upon the Comanches came when they were returning stolen horses to Fort Arbuckle as part of their agreement with Lieutenant Powell. The attackers figured that the Comanches had stolen more horses, and they were determined to punish them for it. Indian retaliation followed, and soon the frontier was aflame with violence.

In the face of new threats to their security, Ross and other Texas leaders again turned to General Twiggs for aid. General Twiggs responded quickly in the face of the increasing difficulties. Thinking only in terms of a military solution, he reported the crisis to the War Department, requesting the use of his troops to bring an end to the hostilities. The Second Cavalry was still at Fort Belknap awaiting transportation to Utah. Why not use them in Texas? Twiggs boldly asked that he be allowed to drop the ineffective policy of the defensive and take the fight directly to the camp of the marauders. He would follow the Indians "winter and summer, thus giving . . . [them] something to do at home in taking care of their families and they might possibly let Texas alone."[22]

Secretary of War, John B. Floyd, viewed the request and answered in favor of Twiggs's proposal. The Mormon problem had eased sooner than expected, so Floyd authorized Twiggs "to make such change in the disposition of the Second Cavalry as the state of the service and of our Indian relations might require."[23] General Twiggs acted while his regiment was still assembled at Fort Belknap. He interpreted Floyd's directive liberally and decided to send out an expedition as early as September that would "follow up the Comanches to the residence of their families."[24] It was his belief that the expedition could be made with little expense since he expected the troops to feed their horses off the land. With soldiers bringing the war to Indian country, he envisioned permanent peace and quiet in Texas. Whether Twiggs knew of Lieutenant Powell's concurrent actions or not, he continued to plan independently of the Department of Interior.

For his expedition General Twiggs chose Companies A, F, H, and K, a detachment of the First Infantry, and sixty Caddo and Delaware warriors. Colonel Lee was in Virginia on leave at this time, so Major George H. Thomas expected to command the expedition. Major Thomas was the ranking officer on duty in the Second Cavalry, but he was not one of Twiggs's favorites. It appears that the old "war horse" never forgave the junior officer for his strenuous opposition during the Mexican War. Whether this is true or not, Twiggs did not offer the assignment to Thomas but gave it to his close friend, Earl Van Dorn. "I intend if the permission is given," he wrote, "to put the command under Major Van Dorn, as I have every confidence in his capacity and energy to conduct such an expedition."[25]

Twiggs's personal attachment to Van Dorn seems to have been strongly related to the younger officer's personal involvement with the Southern cause. Twiggs liked Van Dorn's ardent defense of the South, and the two men had continued on intimate terms since their Mexican War association. They seem to have discussed the Southern position

22. General Twiggs to Army Headquarters, July 6, 1858, *Senate Executive Documents*, 35 Cong., 2 Sess., Doc. 1, p. 258.
23. Assistant Adjutant General McDowell to General Twiggs, July 22, 1858, *ibid.*, p. 259.
24. Twiggs to the Adjutant General, July 27, 1858, *ibid.*
25. *Ibid.*

occasionally, and the older man later helped the major make the decision that led to his resignation from the United States Army. This choice assignment of leading an expedition against the Indians was just one of many favors that Twiggs offered Van Dorn in their years of service together.

Accompanying Van Dorn on his new mission was Lawrence S. Ross, the twenty-year-old son of S. P. Ross, one of the instigators of the earlier citizen action against the Indians. "Sul" Ross, who had lived most of his life on the Texas frontier amidst the Indians, was a student at Florence Wesleyan University in Alabama. During his summer vacations he always returned to Texas and often engaged in actions against the Indians. In the late summer of 1858 he signed with the Army to accompany the Van Dorn expedition as the leader of the friendly Caddo Indians.

On September 15, Van Dorn and Ross, also ignorant of the Fort Arbuckle negotiations, marched their men northward from Fort Belknap to Otter Creek in the northern part of what is now Tillman County, Oklahoma. By September 26 they had a supply depot under construction beside the creek near the present site of Tipton. Instead of building permanent fortifications, they put log and turf walls around tents as protection against Indians and the elements. Van Dorn named his makeshift post Camp Radziminski after a Polish lieutenant of the Second Cavalry who died of tuberculosis earlier in the year. While the men struggled to complete the shelter at the earliest possible date, Ross's Indian scouts searched the country roundabout for signs of hostile Indians.

The one sizable Indian camp in the area was a Kiowa settlement at Wichita Village due west of Camp Radziminski. Near the Kiowas in a hastily constructed camp, a band of Comanches under the notorious marauder, Buffalo Hump, was also in residence. After negotiations with Lieutenant Powell, Buffalo Hump had brought his people to Wichita Village to make amends to the Kiowas and return some horses which the Comanches had stolen from the Kiowa village earlier. The Kiowas had received the Comanches well, and the two Indian bands had gotten on well together. The Comanches were planning a trip to Fort Arbuckle, but they had delayed their departure from Wichita to trade and gamble with the Kiowas. They did not suspect the Army's intent toward them.

Van Dorn's Indian scouts brought him word of the Comanche settlement on September 29. Camp Radziminski greeted the news with enthusiasm, and troops readied themselves for action. The commander ordered the four cavalry companies and the friendly Indians to saddle up, and they departed for the Comanche camp on the afternoon of the same day with two days rations. During their absence the other troops, animals, and supplies were to remain inside the newly completed stockade.

Van Dorn rode ahead of his troops as they moved away from the setting sun. This was the action he craved. He figured that it was only forty miles to the camp of his enemy, and he planned to lead an attack against the Comanches at dawn.

Forty miles was too conservative an estimate. Dawn came and still there was no Indian camp. The sun rose in their faces, blurring out the rugged landscape, but the troops rode on, pushed relentlessly toward their objective by their commander. They ate their jerked beef in the saddle and traveled over the wild country all day. Finally after sundown Van Dorn halted his troops to boil coffee and to feed their tired horses.

As the weary troops rested on the hard ground, a Comanche spy from Buffalo Hump's tribe observed them and reported their presence to his chief. Buffalo Hump called a council, and the Indians deliberated the course of action to take. They finally decided that these were friendly troops, and they had no cause for alarm. Had they not been assured by the Fort Arbuckle authorities that they were in no danger? Secure in these thoughts the Comanches retired for the night without even putting out their usual camp guards.

Sometime after dark, one of Van Dorn's scouts brought him word of the location of the Comanches' camp. He pondered the matter briefly; then he decided to move as close as possible to the Indians to make a dawn attack. He roused his men. Silently they moved in the night advancing over very rough and broken terrain at a snail's pace until just before daybreak on October 1, when they arrived on a large prairie. Informed by his scouts that the Comanche camp was just over a crest of hills, Van Dorn split his command into four columns and set his attack plan. The men would ride toward the village in pairs with intervals of one hundred yards between each pair. The Major then ordered his company commanders to "deploy and charge" when they sighted the camp.

The troops rode slowly and quietly over the hill. The night air was cool and foggy; there was an excitement among the men that pressed them on despite their saddle weariness. Daylight appeared directly in front of them still blurred by the fog, and some turned anxiously toward their commanding officer. The tired troops crossed four ridges before the sun appeared on the horizon. Then through a slight haze over a crest of the prairie in a clump of trees, they saw the Comanche village. The village stretched out several hundred yards along the banks of a branch.

Van Dorn halted his advancing column in a slight clearing out of sight of the village and gave his men last minute instructions before the attack. He detached Ross and his friendly Indians from the main force to move ahead of the attacking unit and cut off the Comanches' horses before the battle began. There was a stillness in the early morning air as Ross's men moved toward the edge of the village. The other soldiers waited expectantly. Suddenly Van Dorn's bugler blasted the still calm with an order to charge. The troops responded as a man, dashing quickly and furiously into the village.

Inside the Indian settlement, the sleeping Comanches, women as well as men, suddenly came to life. They sprang into action, but it was a spontaneous reaction and not the well-organized endeavor of Indian warriors. Prevented from using their horses by Ross's successful action, the Comanches fought desperately on foot from a ravine in and around their village in hand-to-hand combat with an outnumbered but superior foe. First Sergeant John W. Spangler killed six Indians. Lieutenant James P. Majors, an 1856 West Point graduate newly assigned to the Second Cavalry, accounted for three more. Warriors fought on despite heavy losses, desperately covering the withdrawal of their families. For two hours the sounds of battle rang through the ravines. Even the Indian women took part in the battle; they proved very effective with bows and with rifles. Some troops dismounted and fought on foot in thick underbrush, while mounted troops defended flanks and closed off escape routes down the ravines. The fog lifted, but fighters on both sides continued to grapple in bloody combat. Then almost as suddenly as it had begun, the battle ended. Outnumbering their attackers two to one, the Indians were decisively beaten and fifty-six of their number were dead on the field. Captain Charles Whiting counted four dead and twelve wounded in Van Dorn's command. The element of surprise and the cavalry's firepower had been too much for the Indians. Although the battle was over, the soldiers were not finished with them. Before departing from their scene of triumph, they burned the remaining lodges and seized 300 horses. Believing they had been betrayed by the whites, the Comanches who had escaped the wrath of the cavalry vowed revenge.

During the battle Earl Van Dorn had constantly been in the midst of the fiercest action and almost lost his life. The major led three companies to engage the enemy on the left flank. Late in the battle when the Indians were in full flight, he along with Ross, Lieutenant Cornelious Van Camp, and a private tried to round up a group of fleeing Comanches. Van Dorn, accomplished horseman that he was and mounted on a "splendid gray" which stopped at neither branch nor marsh, soon outdistanced the others. Out ahead of his comrades, he found himself alone, charging into the rear of the retreating Comanches. Undaunted by his position, he foolishly advanced into range of two Indians riding double and fired at them. His shot killed their horse and threw the riders to the ground. Seeing their pursuer rushing upon them, the Indians fell to their knees and shot deliberately at him. He reacted instinctively by throwing up his arm and taking the initial force of the flying arrows in his hand, but one arrow passed through his wrist and penetrated his body. He later described these wounds in some detail in a letter to his wife:

My first wound was in the left arm, the arrow entered just above the wrist, passed between the two bones and stopped near the elbow. The second was in my body; the arrow entered opposite the ninth rib on the right side, passed through the upper portion of the stomach, cut my left lung, and passed out on the left side between the sixth and seventh rib.[26]

Sorely wounded, the major fell from his saddle and would have been killed then and there had not his troops appeared on the scene before the Indians could fire again. According to one report, a sergeant saved his life by throwing himself between his commander and the Indians. Van Dorn himself later admitted in picturesque language that if his troops had not appeared when they did he "would have been stuck as full of arrows as Gulliver was by the Lilliputians," and his best friends could not have picked him out "from among a dozen porcupines."[27]

But even in his agony, Van Dorn was not inactive: "I killed the

26. Van Dorn to his wife, October 12, 1858, *A Soldier's Honor*, p. 125.
27. *Ibid.*, p. 40.

Indian that shot me," he recorded triumphantly. Nevertheless, it was a bad experience. He left the following description of his inward feelings:

When I pulled the arrows from me the blood followed as if weary of service, and impatient to cheat me of life—spilling like red wine from a drunkard's tankard.

It was sublime to stand thus on the brink of the dark abyss, and the contemplation was awful. . . . I had faced death often, but never so palpably before—I gasped in dreadful agony for several hours, but finally became easy.[28]

"It was a bad day for the Vans," he concluded. Van Camp's wounds were mortal, and Van Dorn's were severe enough to force him from the field. The troops waited at Wichita Village for five days after the battle before their wounded commander could be moved. On the sixth day the troops made a litter, which they strung between two horses, and carried him back to Camp Radziminski. Though painful, the wounds were less severe than originally believed, and Van Dorn was soon on his feet again. Weakened by his ordeal, he took a five-week recuperation leave at his Mississippi home where he was feted royally by the citizens of his state for his contribution to the conquest of the Indians in Texas. His friends and admirers presented him with a splendid silver service, and the newspapers published glowing accounts of his military achievements. One of his sisters celebrated his triumphant return home by composing a martial air entitled "Wichita March" which she dedicated to him. This march was later a special favorite with the Second Cavalry.

Wichita Village had been Earl Van Dorn's most important personal military action. His reports of the battle reflect his pride in this successful attack. He complimented his troops for spending "more than sixteen consecutive hours in the saddle, with only a *hope* of meeting the enemy."[29] He also took special note of "the spirit, activity, gallantry, and cool courage" displayed by all his men. These men were a reflection of their commander. Their virtues were his, and he was proud of their success. He concurred fully with General Twiggs's evaluation that it was rare when "a command so efficient is assembled."[30]

28. Van Dorn to his wife, October 12, 1858, *ibid.*

29. Orders Number 5 from Headquarters of Wichita Expedition from Camp Radziminski, October 12, 1858, found in Van Dorn Collection, Montgomery, Alabama.

30. General Twiggs to Army Headquarters, October 18, 1858, *Senate Executive Documents,* 35 Cong., 2 Sess., Doc. 1, p. 268.

Army officials also felt that the success against the Indians was an important victory and a step toward final conquest of the Comanches, despite the escape of Buffalo Hump and two-thirds of his warriors. Twiggs complimented his young friend by saying that seldom was a command so well handled. Major Hardee also registered approval of the victory. He wrote from West Point of the "handsomest affair with the savages" of which he had knowledge.[31] Many of those engaged were men he had personally trained for such engagements. Meanwhile, Buffalo Hump and his surviving warriors "disappeared as a mist" into the Kansas frontier.

While the military officials heaped praise on the initiators of offensive warfare, the Department of Interior viewed the action with deep concern. One of the Department's spokesmen charged that the border military forces were frustrating their peace plans. Little impressed by this criticism the army continued its aggressive policy. General Twiggs did express some concern for the dual program of dealing with the Indians when he admitted that there should have been a "concert of action" by the two different agencies. "One of us has made a serious blunder," he wrote, "he [Powell] in making a treaty, or I in sending out a party after them."[32] But the implications were directed against the actions of the Department of Interior. The War Department continued to applaud Van Dorn's action and herald it a "brilliant victory," meanwhile approving a "follow up" campaign with reinforcements.

Major Van Dorn was in perfect agreement with the general policy of the War Department. Because of his interest and his great vitality, he was back with his command at Camp Radziminski in late November. He found his troops tired and his horses underfed, so he decided not to initiate another offensive until spring. The winter was a hard one on all concerned. They remained at Camp Radziminski and patrolled the countryside and made ready for spring. Twice during the winter Van Dorn had to move the camp's location in the face of a forage shortage. Troops and horses suffered. Many of the horses died, and a sizable number of men were invalided back to Fort Belknap before spring's sun made its appearance.

31. W. H. Hardee to Van Dorn, November 4, 1858, Miscellaneous Manuscript Collection, Library of Congress.

32. General Twiggs to Army Headquarters, September 27, 1858, *Senate Executive Documents*, 35 Cong., 2 Sess., Doc. 1, p. 267.

Life on this remote frontier was dismal and hard on too many occasions, but at its most trying it still had its lighter moments. Both officers and enlisted men kept their senses of humor even in a Kansas winter. Major Van Dorn called his orderly in one cold day and told him to save out enough food for himself before he served the officers. "Oh, that's all right, Major," said the orderly, "I always eats first. You gents only get what is left."[33]

It was the monotony and the loneliness that spoke loudest at Fort Radziminski. Troops and officers alike searched ways to pass the weary hours. Poker chips and champagne bottles recently discovered in a cornfield site of the third camp may indicate something of how the troops spent the long cold days in the camp. There were also horse races as usual, and the commander was not above cheering his favorite mount to a hard-earned victory. He probably regretted that his own physical condition restricted his riding for several months. Troops then, as on many other occasions in American military history, never missed an opportunity to add spice and variety to dull garrison life.

During the winter months at Camp Radziminski, the post commander and his men worked hard in preparation for their spring offensive. They drilled often. They scouted for Comanches and Kiowas when the weather permitted. They trained their horses so that when the animals were turned out to graze they would return to camp at any alarm; this valuable practice could prevent the Indians from stampeding them before an attack.

Van Dorn also requested reinforcements. When the recruits arrived, the veteran noncoms drilled them and prepared them for the rigors of Indian warfare. Supplies trickled in to refurbish the depleted stocks of the camp, and the Radziminski command began to take on the appearance of a first-class unit.

Obviously Van Dorn favored a policy of sustained action against the Indians rather than pettifogging negotiation. He expressed these views in no uncertain terms when he heard of the Department of the Interior's criticisms of his Wichita Village attack. Too many of the marauding Indians received gratuitous shelter in the Indian reservations, he protested. Why should this be when he and his troops were encamped in wild Indian country in winter's coldest weather because of them? While

33. William S. Nye, "Battle of Wichita Village," *Chronicles of Oklahoma*, XV, 226.

his men froze before the fury of a prairie norther, the Indians smoked "in quiet security on the parade ground of some military post." "If something better is not offered them as the boon of peace and friendship," he complained, "I am afraid our difficulties with them will be resolved into a war of extermination." But to Van Dorn, force came first.[34]

With the approach of warm weather, the War Department again focused its attention on Indian problems. In a directive to General Twiggs, Secretary Floyd ordered the general to "enforce hostilities against all Indians off their reserves."[35] Then as if tempered by the critics from the Department of Indian Affairs, or suspect of Van Dorn's motives, Floyd added: "This rule should be applied with some discrimination, however, with reference to tribes or bands generally peaceful."[36] Twiggs and Van Dorn showed little concern for the reservation.

Spring came slowly and Van Dorn was reluctant to push his offensive into winter's harshness. The weather reached its worst peak during March. When John S. Ford visited Camp Radziminski on March 1, 1859, he found the troops huddled in their shelters, driven back to their tents by a hearty blizzard. Ford, also anxious for a decisive offensive against the Comanches, discussed the possibilities of a combined effort between the cavalry and his Rangers. Van Dorn listened for several days to Ford's plans, and then another cold wave struck. Heavy snows on March 6 and 7 "chilled" his enthusiasm for Ford's suggestion. He concluded that any offensive must wait for clear signs of warm weather. Ford left Camp Radziminski on this note. It is possible that Van Dorn welcomed his departure, for, regular army officer that he was, he may not have relished thoughts of working with the Rangers. He had plans and hopes of his own.

The major finally chose April 30 as the day when the penetrating cold winds would have abated and the grass would be sufficiently matured to sustain his animals. Early that morning the troops made their long-awaited departure from their winter camp to scout "north." Van Dorn would cross the Washita, the Canadian, and the Cimarron rivers if the situation demanded it, but he would take the war to the Comanches. Friendly Indians rode as his scouts ten miles in advance of his main body.

34. Van Dorn to the Assistant Adjutant General, December 28, 1858, *Senate Executive Documents*, 36 Cong., 1 Sess., Doc. 2, pp. 356–357.

35. Secretary of War Floyd's Directive, April 5, 1859, *ibid.*, p. 358.

36. *Ibid.*

On their fourth day out the scouts captured a stray Comanche boy who soon admitted that he had been a member of a party going to Texas to steal horses. He told the troops that his own people, also part of Buffalo Hump's tribe, were encamped on a small stream about two days ride beyond the Cimarron River or about a week's ride from their present position. "Full confidence was not given to this statement," said Van Dorn later, "but I . . . thought it advisable to extend my march into that section of the country."[37] Without longer pause than necessary, he pushed on toward the Cimarron with the Comanche boy as his guide, threatening to shoot the youngster if he misdirected his troops.

They arrived at the Cimarron River five days later and waited there for a freshet to subside. Impatient at the delay, Van Dorn finally "corralled" his provision wagons and pushed his mounted troops across the stream and on toward the north. The next day their hopes rose when they encountered a small Comanche band, and in a short running fight they killed one Indian. Searching for a larger Indian band, they went on their way immediately after the skirmish. Early on May 11 they struck fresh trails which their Comanche guide believed to be those of his people. Van Dorn halted his troops about two o'clock in the afternoon to rest the men and horses for what he hoped to be an impending engagement. His troopers unsaddled their mounts and put them in a lush field to graze; a detachment of 30 riders under Lieutenant William B. Royal guarded them. Above the sky was darkening and a rainstorm appeared imminent.

Within an hour three Comanche warriors slipped into the field and attempted to stampede the horses. Fortunately for Van Dorn, the well-trained animals refused to stampede, but instead they returned to their riders. The men saddled up quickly and followed the guards chasing the Indians. The unsuspecting Comanches led the pursuing troops directly to their camp. The troops discovered the Indians' horses first, and Van Dorn immediately halted his main force while Lieutenant Royal successfully stampeded the Indian horses.

The Major reported that the Comanches "had taken a strong defensive position, being in a deep ravine, densely covered with a stunted growth of timber and brambles, through which a small stream with abrupt banks, meandered from bluff to bluff on either side."[38] They

37. Van Dorn's Report, May 31, 1859, *ibid.*, p. 369.
38. *Ibid.*

could not see the enemy in these surroundings, and they hardly suspected their presence but for the "twang of the arrows which came forth to challenge the white soldiers' advance."[39]

Van Dorn's plan of attack was simple, not unlike the one he had used at Wichita Village. It was a small-scale model of the same plan he had learned at Monterrey and the one he often used in his Civil War experiences. It did not follow Jomini's principle of concentration precisely, but it had the advantage of offering several fronts to confused Indians. He divided his six companies into three squadrons of equal strength. A squadron of mounted troops was placed at either end of the small valley, while the other squadron dismounted and pushed ahead in a frontal attack.

Part of this plan backfired as soon as the movement began. One of the mounted squadrons moved directly into the line of fire of the other mounted unit and delayed the attack until the situation was corrected. Then the dismounted troops charged, sweeping down into the valley with all their pent-up fury of the past winter escaping in wild yelling and fast shooting. Just as at Wichita Village, the surprised Indians quickly sought shelter and fought back. Captain Kirby Smith spearheaded a supporting attack from the flank. When he fell, severely wounded, in the early minutes of the battle, his troops continued their furious assault as the Comanches, warriors and squaws, fought desperately in defense of homes and families. Lieutenant Fitzhugh Lee also went down with serious wounds. Although both sides fought hard, the Comanches were no match for the guns and strength of their attackers. Van Dorn complimented the Comanches for their courage in his official report of the battle, but he also reflected his own prejudices:

The Comanches fought without giving or asking quarter until there was not one left to bend a bow, and would have won the admiration of every brave soldier of the command but for the intrusive reflection that they were the murderers of the wives and children of our frontiersmen, and the most wretched of thieves.[40]

Because of the numerous casualties among his troops, Van Dorn had to divide his forces into two groups for their return to Camp Radziminski nearly 200 miles away. He placed the sick and the wounded under

39. Thoburn, "Indian Fight in Ford Country," p. 321.
40. Van Dorn's Report, May 31, 1859, *Senate Executive Documents*, 36 Cong., 1 Sess., Doc. 2, p. 369.

Kirby Smith and dispatched them directly to Fort Arbuckle. He took the able-bodied men and scouted to the southwest for several days before returning to Camp Radziminski. His two blows had been effective; for a time the Comanches ceased to be troublemakers.

After his return to Fort Belknap in early June, Van Dorn was relieved of the command of his company and his squadron and was sent to Fort Mason for a new assignment. Here he served as assistant regimental commander until November 1, 1859, when he took a much-deserved four-month leave of absence back to Mississippi. Upon his return to Fort Mason in March, Lieutenant Colonel George H. Thomas, acting commander of the Second Cavalry, immediately invited him to join in a search for another Indian camp supposedly situated near the headwaters of the Brazos River. Van Dorn took to the field this time for over a month, but this expedition was a fruitless one since they discovered no hostile Indians. As far as the records show, this was the last lengthy mission of Earl Van Dorn into Indian country, for his assignments reveal his presence at Fort Mason until his departure for Mississippi on Christmas Day, 1860.

Personal ambition never waned in Texas, even after the Indian menace faded. Shortly after his return from the expedition with Colonel Thomas, he wrote his wife that he would become a regular major of cavalry if his friend Colonel Albert S. Johnston had his way. "Now," he wrote with youthful enthusiasm, "there is some reason for the hope that I shall one day be 'General of the Army.'" He was still a few days from forty, and he took pride in stressing the fact that he had no "gray hairs."[41]

Earl Van Dorn need not have worried about his majority. His was one of the brightest names in the United States Army. His new rank had already been confirmed as of June 28, 1860. New and exciting days were ahead, and his hopes to become a general would reach fruition even faster than he could hope.

41. Van Dorn to his wife, July 18, 1860, *A Soldier's Honor*, p. 340.

CHAPTER FOUR

A New War

*P*ROFESSOR Allan Nevins has called the summer of 1860 in the South a time "of unprecedented excitement with subterranean upheavals and rumblings."[1] Talk of secession was on the lips of citizens throughout the slaveholding states. As far west as Texas incendiary fires replaced reason as the Presidential election focused public attention on the divisive issues of sectionalism. Nevins spoke of the "wave of hysteria" in the Lone Star State as the worst ever. While much of the apprehension of the Texans may have been "unreal," the sentiments of Southernism as against Unionism were in sharp confrontation.

Even troops in the forts and distant outposts felt the intensity of the struggle, and they too became involved in the clash of opinions. West Pointers, in particular, their army careers always in the balance, discussed the crisis with varied degrees of enthusiasm as rumors of war persisted along with secession talk. As if awaiting some signal many of them watched closely the grave-faced Robert E. Lee. Others were more positive in their actions. Some presented their views guardedly in the privacy of their tents or barracks. Some spoke their sentiments only in the written word to loved ones back at home. But others were more belligerent in their feelings, lauding the Southern position, haranguing it constantly before their fellow officers. Three of the leading fire-eaters appear to have been Earl Van Dorn, John B. Hood, and Fitzhugh Lee.

No voice was more consistent or sincere in its support of the Southern position than Mississippi's Van Dorn. He represented an extreme case of what H. J. Eckenrode has called the "tropic nordic."[2] At a time when

1. *The Emergence of Lincoln*, II, 306.
2. H. J. Eckenrode, *Jefferson Davis: President of the South*, p. 4–28.

most of the officers of Southern birth were debating whether secession was justifiable under any circumstances, he was taking a leading role in expressing a pronounced sympathy for the slave states. At Fort Mason he was soon recognized as "an ardent advocate of the right of secession."[3] To his wife he wrote that he was "for secession at every cost."[4]

After Lincoln's election in November, the Lone Star flag flew in defiance over a number of Texas communities, and the secession ferment in the state reached a crisis. At Fort Mason the increasing expressions of dissension threatened to disrupt the discipline of the post. In the dilemma of the moment, Van Dorn turned to his friend, General Twiggs, for advice. General Twiggs's sentiments can be determined from a letter he wrote to General Scott not long after Lincoln's election in which he said: "I think there can be no doubt that many of the Southern States will secede from the Union. The State of Texas will be among the number, and . . . it will be an early day."[5]

Twiggs repeated these alarming views to Van Dorn and advised him under the circumstances to return to Mississippi as soon as possible and settle all his personal affairs.[6] Van Dorn accordingly sought and received a two-month leave of absence with permission to apply for an indefinite extension. His plans took shape rapidly. His sword was for Mississippi, and Mississippi was loud in her praise of South Carolina's secession convention. Van Dorn's hopes soared high. "I am fortunate at this time in having a good military reputation," he wrote his wife, as if already anticipating high command.[7] Patriotism and ambition pushed him on, and he rushed into the future with great abandon.

Arriving in Mobile by boat in late December 1860, the Major greeted his wife who came down from her Alabama home to meet him. As usual their meeting was a brief one. Things of greater importance loomed ahead for the soldier. Mississippi called, and a true son of the

3. Price, *Across the Continent*, p. 276.
4. Van Dorn to his wife, December 14, 1860, Van Dorn Collection, Montgomery, Alabama.
5. Quoted in Robert U. Johnson and Clarence C. Buel (eds.), *Battles and Leaders of the Civil War*, I, 38.
6. General Twiggs to Van Dorn, September 23, 1859, Manuscript Collection of the Confederate States of America, Library of Congress.
7. Van Dorn to his wife, December 14, 1860, Van Dorn Collection, Montgomery, Alabama.

state must answer. On January 3, 1861, Earl Van Dorn severed his connections with the army in which he had served with distinction as an officer for eighteen years. He then awaited Mississippi's decision which came on January 9, when she joined South Carolina in secession. Van Dorn promptly offered his services.

Mississippi was proud to receive the services of a man with such a fine reputation. Early in February he became a member of the first Mississippi volunteers, and when the State Convention elected Jefferson Davis its major general of state troops, Van Dorn became the chief of the brigadiers assigned to Davis's staff.

It is difficult to ascertain the extent of the personal friendship that developed between Davis and Van Dorn during this period of their association. Earl referred to Davis on at least one occasion as "without doubt a strong friend."[8] There is little remaining correspondence between the two men except that of an official nature, but even in the remaining letters Davis gives unmistakable evidence of his high regard for a fellow Mississippian. Davis admired Van Dorn's reputation, and he took pride in the fact that both were Mississippians. When Earl was elected to his staff, Davis sent him a personal letter of congratulation, inviting his new chief brigadier to dine at his home so that Earl might "make the acquaintance of Mrs. Davis and his children." Long after Van Dorn's death Davis wrote of his colleague: "He was associated with me in the organization of the army of Mississippi, immediately after the secession of our state, and I was sincerely attached to him."[9] These friendly relations were later to be strained by Van Dorn's military reverses in the field, but despite all this President Davis always kept a special interest in a Mississippian whose belief in states rights was so much like his own, even if on less intellectual foundations.

Brigadier General Van Dorn's first assignment called for him to travel to the western district of Mississippi to aid the governor in organizing and equipping the state troops. He was placed in charge of the quartermaster, commissary, and ordnance departments of the state. As a traveling emissary for the new state government, he made a good impression wherever he visited, and he was well received by enthusiastic admirers. A group of ladies in Columbus even made a flag for him.

8. *A Soldier's Honor*, p. 48.
9. *Ibid.*, p. 286.

Elated at his success and at the prospects for position and prestige, he bubbled over with excitement. To Carrie he charted his future:

> Who knows but that *yet* out of the storms of revolution . . . I may not be able to catch a spark of the lightning and shine through all time to come, a burning name! I feel a greatness in my soul—and if I can make it take shape and walk forth, it *may* be seen and felt. Heaven guide my footsteps through the labyrinth ahead. Pray for me.[10]

The mention of prayer in this letter is interesting in that it is one of the few references made in all his correspondence to any religious interest whatsoever. If his letters present a basis for judgment, it must be said that religion played an inconspicuous role in his approach to life. During the crises of the first months of the war, while things were still in a state of flux in the Confederacy, more references to things of the spirit appear in his writings than at any other time. "God will be with us," he wrote his wife in April. "Bear up and hope for us and pray for us. If Heaven carries me safely through these coming storms, I shall be the more valuable to you and yours," he continued.[11] In the very next sentence of the letter, he again focuses attention upon his own career: "I shall win honors and reputation and a name. . . ."

The election of Jefferson Davis to the Presidency of the Confederacy left the position of major general of state troops vacant, and the Convention deliberated very little in choosing Van Dorn to replace him. Only one member of the Convention voted against him on the grounds that he was too young for such a responsible position. This member later reversed his vote when he learned that the general was forty years old. Earl received this assignment with a humility not always associated with his nature. He even admitted that he might have some deficiencies when it came to leading a large army. He sounded more confident when he added that in time he would equip his troops and "lead them where they will get well peppered."[12] His prophecy in regard to equipping the Mississippi state troops never came true, but in his Army of the West in 1862 his troops were indeed "well peppered" in several important engagements of great importance to the Confederacy. Indeed, this was a fate that was too often his fortune during the course of the war.

10. Van Dorn to his wife, February 3, 1861, *ibid.*, p. 48.
11. Van Dorn to his wife, April 14, 1861, *ibid.*, p. 47.
12. *Ibid.*, p. 44.

To be elected commander of troops in his native state was a compliment to Van Dorn's record of achievement, but the duties that descended upon him were not so desirable. Besieged by requests for staff appointments and other personal favors, the man of action soon tired of the world of politics, office work, and state militia affairs. By March he could bear up under the strain no longer. He longed for a field command so much that he finally relinquished his state commission and reported as a volunteer to nearby Fort Jackson. Sworn in as a colonel of infantry in the Army of the Confederacy, he was first assigned to Texas to help round up as many members of the regular army in which he had served as possible.

At New Orleans on March 16, Colonel Van Dorn boarded one of the South's most luxurious vessels, the *Southern Republic*, for his trip to Galveston. As he set forth upon an assignment regarded as momentous and desperate, he was the hero of the hour, and he basked in the glory of it. He made an impressive figure standing there on the deck with the sunlight bright on his peaked mustache and short clipped beard, his eyes aflame with the glory of the moment, a smile of appreciation cutting his finely chiseled features. Young ladies thronged to the dock to catch a glimpse of their handsome hero. They waved their handkerchiefs, and men doffed their hats while the well-dressed colonel stood proudly on deck with one hand resting on the rail of the upper deck and the other lifting "his broad sombrero" in proud salute. As the *Southern Republic* moved away from the city, the vessel's calliope, "the best and least discordant on the river," played martial music in honor of the important passenger.[13]

Since the colonel's departure as a mere major in 1860, several important events had occurred in Texas which had a direct bearing upon his new assignment. Early in January his old friend, General Twiggs, had officially expressed sympathy for the secession movement and requested relief from his Texas assignment. Late in January General Scott selected Colonel Carlos A. Waite, a Northern sympathizer, to relieve Twiggs, but on February 18, three days before Waite's arrival in Texas, Twiggs surrendered the military posts and property under his command to a Texas Southern sympathizer, Benjamin McCulloch. For this offense the Federal War Department dismissed General Twiggs from the service.

13. T. C. DeLeon, *Four Years in Rebel Capitals*, p. 43.

Meanwhile, sentiments for secession continued to build up in Texas after the eastern states began to leave the Union. There was much wild talk in Texas, even to the extent of annexing several Mexican states when they seceded. Secession finally came on February 1, 1861, but the situation in the state still remained at fever pitch. With Twiggs gone and the state in such a turmoil, the Confederate Government saw need for a strong commander. The Second Cavalry was still in the state, and many of its members represented possible recruits for the new Southern army. The Confederates needed a commander in Texas who had lived and fought with these men, one who would have personal appeal to them, one who could swing their loyalty to the South. Texas also needed a commander who was familiar with the activities of the various Indian tribes, for sectional controversy had prompted the border savages to renew their predatory activities. Many leading Texans headed their lists of prospects for this assignment with the name Earl Van Dorn. When the Confederate War Department announced him as its selection, Texans everywhere applauded the decision.

By March 26 Van Dorn was in Indianola, Texas, twenty miles from the major concentration of American troops in the state. At Indianola he met two of his former subordinate officers of the Second Cavalry, Major Kirby Smith and Lieutenant Thornton Washington, who were enroute to Montgomery to offer their services to the Confederacy. From these men he learned that many of the soldiers at Green Lake, the point of concentration, sympathized with the South but had not definitely decided upon a course of action.

Van Dorn found the Texas situation troublesome to say the least. Several well-meaning leaders had already attempted to restore some semblance of order, but they had done very little to stabilize the frontier. The old line of Indian defense had been divided into three districts with a Texan over each district. These men were former acquaintances of Van Dorn and included John S. Ford, Ben and H. E. McCulloch. These men had done creditably in their recruiting efforts among Texans for state service, and Van Dorn hoped his task would go as well among the regular army soldiers.

The colonel's mission failed from the beginning though not because of his efforts. North and South were not yet in war, and most of the soldiers preferred to remain in the Union under the existing circumstances. Van Dorn pleaded and cajoled but to little avail. In the midst of his actions, the War Department recalled him to New Orleans to assume command of the defenses there.

Hardly had he departed from Texas when the crisis at Fort Sumter abruptly changed the attitude of the Confederacy's military authorities toward Texas. Before Van Dorn could arrive at New Orleans, he received a telegram directing him to Montgomery posthaste. When he arrived at the new Confederate capital, President Jefferson Davis personally greeted him and enthusiastically announced his reassignment to the Texas theater to "intercept and prevent the movement of the U.S. troops from the state."[14] He was to regard all Union soldiers as prisoners of war unless they joined the Confederate army, and he was to draw upon what resources Texas could offer in men and supplies to aid him in his task. Federal troops in Texas still loyal to the Union were already scurrying around in hurried attempts to get out of the state. More than 500 of them assembled at Saluria in late March, awaiting transportation home in Federal vessels that were supposed to pick them up later in the month at the port city, Indianola. Davis directed Van Dorn to deal with the darkening situation without delay.

President Davis's personal attentions to the Colonel show his continuing interests in one of his favorites. "I was made quite a Lion of at the seat of Government by his manner to me," Earl wrote proudly to his wife. "He even walked down to the boat with me to see me off, and I was of course the observed and envy of man," he continued.[15]

As he did so often, Van Dorn neglected his family for duty, and on April 14 he again departed New Orleans for Texas without visiting his home. He wrote Caroline a short letter from New Orleans and explained his predicament to her with a touch of tender sentimentality: "Yours has been a trying life," he wrote. "I hope you will be happier with a good cause." In the same letter he enclosed a hundred dollars. He also notified Carrie of a horse he had left in New Orleans to be sold for her. Finances were always a pressing matter to the Van Dorns and nearly every letter Earl wrote his wife during the course of the war years makes some mention of his shortage of funds. Whether she demanded more than he could send or not is impossible to ascertain since hardly any of her correspondence is available. His own comments to her indicate that her needs may have been many. "Write to me when you need

14. *Official Records Army*, I, 623.
15. Van Dorn to his wife, April 14, 1861, *A Soldier's Honor*, p. 46.

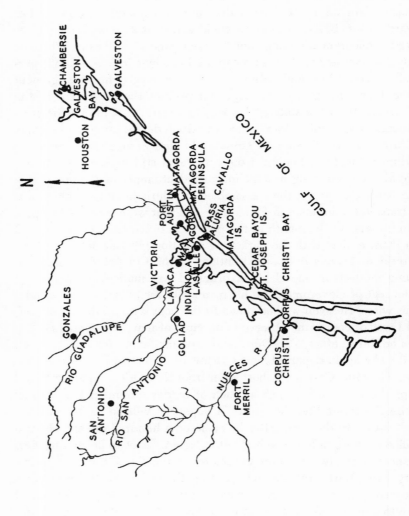

N

TEXAS THEATER – 1861

GULF OF MEXICO

CHAMBERSIE
GALVESTON
GALVESTON BAY
GALVESTON
HOUSTON
MATAGORDA
MATAGORDA PENINSULA
PORT AUSTIN
MATAGORDA CAVALLO
PASS CAVALLO
SALURIA
VICTORIA
LAVACA
INDIANOLA
LA SALLE
MATAGORDA IS.
MATAGORDA IS.
GONZALES
RIO GUADALUPE
GOLIAD
CEDAR BAYOU
ST. JOSEPH IS.
CORPUS CHRISTI BAY
SAN ANTONIO
RIO SAN ANTONIO
NUECES R.
CORPUS CHRISTI
CORPUS CHRISTI
FORT MERRIL

more [money]," he once wrote. "I will send . . . all I can spare. Be
still patient, for we are in hard times."[16]

On April 15, 1861, the Colonel arrived at Brashier City, Texas, where
he boarded the steamer, *Matagorda*, en route to Galveston. His intent
was to intercept the seven companies of Union troops that were moving
toward Indianola to board their vessels. Arriving in Galveston on
April 16, he issued a call for volunteers. Only sixty men responded from
the large body of troops converging on Indianola. He issued another
call and finally assembled 125 men, a strange conglomeration of Galveston Irish and Island City Germans. A Texas officer at Galveston
offered him 400 more men if he would wait until morning to get them,
but speed was too important for him to permit such a delay. On the
night of the sixteenth the 125 recruits boarded the *Matagorda*, and
at midnight the vessel sailed for Indianola with Van Dorn in command.

Early the next morning as the *Matagorda* approached Pass Cavallo,
the entrance to Indianola Bay, its officers discovered a large enemy
steamer lying at anchor out in the bay. Van Dorn looked it over and decided to move the *Matagorda* out into the bay for a better vantage
point. He ordered his men to get out of sight below deck, and when the
Matagorda stopped in the bay he observed the enemy through a glass.
Alarmed by the large number of men he saw, he ordered his own vessel
back to Saluria two miles up the bay. Thinking the *Matagorda* to be
only an innocent old freighter, the Union troops aboard the steamer
and on shore allowed it to proceed on its way unmolested.

At Saluria Van Dorn seized a lighter and faster vessel, the *General
Rusk*, and transferred his troops to it. The captain of the new vessel
informed Van Dorn that the steamer lying off Pass Cavallo was the
Star of the West, already famous for its role in the early action in South
Carolina, now in Texas to pick up all Federal troops loyal to the Union.
Van Dorn absorbed this information eagerly, and after careful thought
he decided upon a ruse to capture the *Star*. He must count on surpris-
ing the enemy vessel. The *Star* was in no position to receive reinforcements from the shore without great delay, and so Van Dorn felt that
his small band of Confederates would be assured of success if they
applied haste and proper precaution to a daring plan. As night approached, the *General Rusk*, with Van Dorn's men aboard, crossed the
bar and moved up alongside the steamer.

16. *Ibid.*, p. 47.

A complete and accurate record of the events from that point on is not available, but Mrs. Samuel Posey, writing later in the often inaccurate *Confederate Veteran*, leaves the most interesting record of the capture. According to her account, the *General Rusk* pulled up alongside the Federal vessel. Then through the still of the night a voice sounded from the *Star of the West* demanding identification. Van Dorn informed the *Star's* captain that he was from Indianola and had troops to be loaded. The captain questioned the use of the *General Rusk*; he said he had expected the *Fashion*. Van Dorn replied that the *Fashion* would bring more troops on the morrow when there would be more water on the bar. Convinced that he was dealing with friends, the captain of the *Star* finally threw a line over to the little freighter and ordered the men aboard his own vessel.

This was the opportunity for which the Confederates had hoped. Quickly and quietly they boarded the *Star*. By squads they scattered over the ship to put down any resistance in an orderly manner. Van Dorn then demanded the surrender of the enemy vessel in the name of the Confederate States of America. The captain was much displeased over this development and answered Van Dorn roughly:

"The hell you say!" he exclaimed. Then as if realizing his predicament, he continued in the same tone: "I suppose I have no choice, as your men far outnumber mine, but I call this a damned scurvy trick."

Van Dorn was flippant in his reply: "You can consider it the fortunes of war," he said. "All things are fair when you play that game."[17]

With the *Star of the West* in his possession Van Dorn turned his attention to the Federal troops in Indianola. Part of this contingent had arrived at the port on April 13, followed four days later by four more companies. As the troops entered Indianola they became part of the command of Federal Major Caleb C. Sibley. On April 17 the major, unaware of Van Dorn's success, marched his troops, about seven companies, to the Indianola wharf in hopes of transporting them in small vessels to the *Star of the West* for the return trip north. Unaware that the *Star* now served the Confederacy, Sibley and his men slept on the wharf that night. The next morning they embarked on their two vessels in search of the *Star*. Frustrated in their efforts, they returned to Indianola.

17. *Posey,* "Capture of the 'Star of the West,'" *Confederate Veteran,* XXXII, 174.

On April 21 Major Sibley managed to charter two small schooners in which he hoped to be able to transport his men away from Texas. Finding these additional vessels still inadequate for his needs, Sibley then dispatched one of them, the *Fashion*, to search for an additional transport. Unknown to Sibley, Van Dorn had seized the *Fashion* late in the evening. At Indianola Sibley waited anxiously for the *Fashion* until about eleven o'clock. Then suddenly on the dark horizon he spotted three vessels to his windward. He tried desperately to identify these dark forms on the bay, but the night was cloudy and the mystery of the vessels remained unsolved. Perturbed by this mystery, he had no choice but to await the dawn to establish their identity. If the vessels were hostile, retreat for his troops was out of the question anyway.

The vessels were hostile, and dawn revealed them as such. Again Van Dorn and his Texans were at work. It was the *Fashion*, in company with the *United States* and the *Mobile*, two other vessels the Confederates had recently seized, armed, and put to sea against Sibley's attempt at escape. Van Dorn had moved these three vessels in front of Pass Cavallo despite the threat of a storm, and they successfully deterred Sibley from leaving Texas. Shortly after dawn when a fourth Confederate vessel, a larger one armed with heavy cannon, appeared, Van Dorn dispatched a personal messenger to Sibley requesting an interview. Sibley reluctantly agreed, and the meeting took place in the parlor of a Judge Hawes in Saluria. Van Dorn appeared at the meeting in full dress uniform, confronted there by Sibley, W. H. L. Wallace, and George Granger. After a brief discussion, Van Dorn announced the surrender terms as authorized by his Government. He declared all Sibley's troops to be prisoners of war, but he offered paroles to all who would take an oath not "to bear arms or exercise any function" against the Confederate States of America unless properly exchanged.[18]

Another major Southern success in Texas was the capture by Confederate Captain John A. Wilcox of Colonel Carlos A. Waite's troop unit. Van Dorn offered these prisoners the same terms prescribed for Sibley. In April and early May Van Dorn found more Federal sympathizers so he set up headquarters at San Antonio where he made life uneasy for all the Union supporters in Texas. On May 4 he reported that a train of wagons and supplies being sent to Union forces in Ari-

18. *Official Records Army*, I, 562.

zona had been captured by his Texans. Then on May 9 he forced the surrender of the last Union contingent in Texas, that of Lieutenant Colonel Isaac V. D. Reeve.

At the time of his capture, Colonel Reeve was marching his 350 troops from the northern part of the state toward San Antonio under the terms of an agreement made in February 1861 between General Twiggs and Colonel Waite. Colonel Waite had agreed to surrender all public property in Texas to state authorities and evacuate all Federal posts in return for permission to evacuate his troops by way of the southern coast. To the Confederates, General Twiggs's agreement had lost its force when Fort Sumter was fired upon, and the War Department specifically ordered Van Dorn to prevent any such movement of Union troops from the state. Van Dorn complied with this order by placing himself at the head of an expedition to prevent Colonel Reeve and his force from leaving Texas. In the hills near San Lucas Spring in the vicinity of San Antonio, he surprised the Federals and placed his troops between them and San Antonio.

At nine o'clock on the morning of May 9, two officers approached Colonel Reeve with a white flag and a message from Van Dorn. The message demanded unconditional surrender. Still deluded by Twiggs's agreement, Reeve demanded verification. Van Dorn responded with a show of force over a hill separating the two commands. Seeing that the Confederate general was serious in his intentions and observing that his own force was greatly outnumbered, Reeve did what the other Union officers in Texas had done—he surrendered. Van Dorn then withdrew his force and allowed the Union troops to march on to San Antonio at their leisure. Reeve later commented that he and his command were treated generously and with delicacy by their captors under very trying circumstances.

Van Dorn was the first Confederate general to face the problem of war prisoners, and it proved to be a major operation for him in the first summer of the war. The Confederate policy itself was vacillating as authorities dealt with problems of allowances, quarters, and rules of conduct. At first the policy had been to release prisoners on the promise of nonparticipation for the remainder of the conflict, but as this proved impractical commanders in the field were ordered to hold captured personnel until further notice. Van Dorn lacked facilities for holding large numbers of prisoners, but the Confederacy offered him no solution to his dilemma even as his numbers mounted in the roundup of Yankee soldiers.

The capture of Colonel Reeve's force completed the roundup of Federal troops within the bounds of Texas. Union forces no longer a menace, Van Dorn extended his operations. In hopes of capturing Federal sympathizers in New Mexico and other areas in the vicinity of Texas, he mustered into service more and more troops and distributed them into strategic locations. For the protection of Texas against "Yankee" and Indian invaders, he established two main lines of defense: the first line was a series of forts from the Red River to the junction of the North and Main Conchos; the second line went from Fort Inge to Fort Bliss. With the Texas frontier secured and the Federals on the run, the commander responsible then settled back in his chair and wrote a glowing letter to his wife:

I have taken all the U.S. troops in Texas prisoners of war, and now lean back in my chair and smoke my pipe in peace, so far as campaigning is concerned, for the present.[19]

"For the present!" As always Earl Van Dorn detested garrison duty in a theater of police activity. He said he felt "as restless as a panther" in his office where he was "caged" like an animal. In June he expressed similar thoughts to the Confederate War Department:

I have executed my orders in regard to the capture of the U.S. troops, and at the same time that I do not wish to be considered as shrinking from my duty that may be imposed upon me in times like these, I must say that I would prefer being where I might have active service suitable to my age and inclinations.[20]

Though he had embellished his reputation in his Texas assignments, he realized that possibilities for further enhancing his prestige while on the border probably did not exist. Already the sounds of battle came from the East, and it was there that the fighting man wished to be.

As he sat at his desk smoking his pipe and anticipating greater glory, Earl Van Dorn might well have reflected upon his Texas service. In the Lone Star State he had earned a reputation for good character, energy, and ability. The South hailed him as a hero, and Texas in particular sang his praises. Because of his success in the Southwest, the

19. Van Dorn to his wife, May 10, 1861, *A Soldier's Honor*, p. 52.
20. *Official Records Army*, Ser. II, I, 60.

North "honored" him by placing a five thousand dollar price tag on his head, the same as that offered for President Jefferson Davis.[21] Confederate troops in Tennessee expressed a desire to have him become their commanding officer. Sister Emily wrote him of remarks she had heard which expressed the belief that had he been present at Manassas, "he would have had Washington City before dark" that day. "You head the list of Southern miracles performed in 1861," she said in summing up his reputation.[22] Then as a concluding remark she pointed out to her brother that his wife was also proud of him.

Earl's success in Texas was much appreciated by the Governor and the citizens of the state. Already lionized because of his actions with the Second Cavalry, his reputation gained apace with his new achievements. Texans, said one writer, liked an officer "when he proved a better fighter than the men he led." Van Dorn not only qualified in this respect, but he was also reputed to be "a splendid horseman, an enviable fist-fighter, and a good shot with a six-gun."[23]

When he visited the Governor in Austin on July 4, 1861, Earl was met enroute by the Austin City Light Infantry and escorted into the capital for a private meeting with the Governor. Austin greeted his arrival with a stirring reception featuring a German choir and the Austin String Band. Governor Clark also appreciated his state commander and was always co-operative with him during his entire tour of duty in Texas.

Of more tangible importance to the ambitious Mississippian, however, was the official praise for his service that he received from the Confederate military officials. Their recognition came first in June in a letter announcing his promotion to brigadier general. Official praise followed. One of the top ranking officers in the Confederacy, General Van Dorn had begun to make his mark.

The new general took great pride in his achievements and in the praise received. He was happy about the promotion and pleased about the indirect recognition from President Abraham Lincoln. Because of the successful Texas roundup, Lincoln had called him a pirate and had

21. Emily Van Dorn Miller to Earl Van Dorn, July 1861, Van Dorn Collection, Montgomery, Alabama.

22. Emily Miller to Earl, August 1861, ibid.

23. Oates, "Texas Under the Secessionists," Southwestern Historical Quarterly, LXVII, 194.

suggested the large reward for his head. Van Dorn laughed at the Union President's concern, declaring before his friends that he would just have to dance at the victory ball with all "the dignity of a corsair."[24] If the general had any regrets in the summer of 1861, they were only passing ones. He was sorry if the war meant he would have to fight some of his old comrades of earlier army days, but he had a ready answer for this. He would raise such a large force that the South would win quickly and end the hostilities. The Mississippian was dreaming again. His dreams appear again and again under the strains of high command.

By July 1861, the war had definitely shifted to the East. Van Dorn knew this and resented the fact that he was being left out of it. His own command was diminishing in importance as the clash of arms sounded in Virginia and Tennessee. In his Texas office Van Dorn battled his prisoner problem and thought of the possibilities of being transferred. Certainly an older man could handle the prisoners and manage the dull office routine that he so hated. "The free air, a brave troop, and a bright sword . . . and I breathe again," he wrote home.[25] This was the kind of thinking that permeated his letters all summer.

The Confederate War Department had its own problems during the war's first summer, so Van Dorn's "breathing again" was postponed. Texans continued to look to him for leadership, and so at San Antonio he sweated and fumed and almost belligerently continued his defense preparations. He spent most of his time recruiting soldiers for the armies across the Mississippi River, and for the most part he worked on his own, meeting his particular problems as he saw fit and was able. His efforts to build up a strong defense in Texas proved far more successful than his recruiting efforts, however, and there was increased pressure from Richmond for more troops.

The summer months dragged on slowly for the commander. From time to time he was besieged with chills and fever; he suffered from eye trouble; he continued ill at ease in garrison. He recruited, armed, and equipped able young soldiers, dispatched them to armies far away, and then filled his own depleted ranks with older soldiers. He was so short of funds at times that he had difficulty in holding even the older

24. An undated, untitled newspaper clipping in the Van Dorn Collection, Montgomery, Alabama.

25. Van Dorn to his wife, July 23, 1861, *ibid.*

men. The glamor of military life lost much of its luster that summer. "We are badly armed and poorly equipped," he wrote. "We hear that 500,000 men are being raised to send against the South. What a future is before us! What an infamous war!" he lamented. "I am fatigued to death in mind and body." It was as though the fate of the entire Confederacy rested on his shoulders. "I feel the weight of my responsibility," he continued. "*I must win*—There can be no such thing as fail—"[26]

Intimate relations in the Van Dorn family are obscured in this period by the dearth of the remaining correspondence. Something seems to have been troubling Carrie. Her correspondence to her husband was irregular. She remained in obscurity at her Alabama home for the entire summer. Was she lonely for an errant husband, for the security of a home? Emily hints of this in a letter to Earl in August: "Don't think of [buying] a piano till after the war," she wrote, "then after you settle Caroline in a palace, or Eden as a *home* will be to her, then I will make you pay up." Caroline had been married to her roving warrior for nearly two decades and never yet had he provided her with more than temporary quarters. One can only guess who was to blame. An ominous note appears in Emily's letter which may have some bearing on the matter: "I am glad that you have such nice female friends," she confided. Meanwhile, little Livy stayed at Port Gibson with Aunt Emily, "quite reconciled to be away from [her] Mother."[27] It was a strange family, and one longs to remove the shutters from long-closed windows to better understand an officer who appears so often and in such important roles in Confederate operations.

Relief from Texas garrison life finally came to General Van Dorn in mid-August, when the War Department ordered him to report to the Adjutant General in Richmond for a new assignment. Brigadier General Paul Octave Hébert replaced him in his San Antonio office much to the chagrin of the Texans. Van Dorn held the respect and affection of citizens and soldiers alike. The less congenial Hébert would soon have trouble with both groups. Later, at Corinth, Hébert's frailties would jeopardize an attacking Confederate command, Van Dorn's.

Delays in travel detained Van Dorn in Texas for nearly a month after his reassignment. Finally on September 17, he arrived in New Orleans, his first stop on his way to Richmond. He was excited to leave

26. Van Dorn to his wife, July 23, 1861, *ibid.*
27. Emily Miller to Earl, August 1861, *ibid.*

Texas, so excited in fact that he again neglected his wife. He informed
her that he was so preoccupied with military business that he could
not stop by her Alabama home to see her and little Earl. Certainly
she would understand that his first duty was to his country, he said. It
was a "point of honor" for him to hurry on. "I wish you were more
accessible that I might stop a day or two with you; but you know how
much I would lose by going to your father's," he wrote.[28]

He did schedule a visit with Livy at Emily's, but floods prevented
this reunion. Emily regretted the floods. Somehow she sensed that her
soldier brother needed her more than he needed Carrie: "I know from
your wife that you never have worn clothing heavy enough for that
climate [Virginia]. You are a little over 21 now and cannot endure
the exposure you once could . . . ," she cautioned.[29] Was she still mother-
ing the younger brother whom she had helped raise in those trying
Mississippi days before West Point?

On September 23 Van Dorn arrived in Richmond. There a real surprise awaited him. He had been promoted to major general and given
an assignment to a command in Virginia. His happiness was complete,
but one wonders if in the excitement of the moment he forgot his old
Texas friends. He had promised the Governor that he would see President Davis and solicit the services of the most competent officer available to command at Galveston, a key link in the chain of defense in
the Lone Star State. From Davis's reply to a letter from the Governor,
it appears that Van Dorn neglected to make the promised contact.

The new major general arrived in the East in the midst of a program
of army reorganization. In September the Confederate War Department formed the thirteen brigades in that area into four divisions.
General Joseph E. Johnston, the commander of the Virginia army, requested the assignment of Van Dorn to one of these new divisions,
which of course gratified the wishes of the Confederate President for
his fellow Mississippian. The other division commanders, also recently
promoted major generals, included two of Earl's West Point classmates,
James Longstreet and Gustavus W. Smith, in addition to Thomas J.
Jackson. "No army composed of new troops ever had general officers
of more merit," General Johnston wrote several years after the war.[30]

28. Earl Van Dorn to his wife, September 17, 1861, *A Soldier's Honor*, p. 341.
29. Emily Miller to Earl, September 16, 1861, *ibid.*, p. 342.
30. Joseph E. Johnston, *Narrative of Military Operations*, p. 73.

Confederate history for several months after the first battle of Bull Run reveals the rise of a series of petty rivalries and disputes that might well have been avoided for the best interests of the Confederacy. Too many ambitious men vied for positions in a newly organized army, and they quibbled too often about rank and assignments before they had proved their mettle in the severest test, the battlefield command. By fall the Virginia theater was a seething hotbed of jealousies and misunderstandings. Van Dorn had hardly joined them when he, too, became involved in one of these disputes. The question of rank provided the spark.

In October the Confederate War Department organized its four Virginia divisions into two corps—the First Corps to be commanded by General P. G. T. Beauregard and the Second Corps, by Major General Gustavus W. Smith. Van Dorn, who outranked Smith by a few hours, remained commander of the First Division in Beauregard's corps. This shuffle greatly disturbed the ambitious general. He had anticipated the command of the Second Corps himself, and he lost no time in expressing his feelings to his friend, President Davis, and to his West Point classmate, General Smith. To General Smith he wrote:

I handed in a protest and appeal to the President this morning in regard to my position. I would not have you think from it that I feel in the slightest degree any unkindness toward you. I am rather sorry, indeed, that the President did not date your appointment a day or so before mine—but a man of good sense can well perceive that it is my duty to myself and friends that I should maintain my position according to the rank given to me by the President.[31]

Pride fell hard. Van Dorn resented being constantly questioned by friends and acquaintances as to why he only commanded a division while General Smith had a corps. Such a turn of events was unthinkable. "These things mortify me," he wrote to Smith, "and I can't stand it. I am sensitive and proud, and you would do as I am doing—this I know."[32]

To his ever-understanding sister he expressed his feelings even more adamantly:

[I]t is the first time in my military career that I have ever been in a false position, or that I ever had my pride as a soldier wounded. . . . But I take

31. Gustavus W. Smith, *Confederate War Papers*, pp. 316–317.
32. *Ibid.*, p. 317.

it, and shall endeavor in a fight to make my small command so noisy and hot that I shall make up for lack of numbers that *ought* to be mine.[33]

He was in good company in Virginia in his conflict over rank. Jefferson Davis and Judah Benjamin had a penchant for antagonizing the sensitive generals. Johnston, Beauregard, and even "Stonewall" Jackson also had their moments of uncertainty and chagrin in the late months of 1861 as the new nation organized its military force in preparation for a full-scale war.

In Van Dorn's case President Davis confessed that he knew all about the situation, had even created it purposefully. By letter he assured his friend that he was well aware of the date of his rank; this had also been deliberate. As to the Mississippian's dissatisfaction, the President said that he was under the impression that Van Dorn preferred a cavalry command to a corps assignment, and the War Department would soon organize such a command by transferring all the cavalry in Virginia to the First Division.

Actually Davis seems to have had another motive for his actions. He had long been anxious to place all the troops from Mississippi into one division under the command of a prominent officer from that state. Van Dorn was certainly that officer. Though he had missed the battle of Bull Run, his reputation rated with the heroes of that battle, and Davis insisted on a man with rank and prestige for the Mississippi command.

Shortly after his communication to Van Dorn, Davis ordered all the Mississippi troops into two brigades and assigned to the First Division. Next he ordered all the cavalry transferred to the same unit. Then he informed his disgruntled general that he now possessed a command commensurate with his rank. He further assured Van Dorn that his military reputation had received no blemish as a result of the new arrangement. "Soldiers are properly sensitive," the President wrote, "but you must not permit scratches to be mistaken for scar-bearing wounds."[34]

Other important changes also took place in the Virginia command with the creation of the Department of Northern Virginia under General Joseph E. Johnston and its three subsidiary districts, the Potomac District under General Beauregard, the Aquia District under General T. H. Holmes, and the Shenandoah Valley District under General Jack-

33. An undated page from a memorandum of Van Dorn in his handwriting found among the papers in the Van Dorn Collection, Montgomery, Alabama.
34. Dunbar Rowland (ed.), *Jefferson Davis*, V, 154.

son. After these shifts in troop assignments had been completed, Van Dorn's new command consisted of nine Mississippi regiments, the army's cavalry, and General Wade Hampton's Legion. When the division was organized, orders placed it on the extreme right of the Confederate line that then stretched from Union Mills through Centerville to Stone Bridge. Van Dorn established his headquarters at Union Mills, about three miles from Manassas.

General Johnston's reaction to the assignment of all the cavalry to one division was spontaneous. On October 23 he wrote to the War Department expressing his opposition to the move. His theory was that placing all the cavalry with an infantry division weakened both the army and the division. "Should the cavalry be placed with a division of infantry," he wrote, "it must be kept out of position, either for its daily service of observing the enemy or to play its part in battle."[35] Johnston suggested that the War Department remove the cavalry from the First Division and make it a separate unit, meanwhile adding an equal force of infantry to replace the cavalry. Van Dorn agreed wholeheartedly with Johnston's position and suggested that Texas troops be used to replace the cavalry since he had been so long identified with many of the men.

Fortunately for later Confederate operations, the War Department accepted Johnston's suggestion. It removed the cavalry from the First Division and assigned it directly to the theater commander. It was in this relationship that the cavalry operated in many of the engagements during the remainder of the war. It was in this arrangement that General J. E. B. Stuart earned his great fame.

Meanwhile, Van Dorn's division became a five-brigade unit with two brigades from Mississippi, two from Alabama, and one from Louisiana. For the remainder of the year the First Division continued to occupy a defensive area to the rear of the old Bull Run battlefield where railroads and ford were their first line of observation.

Although never engaged in combat in Virginia, Van Dorn seems to have constantly anticipated an attack. As autumn ended he became more and more convinced that the enemy would strike near Manassas. On one occasion poor reconnaissance, a weakness of his during the first year of his Confederate service, convinced him that Federal General Samuel P. Heintzleman was advancing toward his lines with 12,000

35. *Official Records Army*, V, 890.

troops. He publicized this fallacious information so convincingly that before the truth came out, the Confederate Secretary of War was accusing General Johnston of having failed to destroy a large army when there was an opportunity to do so.

Autumn passed and winter began. Across the Potomac General George B. McClellan continued to train his troops and enlarge his force. The Confederates awaited an attack; some even hoped for it, but none came. Life was dull in their makeshift camps. There was also too much daily parade and drill for all concerned. But once the parade was over, it was a different matter, especially in Van Dorn's command. Many of his officer friends and some of the citizens of the area were often guests in his quarters "where around his hospitable board, the dangers of the field were forgotten for a time, giving place to the feast of reason and the flow of the soul."[36] What the "feast of reason" and "the flow of the soul" were, the author of the picturesque letter that suggested them did not explain, but G. Moxley Sorrell, a frequent participant, records an interesting story of life among these officers of Virginia that may throw some light on the matter.

At a great banquet given by General Longstreet, an argument developed among the officers present as to what tune they preferred for the Southern anthem. *My Maryland* and *Dixie* were among the suggestions that were offered, but Van Dorn enthusiastically defended the Liberty Duet from *I Puritani*. When his enthusiasm bubbled over and he began to sing the strains at the banquet table, General Longstreet shouted out in his gruff voice: "Upon the table and show yourself, we can't see you."

"Not unless you stand by me," returned Van Dorn.

Longstreet's leap to the table top was followed quickly by Van Dorn and General Smith. In the midst of the merriment, three generals clung to each other atop the narrow banquet table roaring out the majestic strains from Vincenzo Bellini's great opera. The words must have been well received by those who now loved another country:

Let the words: Country, victory and honour awaken terror in the enemy!
Let the trumpet sound and fearlessly
I'll fight courageously.
It is a fine thing to face death crying: Freedom!

The witness to this affair said that while the officers sang, two higher-

36. *A Soldier's Honor*, p. 58.

ranking generals, Johnston and Beauregard, "stood nearby with twink-ling eyes of amusement and enjoyment." More dignified General Kirby Smith departed from this robust group and when requested to return and make a speech, he refused on the grounds "that he could not speak soberly to a drunken audience."

"So much for wine and 'entoosy moosy' as Byron calls it," concluded the approving witness.[37]

Handsome, dashing Earl Van Dorn was popular among the Virginians just as he had been popular among the Texans. Virginia welcomed the Westerner to her theater, and he basked in the warm feeling of the people of that state throughout his short tour of duty there. In November the Confederate Government selected three young ladies of Richmond to make the first flags for the new nation, each to present her finished product to a hero of her own choice. Miss Constance Cary, later Mrs. Burton Harrison, presented her flag to the Mississippian. The flag arrived at his headquarters with the following note:

Will General Van Dorn honor me by accepting a flag which I have taken great pleasure in making, and now send forth, with an earnest prayer that the work of my hands may take its place near him as he goes out to a glorious struggle, and, God willing, may one day wave over the recaptured batteries of my ill-fated home—the down trodden Alexandria.[38]

Mrs. Harrison is one of the very interesting women of the Confederacy. Described as a very lovely woman by a contemporary, she was also a native of Mississippi having been born at Port Gibson near Van Dorn's own home. Her father, a distinguished lawyer and near kinsman of Thomas Jefferson, had moved to Port Gibson from Virginia in the early 1830s and had edited the town's first newspaper. The Carys had returned to Virginia in the 1840s.

Van Dorn received Miss Cary's flag as a token "as eloquent as the alluring promises of glory."[39] He and his troops then adopted it as their division colors with all the fanfare and eloquence so typical of the day and of the person. All swore knightly oaths to Miss Cary, and then they all drank to the flag and its designer, pledging an oath to liberate the town of Alexandria as she had requested. Circumstances would not al-

37. G. Moxley Sorrel, *Recollections of a Confederate Staff Officer*, p. 57. Part of the story is also recorded in Williams, *P. T. G. Beauregard*, p. 110.

38. Harrison, *Recollections Grave and Gay*, pp. 62–63.

39. Van Dorn to Miss Cary, November 12, 1861, *A Soldier's Honor*, p. 56.

low these gallants to fufill their rash promise, but Van Dorn was able
to send the young lady a token of his personal esteem, a valuable blue
and white wrap. Miss Cary thanked him for the present with the hope
that at some future date she might have the opportunity to express her
appreciation in person. No record remains of Van Dorn's reaction to this
statement, but when he departed from Virginia the flag went with him,
to follow him through his campaigns until his untimely death. It was
then returned to the designer, now the wife of Burton Harrison, President Davis's private secretary, by the late general's nephew and aide,
Captain Clement Sulivane.

The Virginia life was good during those last days before active campaigning began in the Spring. At least Van Dorn seemed to think so.
Too busy to write Carrie, he entrusted this task to young Sulivane, recently appointed as his aide as a special favor to sister Octavia, the
young man's mother. "He sends much love to you all," wrote the aide,
"and takes the greatest delight in the likeness of his admirable little
girl."[40]

Finally in late November he wrote Carrie himself, explaining his
negligence in writing by saying that he had been trying to raise some
money to send her. He made no mention of the "feast of reason," but
he did assure her that he missed his family. "I wish I could fly that I
might come and spend the evenings with you and the days with my
country," he wrote, but he seemed more interested in telling her of the
beautiful flag and the publicity it received.[41] He did express his concern
over Carrie's recent illness and suggested that she join Emily in Port
Gibson.

In November the general also corresponded with President Davis
in hopes of obtaining an appointment for his father-in-law in the War
Tax Office of Mobile. Mr. Godbold did not get the job, but President
Davis said it was only because the job was filled.

Near Manassas General Van Dorn continued to play an active and
important role in the preparations for defense. His men built bridges,
repaired railroad lines, and constructed cottages. Always there was
drill, and day after day the First Division marched in review before its
"youthful looking field marshal." Van Dorn was an impressive figure as

40. Letter of Clement Sulivane, November 19, 1861, Van Dorn Collection,
Montgomery, Alabama.
41. Van Dorn to his wife, November 29, 1861, A *Soldier's Honor*, pp. 58–59.

he surveyed the troops he longed to lead in battle. He sat astride his horse "as though he were part of it."[42] His uniform was a gray tunic with heavy gold braiding on the sleeves. On each collar gold stars portrayed his rank. Embroidered in scarlet silk on his handsome gloves were crosses, ancient symbols of rank. He wore his chestnut hair long and wavy; his mouth and chin were now covered by a brown mustache and imperial described as being of "uncommon beauty." His complexion, often exposed to the sun, was dark red, almost like that of an Indian. But it was his eyes that commanded attention: dark, sometimes almost foreboding, they could sparkle with good humor or flash in anger at the slightest provocation. This was one of the South's important major generals in late 1861.

As could be expected, Van Dorn soon tired of inspection and drill and work behind the front lines. War was a serious business to him, and he had not come to Virginia to repeat the monotonies of Texas. A daring dash into the enemy's camp; conquest; the glorious return of the conquering hero—this was war. Across the river sat the enemy. Van Dorn was always among those eager officers who continually pestered the higher authorities for action. And action there would be, and soon, for this officer and many others, but Van Dorn would not find his action in Virginia! He had made his reputation across the Mississippi River. To the West he must return. His honor and his good name were soon to be at stake in a theater of war already rent by confusion and internal conflict. Van Dorn's duty lay just ahead but, in Arkansas!

42. *Ibid.*, p. 265.

CHAPTER FIVE

Across the Mississippi

*N*EVER throughout the Civil War did the Confederate authorities at Richmond really show that they grasped the true significance or the strategic importance of the trans-Mississippi River region. From the beginning of hostilities the states and territories in that vast expanse offered a complex of problems that were too much for officials already harassed on too many sides by the exigencies of a war for which they were ill prepared. Priority of goods, men, and services went to the theater involving the Confederate capital, and too often the West fended for itself; its policies were unclear, its strategy was confused, its leaders were limited by lack of weapons and manpower.

In the first year of the war, no part of the trans-Mississippi River region offered more consternation to the Confederacy than Missouri and Arkansas. Loyalties within these two states were so divided that the status of communities and individuals was still uncertain even after the Confederate Government had formed in Arkansas. In Arkansas the confusion of loyalty was compounded by a struggle for control within the framework of the Confederate organization as those who supported Richmond vied with states' righters for control of the military. In Missouri the struggle was strictly between Confederate sympathizers led by Governor Claiborne F. Jackson and General Sterling Price and Union troops under newly promoted Brigadier General Nathaniel Lyon. On June 11 a final conference between Price and Lyon failed to solve Missouri's secession crisis, and open warfare between the two motley armies began.

Under the forceful leadership of the red-bearded energetic Lyon, the Federals pushed so hard against Price's outnumbered army as to press it deep into the southwestern part of the state. Against what often ap-

peared as overwhelming odds, Price held on during the early summer
months, hoping always for a juncture with a strong Confederate army
stationed just across the Missouri line in Arkansas. Price wanted a combined offensive against Lyon which he hoped would clear his state
for secession. General Ben McCulloch, commanding the Confederate
troops, sympathized with the harried Price, but he was reluctant to
leave Arkansas. His orders, he said, confined him to a defense of that
state and the Indian territory to its west, and nothing had been said
about Missouri except that he was to prevent an invasion from that state.
Communication with Secretary of State Leroy P. Walker confirmed this
attitude when Walker instructed him to give the Missourians "active
and direct assistance" only when "necessity and propriety unite."[1]

General Price did not receive this news gracefully, and he and Governor Jackson continued to insist upon the priority of the defense of
Missouri. McCulloch remained adamant in his insistence upon fighting
the war in his own way. As this disagreement between Price and Mc-
Culloch intensified, a personal altercation was triggered that lasted for
more than six months and further complicated the dismal situation
across the Mississippi.

Sterling Price and Ben McCulloch were two men who by their very
natures seemed destined for conflict. Each was a strong-minded indi-
vidualist, possessed of his own concept of fighting the war, pursuing his
own policy whatever its effects on the total situation. The two generals
not only disagreed on the strategy of defense against General Lyon, but
their own personalities and ambitions clashed in that region so far-
removed from centralized control and counsel. General Price was a tall,
handsome, well-educated and accomplished officer, described by his
friends as a gentleman. He had served with distinction in the Mexican
War and had been governor of Missouri shortly thereafter. Highly regarded by the people of his state, he was described as "unquestionably
the most popular man" in Missouri. But lacking vision to see portents
of the future, Price felt that he must defend Missouri in his own plod-
ding way. He was a major general of Missouri State Troops, which according to him ranked over Brigadier General McCulloch even though
the latter held his rank in the regular Confederate army. Trusted instinctively by his own troops, Price had assembled a sizable force,

1. *Official Records Army*, II, 603.

though it was hardly enough to defend against Lyon's larger, better-equipped units.

Ben McCulloch was one of the most colorful soldiers to come out of L Texas during the war. Flamboyant, headstrong, intelligent, coarse, sometimes brutal, usually profane, he became a Texan just before the Texas Revolution. He served under Sam Houston during the Revolution, distinguishing himself for gallantry at San Jacinto. As a Ranger he fought Indians in Texas and Mexicans in the Mexican War, and for gallantry in action President Pierce appointed him United States Marshal of Texas. Later he served as a peace commissioner to Utah during the Mormon rebellion and was even considered for the role of military governor of the territory. He was one of Texas's most famous men at the outbreak of the Civil War, and when Texas seceded he was immediately in action against Federal sympathizers in the state. Promoted to Brigadier General in the Confederate Army soon after Van Dorn took over in Texas, he was sent to Arkansas with orders to organize the troops there. A thin spare man of great strength, McCulloch was mild and courteous in his manners until riled by those with whom he differed. William Watson, a private soldier who served in his Arkansas command, characterized him as "a thoroughly practical general . . . [who] made himself acquainted with every road or passage through which an army with trains could pass or operate in."[2] Dabney Maury, who also was with him in Arkansas for a time, was not so complimentary as he described the Texan as "undemonstrative, reticent . . . and even cautious."[3] Whatever the judgment of his peers, Ben McCulloch was always the soldier. He believed in discipline, organization, and scientific planning for battles, and to him Price was an "old militia general" leading "a half-armed mob."[4] It is little wonder that these two stubborn officers clashed in a theater already disorganized and confused.

In late July Lyon's army finally pushed Price's troops so close to Arkansas that the Federal force became a distinct threat to McCulloch's T position. When Price agreed to subordinate himself to McCulloch for a concerted action against Lyon, the Texan accepted the offer and emerged from his hibernation long enough to offer "active and direct"

2. *Life in the Confederate Army*, p. 281.
3. "Recollections of the Elkhorn Campaign," *Southern Historical Society Papers*, II, 183.
4. Johnson and Buel, *Battles and Leaders*, I. 269.

aid to the struggling Missourians. On August 10 at the battle of Wilson's Creek, just southwest of Springfield, the combined Confederate force severely chastised the Federal army, killing Lyon in the process.

With the Federal offensive halted, McCulloch and Price resumed their bickering. McCulloch refused to follow Price in a move toward northern Missouri. When Price insisted, the Texan returned with his troops to their Boston Mountains fortress. Price raged in vain at this withdrawal. Disgusted at McCulloch's refusal to co-operate and certain that a joint operation could wrest Missouri from the Unionists, Price and Governor Jackson now turned to Richmond, appealing time and again to President Davis to intercede in the affairs across the Mississippi River. They urged the President to accept Missouri into the Confederacy, to unite all the troops west of the Mississippi, and to place Price over these troops to direct whatever offensive he saw fit. Davis refused to become involved, and the difficulties between the two antagonists intensified.

Meanwhile, as Davis procrastinated, the two armies missed a good opportunity to carry the war into Federal territory when David Hunter replaced John C. Fremont as commander of the Union force in Missouri. The Federals were also having their difficulties, and Hunter, unfamiliar with the military situation, withdrew toward St. Louis, convinced in his own mind that he could best defend and reorganize at that point. After more wrangling in the Confederate command, McCulloch again agreed reluctantly to leave Arkansas and move toward Springfield, but he arrived with too little too late to do any damage to the retreating Federals. The Confederates might have inflicted real damage against the disorganized Unionists at this point, but Price preferred to move toward Lexington rather than to pursue Hunter as McCulloch suggested. Any hopes for a sustained offensive disintegrated in this disagreement. Price continued on toward Lexington while the Texan returned to Arkansas.

Even Secretary Benjamin was upset at this display of mismanagement of forces. "I cannot understand," he wrote sharply to McCulloch, "why you withdrew your troops instead of pursuing the enemy when his leaders were quarreling and his army separated into parts under different commanders. Send an explanation."[5]

McCulloch resented the rebuke. "It is impossible to explain by tele-

5. *Official Records Army*, VIII, 699.

gram," he fired back. He then insisted on a conference with Confederate officials. Benjamin reluctantly concurred and invited him to Richmond to explain.[6]

In reviewing this part of the Civil War, one wonders why the War Department or President Davis did not take a firm position with the Trans-Mississippi leaders earlier. By November they decided that they could ignore this theater no longer. Late that month Davis finally decided to act. He would solve the dilemma by commissioning the Missourians into the Confederacy and placing over them and the Confederate troops in Arkansas one of his own young favorites from the Virginia theater, Colonel Henry Heth. Heth was to be promoted to brigadier general to command over both Price and McCulloch.

Missourians objected strenuously to Heth's appointment. To them there was only one commander, Sterling Price. The Western newspapers, always "old Pap's" supporters, rallied strongly to his defense by sharply joining in the criticism of Heth. In the face of such opposition Heth declined the appointment.

The Missouri reaction to his appointment caused the Confederate President to reply forcefully against a slur of Heth's West Point training by Missouri Congressman W. P. Harris. He defended Heth's appointment in a tart statement to the Congressman, and then he lashed out in defense of professional soldiers:

The Federal forces are not hereafter, as heretofore, to be commanded by path-finders and holiday soldiers, but by men of military education and experience in war. The contest is therefore to be on a scale of very different proportions than that of the partisan warfare witnessed during the past summer and fall.[7]

With this outburst, Davis again delayed action. The bickering between the two officers continued, and the Missourians expressed new demands for appointment of Price to supreme command. Why Davis "can't give you the appointment at once I am utterly at a loss to determine," Governor Jackson wrote Price. "If, then, the President had the power to appoint Colonel Heth, I cannot see why he has not the authority to appoint you."[8]

By late December the President's patience reached its breaking point.

6. *Ibid.*, p. 701.
7. *Ibid.*
8. *Ibid.*, p. 725.

He would never appoint an unprofessional like Price. He must appoint an outsider, a real soldier. Albert Sidney Johnston was the man, but he was occupied in a greater task. At the suggestion of Governor Jackson and others, Davis turned to another of his favorites, General Braxton Bragg. Bragg was in Florida and seemed ripe for reassignment. He read Davis's telegram and made his decision immediately. "The field to which you invite me is a most important one, but, under present aspects, not enticing," he wired back. He had no desire to risk his reputation in such a complex theater of operations. He declined the appointment with the following explanation: "So much has been lost there, and so little done in organization and instruction, that the prospect of retrieving our ground is most gloomy."[9]

Bragg's refusal to accept the assignment not only revealed the confusion as to ultimate authority in the Confederate command system, but it also pointed up the need for an especially strong officer to take the Western command. Davis insisted on a man with military education and experience, but he also needed an officer who knew the West and understood its type of warfare. He must have an officer who would outrank Price and McCulloch and who would quickly seize the initiative against a threatening Federal army. Again Davis looked to a favorite, a major general commanding in Virginia, a man already dissatisfied with the inactivity of the Eastern front, a fellow Mississippian, Earl Van Dorn. Van Dorn had fought Indians on the frontier, he had distinguished himself in Texas in the early stages of the war, and he was respected by men on both sides of the Mississippi River. On January 10, 1862, orders from the War Department assigned him to the command of a newly created unit, the Trans-Mississippi District of Department Number 2 including Louisiana north of the Red River, the Indian Territory west of Arkansas, Arkansas, and most of Missouri.

Confederate leaders applauded this appointment. Van Dorn's strengths still outweighed his weaknesses in the hearts and minds of a still optimistic South. He had the rank and the experience to seize control of the department, and he had the courage to fight. Certainly he could bring unity and harmony to the divided command and then exert a force against the Federal force already pressing hard against several Confederate positions in the West.

What arrangement Davis or Benjamin made with their new com-

9. *Ibid.*, VI, 797.

mander before he left Richmond is not on record, but one can surmise that it had something to do with an offensive. Davis later admitted "the object of Van Dorn had been to effect a diversion in favor of General Johnston," but it is doubtful that the "diversion" was to be spelled out until Van Dorn met personally with General Johnston.[10] in fact St. John R. Liddell reported that neither Davis nor his Secretary of War, Judah P. Benjamin, communicated with General Johnston at this time about the exact nature of Van Dorn's assignment. Van Dorn was definitely thinking of something big from the beginning; otherwise he would not have accepted an assignment so fraught with chances of failure. He spoke of an invasion to his wife even before he met with Johnston. "I am now 'in for it,'" he wrote Carrie, "as the saying is—to make a reputation and serve my country conspicuously or to fail. I must not, shall not, do the latter. I must have St. Louis—then Huzza!"[11]

Davis had probably not given him this specific assignment. Benjamin informed General Johnston that he was sending Van Dorn to receive his orders "in relation to the movement of forces to New Madrid" as Johnston himself had suggested. In his service in the Trans-Mississippi District, however, Van Dorn appears to have worked very much on his own, guided more by his instinct than official sanction.

The new commander departed from Virginia without delay. By January 18, 1862, he was in Knoxville, Tennessee. In his letter to Carrie from Knoxville, he swelled with pride as to his new prospects, but he expressed regret that duty again was hastening him to his new post. President Davis and Secretary Benjamin had so stressed the urgency of the situation that he felt compelled to put his assignment ahead of his wife and children. "Great events were hanging on the times," he reported enthusiastically enroute to his new command. He did not want to miss a possible rendezvous with destiny. Then in a bit of a personal note he chided Carrie for not living with Emily at Port Gibson, but he did promise to send her a hundred dollars a month. He soon found it impossible to fulfill this promise.

From Knoxville Van Dorn journeyed on to Nashville and finally to Bowling Green, Kentucky, where he met his new commanding officer, his old friend from Texas days, General Albert S. Johnston. No record remains of Johnston's conference with the Mississippian, but

10. Jefferson Davis, *The Rise and Fall*, II, 51.
11. *A Soldier's Honor*, pp. 62–63.

he must have pointed up the dangerous position of the Confederate military units in Tennessee and Arkansas. This was a front stretching over six hundred miles, and there were many points of entrance for an aggressive enemy. Of special importance was the Mississippi River, and Johnston must have stressed this. Earlier he recorded his own impressions of its importance:

The Northerners have justly comprehended that the seat of vitality of the Confederacy, if to be reached at all, is by this route. It is now palpable that all resources of that government will, if necessary, be employed to assure success on this line.[12]

The meeting between the two officers was brief, and Van Dorn was soon on his way. He arrived in Little Rock on the evening of January 28. Meanwhile Johnston began to feel the pressure of defending such a long line as a strong Federal army began to follow up its January 18 Fishing Creek success.

Earl Van Dorn entered Arkansas with the confidence of a man who hardly expected a disorganized command. "He is a man of energy and Napoleonic celerity of movement," said a newspaper editor soon after his arrival.[13] As if to prove this claim, the new commander acted quickly. First he announced his headquarters as Pocahontas in the northcentral part of the state. Here he would assemble his troops for the St. Louis march. Then he requested troops from the states in his district on a scale unprecedented in that backward region. From Arkansas alone he expected ten regiments of infantry and four companies of artillery in addition to the troops already in the field. To the governor he confided his hopes of using these troops to drive the enemy from Missouri. The Little Rock *True Democrat* rang out in praise for the new leader: "His acquaintance and familiarity with the people will afford him the facilities of rallying hosts of men who will take the field and follow their gallant leader to victory."[14]

A week later Van Dorn wound up his business in Little Rock. His hopes were still high, and Little Rock had encouraged him toward great deeds. His only concern as he left the city was over some debts that General Hardee had contracted for the Confederacy and had

12. Charles P. Roland, "Albert Sidney Johnson," *Journal of Southern History,* XXIII, 53.
13. Little Rock *True Democrat*, February 6, 1862, p. 1.
14. *Ibid.*, February 13, 1862, p. 1.

failed to pay. "I desire to succeed in what I have undertaken," he wrote, "and hope I may be enabled to commence operations untrammeled by such obstacles."[15]

Before leaving Little Rock, Van Dorn made a spirited speech to the citizens of the city; he solicited their support and co-operation in the momentous work ahead. Then he was off to Jacksonport and Pocahontas; he rotated his service between these two towns for nearly three weeks.

Van Dorn was now facing the severe test of bringing some order into a heterogeneous mob to face a determined invading army successfully. He did not succeed in accomplishing what he hoped because he was a victim of circumstances; many are related to the lack of communications among the various regions of the South. Though he was a part of Johnston's long defensive line, Van Dorn worked in near isolation in Arkansas. Too often he operated without proper knowledge of what was happening either to the east or the west of his position.

Johnston was aware of the weaknesses of his widespread command structure, but there was little that he could do about it with his limited supplies and troop strength. A recent evaluation of General Johnston criticizes this "mission" operations: while it "works splendidly with lieutenants of great skill . . . with lesser soldiers it can be dangerous."[16]

At Pocahontas Van Dorn seemed unconcerned about his communications problem with his commanding officer. With all his energy he prepared for invasion. He still dreamed of a victorious march into St. Louis. Johnston had written once of an advance to the Great Lakes by the Confederates, but he never seriously planned such an offensive. Besides, writes a recent critic, "such an audacious undertaking would have violated the defensive concept of the war that prevailed in Richmond."[17] If his Trans-Mississippi commander considered such a defensive concept, he paid it little heed. He wanted St. Louis, and he was in good company. Generals Price, Leonidas Polk, and Gideon Pillow all seem to have had designs on this city in early 1862. Their

15. Van Dorn to Colonel William Mackall, January 20, 1862, Van Dorn Papers, Library of Congress.
16. Rowland, "Albert Sidney Johnson," p. 55.
17. *Ibid.*, p. 57.

reasoning was much simpler than the action involved. Why could not troops be assembled at a point in the northern part of Arkansas and then be marched toward St. Louis so swiftly and secretly that they would bypass the large Federal force in southern Missouri? Van Dorn believed he could do this, and then he would carry St. Louis by a coup de main. He could thrust most of the Confederate command across the Mississippi into Illinois and Indiana and thus carry the war into enemy territory. St. Louis in Confederate hands would be a great loss to the North. A Confederate army operating in enemy territory would jeopardize the Union bases in Kentucky and the other border states and threaten their lines of communications. Then the enemy would have to modify his own invasion plans and thus relieve the pressure on Johnston's forces in Tennessee.

The first step in this great venture was to assemble the greatest possible troop strength. Van Dorn's main sources of experienced troops consisted of the command of the two Confederate antagonists, Generals Price and McCulloch. General Price was at Springfield, Missouri, with about 7,000 men. McCulloch's force, stationed in and around Fort Smith and Fayetteville, reported an effective strength of 8,767. Also included in the Trans-Mississippi District was the command of Brigadier General Albert Pike. Early reports from Pike led Van Dorn to think erroneously that this force might add as many as 10,000 additional white and Indian troops to his totals. Optimistically he also hoped for enough troops to be recruited from his district to bring his total up to 45,000 men to be available for the invasion. Realizing that Confederate troops hated to leave their native states, he made his position clear to all his men. "The destination of troops mustered into service under my call will be entirely under my orders," he warned them.

Confederate hopes for increased troop strength received severe setbacks daily. Texas sent some troops, but they did not send their quota. More despairing was the letter from a Texas official in which he expressed his feelings about the situation throughout his district as follows:

It is utterly impossible to recruit infantry and throw it to the point of rendezvous within time to be of service in the anticipated campaign . . . I can assure you . . . that it chagrins me not to be able to comply with this requisition in terms and to the letter, but it is a matter of impossibility to do so. . . .[18]

18. F. R. Lubbock to Secretary Benjamin, February 12, 1862, *Official Records Army*, LIII, 784.

The estimate of troop strength among the Indians in Pike's command was also much too high. When that officer had been assigned to command the Department of Indian Territory on November 22, 1861, the troops of his department consisted of only a few whites and several Indian regiments. Even though his potential strength may have reached 10,000, the troops actually available for combat duty numbered about 1000. When finally brought into action, this group did little more than add to Van Dorn's woes.

Conditions among the troops of Price and McCulloch further weakened the troop strength for which Van Dorn had hoped. Reports from Price's command revealed little discipline among the ill-trained Missourians, and someone even suggested that General Price was drinking too much. Van Dorn would have to visit Price as soon as possible and straighten up matters in his command. But the situation seemed just as appalling in McCulloch's camp where the troops lived in crude huts in the midst of rugged winter conditions with smallpox rampant in their ranks.

Unaware of just how much his troop strength was being cut by these developments, Van Dorn continued his preparations with a light heart. Hailed by a Pocahontas crowd, he mounted a platform and made a stirring speech to the citizens and soldiers that assembled before him. Handsome, with features almost too delicately refined for a soldier, yet possessing a charm that appealed to officers and men alike, the speaker contrasted sharply with the frontiersmen before him. Some of them were in crude military attire; others were in civilian clothes. The speech was meant for all of them. The words ring with the commander's optimism; it also bespeaks his naïveté. In rhetoric of the Victorian Age he brazenly presented the Southern Cause, calling on his audience to organize, to "arm and march to join the Army of Missouri, and battle for independence on her soil."[19] He spoke of the new Confederate flag, "waving on the southern borders of Missouri," placed there by fellow countrymen. "We have voted to be free. We must now fight to be free . . ." he exhorted. Then as if impassioned by his own words, this fiery partisan for states' rights concluded dramatically:

Awake! Young men of Arkansas, and arm! Beautiful maidens of Louisiana smile not upon the craven youth who may linger by your hearth when the rude blast of war is sounding in your ear! Texas chivalry, to arms! Hardships and hunger, disease and death are preferable to slavish subjection, and a

19. Little Rock *True Democrat*, February 20, 1862, p. 1.

nation with a bright page in history and a glorious epitaph is better than a vassaled land with honor lost and a people sunk in infamy.

Work piled heavy on the little commander's shoulders as his plans for invasion took shape. Postponing his plans to visit Price because of the exigencies of his immediate situation, he nevertheless wrote the Missourian of his progress. He told Price that St. Louis was definitely their goal, to be taken "by rapid marches and assault" by a Confederate army of at least 25,000 troops to be composed of the commands of Price, McCulloch, Pike, and his own units from Pocahontas. The troops would come together in Missouri and advance on St. Louis as a unit.

A week later his estimate of his troop strength was more realistic. To Price he confided that 15,000 would be a better estimate. There would also be 8,000 from Pike's command, but they were "intended for defense alone or as a corps of observation on the Kansas border."[20] He told Price that he hoped to move as soon after the first of April as possible. "I design attempting St. Louis," he reiterated.

Van Dorn's invasion hopes centered around a series of very complicated actions involving all the different troop units he had identified to Price. Stressing speed and secrecy, he originally planned to move McCulloch from the Boston Mountains to Pocahontas in early March. There he would take command of those troops and his own and lead them across the state line toward a juncture with Price. Price was to march from Springfield directly through Salem, Missouri, and join Van Dorn about April 1 somewhere between Salem and Potosi. Plans for Pike never became firm, but the Indians would probably have been attached to Price's army for the march.[21] Sometime before Price joined Van Dorn he was to feint a blow in the direction of the enemy position at Rolla and check any Federal intention of halting the advance.

On the march toward St. Louis, Van Dorn's main column would destroy the main railroad bridges along their route while the cavalry units fanned out and ranged through the countryside to destroy com-

20. *Official Records Army*, VIII, 750.
21. Van Dorn ordered Pike to move his forces into Lawrence County, Missouri, near Price. Pike resented this order. He said that his job was to command the Indian Territory. It was his responsibility to keep the Indians on the side of the Confederacy and to protect their holdings. Pike did not feel that the Indians should be involved in any sort of Confederate offensive.

munication and supply lines, especially railroad spurs. When he reached St. Louis, Van Dorn hoped to entrench on both sides of the river, and with the co-operation of the friendly population he expected to find in the city, he believed he could force the surrender of the garrison. As for his own supplies and extra equipment he would limit them to a minimum, taking only that which was absolutely necessary. He would resupply at the Federal larders and arsenals once they had gained their objective.

Every aspect of this planning focused on speed and surprise. As Van Dorn made his plans he must have remembered from his West Point days the interpretations of the strategy of Baron Jomini by Dennis H. Mahan. Professor Mahan's stress to a generation of cadets was for the offensive, "executed by celerity of movement."[22] In his writings, which were the heart of his classroom lectures at the Academy, Mahan presented his views in some detail:

Speed is one of the characteristics of strategic marches . . . in this one quality lie all the advantages that a fortunate initiative may have procured . . . by rapidity of movement we can, like the Romans, make war feed war. . . . No great success can be hoped for in war in which rapid movements do not enter as an element. . . . We may here attempt any blow; no movements can fail to turn out well except those which are too slow and methodical. . . .[23]

This strategy of speed and surprise, Van Dorn learned well. Would it work in such a grandiose scheme? Actually this strategy had merit. Numerically the Confederate force had an advantage over the enemy in Missouri. Also there was considerable sympathy for the South in and around St. Louis. Command had at last been unified under a single officer, and the disputes that had disrupted the Trans-Mississippi District had been laid to rest. The line of advance that Van Dorn had chosen was free of Union troops, and the Confederates, with enough speed, might possibly have reached St. Louis before a large army could have assembled to stop them. St. Louis may not have yielded to the Confederates, but the war would have entered enemy territory and relieved pressures and raised morale as in other theaters of activity.

Whether Van Dorn's tactical operations could have kept pace with

22. Quoted in T. Harry Williams, *Military Leadership*, p. 9.
23. Quoted in Depuy, *West Point*, p. 196.

his elaborate strategy is another matter, but certainly his most important mistake was to reckon without knowledge of the character of Federal Brigadier General Samuel R. Curtis, the new commander of the Southwestern District of Missouri. Since his appointment to that post on Christmas Day, Curtis had been making his presence felt at Rolla as he reorganized his army and prepared for anything the Confederates might offer. He scouted Price's position regularly, and he seemed to know exactly what the Confederates were doing from day to day. Van Dorn had planned his great blow with thoughts of a Fremont or a Hunter as his opponent. Curtis was no such "pathfinder" soldier. He, too, was a West Pointer, a veteran of the Mexican War, and a former Congressman from Iowa. An engineer by trade, he knew his trade and how to utilize it in military planning. He was a meticulous organizer, reserved in his judgment, thorough in his planning. He was just the man the Federals needed to bring order out of their Missouri chaos. One of the most underrated generals in the history of the Civil War, Curtis was as much responsible as any single force for rejuvenating the demoralized Union army into a fighting unit.

In February, while Van Dorn was furiously planning to bypass his Rolla position, Curtis gave orders for a general advance of his unit against all Southern sympathizers in southern Missouri. "We must strip for a forced march and final conflict," he had warned them two days earlier, referring specifically to General Price's troops at Springfield. His words strangely echoed Van Dorn's at Pocahontas.

On February 12 Curtis's army of 9,585 infantry and 2,510 cavalry, recently reorganized into four divisions by its new commander, attacked Price at Springfield. Outnumbered nearly two to one, Price evacuated the city and retreated south with his small force. Curtis, more interested in Price's army than in Springfield, followed closely in pursuit. Price, seeing little to be gained by a show-down fight with the Federals, accelerated his retreat, seeking refuge in northern Arkansas. At Cross Hollow, an "extensive cantonment" located about fifteen miles northwest of Fayetteville, he halted his troops, hoping that General McCulloch would join him in a counterattack against Curtis. McCulloch failed to respond. With Curtis's cavalry threatening his security at Cross Hollow, Price resumed his retreat. His demoralized men moved out in such haste that they allowed many of their sick and wounded and a large amount of commissary stores to fall into enemy hands. Price continued on to the Boston Mountains where he encamped on Cove Creek on February 21, out of immediate range of his pursuer and within thirty miles of McCulloch's headquarters.

Price and McCulloch were together again, and this time their backs were to the wall. From his Cove Creek camp, Price sent Van Dorn the bad news, suggesting that the Mississippian come to western Arkansas immediately to take over the command of the troops there and lead an invasion back into Missouri. Anxiously he awaited word from Pocahontas.

Meanwhile, Curtis's pursuit carried his advance troops under Brigadier General Alexander Asboth into Fayetteville, Arkansas, where "in conformity" with the orders of General Henry W. Halleck, his departmental commander, he halted his advance in anticipation of what he believed would be a counterattack by Price and McCulloch. Though many of the citizens of Fayetteville welcomed Asboth's troops, Curtis decided that an outpost there would be untenable. He then set his major defensive concentration near Sugar Creek, a meandering little stream running just south of an irregular mountain range, the Pea Vine Ridge. Curtis set this spot "as the strongest of several strong places taken from the enemy to make a stand against any and all odds."[24] Because of a shortage of forage, he spread out his troop units from Sugar Creek in a wide radius of defense with three main centers of control. He placed the First and Second Divisions, under Generals Franz Sigel and Asboth, at Cooper's Farm, four miles southwest of Bentonville, fourteen miles east of his Sugar Creek position. The Third Division, under Colonel Jefferson C. Davis, took position on Sugar Creek; and the Fourth Division, Colonel E. A. Carr commanding, moved to Cross Hollows, where Curtis established his own headquarters.

The shocking news of General Price's retreat reached Van Dorn on February 22 just at the height of his invasion plans. He had heard rumors of a rejuvenated Federal force, but Price's precipitous retreat he had not expected. About the same time that he learned of Price's debacle, he also received an interesting note from General P. G. T. Beauregard in Tennessee. Beauregard suggested that he and Van Dorn join their forces and move against Cairo, Paducah, and St. Louis. As

24. *Official Records Army*, VIII, 196.

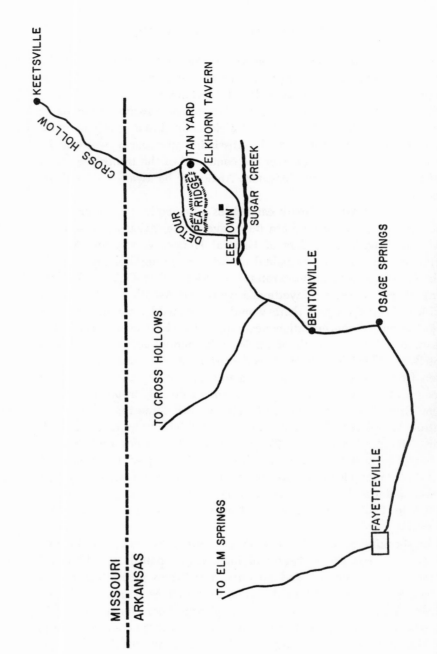

NORTHWEST ARKANSAS

enticing as this offer appeared, Van Dorn chose to ignore it and rush to western Arkansas. Sizing up the situation, he decided that an advance into Missouri was impossible as long as Curtis held Price and McCulloch in check. Though unwilling to abandon his St. Louis plans, he saw that he must first push the Federals out of Arkansas, and he planned accordingly. He would attack with the troops already facing Curtis. The force stationed at Pocahontas would stand by to keep additional enemy forces from penetrating the state, poised for an advance toward St. Louis when he cleared Curtis from his path. He then assembled a small staff at Pocahontas consisting of his adjutant, Colonel Dabney Maury; his nephew and aide, Lieutenant Clement Sulivane; and a Negro servant named Milton, and prepared to travel across the country to join Price and McCulloch near Fayetteville. For his own purposes he saddled his best black thoroughbred mare, a horse he had purchased in Virginia, to make the rugged trip. With a native guide, the general and his staff boarded a steamer near Pocahontas and proceeded down the Black River to Jacksonport, arriving there on February 23. Unable to travel further by boat, they delayed one day and then mounted their horses for a long cross-country ride.

The ride across northern Arkansas was a trying one. Roads were poor, and the riders were in a hurry. They made every effort to avoid delay. Dabney Maury later commented on the harshness of the winter weather and the long hours they spent in the saddle. With more seriousness than humor he reminisced: "Had it not been that we slept every night in a feather bed . . . we could have been permanently disabled for cavalry service forever."[25] Spending the nights in hospitable farm houses each night on the trip across Arkansas certainly made the ride more endurable.

One day out from Pocahontas, Van Dorn lost his sword from its sheath. Lt. Sulivane finally found it, but the men lost valuable time in the search. Someone mentioned a bad omen, but Van Dorn only spurred them on to a faster pace. Arriving at a turbulent stream, the men constructed a crude boat to cross the icy waters, but again there was trouble. When the guide tripped getting into the boat, Van Dorn was flipped into the stream. "Encumbered with his heavy cavalry cloak, boots, spurs, and saber . . .", the "bad omen," Van Dorn was thoroughly

25. "Recollections of Earl Van Dorn," *Southern Historical Society Papers*, XIX, 194.

drenched. Despite his condition, he seemed in good spirits and lustily swam ashore without aid from his comrades. He was supposed to have emerged from the stream with such a light-hearted air that he recited this poem to herald his mood:

> Once upon a raw and gusty day
> The troubled Tiber chafed within her shores:
> Accoutered as I was, I plunged in,
> The torrent roared, and I did buffet it
> With lusty sinews.

This mood changed quickly. The sudden drenching, his ineffectual efforts to dry his clothing, and his exposure to the sharp cold winds for the rest of the day brought on an attack of colds and fever which plagued him for several days until after the Pea Ridge campaign. Often during that campaign illness forced him to ride in an ambulance. Naturally this limited his effectiveness as a commander, and it even aroused the contempt of many of his hard-bitten troops. These men resented seeing their commander riding in an ambulance, and they passed the word down the ranks that Van Dorn had been drinking too much.

The remainder of their trip across Arkansas was uneventful. The people they encountered along the way were friendly and hospitable to them, sheltering and even entertaining them on occasion. Sergeant Watson, a severe critic of Van Dorn, suggested in his journal that the "entertainment" along the way probably consisted of all-night poker playing and whiskey drinking.[26] Be that as it may, the weary travelers arrived at Van Buren on the evening of February 28. One suspects that the trip pushed Van Dorn's endurance to the limit. He must meet the rivals, Price and McCulloch, in his weakened condition and plan an attack. His courage and his ability were in for a severe test.

26. *Life in the Confederate Army,* p. 284.

CHAPTER SIX

Commanding an Army

*T*HE wind blew cold and blustery as Earl Van Dorn and his staff rode into the little frontier town, Van Buren, on the first day of March.[1] Fatigue lined the faces of the weather-beaten riders as they dismounted and then waded through Arkansas mud to the rudely constructed military telegraph station. Stopping briefly to issue orders to his aide as he warmed himself before a roaring fire, Van Dorn then dictated telegrams to be sent to the two army commanders who were encamped in the Boston Mountains just north of the town. The message to each was a simple one. Were the troops prepared to march against Curtis? Then a command: if they were not ready, make preparations at once.

General McCulloch's reply indicated his enthusiasm for the move: "We now have force enough to whip the enemy," he said optimistically.[2] Private Watson, viewing the situation from the ranks of the same command, was not so sure. Later he wrote of his fears:

It seemed evident to the more thoughtful that [Van Dorn] . . . was giving his orders from a distance off a book or map, without much knowledge of the position or condition of his army, the strength of the enemy, or the nature of the country in which his army was going to operate.[3]

There is merit to this criticism, but Van Dorn was still more interested in speed than intricate planning, and at this point he was counting heavily upon the element of surprise.

1. Dabney Maury reported this date as February 28, but the preponderance of evidence supports the March date. Maury was writing some fourteen years after the campaign, and his articles are filled with errors of minute details. *See* Maury, "Recollections of Elkhorn," *Southern Historical Society Papers*, II, 184–185.
2. *Official Records Army*, VIII, 763.
3. *Life in the Confederate Army*, p. 283.

Van Dorn finished up his business in Van Buren quickly. After a short night's sleep in the crude quarters of a Van Buren resident, he and his staff and several guides began the thirty-mile ride to the Cove Creek camp of General Price and the Missourians. All day the saddle-weary travelers pushed over an ascending mountain road that was covered with ice and freezing slush, often in the face of a blinding snowstorm. They finally arrived at Price's farmhouse headquarters just after dark on that dismal Sunday.

Price greeted the new arrivals cordially, at once offering them the bounty of his own larder. For an hour or so the hungry visitors forgot the horrors of war as they partook of their first decent meal since Pocahontas and one of the last hearty ones they would face for several trying weeks. The "kidney stewed in sherry" made a lasting impression on staff-member Dabney Maury.[4]

Van Dorn's initial discussions with Price did little to dampen his enthusiasm for his offensive. This enthusiasm was contagious. When price made the announcement to his men that they were going to attack Curtis, they "grew hilarious and enthusiastic, and all voted their new chief a success from the beginning."[5] A closer look at these men by their new commander might not have been so encouraging. The Missourians had given the impression of being little more than an armed mob when they had passed through Fayetteville several days earlier, and they had changed little during their brief sojourn on Cove Creek. They were willing to follow Price, however, and they were anxious to return to Missouri. It was their enthusiasm that encouraged Van Dorn, but he might have considered their physical condition a little closer in his planning. Raw troops are usually an undisciplined mob, making complex tactical operations difficult if not impossible.

The next step was to visit McCulloch and make the final arrangements for the attack. Joined by Price and followed by the Missourians, Van Dorn proceeded on to the Texan's headquarters on Monday. They arrived at McCulloch's camp late in the day. Van Dorn was cold, tired and probably feverish, but he was determined not to permit any delay.

McCulloch's command greeted their new chief with mixed emotions. A forty-gun salute boomed, and many of the men rejoiced openly as

4. "Recollections of Elkhorn," p. 184.
5. Victor M. Rose, *The Life and Services of General Ben McCulloch*, p. 200.

the little general rode into camp on his beautiful black mare. Ephriam M. Anderson has left a vivid description of Van Dorn as he rode in:

[H]is age seemed to be between 35 and 40 [he was nearly 42], though some deep lines were marked upon his face: he was of medium height, slender, free in his address and movements, with a gay, dashing manner about him: sitting his horse in an easy and careless style: his features were regular, his forehead rather high, eyes black and fiery; lips thin and compressed: the chin was large and the jaw-bone prominent. He wore a blue uniform coat, a cap of the same color, embroidered with gold lace, dark pants, and heavy cavalry boots.[6]

His supporters generated the same sort of enthusiasm for him that he had noted in Price's camp. They believed he "would fight," and of that they approved.[7] Many of these soldiers knew of his Texas fame firsthand, while others had heard of his bold and daring deeds against Mexicans and Indians. These traits appealed to many of the frontiersmen who accepted courage as the highest of virtues. A Missourian expressed his feelings this way, "we now have a chief that possesses energy and courage."[8] Colonel Thomas L. Snead, one of Price's staff officers and later a critic of Van Dorn, also spoke for many of the men when he said: "We Missourians were delighted; for he was known to be a fighting man, and we felt sure he would help us to regain our State."[9]

Support was not unanimous; some found him hard to accept. The contrast between the West Pointer and McCulloch was too obvious to many of the Westerners. The Mississippian was spit and polish; the Texan was a "thoroughly practical officer," very popular among the people of Arkansas and Texas, and especially so among his own troops where respect bordered on adulation. Van Dorn had yet to prove him-

---

6. Ephriam McD. Anderson, *Memoirs: Historical and Personal: Including the Campaign of the First Missouri Confederate Brigade*, quoted in Edwin C. Bearss, "The Battle of Pea Ridge," *Arkansas Historical Quarterly*, XX, 82.

7. Back in Little Rock the *True Democrat* sensed some of this excitement that ranged around Van Dorn. "We are more and more pleased with [his] . . . action," this newspaper reported on March 6. "One day we hear of him at Pocahontas . . . on the next at Jacksonport. A few days later at Clarksville . . . and anon he is reported at Boston Mountain. . . . Every department seems to have caught [his] . . . activity." March 6, 1862, p. 2.

8. John W. Noble, "Battle of Pea Ridge," *Commandry of Missouri*, p. 220.

9. Johnson and Buel, *Battles and Leaders*, I, 275.

self, and many would reserve their respect until he showed courage and energy. To at least one member of McCulloch's command, the indomitable Watson, all that Van Dorn meant to him was that he came from Virginia and was a good poker player. Others grudgingly accepted him, but without McCulloch to intervene, he would have a difficult group to control.

General Van Dorn greeted McCulloch's command in a stirring voice with that flowery rhetoric he employed so freely:

Soldiers: Behold your leader! He comes to show you the way to glory and immortal renown. He comes to hurl back the minions of the despots at Washington, whose ignorance, licentiousness, and brutality are equaled only by their craven natures. They come to free your slaves, lay waste your plantations, burn your villages, and abuse your loving wives and daughters.[10]

It was the same medicine—but strong tonic to the men before him.

In McCulloch's rude headquarters the commanding general conferred at length with his new colleagues and learned from them all he could in a brief time about his new army and the enemy before him. The two officers were co-operative and gave him as clear a picture as they could. Their most shocking news was a report that the troop strength would be only 16,000 instead of the more than 20,000 that Van Dorn had expected. The troops were distributed as follows: General McCulloch's command, 8,384; General Price's Missourians, 6,818; and General Albert Pike's unit, probably about 1,000. McCulloch had a cavalry and an infantry brigade and four batteries of artillery. As of March 1, recently promoted Brigadier General James McIntosh commanded his cavalry and the unpredictable Louisianan, Colonel Louis Hébert, led his infantry. Price's forces consisted of two brigades of Missouri Volunteers under Brigadier General William Y. Slack and Colonel Henry Little, a battalion of cavalry, several under-strength divisions of Missouri State Troops, and several small artillery units.

General Albert Pike's force was the unknown quantity—no one seemed to know either the exact number or the composition of this unit. Van Dorn had continually downgraded his estimate of Pike's troop strength after an initial optimistic 10,000. When he learned that the actual figure might even fall below a thousand and that these troops were Indians except for one white squadron, he must certainly have

10. Arkansas *Gazette*, March 6, 1887.

been disappointed in Pike. The two men were not on good terms as it was. Pike had protested bitterly to the War Department about the battle at Wichita Village in 1858; he accused Van Dorn of duplicity and barbarity for attacking the Comanches after Fort Arbuckle had signed a nonaggression pact with them.

Whether the two men showed this animosity in their first meeting at Little Rock in early February is not known. At that time Pike accepted a working arrangement of some sort with Van Dorn, agreeing to co-operate as best he could. Pike then proceeded to Indian Territory to serve as paymaster to the Indians. The arrangements between Pike and Van Dorn were ill-defined from the beginning. Pike's command was actually a separate department in the Confederacy and was never officially assigned to Department Number 2. There was enough vagueness in the various War Department orders to confuse both commanders and create a situation unproductive to Van Dorn's best interests in his plans for an attack against St. Louis or General Curtis.

On February 7, Van Dorn had reported to General Price that Pike and 10,000 troops would co-operate with the Missourians in any emergency in the projected St. Louis invasion. On February 14, he revised this statement by saying that Pike's "8,000" could be used only for defense or observation. By February 24, he had lowered his estimate to 6,000. In the meantime he ordered Pike to Neosho, Missouri, to work with Price. Pike, adamant in his opposition to this order, stated that the Indians were never to fight outside their own territory without their consent. He felt that the Indians were incapable of fighting the white man's type of war and would suffer undue hardship if they should be forced to participate. Some of the Indians also resented having to leave their territory to fight for fear of losing their lands during their absence. Pike shared this belief. Curtis's unexpected advance at this point prevented a showdown between Pike and Van Dorn, but both men seemed to harbor new ill-feelings over the incident.

Meanwhile, in his conference with Price and McCulloch, Van Dorn was not only obtaining information about his own troop strength, but he was also learning much about the enemy's strength and position. Both officers were helpful since they had been in the presence of the enemy time and time again during the hostilities of the first year of the war. McCulloch, however, was especially helpful for he seemed to know every road or trail in the area. In providing a rear guard for

Price's troops as they had retreated from Cross Hollow, he had dispatched his cavalry to deploy behind the enemy to harass supply lines and to take the pressure off the retreating Missourians. From his cavalry commanders, McCulloch learned much of the defensive positions of Curtis's various units. Of special interest to the three generals who now planned the battle strategy was the Union position on Sugar Creek, the strong point in Curtis's line of defense. Just how should this position be approached? Van Dorn questioned his lieutenants on their views.

General Price was the first to speak. The doughty Missourian spread a rough map out on the table before them and, drawing imaginary lines with his finger, he advised an advance by the combined force directly toward Curtis's position. They should first move to Fayetteville, a day's march. From there he would drive on Sigel's position south of Bentonville, but just before the main army struck Sigel, Price would have the Confederate cavalry mask this attack by a feint against Curtis's front. This would cut off Sigel's retreat, split the enemy force, and also prevent Federal reinforcements from being directed to Bentonville. With Sigel's troops out of the way, McIntosh's cavalry would then flank Curtis's position to the north and cut off the enemy's line of retreat. At that moment when Curtis was bottled up, Price and McCulloch would launch a heavy frontal attack on Curtis's main position with both artillery and infantry. Price's plan relied on speed and secrecy and the numerical superiority of the Confederate force.

McCulloch offered strenuous objections to Price's scheme. His objections were similar to those he had used for not joining the Missourian earlier. The Confederate troops were too raw, he warned, too poorly drilled, not well-enough armed, to send against the well-organized army of Curtis. Why not delay a bit? Keep the infantry in camp until the men were thoroughly drilled and seasoned for an offensive. If Curtis attacked, the Confederate command would be ready for him, but meanwhile, McIntosh's cavalry could drive Sigel into Indian Territory and harass Curtis's supply and communications lines.

McCulloch's plans never had a chance with Van Dorn. Maybe his conversations with General Johnston had convinced him that his first responsibility in Arkansas was to take the pressure off the Confederate army in Tennessee. Maybe it was an insatiable desire just to get on toward St. Louis. He was always impatient with delay. Whatever the case Van Dorn "resolved to attack at once," believing that the Federals held up their own offensive only because they awaited supplies and reinforcements. He was most optimistic, as he usually was before a great campaign, and held strong hopes of "effecting a complete surprise and attacking the enemy before the large detachments encamped at various points in the surrounding country could rejoin the main body."[11] The late Kenneth P. Williams said that at this point Van Dorn "was luxuriating in the dream of every commander, that of gobbling up the enemy piece by piece,"[12] but like many other officers throughout the history of organized warfare, he found to his chagrin that this type of dream can often be complicated by an enemy who does not wish to be gobbled up. Curtis was of this particular state of mind.

Van Dorn terminated the conference and proceeded to issue orders for an advance to begin the next day. Price and McCulloch were to advance together to Bentonville via Fayetteville and Elm Springs. To Pike, somewhere in Indian Territory, marching orders were not so explicit. The first order of the day was for Pike to move his entire unit "along the Cane Hill road" until he could join the rear of Van Dorn's advancing force.[13] Later in the day Van Dorn realized that Pike was to take the long way if he followed these orders, so he corrected the line of march to get him into position earlier. Actually Pike was too far from Fayetteville to join the main force when he was expected, and he would be delayed until the very eve of battle.

Van Dorn's dream of marching on St. Louis was set to begin, not quite as he had originally planned it, but he still held high hopes of success. If Generals Hardee and John Porter McCown had been present to add their commands to his attacking force, fate might have been kinder to Earl Van Dorn!

At dawn on Tuesday, March 4, the main body of the ragged Confederate force moved out from the Boston Mountains toward Fayetteville. Each man was carrying a single blanket and a minimum of food and equipment. It was a colorful if pathetic sight as "every species of wheel vehicle, from the jolting old oxcart to the most fantastically painted stagecoach, rolled along the road."[14] All morning the troops battled blinding snow and sleet, but Van Dorn only pushed them

11. *Official Records Army,* VIII, 283.
12. *Lincoln Finds a General,* III, 289.
13. *Official Records Army,* VIII, 764.
14. Watson, *Life in the Confederate Army,* p. 283.

harder. Many began to grumble that their commanding officer did not realize that they were walking while he rode. By noon many were staggering, and some actually fell along the wayside. Jay Monaghan presents a poignant picture of events along the road:

> Cavalrymen tried to warm numbed fingers between saddle blankets and their horses' backs. The hot sweat felt good at first but finally left their hands colder than ever. Infantrymen fared better by swinging their arms and legs naturally.[15]

Sixty pieces of artillery, including a famous old artillery piece, ox-drawn "Ol' Sacramento," rolled along behind the expedition.

In the saddle at dawn, Van Dorn supervised operations as his troops moved on. He rode hard all morning, but new attacks of fever and chills struck and sapped his strength. He finally gave in and mounted a horse-drawn ambulance much to his own disgust as well as that of some of his troops. Not so with colorful, rugged Ben McCulloch. Dressed in his black velvet suit and Duke of Wellington boots, he rode immediately behind his own skirmishers and ahead of the Sixteenth Arkansas Infantry Regiment, recognizable to troops all along the line. Cold, frost-bitten infantrymen cheered him again and again and reserved their contempt for the little man in the ambulance.

Fortunately for the advancing army, the sun came out during the early afternoon and helped dry out their clothing. But the march continued. Late afternoon found them at Fayetteville, as scheduled, where they ate hard bread, drank their coffee substitute, and then settled down to rest in whatever shelter each could find or construct. Snow fell steadily during the night, covering the men in their sleep.

From Fayetteville, the main route toward Sugar Creek was over the highway that connected Springfield, Missouri, and Fort Smith, Arkansas, a thoroughfare known as the Telegraph Road. This highway followed a northeastern direction toward the Missouri state line from Fort Smith and crossed Sugar Creek about four miles south of the Pea Ridge Mountains. Besides the Telegraph Road, another highway veered northward through Fayetteville. This road, the Bentonville Road, passed through Elm Springs and Bentonville and finally rejoined the Telegraph Road just south of Sugar Creek.

Propped on an elbow in his ambulance bed, Van Dorn again looked

15. *Civil War on the Western Border*, p. 234.

over these roads. Following Price's suggestion, he would use the Bentonville Road as planned. In this way he could soon threaten Sigel's position just south of Bentonville.

Early Wednesday morning Van Dorn ordered all his troops, with the exception of McIntosh's cavalry, to move out from Fayetteville on this road in the direction of Elm Springs. To familiarize himself with the enemy outposts between his army and the Missouri border and to reconnoiter the ground directly in front of him, he directed McIntosh's cavalry to proceed four miles northward up the Telegraph Road. At that point McIntosh, too, was to divide his own command. Part of it he was to lead off the Telegraph Road and carefully reconnoiter the countryside before rejoining the main command at Elm Springs late in the afternoon. The other unit, the Sixth Texas Cavalry under Colonel B. Warren Stone, was to continue up Telegraph Road and threaten suspected Federal outposts at Mud Town and Cross Hollow before it finally bivouacked on that road during the night. Then on Thursday they were to ride across the country and join the main army. Van Dorn was convinced that the Federals were unaware of his progress, and for a while he was right. His plan to this point was a good one especially in his use of cavalry and his selection of roads for his movement. Other factors were not so favorable to his hopes for success. The heavy loss of sick and weary men cost him his numerical advantage. McIntosh also jeopardized his offensive by getting lost in unfamiliar mountain country. Union troops killed or captured many of his troops before he again found his way through the hills. His services were lost when they were most acutely needed.

On Wednesday sunshine again brought to the marching troops some relief from the intense mountain cold. Taking advantage of this sudden break in the weather, Van Dorn left his ambulance, and on horseback he rode up and down the long line of marching men. Cheers greeted him at every unit although the enthusiasm was less spontaneous in McCulloch's command where those hardbitten regulars still figured him for a West Point dandy.

The forward progress of the main army on Wednesday ended late in the afternoon at Elm Springs. Joined by part of McIntosh's reconnoitering unit, the commanders selected their bivouac areas. After a miserable meal of uncooked corn meal and water, the men bedded down in their single blankets. Again the snow fell, and for the second straight night the troops shivered and suffered, getting very little needed rest.

Van Dorn's belief that Curtis knew nothing of his advance was true until about two o'clock Wednesday afternoon. Then as the Confederates trudged their way through the ice and cold toward Elm Springs, "Wild Bill" Hickok and his scouts brought news of the advance to Curtis's headquarters at Cross Hollow. They correctly informed the Federal commander that the Confederate cavalry would be at Elm Springs by nightfall, and that Van Dorn's artillery was on the road moving in that direction.

Shocked by this news, Curtis saw visions of his divided command being absorbed piecemeal by the enemy. But acting coolly, he dispatched couriers to Sigel and the Union commanders at the other outposts and ordered them to concentrate on the high ground north of Sugar Creek at the earliest possible moment. Then he too moved twelve miles up the Telegraph Road to Sugar Creek where he joined his main unit about two o'clock on Thursday morning.

All Curtis's outpost commanders received their orders for the Sugar Creek concentration, and all complied immediately except General Sigel who delayed action until one of his detachments at Osage Mill, about four miles south of Bentonville, reported that its pickets had been fired upon by advancing Confederate scouting parties. Feeling it necessary to concentrate his and General Asboth's troops to meet the Confederate advance and contrary to Curtis's orders, he directed part of his force under Colonel Frederick Schaefer back to Bentonville to await further instructions.[16] The remainder of the two divisions he ordered to begin deploying toward Sugar Creek via Bentonville at two o'clock on the morning of March 6. General Asboth's division left its outpost position at McKissick's farm promptly at the hour scheduled. They arrived in Bentonville two hours later and there awaited the arrival of Sigel's division. Meanwhile, the Confederates occupied Elm Springs, and Van Dorn planned an early morning march and attack against Sigel's First Division.

16. Johnson and Buel, *Battles and Leaders*, I, 319. After the battle General Halleck expressed concern over Sigel's action. "It was precisely in keeping with what he did at Carthage and Wilson's Creek," he reported. "I anticipated that he would try to play you a trick by being absent at the critical moment." Halleck then promised Curtis to transfer the German general to another department. Thus Van Dorn had no monopoly on confusion and divided command during the Pea Ridge campaign. *Official Records Army*, VIII, 626.

Again Van Dorn figured without weighing his enemy's possibilities for action. Scouting reports alerted Sigel to the fact that Van Dorn's army was too strong for him, so when he arrived at Bentonville, he ordered all his command but a rearguard of about 600 men to depart for Sugar Creek at once. He and his small detachment remained in Bentonville "for the purpose of defending the main column on its retreat."[17]

The Confederate commander, still basking in the thoughts that Curtis had no knowledge of his position, had his men on the road to Bentonville by three o'clock Thursday morning. He would catch Sigel before the wily German could get on the road to the creek, or so he believed before he was beset by trouble. Hardly were his troops on the road when he was struck again by his illness and was back in the ambulance for the march.[18] His troops, cold and near the point of physical exhaustion, missed his personal leadership. As morning passed and he failed to appear before them, they began to straggle. Their marching became so slovenly that it was nearly noon before the head of the leading division swung into view of the town. From his sickbed Van Dorn saw the rearguard of Sigel's detachment departing from Bentonville. Thinking it was Sigel's entire command, he hurried his men on. He later reported that had his own force arrived at Bentonville an hour earlier, he could have captured the Federal general and 7,000 men and thus changed the complexion of the entire campaign. Actually Sigel's main force had never been in danger.

Van Dorn then seriously misjudged the capabilities of his men. Anxious to make up what he felt had been a missed opportunity at Bentonville, he relentlessly pushed his fatigued troops after the retreating Yankees. He also placed McIntosh, who had returned from his scouting expedition of the day before, on a flanking movement to get behind Sigel's army near a place called Camp Stephens on Sugar Creek about three miles west of Curtis's position. McIntosh attempted this operation, but once behind enemy lines he foolishly divided his command to attack Sigel from two sides. Losing his way in an entanglement of trees and underbrush, McIntosh arrived too late to make his move behind Sigel. The impetuous officer then tried to make up for his delay. With practically no precautions, he and "his wild men on wilder

17. Johnson and Buel, *Battles and Leaders,* I, 320.
18. Many of the officers and men were duly concerned over this illness for the campaign was all Van Dorn's, and without his personal leadership, plans could and did go awry.

horses" charged directly into Sigel's retreating troops. Amid a shower of bullets, McIntosh ordered his troops into the very face of the enemy's guns. Grasping his battleflag, the daring officer waved it above his head, imploring his men to follow him into the thick of the fight. Courage of this sort could mean the difference in a battle, but it could also result in a leaderless army. Sigel, reinforced by some heavy weapons from Curtis's position, met this charge with several heavy volleys. McIntosh lived to fight another day, but the Federal shot dispersed his men and ended the attack.

After this repulse a Captain Hale, a sort of "elder statesman" for the Sixth Texas Cavalry, one of McIntosh's units, decried the rout: "This here rigiment are disgraced forever! I'd a ruther died right thar than to a give arry a inch!"[19]

Colonel Elkanah Greer, one of McIntosh's regimental officers, defended his commanding officer. McIntosh was actually trying to get behind Sigel's troops as they retreated up the Camp Stephens Road toward Sugar Creek, he said. They failed because of the mountainous terrain and rocky roads. "This was done as effectually as possible under the circumstances," he wrote. "Considering the ambuscade they had prepared for us . . . it seems almost like a miracle that more of my men and horses were not either killed or wounded."[20]

A visitor in the Pea Ridge area today can sympathize with the Confederate apologists in their difficulties. This is still rugged, overgrown country with hills and precipitous valleys dominating the entire landscape. Better reconnoitering and more detailed planning might have cost Van Dorn some time, but it would have better informed him of the terrain whereon he would fight.

Despite McIntosh's or Van Dorn's poor judgment or just plain Confederate bad luck, Sigel still remained in a desperate plight at this point. Van Dorn's main unit was approaching, and Sigel still had several rough miles to cross with his own unit. His commander was better prepared. Ever diligent, Curtis dispatched part of Colonel Peter Osterhaus's command to his aid. After rescuing the retreating Federal unit, Osterhaus then joined Sigel enroute to Sugar Creek. Their retreat continued in an orderly manner ever followed by Van Dorn and the main body of his troops. Time and again Sigel and Osterhaus paused to fight

19. Rose, *Ross' Texas Brigade*, p. 57.
20. *Official Records Army*, VIII, 297–298.

a brief rearguard action with the Confederate advance patrols or to place obstacles in the road to block the Confederate vehicles. Their artillery never missed an opportunity to place well-directed fire into the advancing column and further add discomfort to their pursuers. These tactics and cavalry protection on their flanks took Sigel and Osterhaus safely into Curtis's camp long before sundown. By nightfall their troops were in position in Curtis's front lines awaiting the expected Confederate attack.

Van Dorn doggedly continued his pursuit, rapidly committing himself to a battle on the enemy's choice of terrain. He halted his advance short of Curtis's outpost units just after dark. His main units were in and around Camp Stephens. They all knew that the morrow meant the big fight. Van Dorn also knew it, and he was as confident of a victory as ever, or so it appeared.

But behind Confederate lines, disorganization and the relentless pressures of three hard days were beginning to tell. Eating parched corn, sleeping in the snow, marching through rain and mud had their ill effects. Pike's late arrival did little to improve morale. One of Price's Missourians left a picture of the arrival of Pike's troops and the confusion they created:

They came trotting by our camp on their little Indian ponies, yelling forth their wild whoop. . . . Their faces were painted, and their long straight hair, tied in a queue, hung down behind. Their dress was chiefly in the Indian costume—buckskin hunting-shirts, dyed of almost every color, leggings, and moccasins of the same material, with little bells, rattles, ear-rings, and similar paraphernalia. Many of them were bareheaded and about half carried only bows and arrows, tomahawks, and war-clubs. . . . They were . . . straight, active, and sinewy in their persons and movements—fine looking specimens of the red men.[21]

Before them rode bewhiskered Albert Pike, the Arkansas poet, long-time friend to the Indian. With him was Stand Watie, the only Indian to become a general officer in the war.

When the Indians entered the Confederate lines, they broke ranks, yelled savagely, fired their guns in the air, and created bedlam. This group added little but color to Van Dorn's command, but certainly they presented "as bizarre an army as ever rode into an American

21. From Ephriam Anderson's *Memoirs* quoted in Bell I. Wiley, *The Life of Johnny Reb*, p. 325.

battle."[22] Though Pike later wrote voluminous letters to justify his and the Indians' conduct in this campaign and in subsequent operations in Arkansas, he more accurately summed up their importance for Earl Van Dorn in a letter he wrote on May 4, 1862:

> The Indian troops are of course entirely undisciplined, mounted chiefly on ponies, and armed very indifferently with common rifles and ordinary shot-guns. When they agreed to furnish troops they invariably stipulated that they should be allowed to fight in their own fashion. They will not face artillery and steady infantry on open ground, and are only used to fighting as skirmishers when cover can be obtained.[23]

More would be heard from Pike and his Indians before this campaign ended, but it seems certain that Van Dorn, who had expected so much from Pike earlier, now saw his Indians as only another source of trouble.

After all the difficulties encountered on his march to Camp Stephens, a general less insistent upon a battle than Earl Van Dorn might well have discounted his prospects for victory against a force as formidable as Curtis's. Just a casual glance at the men in his own ranks would have disheartened a lesser man. Tired, hungry, and ill, many of them were unfit for the rigors of the battlefield. Dysentery and malaria were prevalent among McCulloch's men; many were still recuperating from measles or small pox. Most of the troops in all commands were poorly armed, and morale everywhere was very low. Van Dorn had pushed these men hard for three straight days—too hard! He would have to push them harder. Could human flesh endure? Disciplined, well-organized troops would have had difficulty under the conditions confronting the Confederates. For raw troops the results could be chaos!

Across the precipitous banks of Sugar Creek, General Curtis could well afford to be optimistic about his chances in the impending battle. Though there was fatigue and some disorganization within his own ranks, he could still truthfully report that his army was "generally well armed, drilled, and anxious to encounter the enemy at any reasonable hazard."[24] Certainly they were in better condition than the ragged army pressing an attack in their direction.

22. Monaghan, *Civil War*, p. 235.
23. *Official Records Army*, XIII, 819.
24. *Ibid.*, VIII, 197.

Curtis's men had worked hard under skillful officers preparing their defense—felling timber, obstructing roads, erecting field fortifications, moving artillery pieces into good fields of fire. Curtis had taken pains to occupy the high ground on the northern side of Sugar Creek. His defending army had an important advantage with this position. His Third and Fourth Divisions set up their positions in the hills on the eastern end of his defense line: Davis's Third Division flanked Telegraph Road to its west; Carr's Fourth Division occupied a similar position east of the road. Between these positions Telegraph Road took a sharp turn. An army approaching this position from the south could never see the troops behind this curve until it was too late to defend itself. Curtis had made special efforts to blockade all the roads and thoroughfares on his left when he pulled his units in from their outposts. Convinced that the Confederates would have to attack over the Telegraph Road, he was especially interested in obstructing any traffic that might appear in that sector of the field.

The First and Second Divisions were to occupy the hills on the extreme right wing of the Union position, but delayed by the activity on the Bentonville Road, they were late getting set and were not ready for action until very late Thursday afternoon. On the right end of his line Curtis did not take the initial elaborate precautions that he took on his left. He expected the mountains to deter any efforts the enemy might make there. But when Van Dorn moved down the Bentonville Road late on the sixth and halted at Camp Stephens near Twelve Corners' Church, Curtis realized that the Confederates were a distinct threat to his weaker right wing. He immediately dispatched Colonel Grenville M. Dodge to strengthen this section of his defense by placing obstructions in all the roads and trails. Dodge did a commendable job at great cost to the Confederates. Curtis also shifted some of his cavalry and artillery into supporting positions near the base of the main ridge.

By nightfall on March 6, General Curtis was ready for almost any kind of attack. Terrain advantages, proper dispersion of his troops, and fluid internal lines gave him flexibility to meet an army coming from almost any direction. A frontal attack against his center would be suicidal. A move against his left would be just as foolish. His right lay under the protection of towering Pea Ridge. What course was there for an enemy who was intent upon making an attack?

Van Dorn was not unaware of his dilemma as he halted before Curtis's dispersed troops on Thursday evening. Token reconnaissance had revealed the enemy's strongest points. He realized that he faced a formidable foe in the fortifications behind Sugar Creek. His own advantages were not so obvious, but he must make the most of them. He knew he outnumbered Curtis in effective troop strength by a sizable number. He also realized that Curtis held his position with only a single supply line for his large army, the long road back to Springfield. What could he make of the opportunities in each case?

Calling in Generals McCulloch and McIntosh "who had an accurate knowledge of [the] . . . locality" he questioned them at length as to the best route for his assault.[25] Everything they said pointed toward Curtis's right. On his map McCulloch pointed to the Union positions as his scouts had reported them. Then he pointed to a little-used detour that skirted past and around most of Curtis's fortifications. The Bentonville Detour, little more than a trail, ran directly north from Twelve Corners' Church where it intercepted the Bentonville road. Moving west of a tiny community called Leetown, it passed in a circular route around the western flank of Pea Ridge where it then cut sharply toward the east. It then ran on parallel to the ridge until it struck the Telegraph Road about three miles north of Curtis's headquarters at the Pratt House. The total distance over the detour was about eight miles. "I had resolved to adopt this route," said Van Dorn.[26] He would get behind Curtis and strike the Federals where they least expected it. He would occupy the only road back to Missouri and cut off any hopes that Curtis might have to escape.

Van Dorn liked this daring move from that moment. Again he would depend upon speed and secrecy. Again he sacrificed reconnaissance for a quick movement. Whether Van Dorn intended to move all his combined force over the detour or just Price and the Missourians as it developed, it is not clear from his reports of the battle. The implications are that Price and McCulloch would advance together. Writing years after the war, Colonel Thomas Snead of the Missourians indicates that Van Dorn planned two separate attacks against Curtis on Thursday evening. He concluded that the general unwisely divided his com-

25. *Ibid.*, p. 283.
26. *Ibid.*

mand, personally conducting Price's troops around the enemy while leaving McCulloch and McIntosh to face Curtis's left and center from a position near Leetown. W. I. Truman, also writing long after the war's end, agreed with Snead by saying that Van Dorn divided his forces, sending Price to attack the enemy on the north and leaving Mc-Culloch to face Curtis at the southern end of the Federal line.

Though the eventual battle line developed as these two men suggested, more evidence points to its development through expediency rather than advance planning. General Pike, who trailed all the others on the advance over the detour, presents substantial support for this claim. Pike explained that his forces and all those under McCulloch had proceeded as far as Pea Ridge early on the seventh presumably behind Price toward the Telegraph Road. Suddenly they received new orders about midmorning directing them to countermarch back toward Leetown where they encountered a strong enemy position. Implications from this report are that McCulloch was originally scheduled to attack closer to Telegraph Road than he did, probably in direct conjunction with Price's army, but that plans were changed because of the circumstances brought on by delay and the concentration of a large Federal force at Leetown.

Van Dorn made no mention of a two-pronged attack when he later described the battle, saying only that after he had conferred with Mc-Culloch and McIntosh he was certain that he could reach Telegraph Road in Curtis's rear by making the detour. "I had directed General McCulloch to attack with his forces the enemy's line . . . ," he wrote later, but whether he issued this order on Thursday evening, March 6, or Friday morning the seventh he does not make clear.[27] From the evidence it does appear that he decided definitely on Thursday evening to attempt an encirclement of Curtis's army. This movement was one of the most daring and bizarre of his career. But he had outflanked Mexicans at Monterrey and at Cerro Gordo as a junior officer; he would try similar tactics against Curtis with his own army.

In any case, Van Dorn's plan on Thursday was a daring one. If he were actually trying to strike from two different fronts, his armies separated by a mountain range, he was attempting one of the most hazardous of military operations with the rawest of troops and the most

27. *Ibid.*, p. 284.

inexperienced commanders. If, as was probably the case, he was attempting to fight Curtis from across the Federal supply line, he was gambling on success with two separate armies whose records of cooperation left much to be desired. In either case there was a certain merit in the plan and great risk.

Nightfall near Twelve Corners' Church was a miserable time for the Confederates. Price's troops had crossed the icy Sugar Creek soon after their pursuit of Sigel had ended, and now they rested uncomfortably north of the stream. The other Confederates fretted on the opposite bank where they were being held until final attack plans matured. Hoping to deceive Curtis into believing he would make no move before morning, Van Dorn had put out pickets and ordered fires built as though he were bivouacking for the night. This ruse seems to have worked. Curtis did not commit himself to a new defense line until early Friday morning.

In the Confederate ranks the men grumbled over the dismal weather, the darkness of the night, the shortage of food. Many were completely out of sorts with the commanders who had brought them to such misery. Some chatted in the firelight; some tried to sleep wrapped in their dirty blankets; others just sat, staring into the darkness. While the men waited, Van Dorn dismissed McCulloch and McIntosh and pondered his next move.

General McCulloch moved restlessly among his troops. For a while he stood quietly before a bright fire and made a grotesque shadow in its light. An enlisted man tapped the silent figure on the shoulder. The Texan turned slightly. The soldier handed him a bundle of light wood: "I wish you would light these for me," he said curtly. McCulloch did so; then he disappeared into the shadows to avoid revealing his true identity. Serious and a bit sad-faced, he stood later before a smaller fire with a group of his own men and warned them of a hard battle on the morrow. The battle would "bear decisive fruit," he predicted.[28]

Just after nine o'clock, Van Dorn finally issued his orders. The advance would begin immediately. All troops except General Martin E. Green's Second Division of the Missouri State Guard were to proceed over the detour. Price's command was to lead the way, and the troops of McIntosh, McCulloch and Pike were to follow in that order. Green's troops were to remain near the crossroads to protect the supply train

28. Rose, *General Ben McCulloch*, pp. 202–203.

which had to remain behind until proper precautions could be made to assure its safe disposition behind the Federal lines.

Accompanied by Van Dorn, Price's Missourians departed over the detour immediately upon receipt of the orders. McCulloch remained at Sugar Creek to supervise the crossing of the other troops. Trouble soon beset both forces.

The march of the Missourians began uneventfully. Already across the icy stream, they moved with some speed over the first mile or so of the detour. For about an hour their movement was smooth, their pace, rapid. Then suddenly they began to encounter the obstructions that Colonel Dodge had so diligently placed in their path, and their advance slowed to a crawl. All night they struggled against these obstacles. Panting, cursing, lifting, these men, already weak from hunger, moved trees and boulders and then fell wearily by the wayside to watch others take their places. Van Dorn's hopes for a dawn attack against Curtis's rear died in the pull and strain of human muscles and nerves on a lonely detour less then three miles from their entrenched enemy.

Officers and men alike pushed and pulled artillery wagons and supply vehicles over the rugged terrain. Gradually the Missourians opened the road, and the caissons began to bounce over the half-cleared trail. Instead of being rested and ready for battle, the Confederates faced the prospects of a hard fight tired and demoralized.

All night General Van Dorn tramped through the woods, past the flickering fires around which some of the more exhausted had fallen into fitful sleep. Sometime during the night he sent his ordnance officer for his supply wagons, but it was too late. In the confusion of the night, they had returned to Bentonville.

At Sugar Creek things were also in a muddle. W. L. Gammage summed up the reasons for much of this confusion:

McCulloch's infantry formed at 9 o'clock for the purpose of advancing, but from some unaccountable neglect the creek had not been bridged, and the men only having two little poles laid side by side to cross over on, were delayed from hour to hour until it was after daylight before all had passed over, thus losing six or eight hours of precious time.[29]

It was a bitter cold night and men suffered as they awaited the next move. Gammage said that he stood in the road, sleepy, cold, and out

29. *The Camp, The Bivouac, and The Battle Field,* p. 24.

of patience over the whole affair until he could stand it no longer. Then like many of the others, he rolled up in his blanket and slept until he was rudely awakened for the next move.

This failure to provide proper facilities for the stream crossing was another costly misadventure for the Confederates. Colonel Greer, commanding one of McIntosh's units, said that because of the delay, his troops moved only "a few miles" during the night. General Pike waited behind McCulloch's army, unaware of the cause of the delay, uninformed as to the course of action they were to pursue. It was nearly dawn before his troops crossed the stream. By then many of his Indians were completely out of control. Once the stream had been crossed, the troops ate a stinted breakfast of coffee substitute and cold meal bread and moved into the detour.

Van Dorn was on the eve of his first great battle as an army commander. By his own estimate he had about 16,000 troops against Curtis's 10,500. Already his planning had shown both brilliance and inconsistency. He would have to pay dearly for his mistakes and those of the Confederate War Department upon a battlefield that would be recorded in history as Elkhorn Tavern or Pea Ridge.

CHAPTER SEVEN

Struggle for a Tavern

*T*HE region over which the commanders in both camps were so concerned on the night of March 6 was a parallelogram bounded on all four sides by vital thoroughfares. Telegraph Road, the main highway through the area, formed its eastern edge. The line on the south was the Bentonville Road parallel to Sugar Creek and to Curtis's original position. On the west and north the Bentonville Detour formed the other two sides of the figure by making its sharp turn eastward around Big Mountain, the most prominent peak in the Pea Ridge range. Within the parallelogram the terrain was heavily wooded and broken throughout by high ridges and deep hollows. Some of the ridges stood as much as 150 feet above the rocky fields and valleys below.

Besides certain physical features, the most prominent landmark in the area was Elkhorn Tavern. This tavern, a two-story frame house with a broad south porch and large chimneys at both ends, was located on the west side of Telegraph Road, facing the southeast, about a mile and a half behind General Curtis's original lines. Famous in Arkansas for housing the first telegraph station south of Springfield, it was a popular assembly point for the residents of the northwestern part of the state at the time of the Civil War.[1]

In front of the tavern was a level ridge on which the Huntsville Road from the east joined the main highway. Beyond the junction the country was rough and broken again, finally sloping down into lesser

1. The original tavern was burned by bushwackers soon after the battle of Pea Ridge. After the war was over the building was reconstructed around the remaining two chimneys in much the same pattern as the original building. The tavern, recently renovated, is one of the main centers of interest in the new Pea Ridge National Park.

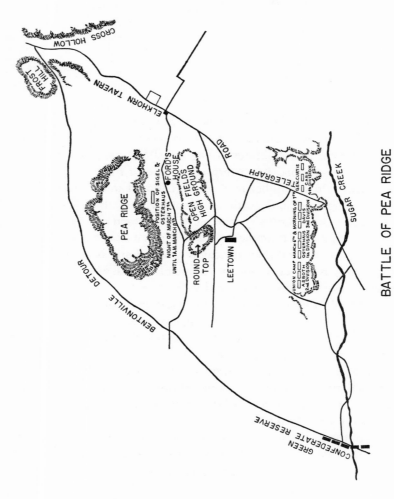

BATTLE OF PEA RIDGE
or
ELKHORN TAVERN

hills and valleys before striking Sugar Creek. Behind the tavern to the west and northwest was a rocky ridge, the main line of the Pea Ridge chain, a formidable obstruction. The tavern stood at the head of a long gorge known as Cross Timber Hollow which cut sharply through Pea Ridge for a distance of about seven miles toward Springfield. Telegraph Road wound its way northward through this gorge. A series of smaller but equally rugged gorges branched out irregularly from the Hollow on both sides and gave the entire countryside a cut-up and uneven appearance. The Bentonville Detour entered the main highway through one of these gorges just behind Sugar Mountain or Trott's Hill as it was called locally. Trees and heavy undergrowth further complicated the area by obstructing visibility and limiting movements of men, horses, and vehicles. The region was so densely covered with woods, vines, and steep defiles that anyone leaving one of the many trails or roads was in real trouble. An army maneuvering in this area would be hard-pressed to hold its units together. Maintaining supply and communications lines, even between field units, could be a major problem.

Besides the tavern there were several other buildings in the area. Among them were Pratt's Store, about a mile down the main highway from the tavern where Curtis first had his headquarters; and the Tannery, a tanyard three quarters of a mile up the gorge from the tavern on the same side of the road. There were a few other scattered residences around, but the only concentration of dwellings was at Leetown, a sleepy little village near the center of the parallelogram. Leetown had been settled by and named for John W. Lee, a first cousin of General Robert E. Lee. The little village was situated on a long slope leading down from Big Mountain to Sugar Creek. It lay less than a mile west of the main highway and was connected to it by two rocky roads.

Late afternoon of the sixth found Leetown deserted of its citizens. While armies maneuvered for positions among the surrounding hills and valleys, the inhabitants of the one community in the area, deciding they wanted no part of the threatening drama, departed posthaste. Not so the three members of the Jesse Cox family who lived in Elkhorn Tavern. They remained in the tavern throughout the battle, hovering in fear in the basement while shot and shell whistled overhead and men died on the first floor of their home.

Confederate patrols leading the Missourians behind Big Mountain made the first contact with the enemy about 3:00 A.M. on Friday when they encountered the outpost of Company M of the Third Illinois Cavalry. Both units were surprised by the encounter, but the larger Confederate force quickly overpowered the enemy position. Figuring correctly that this was only an isolated picket, Van Dorn and Price did not even slow down their main advance. Toward daybreak one of the prisoners captured at the outpost escaped, but by then Van Dorn had progressed too far to be stopped.

Meanwhile, patrols of Major Eli E. Weston of the Twenty-fourth Missouri Infantry of the Union army brought in sporadic reports of Confederate activity in the vicinity of Sugar Mountain. Though Weston identified enemy cavalry and some infantry in this area, he never seemed to realize that he had discovered more than just a token force of Confederates. At daybreak he was still attempting to block what he considered just an unusually large "scouting party" when reinforcements from Colonel Eugene A. Carr's division began to arrive on the scene.

Carr's movement had been prompted by General Sigel's discovery that the advancing Confederates were really a part of one of the enemy's main forces. Early Thursday night, fearing some move by the Confederates on the Federal right, the German general had dispatched two of his guides and some cavalry "to proceed as far as possible toward the west and north-west and report any movement of hostile troops immediately."[2] These scouts brought him word of Van Dorn's movement toward Cross Timber Hollow. After seeing them himself, he reported to Curtis just after dawn the presence of a sizable enemy force moving toward the Federal rear.

Before this report reached him, Curtis had been fooled by Van Dorn's maneuver. Sigel's information came to him as a shock, but here he showed the qualities of leadership that marked him as a fine officer. Recovering quickly from his surprise, he assembled his division commanders in General Asboth's tent near Pratt's Store and made plans to meet the new threat. First he made it clear to his officers that he was still in command of the situation despite this unexpected development. Then he spoke of what might be called a "task force," a detachment of cavalry and light artillery supported by infantry, which could strike quickly at the Confederates still south of Big Mountain on the Benton-

2. Johnson and Buel, *Battles and Leaders*, I, 321.

ville Detour.[3] This action would split the enemy and force him to fight on two separate fronts. Curtis placed Colonel Peter Osterhaus, a fine officer from Sigel's division, in command of this task force.

Then as his major action, Curtis outlined to his commanders the realignment of his divisions to face a new front. Sigel's and Asboth's divisions, still resting on Sugar Creek, would shift slightly toward Leetown and become his new left wing. Osterhaus with the task force and part of Davis's Third Division would form the center of the line just above Leetown. Colonel Carr would make the hard move up Telegraph Road to face Van Dorn and Price as Curtis's new right wing.

Soon after the conference in Asboth's tent had ended, Curtis received word from Major Weston of the Missourians' approach toward Telegraph Road and the impending threat against Elkhorn Tavern. Turning to Colonel Carr, who lingered at the tent for further orders, Curtis said simply, "[C]lean out that hollow in a very short time."[4] Terrain and enemy strength could complicate Carr's assignment; Van Dorn was as determined as Curtis to win the day.

While generals in blue plotted their new strategy, the Missourians cut over the detour. By six o'clock Friday morning they had cleared away most of the obstructions on the trail, and their lead troops were entering the narrow gorge that would take them directly into Cross Timber Hollow. Van Dorn led the main body of Price's command into the hollow about two hours later. They had now cut off Curtis's line of retreat toward Missouri. Could they hold this new line? And where was McCulloch?

Van Dorn and Price hurried their struggling troops as best they could to ready them for an attack down Telegraph Road. Van Dorn had originally hoped for a dawn attack, but it was after ten o'clock before the Missourians were assembled for action. Van Dorn was still confident. Before him only the token forces of Captain Robert Fyan and Colonel Carr's advance troops blocked his path. "The game seemed now to be in our hands," wrote Dabney Maury.[5]

Van Dorn issued orders from the field for his troops to move through Cross Timber Hollow toward their first real objective, Elkhorn Tavern, and to keep as much on high ground as possible. His troops were tired,

3. Edwin C. Bearss, "The First Day at Pea Ridge, March 7, 1862," *Arkansas Historical Quarterly*, XVII, 134.
4. *Official Records Army*, VIII, 259.
5. "Recollections of Elk Horn," p. 187.

hungry, and footsore, but the brightness of the day and their presence behind enemy lines temporarily rekindled their enthusiasm. They moved cautiously but confidently down the road.

At first they met no opposition. Captain Fyan's Missouri infantry blocked their path, but the captain delayed his order to fire. Watching the Butternuts approach his position, their nondescript uniforms visible in the distance, he still could not decide whether they were enemy troops or refugees from Missouri. Suddenly he was sure. He gave a crisp order, and the firing began.

Unable to hold back the strong force before him, Fyan and his troops courageously took up positions as skirmishers behind wooden fences. On came the Confederates, venturing as close to the fence as possible. Some remained in the road; others spread out to either side as far as the terrain permitted.

For a moment it appeared too easy. Suddenly the tempo of the Federal fire increased. New forms appeared behind the fence rows. Colonel Dodge and the Fourth Iowa Infantry had arrived to support the defense. For a moment the Missourians wavered. "Press on," shouted their officers. The tiring troops struggled forward; their strength held in the fury of the moment. Colonel Carr saw his troops recoil before their determined effort. To hold his line he must have more troops. Promptly he dispatched word of his needs to General Curtis, and the fighting continued.

About 11:00 A.M. the Federals' artillery got into action, and the bigger guns began to fire. The night's delay was now becoming costly. Their advance slowed before the six- and twelve-pounders. But Van Dorn was not to be stopped so easily. Still in the saddle despite recurring weakness and fever, he surveyed his situation and then ordered his own artillery forward. His troops spread out more, seeking refuge in gorges, behind fence rows, in thickets, while they awaited the arrival of their own big guns, especially "old Sacramento."

Behind the lines Confederate artillerymen sweated and strained, pushing and pulling their heavy weapons into position. Even the mules seemed to co-operate. The caissons bounced roughly over the road as they neared their new positions. Forty or more weapons were quickly stationed on the available high ground on both sides of the highway. Captain Henry Guibor's battery opened fire first from a ridge about

250 yards from the Federal line. The other guns quickly picked up the tempo.

The sounds of battle reverberated through the rocky gorges, and the smoke of the guns clouded the vision of the troops. From behind the fence rows in front of the tavern, small-arms fire crackled and cut heavily into advancing Missourians. Shot and shell from the Federal artillery also continued to take its toll. Confederate firepower was equally destructive. General William Slack and Colonel Henry Little pushed their Butternuts hard against the strengthened Federal position, and the Yanks struggled desperately to hold on. Slack encountered "a sharp volley of musket and rifle balls" on the left, but his men continued to infiltrate the enemy ranks in spite of the heavy fire, routing the Yanks from their "ambuscade." Confederate artillery moved up quickly to take new positions among the dead and dying. Pushing hard nearby, Colonel Little captured several Union forage wagons that fell behind in the retreat.

As the Union line wavered, Van Dorn advanced his troops forward at a faster pace. Under the warming midday sun, the battle now developed its greatest fury. Horses screamed, guns exploded, and the "rebel yell" swelled the din of combat. General Slack fell, shot through the body, but Colonel Thomas Rosser leaped to the front, and the attack never slackened. Heroism was commonplace in both lines. When the Federal artillerymen set up a "6-pounder" to fire obliquely into the charging Rebs, Lieutenant Eugene Erwin sized up the situation instantly and charged it with his small force. They scattered the gun crew and captured the weapon. When a regiment of Federal infantry threatened Guibor's artillery battery, Captain J. Rock Champion of the Missouri Guard attacked the entire regiment with only twenty-two men. Incredible as it seems, "Rock" halted the Union drive and returned with most of his men to his own lines.

All along the broad front, the Federals took a beating. As their lines weakened, Price continued to drive his yelling Missourians into their midst. Everything in sight was pushed back toward the tavern as sweating Confederates advanced over Federal banners, knapsacks, overcoats, hats, and guns abandoned in hasty flight. The scene was chaotic to the fleeing Yanks as the dead and wounded piled up side by side in the road. But Van Dorn and Price were denied the victory. Just as Price neared a final breakthrough, Federal reinforcements arrived from the original Sugar Creek line. Colonel William Vandever and the Ninth Iowa Infantry joined Curtis's defenders at the moment of their great desperation. Vandever's fresher troops counterattacked effectively, and the lines swayed back and forth in desperate hand-to-hand fighting.

Van Dorn, near the center of the action, ordered up what reinforcements he had, and again the blue line appeared ready to collapse. To the Confederate commander, victory seemed imminent. Elated over his success of the day he later described the moment: "[B]efore 2 o'clock it was evident that if . . . [McCulloch's] division could advance or even maintain its ground, I could at once throw forward Price's left, advance his whole line, and end the battle."[6] In the moment of anticipation, he sent a message to the Texan to press vigorously against the enemy at Leetown and prepare to meet the Missourians somewhere close by after they made their breakthrough. Before his troops he was poised to push on to victory when suddenly cheers sounded from the besieged line before him. Asboth—and Curtis himself—had arrived on the scene with additional troops. The exhausted Confederates held their ground, but the tide had turned. Curtis had successfully shifted the major part of his first defense line in time to frustrate his enemy's major drive. Those agonizing hours of delay on the detour had cost Van Dorn his advantage. But it was not yet over; he would regroup and charge again. As if to complicate matters for him, however, events in the vicinity of Leetown were also taking some unexpected and bizarre turns. McCulloch's troops, engaged earlier in the day by Osterhaus's task force, also began to feel the effects of Curtis's successful shift of front.

McCulloch's problems, which had begun with the difficult crossing of Sugar Creek, continued into Friday morning. As dawn broke, he and General McIntosh were moving their troops up the detour with every hope of getting into proper position to support the Missourians. Additional delays brought on by the bad road and undisciplined troops slowed them so much that by the time they had reached the base of Big Mountain just north of the outskirts of Leetown, Colonel Osterhaus had entered the area with his task force. Whatever hopes the former Ranger had for following Van Dorn's original battle plan were now dependent upon a quick conquest of this new foe. McCulloch requested

6. *Official Records Army*, VIII, 284.

and received permission from Van Dorn to strike Osterhaus before continuing his march.

Properly disciplined troops might have eliminated the task force before additional Federal troops entered the area, but such were not available to McCulloch and McIntosh. Confusion in their ranks delayed them long enough to allow Osterhaus to get a good position and reinforcements to begin moving toward his position. Captain Gammage left an excellent account of the confusion in the Confederate units as they prepared to counter Curtis's latest threat:

> I looked across the field in front and saw a body of cavalry dashing along the fence Northwards, and then a volley of musketry, the clash of swords, the shout of men as if in a charge, and in a little while all was still save now and then a stray shot or a solitary cannon report came booming upon the air. When I looked around, the squad of horsemen who but a few minutes before had been by my side had disappeared, and in the distance the long line of infantry were pushing forward at a double-quick through the fields, over the fences, up the mountain side, into the timber, and they were lost to my sight. A few minutes of anxious suspense, and all at once, as if the whole Heavens were rent asunder, volley after volley of musketry came crashing from the hills across the valley below, whilst the booming of cannon and the bursting of shells kept one continuous roar.[7]

It was McIntosh's cavalry that struck first against the task force. As the lead unit of McCulloch's army, he had been moving up the detour well past Leetown when Osterhaus suddenly appeared to his right. Upon orders from McCulloch, he wheeled quickly and countermarched down the slope. Coming in sight of the Union troops, McIntosh did that which he knew best—he ordered a charge. Waving his saber overhead, he led a furious and irrepressible attack into the midst of the task force. "Like the impetuous rush of an avalanche," wrote one of the Texans, ". . . [his] mad columns swept over the field, in the midst of a tempest of iron hail, the thunders of artillery, the yells of the combatants, and the groans of the dying and wounded."[8] Joined by others of McCulloch's command, including Pike's Indians, the charge passed completely through Osterhaus's force. They captured three pieces of artillery and dispersed the Federal cavalry and infantry in the area.

Suddenly the Indians went wild. For several minutes they danced

---

7. *The Camp, the Bivouac and the Battle Field*, p. 25.
8. Rose, *Ross' Texas Brigade*, p. 58.

wildly around the "shooting wagons."[9] Pike never really gained control of them again. When a shell exploded in their midst several minutes later, they panicked and ran frantically into the woods behind the Confederate lines where they remained for the rest of the day.

For the moment, McIntosh was not concerned about the Indians. Thinking he had routed the enemy with his sudden charge, the daring horseman returned to the main unit and reported his success to McCulloch.

Meanwhile, the Federals were also actively preparing for a continuing engagement. After his initial reverse, Colonel Osterhaus immediately called for reinforcements. Still of the opinion that the Leetown front was the main Confederate attack, Curtis promptly spurred on Davis's troops to Osterhaus's assistance despite the fact that Colonel Carr was already being seriously challenged near the tavern. This proved to be one of the wisest moves Curtis made during that trying day. Davis arrived at Leetown about two o'clock in the afternoon in time to receive McCulloch's next attack.

In the woods above Leetown, McCulloch was in a good mood after McIntosh's success. He was now enthusiastic about his chances for destroying the enemy before him. He told his staff that he must look over the field before renewing the attack. He would go alone. "Your gray horses will attract the fire of sharpshooters," he warned them ironically.[10] Venturing out from his lines, he rode several hundred yards before stopping to view the enemy. All through the area there was sporadic firing, but McCulloch probably figured that he was well concealed by the heavy growth of trees and bushes all around him. There he sat, gazing out across the enemy position, a perfect target in his unusual attire. Suddenly his staff, who had been watching his every move, saw him pitch forward from his saddle and fall near a large tree. The officers who rushed to his aid discovered that a sniper's bullet had found its mark. McCulloch was dead.

General McIntosh, as shocked as his men, quickly dispatched a man to cover McCulloch's body to prevent recognition by his troops, but within an hour the news had circulated through the Confederate ranks. McCulloch's men, so dependent upon his forceful leadership, heard the news with astonishment and disbelief. Colonel Frank A. Rector, who

9. Noble, "Battle of Pea Ridge," p. 227.
10. Rose, *General Ben McCulloch*, pp. 203–204.

rode up from another part of the field to investigate the delay, viewed the cold features of his dead chief with dismay. He exclaimed loudly, "My God! It's old Ben!"[11]

Taking advantage of the lull in the battle, Colonels Osterhaus and Davis began a slow, deliberate move against the Confederates. Colonel McIntosh reacted instinctively to this move and ordered another desperate charge. Though the Confederates were still a bit disorganized and were without their Indian allies, they engaged the Federals in close combat. Across a field the lines of the two armies surged at one another. Five times the Confederates charged, and five times Davis and Osterhaus repulsed the yelling Rebels. In one of the charges, General McIntosh lifted his sword and directed the men straight into an enemy position. The fire was heavy, the Confederates were pushed back, and McIntosh fell before the enemy line. One of his own men sounded his eulogy:

The impetuous McIntosh, who was at home only amidst the raging of wild elements, and who courted the missions of danger with a fondness not surpassed by the affection of a lover for his mistress, led an Arkansas regiment of infantry against the enemy . . . and fell at the very muzzles of their guns, sword in hand.[12]

Colonel Louis Hébert, the ranking officer on the field, had hardly assumed command when the Federals captured him within their own lines. Colonel Greer tried to reassemble the troops, but his efforts were in vain. General Pike, who should have had command, did not hear of the deaths of his two superiors until after three o'clock. Totally ignorant of the country, the roads, and the over-all planning, he also tried unsuccessfully to reorganize the troops. The young, green soldiers had fought well, but they did not respond to new voices of command. Some "completely lost their presence of mind amid the tumult."[13] Federal batteries arrived before them, and the exhausted troops sullenly began to retreat under the heavy fire.

As Pike and Greer worked desperately to reorganize their battered and dispersed commands, the strengthened Federals pushed the demoralized Confederates from the field. The roar of musketry and artillery continued, and the Rebel dead piled high. As a sort of finale, the

11. *Ibid.*, p. 205.
12. Rose, *Ross' Texas Brigade*, p. 58.
13. Comte de Paris, *History of the Civil War in America*, I, 512.

Union artillery poured a murderous blast of shot and shell into the leaderless Confederates, and the Eighteenth Indiana Infantry came sweeping down the Rebel flank to settle the fortunes of the day around Leetown. The Confederates, now commanded inefficaciously and completely demoralized by the losses in their ranks, broke and ran. Van Dorn's right wing had collapsed. His hopes for uniting his two armies on the field of battle faded in the last sounds of the guns from a bloody and costly field. Instead of clasping hands with the Missourians on the field of victory, the surviving Confederates from McCulloch's command streamed through the countryside, their leaders dead, their hopes shattered in an afternoon's holocaust.

Van Dorn received news of the deaths of General McCulloch and McIntosh some time after three o'clock in the afternoon. Though disheartened by this report, he never lost his exuberant hope. "We must press them the harder," was his determined rejoinder to this message of tragedy.[14] He then sent orders to McCulloch's surviving officers to bring their men to join Price's command as soon as possible. Remaining with General Price's army, he continued to make plans for one more major thrust against Curtis before the end of the day.

Action in rear of Elkhorn Tavern tapered off early in the afternoon as both armies paused to reorganize and give their commanders a chance to plot new tactical moves. During much of this interval, the artillery on both sides kept up a steady barrage, but no effort was made for an infantry assault. When the fire slackened, troops rushed about to recover their wounded, and by nightfall nearly every building in the area had become a make-shift hospital. Meanwhile, a few of the troops from McCulloch's command began to find their way into the Telegraph Road area. For the moment the Mississippian's hopes for a reunited army rose.

At five o'clock the Confederate commanders were confident that they were ready for a decisive assault against Curtis. They must break that Federal defense line before darkness settled if they were to carry the field. General Van Dorn would depend heavily upon Colonel Little in this attack. The colonel would lead the first part of the operation with a sharp thrust against Curtis's right wing. Colonel Little was a fine officer, possibly the best one Van Dorn had, and the major general valued his services very much.

A heavy artillery barrage began the new assault. While the big guns

14. Maury, "Van Dorn, the Hero of Mississippi," *Annals of the War*, p. 462.

kept the enemy behind their defenses, Little moved up the regiments of Colonels Benjamin A. Rives and Elijah Gates. Then at his signal came one of the most spectacular charges of the day. Colonel Little himself described some of the dramatic action:

It was very late in the day when the sharp battle of small arms in the direction of our extreme left announced the moment for action. I ordered the charge. My men advanced in one unbroken line. We met the foe. For a few seconds he resisted, and then fell back before our lines, as with a shout of triumph Rives's and Gates's regiments dashed onward past the Elkhorn Tavern, and we stood on the ground where the enemy had formed in the morning.[15]

Elkhorn Tavern! It had become the Confederate symbol for victory. Then in the confusion of the moment, there occurred one of the bloodiest incidents of the day. As the Rebels converged on the tavern, the Iowa artillerymen fled from their disabled weapons, but not before one of them threw a blazing quilt over an abandoned caisson. Seconds later, as the Confederates surrounded the weapon, it exploded in their faces. The ensuing scene was horrible, with "gory tatters of men tossed into the paling sky, some to hang dripping from the trees, others to plummet down through the branches and thud among the mangled bodies on the ground."[16]

It was the Federals who were in the real trouble, though. To avert disaster, Curtis shifted units as rapidly as he could to support his retreating troops. Again the embattled Colonel Carr was everywhere. Though reinforcements only trickled in to his position, he fought on. His persistent refusal to withdraw before the heavy assaults of the enemy cast him in one of the most heroic roles of the day. He lost more than one-fourth of his men, and he suffered a serious wound himself, but he never let up before the enemy's desperate attack.

As Federal reinforcements built up, Curtis artfully attempted a counterattack against Van Dorn's weary troops. With his chances for a complete victory rapidly slipping from his grasp, the Confederate commander reacted in haste. First he ordered his artillery units to enfilade his line for extra protection. Then dismounting his cavalry and adding these men to his force, he initiated the day's final charge.

The sustained force in the Rebels' attack belied their poor physical

15. *Official Records Army*, VIII, 308.
16. Monaghan, *Civil War*, p. 244.

condition. As they closed in on Curtis, some of the most ferocious fighting of the day took place. The Federals had cleared all fences to make breastworks, and they faced the raging Butternuts from a strong position. Was it strong enough? For a moment it appeared that Van Dorn would finally conquer the field. His troops drove their way quickly to General Asboth's position. Asboth had set up a sizable force employing a cannon in front of the Federal position, but the charging Confederates soon put many of these troops out of action. All along their line the Federals yielded to the intensity of the attack. The troops of Asboth and several other units broke and fell back rapidly. Van Dorn, in the midst of his troops, urged them to a final effort.

Suddenly the Confederate general was filled with dismay. General Price had halted his own attack. Price, who had suffered a flesh wound in the arm earlier in the engagement, had ordered his troops to fall back and take up a defensive position for the night. It was too late for Van Dorn to regroup and attack again. The troops were tired; their ammunition was low. In despair Van Dorn halted the attack and set up camp. His new headquarters that evening was Elkhorn Tavern, the same building occupied earlier in the day by the Federals. He had missed his greatest chance. The night ahead loomed dark and foreboding. He must have more ammunition and food. He must have help from McCulloch's army if he expected to beat Curtis on the morrow.

Meanwhile, near Leetown things had gone from bad to worse for the Confederates. After their rout by the Federals, many of the raw troops had fled pell mell into the hills and draws to the north. As night approached many still roamed through the sparce settlements in search of food, shelter, their own units, the route to Van Dorn's army, or just the way home. Many staggered with fatigue; most were desperate with hunger. Said one of them poignantly: "Every byway and highway, mansion and cottage, were filled by hungry men seeking something to eat. They ravenously devoured everything they could procure—raw corn, potatoes, turnips . . . [some] even scrambled over an overturned slop barrel."[17] These were the reinforcements that the commanding general awaited at his newly won headquarters in Elkhorn Tavern.

After darkness had settled, General Greer dispatched a messenger to Van Dorn with information of the day's activities and a request for

17. Rose, *General Ben McCulloch*, pp. 210–211.

orders of what to do next. After a hazardous trip through the mountains the messenger, John N. Coleman, arrived at Van Dorn's headquarters at 1:00 A.M. After hearing Coleman's story Van Dorn instructed the young messenger to inform Greer to withdraw his entire army "and lead it around the enemy's right [left?] flank, to a position occupied by the Missouri division."[18] Coleman returned to Greer with the news about two o'clock, and during the rest of the night the remnants of McCulloch's battered command made their way eastward through the gorges of Pea Ridge toward Elkhorn Tavern, where, tired and discouraged, they joined the other Confederate unit about an hour before dawn. Though Pike and Colonel Watie both joined Van Dorn during the night and took part in the next day's fighting, others of McCulloch's command, including most of the Indians, returned to Bentonville and missed Saturday's action.

Losses during the first day's fighting had been costly for both sides. Van Dorn had learned painfully the dangers of co-operative attack, and he had suffered because his double assault had been carried out ineffectually. Dabney Maury, looking at the results with the advantage of hindsight, complained that Van Dorn should have used all his troops in attacking Curtis's rear. It now appears that a rear attack would have been unlikely if not impossible. By dividing his force, though, Van Dorn had lost his contacts with McCulloch. Separated by hazardous terrain features, the two men found it impossible to co-ordinate their attacks. It was really two separate armies that fought two separate actions on Friday. Through necessity the commander of the Trans-Mississippi District had violated one of Jomini's basic principles by splitting his force before the enemy, and unlike Lee at the second battle of Bull Run or at Chancellorsville, he had no Jackson, only a brave but impetuous McCulloch and an army of raw troops.

Although fighting ended at nightfall on the Elkhorn Tavern front, General Curtis worked late into the night planning for renewing the battle at dawn. He expected a new Confederate offensive at that time, and he needed reinforcements to withstand such an attack. It was imperative, therefore, that he bring the rest of his troops formerly concentrated on Sugar Creek to the vicinity of the tavern. He directed Colonel Davis's troops, who had been so instrumental in turning the

18. Rose, *Ross' Texas Brigade*, p. 60.

tide at Leetown, to move up and occupy the ground at the left of Colonel Carr's regiment. Davis began this movement at midnight and was in line before Van Dorn's army the following morning. Sigel soon joined him in the line. After the arrival of all these new troops, Curtis set up his plan of battle for Saturday. He ordered the forces of Carr, Asboth, and Davis to hold firm the right and center of the line while Sigel's cavalry and infantry were to move to the left so as to flank the Confederate right when they attacked.

In the Confederate camp Van Dorn awaited the dawn "with no little anxiety," and little idea of what to do except to continue his attack. During the heat of Friday's battle, his ammunition wagons had disappeared, and as the darkness had settled he had realized that supplies for his men and ammunition for his guns must be replenished before he could renew the attack. Exhausted troops bivouacked on the ground just taken—cold, hungry, disillusioned. To these half-starved men, there were no longer any meaningful voices of authority. They watched in disbelief as the troops from McCulloch's command drifted in to warm by the large fires and await their turn at reassignment. Many of the Butternuts tried to sleep, but at best it was fitful slumber. Private Watson expressed the feelings of many a "Johnny Reb" that night in these words:

> The darkness of the night, the bleak moaning of the cold wind, and the continued roar of artillery would have suggested a theme for a weird romancer, but we saw no romance about it. We felt it bitter cold.[19]

Early on the morning of March 8, the Confederate line rested along Telegraph Road as follows: One regiment was on the right side of the road. Across the road a battery of artillery rested "in mask." On their left was another regiment and part of a brigade, both weakened by heavy losses the day before. Another Arkansas regiment and a dismounted cavalry unit rounded out Van Dorn's force on his front line. Three hundred yards to the rear of these troops were three regiments of Arkansas troops under Colonel Thomas J. Churchill—Van Dorn's reserve.

After a short night's rest, Van Dorn was up to view the enemy's position well before dawn. His officers had informed him already that Curtis was being resupplied. The scene he saw before him confirmed this news.

19. *Life in the Confederate Army*, p. 303.

The enemy line was too strong. He could not attack as planned; he must just await the enemy's moves. He had not replenished his ammunition, several of his key officers had been lost, and the officer in charge of the ordnance and supplies could not find the wagons.[20]

When Curtis saw that Van Dorn was not going to attack, he decided to take the initiative. About 7:00 A.M. he ordered the artillery of Colonel Davis to fire on the Confederate center. Though its ammunition was low, the gray line answered with devastating effect. The very earth seemed to tremble as the guns on both sides boomed through the hollows. The fire was so devastating that both commanders had to call in reserves to replace their heavy losses.

The exchange continued for some time with both armies seeking to find and exploit any advantage. Gradually, though, the Confederate position weakened. Finally about 10:00 A.M. Curtis began to move his infantry forward. He continued his destructive artillery fire against Van Dorn's strongest positions. "The roar of cannon and small-arms was continuous," Curtis later wrote in his official report of the battle, "and no force could then have withstood the converging line and concentrated crossfire of our gallant troops."[21] Colonel Little felt that the Confederates met the attack with determination but with too little power. "[W]e was like trees in the forest," wrote one of the young Confederates, "[who] . . . stood still till they are cut down."[22]

As the battle raged furiously, Van Dorn's losses in leadership became more apparent. Watson, in the thick of battle all that morning, lamented his fate bitterly: "We were marched hither and thither, and left standing sometimes in range of artillery fire, and sometime out of it, no one seeming to know where we were to go or what we were to do."[23]

The troops became disgruntled, afraid, uncertain. One soldier shouted out his feelings: "Oh hang it! I believe we may lie here all day. I don't believe Van Dorn knows anything about us, or ——"

"Or about anything else," another interrupted.[24]

Though these soldiers may have expressed the sentiments of many of

20. These wagons had been lost by negligent drivers who had not followed orders and had become separated from the main command. They had eventually been directed to Bentonville by mistake by an incompetent quartermaster.
21. *Official Records Army*, VIII, 202.
22. Homer Calkin, "Elk Horn to Vicksburg," *Civil War History*, II, 14.
23. *Life*, pp. 306–307.
24. *Ibid.*

the men facing the reinforced Union line, they were wrong about their chief. In command of the troops all morning, he was often under the heaviest Federal fire.

Relentlessly the Federals continued their assault, gradually pushing the gray line back toward Cross Timber Hollow. Pursuing his new advantage, Curtis sent Sigel into the hills on the enemy's right to drive out troops and artillery in some of the fiercest fighting of the morning. Sigel's infantry poured such a heavy barrage into Guibor's battery that the men fled in panic. There was only one man who remained to meet the attack, nineteen-year-old Captain Churchill Clark, who was decapitated while unlimbering a gun for a final shot.

Everywhere along the line, the Confederates fought diligently. For nearly thirty minutes the battle raged with the Union troops pushing them more and more to the rear. Another gallant and valuable Confederate officer, Colonel Rives, fell as the strong Federal line pushed on relentlessly. The center and right of the blue line advanced methodically; a deep thrust was made into the disintegrating Confederate center. By noon the entire Southern army was within an arc, in danger of being completely surrounded. The collapse of the Confederate right, the exhaustion of supplies and ammunition, and the deteriorating condition of the troops were too many factors to overcome. Van Dorn reluctantly made his decision:

I resolved to withdraw the army, and at once placed the ambulance[s], with all the wounded they could bear, upon the Huntsville Road . . . while I so disposed of my remaining forces as best to deceive the enemy as to my intention, and to hold him in check while executing it.[25]

Much of the disposing consisted of confused retreating in all directions by weary, frustrated, bewildered troops. Many of them escaped by making their flights through the canyons and deep defiles of Cross Timber Hollow. Others, after entering a large canyon in the Hollow, turned sharply to the south and by following obscure ravines came into the Huntsville road several miles east of the tavern. Van Dorn's final general order of the day directed the troops still under his control to retire by this same route if possible. Colonel John T. Hughes, commander of the last unit to leave the field, said that he departed under heavy fire.

25. *Official Records Army*, VIII, 284.

When the Confederate line finally broke and the men began to disperse through the hills, Yankee enthusiasm boiled over. Up and down their lines they cheered wildly as they drove their enemies from the field. Some of the Confederates who were guarding the rear of their position heard this cheering, and they mistook it for the sounds of their own victory. When they finally saw their fleeing comrades, many were critical of their commanding general for ordering a retreat when the final triumph was so near at hand. To keep these troops in line, some of their officers told them that the enemy was retreating over Bentonville road and that the Confederates were going to cut them off on another road seven miles to the east. This seemed to please most of the disgruntled, and one of them commented: "We began to think that Van Dorn was not such a bad general after all."[26]

Others were not easily satisfied. One of the most critical seems to have been General James S. Rains, commander of a division in the Missouri State Guard. Rains is supposed to have argued at length with his chief about the wisdom of withdrawing from the field. On Sunday, as one story goes, Rains was passing Van Dorn's tent when someone in a crowd of soldiers called out: "Who was whipped at Pea Ridge?"

General Rains looked up quickly and replied: "By ——, nobody was whipped at Pea Ridge but Van Dorn!"

Van Dorn promptly took Rains's saber and placed him under arrest. Rains was unrepentent; several days later when Van Dorn tried to release him, the disgruntled officer insisted upon a court martial.[27] In his official report of the battle, Rains wrote: "On arriving at the old field and reporting to Major-General Van Dorn I was ordered by him to march on the road toward Huntsville," he reported. "For the first time I realized the fact—the fight was over; the victory within our grasp was lost."[28]

Some of the voices from the ranks continued to grumble over the retreat as "a shameful piece of bungling and mismanagement";[29] other voices spoke less enthusiastically of the Confederate chances for continuing the battle. "Few . . . had guns, knapsacks, or blankets," wrote

26. Watson, *Life*, p. 311.
27. Faye L. Stewart, "The Battle of Pea Ridge," *Missouri Historical Review*, XXII, 118.
28. *Official Records Army*, VIII, 328.
29. Watson, *Life*, pp. 310–311.

William Baxter of nearby Fayetteville, "the few who had anything to carry were those who had been fortunate enough to pick up a chicken, goose, or pig . . . ."[30] John May, a father of three of the Confederate soldiers, confirmed this opinion: "It was a perfect stampede," he said. "Whole regiments threw down their arms and fled."[31]

Considering all the confusion and chaos that ensued at the end of the battle, Van Dorn seems to have departed the field as well as could be expected. The Federals were as uncertain of his routes of departure as he was, and they made little attempt to pursue the retreating army. To Curtis "the enemy had suddenly vanished."[32] Sigel made a half-hearted effort to pursue and finally captured a few of the enemy when they fell by the road from sheer exhaustion, but the large force he followed toward Cassville escaped from him. The Federals were just about as tired as their foes, and pursuit on every front was soon discontinued.

Despite their stunning victory at Pea Ridge, the North remained wary of Van Dorn and his army. General Halleck warned Curtis from St. Louis to keep his main force strong and his cavalry alert for enemy action. "Be careful of Van Dorn," he counseled. "He is a vigilant and energetic officer, and will be certain to strike any exposed point."[33]

While Curtis surveyed his own situation, Van Dorn encamped ten miles from the battlefield and began to reassemble his broken command. By three o'clock Saturday a large number of his troops were with him, and later that day a large portion of their baggage and artillery joined them. Other stragglers made contact with the army as it retreated southward, and by the time they reached Van Buren, many of the original command had returned to duty. During the time that the troops struggled toward Van Buren, they lived on the land; most of them were tired, cold, and hungry. Many had little or no food for the entire six days that it took them to return to Van Dorn's new headquarters.

The battle was over. The disastrous campaign had been a costly one for the South. Van Dorn had failed in his first great chance for glory. The pen of one of the Missourians caught the pathos of the defeat:

If ever fate . . . was against a man, it had evidently singled out Earl Van Dorn for one of its most distinguished victims. Victory at Elkhorn would

30. *Pea Ridge and Prairie Grove*, p. 98.
31. *Ibid.*, pp. 100–101.
32. *Official Records Army*, VIII, 202.
33. *Ibid.*, p. 611.

have meant the capture of Curtis's army and an open road to St. Louis. . . . What anguish must have wrung the heart of this gallant soldier when he saw the scintillant picture of ambitious hope and well laid plans charred and consumed as a burning scroll in a fire of defeat.[34]

Why such a stunning defeat? What went wrong? These questions remain only partially answered more than a century after the battle. Among other things, the personality of the Confederate commander must be considered. What flaws marked his own personality as a director of armies and a planner of battles? His reasoning was sound as far as the over-all strategy was concerned. It was in his immediate planning that he failed. Both negligence and poor judgment appear in his planning. He never seemed to overcome these flaws in his character. At Pea Ridge he was negligent in his reconnaissance efforts and in his arrangements for keeping supplies and ammunition available for his big battle. He showed poor judgment in his use of ill-disciplined, raw frontier troops, in exposing his own line of supply and communications to the enemy, in extending his own line so far that he lost control of his men, in the selection and use of his staff, and finally in making the attack when he did. Victory against a determined enemy would come hard under any circumstances. These mistakes complicated the actions and assured the final defeat.

The key failure on Van Dorn's part must be related to his inadequate reconnaissance efforts. Speed took precedence over more intricate knowledge of the terrain. Because of undue concern for speed, the march to Sugar Creek became a nightmare to his soldiers when distances and road conditions were not what he had expected. Proper scouting might have opened the door for a successful move against Sigel at Bentonville. It should have prevented the debacle on the Bentonville Road on the sixth. Poor reconnaissance also contributed much to the confusion and frustration in the Confederate ranks during the two days of combat. Van Dorn should have expected obstructions in the Bentonville Detour. He should have had first-hand knowledge of the condition of this road and others as well as of the streams and other terrain obstacles he had to face in over fifty-five miles of marching.

Van Dorn neglected to plan realistically for the physical needs of an army and set up a proper resupply. He hardly concerned himself about his quartermaster until it was too late to do anything. He seems to have

34. Payne, "The Test of the Missourians," *Confederate Veteran*, XXXVII, 101.

made no real effort to discover the condition of his men or animals in the final hours before the army marched on March 4. Rest, food, blankets, tents, extra ammunition, and forage—these were essentials for an army facing a strong and well-organized enemy in the cold and wet of an Arkansas winter.

Certainly Van Dorn cannot be blamed for the physical or psychological condition of his troops. He was handed an army of ill-disciplined, poorly armed, underfed, disorganized troops by McCulloch and Price. His fault is in his poor judgment in handling these troops and in subjecting them to a long march followed too quickly by an intricate attack. He seemed to have learned little from his lessons in Mexico where he had seen firsthand the many problems associated with raw volunteers. To expose his own line of supply and communications and to extend his march out of range of his depots and ordnance stations with troops so ill-prepared for complex operations could only lead to disaster. Did he not realize that when he cut across Curtis's supply line he was exposing his own? His faith in speed and secrecy failed without well-trained, thoroughly disciplined troops.

What Van Dorn's chances for success would have been with proper staff officers to help him in the supervision of his plans, one can only surmise. Much of the blame for the defeat lies with his subordinate commanders and members of his staff, men about whom he knew so very little on the eve of battle. Leaving most of his regular staff at Pocahontas, he felt only contempt for many of the officers in his new command. In his own words he expressed his feelings toward some of them, "I found the want of military knowledge and discipline among the higher officers to be so great as to countervail their gallantry and the fine courage of the troops." Then in sharper tones he added, "I cannot convey to you a correct idea of the crudeness of the material with which I have to deal in organizing an army out here. There is an absolute want of any degree of sound military information, and even an ignorance of the value of such information."[35]

To complicate matters for himself and his staff, he shared his planning with only a select few of the officers, and even to these men he did not reveal his complete plans. Whether this reticence to communicate was a veil for his own ignorance or just distrust of his subordinates, it does not excuse the fact that most of his officers seemed uncertain of

35. *Official Records Army*, VII, 787.

just what was going on at any stage of the battle. Death or injury to a key officer could disrupt tactical operations in the midst of the fight, and raw troops could panic without confident leadership. The deaths of McCulloch and McIntosh were serious losses under any circumstances. They became greater tragedies when their replacements proved to be completely unprepared for command.

If Van Dorn realized the mistakes he made, his own shortcomings as an army commander, he does not say. He did take his defeat hard. In a letter to his sister soon after the battle he wrote that it was with tears in his eyes that he ordered his troops from the field after the battle.[36] Tears or no tears, he had missed his great chance for immortal fame, and much of the blame was his own. One can only speculate as to the consequences of a Confederate victory over Curtis, but they would have changed the course of the war. A victory in Arkansas would also have placed the victorious general high in his country's military circles. But the basic weaknesses of the man prevented such a taste of glory. He could plan, he could dream, he could visualize the improbable; but he could never master all the intricate details that go with the heavy responsibilities of army command. He was to prove this on another battlefield before the Confederacy finally placed him in charge of small cavalry units much more suited to his ability and temperament.

To Van Dorn's credit, one must mention two other factors that contributed heavily to the Pea Ridge fiasco. Van Dorn like Price, Kirby Smith, T. J. Churchill, and others who later faced the frustrations of Trans-Mississippi warfare, was a victim of the Confederate War Department's lack of concern for this important region. Jefferson Davis, Robert E. Lee, Judah P. Benjamin, and others who directed Confederate military planning from Virginia never realized the significance of Arkansas or Missouri to their new nation. Instead of building up the native forces in those states, of encouraging Missouri to join wholeheartedly in an effort to dispell the enemy, they turned a deaf ear to this region except to demand troop replacements for Virginia or more supplies. Their commander in the Trans-Mississippi was victim not only of his own inabilities but of the failure of the Southern government to realize that the war was not limited to Virginia but that it stretched across a vast area even beyond the Mississippi.

36. Earl Van Dorn to Emily Miller, March 16, 1862, Manuscript Collection of Foreman M. Lebold, Chicago, Illinois.

The second factor was the Federal general, Samuel R. Curtis. Since Lyon's death, the Union sympathizers in Missouri had seen only mediocre leadership. Van Dorn probably expected Curtis to follow this same pattern. But Samuel Curtis was a fine officer and engineer who planned and fought one good battle in the Civil War. That battle was Pea Ridge. One of his own men summed up his contributions to that battle:

> Officers and men were all imbued with the earnest feeling that you would lead them only to victory, and you did so at a moment when experienced and brave soldiers admitted the critical character of our position. Allow me to thank you . . . for your skillful leadership and the results achieved.[37]

Despite his failure at Pea Ridge, one must admire Earl Van Dorn for his courage, his dreams, and the soundness of his strategic thinking. He nearly caught Curtis off balance even with inexperienced troops. With disciplined and rested troops and capable subordinate commanders to carry out his plans, his hopes for success might possibly have materialized, at least on this battlefield. Harvey Ford assessed the failure with these words: "Had it fallen to his lot to command a trained and veteran army—the necessary complement to Van Dorn's conceptions of strategy —the result might have been different."[38]

Losses in the battle in terms of killed, wounded, and captured in the two armies were high, though not nearly so high a percentage as they would be in other engagements later in the war. Van Dorn listed 600 Confederates killed or wounded and 200 captured; his was probably a conservative estimate. He made no mention of the number missing after the battle which in itself was a sizable figure. According to Thomas Livermore, Curtis lost 1,384 of his men as killed, wounded, or missing.[39] At least from the standpoint of battle casualities, neither army held a great advantage.

Back in his makeshift headquarters in western Arkansas, Van Dorn regained his confidence and even began to plan for a return engagement with Curtis. The St. Louis dream persisted despite Pea Ridge. But to attack Curtis in the western part of the state without proper supplies or additional troops was out of the question for the time. Therefore, why

---

37. *Official Records Army*, VIII, 240.

38. "Van Dorn and the Pea Ridge Campaign," *Journal of the American Military Institute* (Winter 1939), p. 236.

39. Surgeon Gammage, a participant in the battle, listed the Confederate loss as 525 wounded, 185 killed, and 300 captured. *The Camp, the Bivouac and the Battle Field*, p. 26.

not return to Pocahontas, effect a junction of all the Confederate forces in Arkansas, and then advance into Missouri where he would "fall upon the force of the enemy in the vicinity of New Madrid or Cape Girardeau and attempt to relieve General Beauregard"?[40] Assuming that the enemy could not subsist off the Arkansas countryside, he also planned to dispatch troops to destroy the Springfield, Missouri, supply depot and the supply trains that were running unmolested from that city to Curtis's army. The combined forces would then march toward St. Louis while General Pike operated in the Indian country to the west of Arkansas and Missouri by cutting off enemy units and annoying the Federals as much as possible. Van Dorn was still dreaming lofty dreams, but again his hopes failed to materialize in a maze of circumstances and new developments.

40. *Official Records Army*, VIII, 790.

CHAPTER EIGHT

Return to Mississippi

*T*HE aftermath of a military debacle is usually a time of confusion and
controversy in the camp of the vanquished. Too often commanders
disagree as to the reasons for the defeat, and personal animosities arise
as officers attempt to shift responsibility and blame to the shoulders of
others. One such disagreement mars the aftermath of the battle of Elk
Horn. Generals Earl Van Dorn and Albert Pike had already held their
little differences,[1] but the personal altercation between these two men
intensified in the heat of the campaign. General Curtis informed Van
Dorn on March 9 that some of the Union troops in the battle had been
"tomahawked, scalped, and their bodies shamefully mangled" by Pike's
Indians.[2] Van Dorn expressed his regrets to Curtis over this incident
and countered warily with an accusation that Confederate prisoners had
been murdered in cold blood by Sigel's Germans. Inwardly, he was
rankled by the Indians' actions. From the beginning of his service in
Arkansas, he showed a hostile feeling toward the Indians. He was disappointed by the small number of Indians in Pike's command, and their
actions in the battle sustained his views that they were uncivilized and
lacked discipline in their command. As far as he was concerned the
Indians had done nothing right since his first contact with them. They
arrived late at Twelve Corners' Church on the sixth; they made too
much noise on the night march; they bolted the battlefield in the moment of the army's greatest need.

General Pike felt the intensity of Van Dorn's personal feelings toward
him in the handling of these Indians. He explained his chief's attitude
partially in terms of their earlier relations: "General Van Dorn has been

1. See page 121.
2. *Official Records Army*, VIII, 194.

actuated by personal hatred of me," he later wrote General Hindman, "owing to my reports to the Government, old and new, in regard to his attack ... on a Comanche camp. ..."[3] Though Pike seems to have made an attempt to work with Van Dorn, his resentment for the dapper little general grew daily. In the first place, he resented the Mississippian's authority over him; he felt that his was a special assignment over the Indians. In this connection he opposed from the beginning using the Indians outside their own department.

Pike also resented the way Van Dorn treated him both before and during the battle. He had never been included in the planning of the campaign, and he was hardly treated as a general officer by his commander in the actions in which he participated on March 7 and 8. His antagonism toward his chief increased soon after the battle when Van Dorn made only a cursory reference to him in his official report of the battle. "I regret that no other allusion is made by General Van Dorn in his report ... of the action at Elkhorn to the Indian troops engaged than the simple statement that he ordered me to join him with my force," Pike wrote bitterly.[4] In the same letter he defended the actions of his Indians in the battle: there were other factors in the defeat besides their mistakes.

It was not reasonable to expect much of a small body of Indians . . . in a regular engagement, where the enemy had to be attacked in a position selected by himself on ground to which he had dexterously enticed us and where he had been encamped and preparing to welcome us for three weeks.

Though Pike defended the Indians, he does seem to have realized that they were at fault in the battle for violating certain codes of organized warfare, and he took them to task over the matter. But he had expected some statement of support or explanation from Van Dorn. Northern newspapers were severely censuring him for the Indian atrocities and blowing the incident into spectacular stories of savage barbarity. Pike felt that a kind word from his commander would at least assure the Confederate brass in Richmond and his supporters elsewhere that most of these reports were just sound and fury.

Van Dorn was not so inclined. In fact he added salt to the wounds by writing two other letters—one to the War Department and one to Pike himself. In his letter addressed to the Secretary of War, he explained

3. *Ibid.*, XIII, 954.
4. *Ibid.*, XIII, 820.

the reasons for his Elk Horn defeat: "The death of McCulloch and McIntosh and the capture of Hébert left me without an officer to command the right wing, which was thrown into utter confusion. . . ."[5]

"Without an officer"! What a slam at Pike, the next in line of command! Then three days later, speaking through his adjutant general, Dabney Maury, he urged Pike to restrain his Indians in his further operations "from committing any barbarities upon the wounded, prisoners, or dead who may fall into their hands."[6]

These two firm rebukes distressed Pike very much, but there was more to come. The final straw was Van Dorn's seizure of guns, money, supplies, and some newly recruited troops from Pike just before Van Dorn departed from Arkansas. For this Pike never forgave him. Soon after Van Dorn had left the state, Pike began a series of long letters to Confederate officials justifying his own actions and criticizing those of his commander. There is intense bitterness and much repetition in these letters. Much of their spirit is reflected in this statement to President Davis written on July 31, 1862:

Generals Van Dorn and Hindman [Van Dorn's successor in Arkansas] never reflected and probably never cared that I occupied a somewhat different position from that which one would occupy sent here by them to take mere military command of this country.[7]

Fortunately for the Confederacy, these two generals who detested each other so much were soon parted. After June Pike was no longer under Van Dorn's jurisdiction, if he ever really was. The real tragedy in this situation comes from the realization that much of the tension created by their difficulties could have been mitigated by clearer, more precise orders from the Confederate War Department. Van Dorn and Pike were hardly suited to work together under any circumstances. Under the loosely worded orders from Richmond, their disagreements increased, eventually swelling to greater proportions in the conflicts of interests and personalities of the two men involved. Neither man ever seemed willing to try to understand the problems of the other. Van Dorn was a man of action, always planning daring and often foolhardy ventures. Pike was more conservative. Lacking Van Dorn's vision and daring, he was especially critical of what he termed "Quixotic expeditions

5. *Ibid.*, VIII, 282.
6. *Ibid.*, p. 796.
7. *Ibid.*, XIII, 864.

into Missouri."[8] One regrets the actions of each of these men, but Van Dorn must be especially censured for his treatment of Pike throughout the campaign. His was a personality problem that a greater general would have overcome.

On a larger scale, though, this quarrel between two ranking officers was a reflection of the internal tension in Arkansas which reduced efficiency and limited the state's chances for successfully repelling the invader. Arkansas officials generally sided with Pike in the dispute as further confusion developed in a department already too much involved in senseless debate. Though Van Dorn did not always understand its cause, he was very much aware of this confusion as he planned his new actions against Curtis. He was convinced that he must take drastic action to bring order out of the chaos. Unfortunately the methods that he chose were those employed too often by Confederate commanders, and they brought even greater criticism from the very people he tried to help.[9] This new tactic called for increasing his own military power to prevent wrangling among the many disparate authorities in the state. He tipped off this new venture in an order he issued at Van Buren, Arkansas, on March 21. Though this order was mild compared with his later actions in Mississippi, the context of the message does reveal a startling seizure of power. Part II of his General Orders Number 9 of this date read, in part:

All persons connected with the military service of the Confederate States in this district are forbidden to publish, or to cause or permit to be published, any statements respecting operations or movements of troops, whether past or proposed. All telegraphic operators are cautioned against transmitting dispatches respecting the military movements and events of the district which do not come from authorized sources and are not sent as official communications. And all editors of newspapers are earnestly and respectfully requested to exercise careful scrutiny over their publications, that nothing may be published which can convey aid or comfort to our enemies, or suggest to them the position, condition, or designs of our armies.[10]

8. *Ibid.*, p. 952.

9. President Davis himself later assumed extraordinary powers after getting Congress to suspend the laws of habeas corpus. It must be admitted, however, that he used this right only in certain crucial situations. Other generals who assumed more powers than were generally authorized by their commissions included Braxton Bragg and Thomas J. Hindman. E. Merton Coulter, *The Confederate States of America*, p. 337.

10. *Official Records Army*, VIII, 796–797.

In the same order he also issued severe restrictions against his own troops. He forbade them to depredate civilian property, and he promised severe punishment for those soldiers who took stock, poultry, fencing, or other private property. He also directed his Quartermaster officers to pay fair prices for forage and other supplies. Though all these items are in line with modern military practices and they do seem appropriate for Arkansas's needs, the independent character of the region seemed to resent the power implied in the issuance of such orders. Much of the criticism that followed Van Dorn to his later assignments resulted from opposition to these orders.

These moves were all in the interest of the Confederacy, however, directed particularly toward a new move against Missouri. Alerted to the fact that Van Dorn was again planning big, Confederate Brigadier General John P. McCown at New Madrid watched him closely and awaited his projected advance. A large Union force threatened McCown's position, and Van Dorn's move might offer him relief. But as in February "the best laid plans" were shelved by a pressing emergency from still another front. From Tennessee came news of the threat of General U. S. Grant to push Generals Johnston and Beauregard right out of that state. Notified of the desperate plight of Johnston's position, Van Dorn weighed his projected Missouri invasion and then directed his support toward Tennessee. The letter offering his services and a letter from Johnston ordering him to move his army to within supporting distance of General Beauregard crossed in the mail, and on March 17 Van Dorn began to move his troops out of Van Buren.

Then began one of the slowest, most agonizing movements in the entire war—transporting a scattered army to a new and distant location. The tedious march to Pocahontas was just under way when Van Dorn received new orders from Johnston. A battle with Grant in Tennessee was rapidly materializing. Van Dorn was to move his entire command to Memphis as soon as possible. At Memphis the troops were to join General Beauregard under the new designation, "Army of the West." To comply with these orders Van Dorn decided to concentrate most of his troops at Des Arc, Arkansas, a small town on the White River, where he would reorganize them and then march them overland eighty miles to Memphis. As these troops began the march toward Des Arc, he made a hurried trip to Corinth, Mississippi, during the last days of March, where he consulted briefly with Generals Johnston and Beauregard. In this council, Johnston decided to attack Grant's invading forces before a Federal army under General Don Carlos Buell could arrive from Kentucky. It was hoped that the Army of the West would arrive in time for the battle. There was a drama in this decision—two rival armies racing to a scene of battle, the winner of the race being the decisive force in the battle's outcome. Unfortunately, the Confederates never had a chance.

Not that Van Dorn did not have the best intentions of joining General Johnston at the earliest possible moment; it was not that at all. He expended every effort to move his troops quickly. But his hopes for a fast operation faded, impeded constantly by bad weather, poor roads, and shortages of supplies—food, blankets, shoes, and clothing. His troops were so poorly supplied on this march that General Daniel Ruggles made an appeal to the ladies of Mobile, Alabama, "to take some measures for their relief."[11] Sickness was also prevalent to a crippling degree among the troops. Overexposure and a new measles epidemic took a heavy toll from the ranks and delayed departures from western Arkansas. Operating in the inclement weather of late winter, the hardiest of his troops found it nearly impossible to cover the long distance to their new destination. A visitor in Arkansas about this time recorded his own observations about travel in the state that show some of the problems:

Her public roads are quagmires, and her rivers innocent of any improvement save those afforded by nature. Jogging along over one of those selfsame roads, I broke my buggy trying to drive around a suspicious spot, where some philanthropist had erected a hickory sapling bearing the ominous words, 'NO BOTTOM HEAR!'[12]

One of Van Dorn's soldiers, James Payne, echoed these sentiments. Anyone traveling in Arkansas in the rainy season, he said, "has a fair idea of our trials with Arkansas mud, swollen streams, and general cussedness of badly kept roads."[13] The creeks had become rivers. Men were forced to drag cannon and supply wagons through mud and water. These were hard times for all of them.

Rains and snows made surging torrents out of the White, Arkansas, and Mississippi Rivers as well as many of the smaller streams in central Arkansas. One unit took thirteen days to travel from Van Buren to Little Rock because of the floods. At least three Arkansas regiments

11. Mobile *Register and Advertiser*, March 21, 1862, p. 1.
12. Fayetteville (Tennessee) *Observer*, February 27, 1862, p. 1.
13. Payne, "The Test of the Missourians," *Confederate Veteran*, XXXVII, 102.

were delayed en route to Little Rock until April 20—long after the battle of Shiloh—because of confusion along the way caused by poor traveling conditions. At Little Rock they were halted again because the Memphis road was flooded. Other troops arriving in Des Arc found no vessels available to transport their supplies and equipment down the White River. Other troops failed in their efforts even to get to Des Arc. As late as April 13, Colonel Louis Hébert was still struggling through western Arkansas with his 1,870 men.

These constant delays, though unavoidable, proved disastrous for the Confederate forces facing Grant. Waiting as long as he thought feasible, Johnston decided to attack Grant without Van Dorn's support. Buell was winning the race, and Johnston hoped to terminate the action before his arrival.

President Davis and General Beauregard later criticized Van Dorn for not arriving at Shiloh in time to turn the tide of battle to the Confederates. Davis said that Johnston ordered Van Dorn to join him by the quickest route, but the Mississippian failed him. It does appear, though, that both men made the unfortunate general the scapegoat of some of their own failures and miscalculations, for Johnston fought the battle knowing that Van Dorn would probably not arrive in time to offer him aid. The Confederates had telegraph service with Memphis, and even as Johnston's army departed from Corinth there was no word from Memphis of Van Dorn's arrival there. From Memphis the Army of the West would travel by train to Corinth and that still left them a day's march from the battlefield.

As the battle of Shiloh began, many of Van Dorn's troops were struggling along muddy roads in Arkansas still hoping to join Johnston in time to throw a decisive weight into the battle. This hope was in vain. Only one advance regiment of the Arkansas force arrived in time for part of the battle. The remainder were stopped by the swamps, the swollen rivers, and poor transportation facilities. Even as the battle raged, Van Dorn and many of his men waited impatiently for the floods to subside or for vessels to arrive to transport their supplies and equipment. It was not until the eighteenth of April that most of the new Army of the West finally assembled in Memphis. The battle of Shiloh was over; General Johnston was dead, and his successor, General Beauregard, had withdrawn from Tennessee into northern Mississippi.

Van Dorn left Arkansas after only three months never to return. He would remember the state as long as he lived, for here he had suffered his first great defeat. The battle of Elkhorn had been an important turning point in his career. His advance toward higher rank ended on that dismal field in the Trans-Mississippi District. The people of the state viewed his departure with mixed emotions. Some felt that his withdrawal was a sign that the Confederacy was deserting the state and was leaving it to the wrath of the invading Yankees. Governor Rector, especially critical of this action, said that the Confederate War Department had lost what little interest it had held, and Van Dorn's removal left Arkansas to fend for itself.

Even President Davis expressed unusual concern over Van Dorn's actions in Arkansas. The Confederate President made no mention of the Elkhorn defeat in a letter to his fellow Mississippian, but he suggested strongly that Van Dorn explain to the Arkansas Governor why he had departed from the state so precipitously and with so much of the manpower. Van Dorn delayed an answer to this letter for nearly three weeks; then he justified his action on the premise that what help he gave to General Beauregard would also be beneficial to Governor Henry M. Rector and Arkansas. Why the governor had ever challenged this view which Van Dorn had explained to him so thoroughly, he did not know "unless the dung-hill policy of fighting at every State's threshold was too alluringly pressed upon him by shallow politicians, too weak to see beyond the door and too cramped in patriotism to go beyond it."[14] Although not expressing the idea clearly, Van Dorn was recognizing one of the basic internal problems of the Confederacy: the feeling that each state must first protect its own interests. Other Confederate commanders would be confounded by this same problem throughout the war.

As if to clarify his own position with President Davis, Van Dorn suggested that Price be placed in command of the Trans-Mississippi region. This would mean Price taking the lead in the advance on St. Louis. Magnanimously he wrote:

I see the alluring bait to my ambition—the fall of Saint Louis, the reclamation of a rich segment of our beloved South from the grip of the enemy, and the glory that might be mine, but I shut all this out from me because I think it is the best interest of the country to do so. I drop whatever glory there may be in it on the brow of General Price. . . .[15]

14. *Official Records Army*, XIII, 832.
15. *Ibid.*

In a letter to his wife three days earlier, he had not been so generous. Then he had still hoped to avenge his defeat and invade Missouri. But even then, he was thinking of larger game. "I carry with me about 25,000 men and about eight pieces of artillery," he wrote. "With the addition to them we hope to drive the enemy not only out of Tennessee, but out of Kentucky, and attack Cincinnati."[16]

At Memphis Generals Van Dorn and Price made final arrangements for transporting the Confederate army to Corinth. While there Van Dorn had an interesting encounter with St. John R. Liddell, a somewhat mysterious figure who later rose to the rank of brigadier general in the Confederate Army. Liddell, a self-styled strategist, always full of plans for other Confederate officers and always more than willing to share them, suggested to Van Dorn that he round up a cavalry force of 9,000 troops, ride into central Tennessee and on into Kentucky and disrupt the enemy supply and communications lines behind Corinth. This would be a greater service for Beauregard's garrison than Van Dorn's presence with his troops.

Like so many of the other officers who had encountered Liddell, Van Dorn listened to this proposal with little sympathy. Liddell was chagrined at this indifference. He confided his feelings to his memoirs, ". . . he drew himself up, to my great surprise, with stiff dignity and with studied politeness coolly bowed to me, without deigning to reply."[17]

"There was no mistaking the fact that he considered my suggestions to be presumptuous and unworthy of his notice," he continued. Liddell then beat a hasty retreat from Van Dorn's presence and reported the affair to General Hardee a few days later. General Hardee's reply suggests a touch of diplomacy by the higher-ranking officer: "It was asking too much of Van Dorn to give up a Corps of Infantry for a cavalry command," he said. Liddell accepted this statement for the moment, but he had formed a permanent opinion of General Van Dorn, and he would remain a critic of the little Mississippian throughout the war.[18]

Meanwhile, the immediate challenges from Mississippi commanded Van Dorn's attention. From Corinth, General Beauregard, believing another major engagement pending, ordered Van Dorn to join him at the earliest possible moment. Van Dorn hurried on, but too late. Word

16. *A Soldier's Honor,* p. 71.
17. Unpublished Memoirs of General St. John R. Liddell.
18. *Ibid.*

came from Beauregard that the enemy was withdrawing from in front of his position at Corinth, and Van Dorn need not rush. Instead he was to proceed slowly down the Mississippi River and burn all the cotton within reach of his army. Van Dorn put this "scorched earth" policy into effect. He even gained enthusiastic support of many of the plantation owners by assuring them of the impending advance of the Federal Army. He and the last contingent of his troops finally arrived in Corinth on the last day of April 1862. Headquarters for this new Army of the West was Camp McIntosh, a newly established camp about one and one half miles west of the town, and Van Dorn stopped to await developments. The troops who had fought Yankees at Pea Ridge and at Shiloh were together at last, now facing an ever larger invading force than either had formerly encountered.

The Arkansas experience had not only been a trying one for General Van Dorn but also for his family. They had received news of his whereabouts only through rumor and newspaper reports, and the news of his stunning defeat came as a disheartening surprise to them. Earl told them nothing of his plans or his accomplishments during these dismal days. His mind was closed to all else but military concerns, and he made no effort to write his wife or beloved Emily. Finally about a week after Pea Ridge he did write Emily, to excuse his long silence by what he referred to as bedevilment "by all sorts of troubles."[19] Unsure where his wife was staying, he included money for her in the letter to Emily. He informed his sister that he had been unable to write since leaving Pocahontas in late February and asked her to "please tell my dear Carry to write." Finally on April 6, he wrote to his wife for the first time in more than a month. His main concern even then was in the impending struggle in which he still hoped to redeem himself for his Elkhorn failure. This letter also expressed a deep melancholy, heightened by his own frustrating experiences in Arkansas. "I am getting as short and crabbed as though I had never been a good-natured man," he complained. He also expressed his concern for his beloved South. If she did not win "honor and independence," he was ready to go to Mexico or South America.[20].

His spirits took a turn for the better a few days later. His native state

19. Earl Van Dorn to Emily, March 16, 1862, Foreman M. Lebold Manuscript Collection, Chicago, Illinois.
20. *A Soldier's Honor*, pp. 70–71.

presented him with another sword—this time in recognition of his services to the South. "I have sought to have it made in a stile [sic] worthy of yourself and the state and am pleased to be able to send it to you just now in time to flash defiance in the face of the enemies of Mississippi," wrote Governor John Pettus in a special presentation letter.[21] A few days later Van Dorn received another boost when the Confederate Congress praised him for "valor, skill, and good conduct in the battle of Elkhorn. . . ."[22]

Earl Van Dorn's record of achievement was gaining him another chance. It was ironic that he would return to his native state for his next big opportunity. There he no longer held an independent command, but he was an important army commander in a force larger than any in which he had ever served.

To the casual student who views the Civil War in terms of decisive actions, large armies in the field generally take on the appearances of lumbering, undisciplined giants. These giants either move about over the countryside with no apparent sense of direction or they cower behind earthen or wooden fortifications and await the moves of other giants. Sometimes the heads of these monsters strike against each other, and history records the action as a major engagement. More often the leviathans merely wag their tails or shake their heads over the country-side and bring misery and destruction to the innocent victims in their paths.

The two great armies that faced each other after the affair at Shiloh were such giants. Like great beasts they licked their battle wounds and reluctantly faced up to the realities of a continuing struggle. Only twenty miles of Southern landscape separated their main bodies, but tentacles from both creatures plied the roads, searching out some vul-nerability that would provide a decisive advantage once the struggle was renewed.

Up and down the Mississippi River the shock of the clash of these two armies reverberated. As far north as Ohio the citizenry roused itself to the realities of war's horror and rushed doctors and nurses toward the Federal camps. In Mississippi also the meaning of war in its most primi-tive sense struck home for the first time. Far removed from the early

21. Governor John Pettus to Earl Van Dorn, April 8, 1862, Van Dorn Collection, Montgomery, Alabama.
22. *Official Records Army*, LIII, 803.

scenes of action, residents of sleepy little towns suddenly became aware of the menacing force of the Union army. They had watched favorite sons march off to the colors and then noted familiar names in growing casualty lists, but the threat from a giant army was something else. Businesses, homes, and families were in jeopardy. For many "the conflict was becoming implacable."

If the giant forces assumed an air of impersonality to the observer outside their ranks, such was not the feeling among the blue– and gray-clad soldiers who formed their complements. At Shiloh they had just fought the bloodiest battle in the history of their countries, not just as giant impersonal armies but as individuals struggling for life on a bloody battlefield. Nothing could be more personal than that to the decorated heroes, the skulking cowards, or to the thousands of other young men who had participated in these scenes of violence. Two giant armies lay stunned in soggy fields near the Tennessee River, but it was men of flesh and blood who suffered and feared.

Two giant armies do not lie stunned for long. They revived with increased supplies and equipment, new leaders, and new incentive. As material needs were supplied in both armies, the voices of new leaders sounded firm and fresh. New spirit appeared, and by late April there was talk of action in both camps. Incentive centered around the strategic railroad center at Corinth where Beauregard had concentrated his army. The arrival of 17,000 troops under Van Dorn had been a big factor in infusing "fresh spirit" into his command, but he was still outnumbered two to one by General Halleck's Federal army. Dr. W. L. Gammage, one of the Arkansas contingent who arrived at the new Confederate position on May 4, was impressed by Beauregard's preparations. "Everything seemed to be on a grander and more magnificent scale than we had ever known it before," he wrote.[23] Northern newsmen would later disagree with this evaluation of the Corinth defense, but Beauregard had done a good job in reclaiming a broken army and building a strong defense line.

Life moved at a fast pace in the little railroad center in those late Spring days of 1862. After dreary April rains the sun made a much-heralded appearance, "shedding a balmy warmth" over the countryside. In the city "the whole earth seemed to be teeming with soldiers" as Beauregard made ready to meet General Halleck's anticipated new

23. *The Camp, the Bivouac and the Battle Field*, p. 33.

offensive. Dr. Gammage was caught in the midst of these preparations. "The roads for miles around were crammed and jammed with
wagons, carts, ambulances, caissons and artillery carriages," he wrote
with enthusiasm.[24]

Everywhere in and around the city there were new sounds of Spring
—the clatter of cavalry rattling through the town, rumbling commissary
wagons bouncing over the Main street ruts, marching regiments returning from lengthy picket duty. Even after the sun set, there was no
quiet. Long after the day had ended, the music of regimental bands
echoed through the night air.

Before the city toward the Tennessee border war preparations were
much apparent. There Beauregard's front lines extended for about
three miles from the Memphis and Charleston Railroad line on the left
to the Mobile and Ohio Railroad in the center. This line made an arc
of about 120 degrees north and east of the city. The regiments of Generals Hardee, Polk, and Bragg commanded this arc from left to right.
Van Dorn provided depth to this line by stationing his brigades as near
as practicable to the center of the prospective battle line. Confederate
engineers constructed crude roads between these reserve units and the
front lines to facilitate movement of men and artillery. Meanwhile,
General Beauregard also directed a weather eye toward Halleck's
army with his cavalry which patrolled the country far beyond the extended Confederate outposts.

In front of the Confederate position General Halleck procrastinated
as was his custom. His difficulty was aptly described by a Southern
general who watched his slow, deliberate movement.

> Pre-eminently cautious by nature, and the more cautious now because
> he was sure of ultimate success, and averse always to the unnecessary shed-
> ding of human blood, Halleck, instead of advancing boldly against Beaure-
> gard as Grant would have done and risking all upon the hazard of a battle
> whose issue would have been uncertain, first fortified his position . . . then
> began to strengthen his army. . . .[25]

Late April or early May could have been the decisive time for Halleck.
His army numbered approximately 110,000 fighting men compared
with about 53,000 "present for duty" in Beauregard's force. The Federal
commander could probably have routed the Confederates with a giant

24. *Ibid.*
25. Johnson and Buel, *Battles and Leaders,* II, 718.

massed attack. Instead he chose the slow but determined advance toward Corinth.

Beauregard watched the advance and tried to devise tactics to impede it. His only hope was to build a strong defensive position, meanwhile striking the huge Federal army at its weakest spots as it moved slowly toward him. One of the key officers in his planning was the new arrival, Earl Van Dorn.

Van Dorn's appearance in Beauregard's army had hardly been the spectacular event for which the Mississippian had hoped. He still carried the stigma of Arkansas, and his late arrival at Corinth had hurt him further. One of Beauregard's men recorded his own impressions of the little general the first time he saw him: "He looked to me more like a dandy than the general of an army. He was small, curley or kinkey headed, exquisitely dressed, was riding a beautiful bay horse, evidently groomed with as much care as his rider, who was small looking and frenchy."[26]

Though there was some criticism of his actions in the past, most of the troops seemed to accept his leadership. Even Johnson called him a "distinguished soldier" who "enjoyed the confidence and admiration of his men."[27] Certainly no officer within the Confederate lines was more eager for action than he. Hoping for a chance to redeem himself for the Arkansas debacle, he brooded for action against Halleck. If only he could have his way, he would attack the slow-moving Federal army without delay. Many of his men also seemed eager for action. Confederate morale was high. Many of the men were on home soil. They knew their land, and they would fight for it.

On May 3 the first direct contact occurred between Confederate outposts and Halleck's advance troops. For a few hours another Shiloh seemed in the making. Confederate outposts were drawn in late in the day as Federal artillery found its range. That night the Confederates on Beauregard's right slept on their arms, fearful yet hopeful that the morning would bring on the battle that had been so long in building up. Behind the front lines, Van Dorn chafed for action.

On May 4 nature intervened and changed the plans of army commanders in both camps. Early that morning the rains came in the form

26. William T. Alderson (ed.), "The Civil War Reminiscences of John Johnson," *Tennessee Historical Quarterly*, XIII, 163.

27. *Official Records Army*, X, Pt. 2, 489.

of a cold, penetrating storm which disrupted transportation and communications and led to discomfort and some suffering. As the rains beat down, swearing teamsters pulled supply and artillery wagons from muddy roadbeds; generals who had spent the night in the saddle ordered weary troops to hold their lines and await developments.

On May 6 General Beauregard finally made modifications in his defense pattern which brought Van Dorn's troops a change of position and a brush with the enemy. Closely watching the enemy before him, Beauregard observed that impetuous General John Pope was moving out ahead of the main army. Pope had just completed the conquest of Island Number 10 and New Madrid, and his star was at its zenith. So was his confidence in himself. He was ripe for the kill if only he could be maneuvered into position. Beauregard, always alert to the possibilities of an action against an isolated unit, dispatched Van Dorn around to the right toward Farmington, Mississippi, a village five miles east of Corinth on the road to Hamburg, Tennessee.

With an enthusiasm that demonstrated his desire to engage the enemy again, Van Dorn moved his troops to the dilapidated village. On Beauregard's orders he halted his advance near Farmington and waited for Pope to precipitate the action. Pope would probably have obliged, but heavy rains slowed his advance just north of the community. When the rains were over, he moved closer to the village, hoping to reconnoiter the area immediately to his front, the area occupied by Van Dorn.

The terrain in and around Farmington was treacherous to an invading army, and General Halleck was not as enthusiastic about Pope's move as was Pope. "Do you want any aid from Buell?" Halleck warily asked his impetuous commander.[28]

Pope's reply revealed an unwarranted confidence: "I only want Buell to watch my right carefully during the reconaissance, that no force may interpose between us," was all he had to say.[29]

General Pope moved into Farmington on May 8. By early morning that day his pickets were in front of the town. Halleck, still worried over these tactics, directed Buell to keep an eye on his impulsive general: "Be prepared to cover the retreat of Pope's reconnoitering party if it should be driven back and pursued," he warned ominously.[30]

28. *Ibid.*, p. 169.
29. *Ibid.*
30. *Ibid.*, p. 171.

That same evening at Beauregard's command Van Dorn moved his troops down the Danville Road toward Farmington. Scouts preceded the unit's advance to ascertain the enemy's exact position. Just outside the town, Van Dorn halted and set up a battle line. Before dusk his advance troops drove in Pope's pickets, and Halleck promptly warned the rash officer to avoid any "general engagement." Pope's reply typified the temperament that later contributed to his tragic defeat at Manassas Junction. "I am not likely to be taken at a disadvantage and trust you will not be uneasy about me," he wrote his commander. Of course this did nothing to soothe the agitated Halleck's feelings.[31]

Despite his jaunty attitude, Pope maintained some caution and at Halleck's request he avoided a general engagement by retreating into the village. This maneuver seemed to have caught Van Dorn off guard, and he responded with uncertainty. He had intended to launch an attack immediately after he had moved his troops into a strong position, but he lost valuable time getting his army ready and night came before he was ready to move. That night the Confederates rested on their arms in battle formation almost within the Federal bounds of defense. Van Dorn's left flank reached to the crest of a hill above the marshy bottom of a small creek that ran in front of the Corinth trenches; his center rested on the Danville road at a point about a mile in advance of the crossing of that road and the Charleston and Memphis Railway; his right flank was parallel to that same railroad.

Early on the following morning, May 9, the Confederate commander moved his line of battle abruptly to cut off aid to Pope's front from north of the town. He cut off three avenues of approach into Farmington—the old Jacinto, the new Jacinto, and the Danville roads. Then he ordered an advance upon Farmington. General Daniel Ruggles opened an attack on the center, and Van Dorn soon joined him with the main elements of his command. Pope, now directly under Halleck's command, avoided a major engagement by quickly withdrawing his forces. He crossed Seven Mile Creek and then massed his troops near the other Federal units in the vicinity in hopes that the Confederates would cross the creek and continue the attack. Van Dorn suspected the ambush and ordered his troops to halt their pursuit at the creek bank. After burning the only bridge across the small stream, he re-

31. *Ibid.*, p. 176.

turned with his troops to their headquarters in the Corinth defense line.

The results of the skirmish disappointed Van Dorn. He blamed swamps, thickets, and ravines for preventing his right flank from reaching the Hamburg Road in time to cut off Pope's retreat. Again he had neglected the all-important reconnaissance. A scouting party might have found the terrain obstacles and speeded up the approach of his right wing, but, as was too often the case, Van Dorn conceived his plans in haste and without proper concern for the complexity of the situation.

General Hardee, who was with Van Dorn at the time of the skirmish on the ninth, said that all the fault of the failure did not belong to his colleague. He said that Van Dorn arrived at the spot to which Beauregard had directed him, but that Beauregard did not know the topography of the countryside well enough to anticipate the rugged terrain. Beauregard in turn attributed the failure to the Confederate guides who led their troops in the wrong direction. Later, Colonel William P. Johnston, as special investigator of the affair, concluded that in the final analysis, "success was improbable" in the first place. The over-all plan of the battle was a good one, but tactical planning by both Van Dorn and Beauregard was faulty. By the time the Confederates could move into their anticipated position, unanticipated delays had cost them their advantage. Before Van Dorn could attack, Pope was ready to receive the attack, so the Confederate general decided against a rash assault into the face of a well-organized enemy position.

There were not many casualties in the skirmishing of the day. Union losses totaled only 16 killed, 148 wounded, and 14 captured. Van Dorn reported only nine Confederates killed in the brief engagement. The major result of the little fray was to stress the fact that General Halleck was waiting for certain success before attacking full-scale. Even though his troop strength was greater than Beauregard's, he would set the battle on his own terms. The Confederates showed good sense in not pressing their attack, for had they continued on the offensive they would have had to fight Halleck's large army in its well-prepared trenches.

Thus what could have become a major engagement of the war in Mississippi ended with a few casualties and both armies in nearly the same positions as before the skirmish. Even Northern newspapers credited Van Dorn with a victory, but the withdrawal of the Confederates to fortified Corinth again allowed detachments of the Union army to occupy Farmington. Back at Corinth Van Dorn spoke out strongly for initiating an attack on Halleck's army, but General Beauregard wisely warned that the time and place were inappropriate and refused to sanction another offensive at the time.

For the remainder of May, two great armies faced each other across a few miles of Mississippi soil, each awaiting an attack by the other. From each headquarters every action of the opposing force was observed, and generals in both camps awaited anxiously the movements across the lines. Every day the artillery fire was intense, but no grand assault was ordered. This was a new type of war, unknown to the dashing veterans of Mexico; many of them including Van Dorn found it impossible to understand or to accept.

Occasionally one of these impetuous officers temporarily broke the siege by an attack, always on a very small scale. On May 13 a group of Van Dorn's troops exchanged a few shots with Federals on the Danville Road, and a few casualties resulted on each side. On May 17 scouts brought in warnings of a pending offensive by Halleck's forces. The next day General Beauregard ordered Van Dorn to cover the Confederate right for a defensive-offensive action against the Federal attack. Van Dorn formed a battle line south of the railroad facing the expected attack. When action became general along the front, he was to push forward across the Corinth-Burnsville Road and attack the enemy on his left flank; then he was to press in and drive the Federals from their artillery.

From its beginning Van Dorn opposed this move. "The movement is without possibility," he complained to his commanding officer.[32] Bad weather threatened. The Federals had closed the crossing at Clear Creek, and the terrain ahead of him was so bad that it offered little chance of a smooth advance. General Hardee agreed that much of the route of the Confederate march had not been examined, but General Beauregard insisted upon an attack.

The enemy moved forward slowly. On May 23 after several days of heavy skirmishing among the pickets, Van Dorn prepared to strike. Ordered to be in position for an attack at three o'clock that morning

32. *Ibid.*, p. 532.

or by early dawn at very latest, Van Dorn finally was ready just after noon. By that time it was too late to attack, and the enemy had halted his advance.

Terrain difficulties combined with poor reconnoitering efforts halted both armies short of combat. After failing to make a push against the Union position, Van Dorn excused his failure to press forward by saying: "I have been delayed by bad management and stupidity of officers . . . and I am sick with disappointment and chagrin."[33] Though lacking magnanimity of character, he again revealed his old lust for battle as he added: "I feel like a wolf and will fight Pope like one." His hope to fight Pope never materialized. He found "unexpected difficulties, topographical and otherwise," so after consultation with Generals Hardee and Price, he decided to return to his entrenchments.

Van Dorn returned his force to Corinth after only light skirmishing. Colonel William Preston Johnston later reported that had the general's guides been able to direct the Confederates into position by dawn on the twenty-third, a general attack could have been launched which would have taken the enemy by surprise. This hardly seems plausible for the enemy was well entrenched and much stronger than Van Dorn's force of only 12,900 effectives.

Though General Halleck seemed reluctant to fight the Confederate army in its entrenched Corinth position, the town itself soon proved untenable for General Beauregard. A Richmond reporter described the situation:

The sun pours down its hot and scorching rays; the air is filled with clouds of excruciating fine dust, which . . . penetrates everywhere, the streets are almost deserted of beings, and men and animals move lazily about their tasks. Not even a rumor ripples over the surface of this army ocean, to break the monotony of its calm.[34]

The ranks of the Southern command were constantly being reduced by sickness and desertion because of the heat and poor health conditions. Camp fever began to take a heavy toll. Fresh water was at a premium. "With every pint of fluid one has to drink a half ounce of dirt," wrote the Richmond correspondent attached to the Confederate command.[35] "You feel it scrape the throat as it goes down, and after

33. *Ibid.*, Pt. 1, p. 539.
34. Richmond *Dispatch*, May 30, 1862, p. 1.
35. *Ibid.*

it gets to the stomach it lays as heavy and indigestible as a bed of mortar," continued his dreary report.

General Beauregard also realized that while his own forces were suffering, the opposing army was increasing its strength in men and supplies. The end was in sight. Could he bow out gracefully without the climax of a great and decisive battle? To settle this problem, he called a conference of his leading generals—Van Dorn, Polk, Breckinridge, and Bragg. It was their unanimous decision to evacuate the town. Beauregard then ordered all newspaper correspondents from Corinth, and without further delay he loaded his supply trains and issued orders to prepare the troops for the evacuation. After a brief exchange of fire between Van Dorn's artillery battery and the enemy just south of Farmington, the Confederates began moving out. By June 1 evacuation of the city had been completed, and the Confederate army was moving toward Tupelo. A dilatory pursuit by the Federals enabled Beauregard to successfully elude the enemy.

The evacuation of the city itself deserves some special mention. Though carried out under the surveillance of the Union pickets, the Federals did not discover the movement until the Confederates were well on their way toward Baldwin. During the night of May 29 trains arrived all night long, and the Confederates loaded them with supplies and troops and then sent them on their way southward. Each time a train came into the city great cheers greeted its arrival as though reinforcements had arrived. General Halleck seems to have been completely fooled, for his forces did not enter the city until after seven o'clock the following morning. By that time Beauregard's army was safely behind the Tuscumbia River.

"When daylight appeared," later wrote Dr. Gammage, who was with Van Dorn in one of the last units to depart the city, "not a soul could be seen save here and there a straggling footman who had overslept himself, or a cavalry scout who had been left behind to watch the movements of the astonished and outwitted Yankee host."[36]

General Polk described this interesting withdrawal in a letter to his daughter on June 3. He believed that the Southern forces had retreated at just the right moment. "We have deemed it advisable, after having kept the enemy employed six weeks in digging and embanking all the way from the Tennessee River to Corinth, and just when he had

36. *The Camp, the Bivouac and the Battle Field*, pp. 36–37.

spent millions of dollars, and lost thousands of men by the climate and water, and when he had just got ready to open his heavy batteries—to bid him good morning and invite him down a little farther South."[37]

From "a little farther South" at Baldwin, Van Dorn watched the pursuing enemy. On June 6, after a brief skirmish with an advance Union patrol, he moved his troops into Tupelo where he and the other Confederate commanders awaited General Beauregard's next order.

From Richmond President Davis and the Confederate War Department watched Beauregard's withdrawal in anguish. Though Beauregard reported his evacuation as a victory, Davis viewed the situation with alarm. The loss of Corinth was a bitter blow to the Confederacy, one which they could ill-afford at this crucial stage of the war. Ever since Shiloh, Beauregard's enemies had complained continually of his inability to command. At the evacuation of Corinth their cries increased, and their din became so loud that Richmond had to act. Wrote T. Harry Williams in his biography of the Creole: "The administration was ready to move in on Beauregard."[38]

Though given a chance to explain his actions, the hero of Fort Sumter never convinced the administration that his actions were adequate to the situation at Corinth. Losses in the West had been too great during the first year of the war, and Confederate leaders in Richmond would not tolerate another failure. With Mississippi Governor John J. Pettus appealing desperately to Davis for an increase in supplies, and with Davis already overly critical of Beauregard's actions in the West, the time had come for drastic action. General Beauregard helped bring the issue to a head by taking a sick leave without expressed permission from the War Department. Davis then used this as an excuse to remove him from command and replace him with a favorite general, Braxton Bragg.

At the time of Beauregard's removal, the War Department also made some changes that directly affected General Van Dorn. By the President's direct order, he was detached from the Army of the West and dispatched to relieve his West Point classmate, General Mansfield Lovell, as commander of the Department of Southern Mississippi and East Louisiana, with orders to watch and, if need be, to attack the

37. Polk, *Leonidas Polk*, II, 118.
38. *P. G. T. Beauregard*, p. 156.

Northern forces in the Mississippi valley around Vicksburg and Port Hudson. The War Department had originally intended that General Bragg have this assignment, but when that general replaced Beauregard, they substituted Van Dorn for the Vicksburg position.

President Davis's removal of two leading generals, Beauregard and Lovell, did little to create good will in the already confused Western theater of operations. Both generals accepted their dismissals with bitterness. Beauregard wrote critically of the Confederate chief executive: "If the country be satisfied to have me laid on the shelf by a man who is either demented or a traitor to his high trust—well, let it be so."[39]

Lovell also expressed his own unhappiness in vituperative language: "I learn . . . indirectly that a general officer [Van Dorn] has been directed to supersede me in my command—abruptly and without notice to me—thus indicating a want of confidence on the part of the administration."[40] Responsibility for the loss of New Orleans lay on Lovell's shoulders, and the Confederate brass felt that a stronger leader was needed for the coming showdown struggle for control of the Mississippi River. And as was so often the case, where there was confusion and controversy there also was Van Dorn.

Though displeased at his new assignment, Van Dorn, along with General John Breckinridge's troops, reported to Jackson, Mississippi, under orders to begin preparing a defense for the small stretch of the river still in Confederate hands. Irritated at being relieved as an important commander in an active army and placed over what he considered an obscure department, he entered this new assignment with less enthusiasm than others in his career which had held more hopes of action and glory. But if it was action that he wanted, he would find the Mississippi River—and especially the city of Vicksburg—to be anything but dull places.

Upon arriving in Jackson, Van Dorn found his resources of both men and supplies sorely limited, so he called upon the garrisons stationed in and around Oxford and Holly Springs to unite with him at the earliest moment to aid him in warding off the Northern aggressors. Then he admonished the people in and around Jackson to aid the Southern cause by systematically destroying property that might otherwise fall into the enemies' hands. Warning them to be alert and ever

39. Quoted in Williams, *P. G. T. Beauregard*, p. 161.
40. Smith, *Confederate War Papers*, p. 97.

watchful, he said: "An undisciplined rabble is not dangerous to the enemy, is extremely injurious to the neighborhood where it may be stationed, and is a disgrace to any country."[41] Van Dorn had learned an important lesson in Arkansas. He was rapidly becoming an excellent guerrilla leader.

While in Jackson, Van Dorn discovered that large fleets of gunboats, mortar boats, and loaded transports of the enemy were "ascending and descending the river toward Vicksburg," from New Orleans.[42] Aware of Vicksburg's importance, he then issued orders to all the commanders in the outlying areas to assemble their troops in that beleagured city for a crucial defense against the invader. Maybe there was action here after all. Van Dorn would soon find out.

41. *Official Records Army,* XV, 768.
42. *Ibid.,* LII, Pt. 2, 323.

CHAPTER NINE

Defense of Vicksburg

*E*ARLY in the war the city of Vicksburg, Mississippi, was of great strategic importance in the defense of the Mississippi River because of its unusual location on a high bluff overlooking a prominent bend in the river. The terrain has changed with the passing years, but in 1862 the bluff was an excellent defense barrier, varying in height from 200 to 300 feet above the river. In addition to this important land feature, Vicksburg also possessed natural protection from the water front in trees and underbrush. These terrain obstacles coupled with steep, inaccessible slopes made the possibilities of an invasion from the river virtually impossible. The city was an important trade center of about 5,000 inhabitants and was surrounded by some of the most fertile country in the South. Its annual shipments of cotton before the war usually exceeded 100,000 bales.

Vicksburg first came into prominence in the early Spring of 1862. Soon after the fall of New Orleans, both armies singled out this strategic city because it was one of the important strongholds still blocking the Federals from navigating the river. Captain (Flag Officer) David G. Farragut directed his victorious fleet up the river from New Orleans for a repeat performance of his success at the mouth of the river. Early in June General Halleck offered to lend the Navy a helping hand if Farragut needed him. But a change in direction in Federal strategy after the fall of Corinth caused Halleck to direct his army toward a concentration on enemy territory instead of enemy armies. "The repair of the railroads is now the great object to be attended to," remarked Halleck.

New Federal strategy also affected Confederate planning. The threat before Vicksburg was a victorious navy menacing from one direction

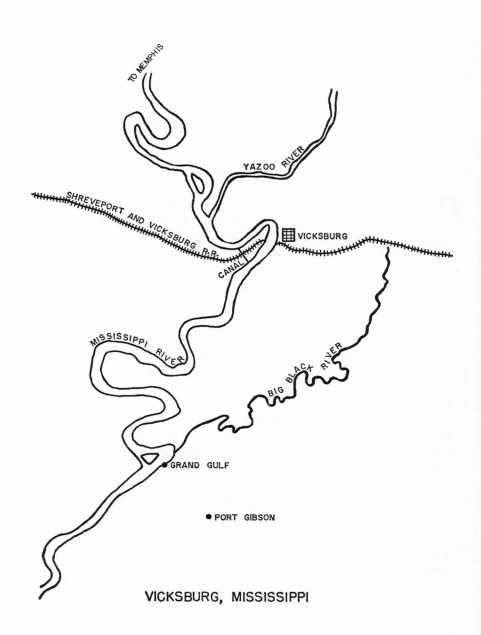

VICKSBURG, MISSISSIPPI

and a giant army threatening from another. The only Confederate army of any size rested wearily near Tupelo, Mississippi. Now commanded by General Braxton Bragg, it was hardly a match for a major Union offensive either against its front or toward its flank at Vicksburg. Could the river port hold on? Bragg and the other Confederate leaders hoped so. The city continued its preparations to carry on its own private war against the Union if such be its need. Her citizens and her military defenders decided that the North would pay dearly for her possession.

Confederate officers had turned to Vicksburg as an ideal defensive position to block a Federal advance up the river even while Farragut's guns were cooling at New Orleans. After his retreat before General Benjamin Butler's advance, General Mansfield Lovell requested permission from General Beauregard to begin fortifying the city. Beauregard, torn between Helena, Arkansas, and Vicksburg as the location for a river garrison, finally decided on the latter as being a more defensible location. In April 1862 in accord with Beauregard's decision, General Lovell sent General Martin Luther Smith to begin setting up strong fortifications. General Smith, an officer in the Topographical Engineers before the war, assumed command of the city on May 12.

Though limited from the beginning in men and supplies, he did a remarkable job in preparing the city's defenses. When he entered Vicksburg he had with him only five infantry regiments, but he began the new assignment with enthusiasm. Inside the city he found three batteries already completed and an additional one in progress. Working day and night he added steadily to these fortifications. He increased the series of batteries to the north of Vicksburg and set up an enclosed battery to the south of the city. The guns north of the port commanded the mouth of the Yazoo River and provided a defense against vessels from Memphis. The southern guns covered a narrow peninsula jutting out across the river and guarded against enemy vessels approaching up the river from New Orleans. General Smith also provided for general defense of the area by skillfully locating guns on the crests of all the high hills overlooking the river. Reinforcements also arrived at the city until a garrison of about 3,000 men guarded its extremities and aided in the building of fortifications by making cisterns and erecting shelters.

The Federal fleet under the command of Captain Farragut and transports carrying General Thomas Williams's division of 3,000 Federal troops from Baton Rouge first made their appearance at Vicksburg to threaten the new defenses on May 18 just as Smith was in the midst of some of his most important preparations. Farragut demanded that Smith surrender the city; Smith emphatically refused. The Federals made no immediate show of force but remained inactive below the city for more than a week.

The Confederates watched the fleet from atop their bluffs with anxiety and continued feverishly working at their fortifications. The Federal commanders, realizing that the city was too strong for them, decided that the time was not yet ripe for an invasion; they bided their time. Unwilling to risk his small army against what he considered a very strong position, General Williams returned with his troops to Baton Rouge where he felt their service would be of more importance to the total Northern offensive. Farragut soon returned to New Orleans for more pressing business, but he left six vessels to keep up a blockade of the river at this point and to keep up an occasional bombardment upon the city.

On May 26 after being increased to ten gunboats, the Federal fleet opened fire on Vicksburg for the first time. The Confederates, still working around the clock building their fortifications, held up their fire during this attack to conserve their limited ammunition supply. Their firing only at infrequent intervals had little effect upon the Federal fleet.

The Federals continued a spasmodic firing until the middle of June, concentrating their heavy weapons on the city itself and on locations where they thought the Confederates had placed their troops. From June 14 to June 18, they halted their bombardment while Farragut and Commander David D. Porter joined them from New Orleans. Farragut had little hopes at this point of successfully opening the river, but in compliance with orders he added his and Porter's mortar-flotilla of sixteen vessels to the attacking force. As soon as the vessels were in line, they renewed their bombardment. For a solid week they kept up the barrage through most of each day and on until about ten or eleven o'clock in the evening.

On June 23, Van Dorn inspected his new Vicksburg command, accompanied by Governor Pettus. Reacting to the precarious situation in the city with consternation and concern, he surveyed the defenses quickly and then returned to Jackson to co-ordinate his command. All efforts were directed toward preventing the fall of this vital center.

On June 24 he recommended that all persons living within eight miles of the Mississippi River move their families to the interior of the state "as it is the intention to defend the department to the last extremity."[1]

While Van Dorn was still in Jackson, the Federal vessels attacking Vicksburg received additional reinforcements. General Williams returned from Baton Rouge and landed his troops and ten field guns on the Louisiana side of the river. Additional vessels from New Orleans brought Farragut's fleet up to a strength of three ships, seven gunboats, and sixteen mortar boats. On June 26 the first Union vessels arrived from a recent victory in Memphis to join in bombarding Vicksburg. By July 1 these vessels under Captain (Flag-Officer) Charles H. Davis had increased the Federal attacking force to over forty gunboats, mortar boats, rams, and transports.

Van Dorn felt a strange challenge in this new command. He arrived at Vicksburg on June 27 to take charge of the defenses. A citizen who rode in the same car with him sensed a seriousness of purpose in the general which showed in his "quiet keen blue eyes."[2] The citizen left an interesting description of his traveling companion:

[H]is hair is what, in a lady, you would call auburn, but in a soldier and gentleman, sandy. He wears it flowing and uncut, and his beard full, though not bushy or neglected. His complexion is soft and blonde, almost like that of a woman, and I was told he could, and at times actually did blush.[3]

The heaviest fire of the campaign greeted Van Dorn's arrival as the Federal vessels pounded away at the city's defenses. The Vicksburg garrison, continually reinforced by troops from the surrounding area, took all the cannonading the Federals could offer and countered with some firing of their own. Though his garrison still numbered fewer than 4,000 troops, Van Dorn accepted the challenge of the moment determined to hold the fortress at all costs. The populace was with him. "Our people generally, and our Vicksburg friends in particular, are restored to a degree of confidence which they have not felt under the recent military regime," confidently wrote a Mississippi native.[4] With the roar of Federal guns in the air, the citizens of Vicksburg listened with enthusiasm to a stirring speech by their new leader:

1. *Official Records Army*, XV, 510.
2. Richmond *Dispatch*, July 16, 1862, p. 1.
3. *Ibid.*
4. *Ibid.*

The enemy are attempting to destroy this beautiful city, and a heroic people have determined to sacrifice it rather than give it up to the invaders of their homes. . . . The contest will commence when the enemy attempts to put his foot upon your soil. Stand cooly by your guns, and deliver your fire only when he comes too near.[5]

As if trying to disparage the new commander, the Federal fleet tested his courage and the courage of the people of the community. The day after the address, five Northern vessels from Farragut's lower fleet bombarded the city mercilessly, but the citizens and the soldiers managed to return the fire. Despite the heavy firepower of the vessels, Van Dorn seemed unperturbed. "They only amuse our men," he wrote to President Davis.[6]

Before the proud river city, Federal grand strategy rapidly unfolded. Vicksburg was one of the last strongholds blocking Union control of the Mississippi River. Though not yet committed to a land attack by the main Federal army in Mississippi, Northern leaders seemed determined to break the city's defense with a naval assault and a small-scale invasion. Vicksburg's collapse would mean that Union vessels could navigate freely in the river from New Orleans to the Ohio. The fall of the city would also cut off the Trans-Mississippi West, land of vast supplies and some reinforcements for a Confederacy that sorely needed every bit of food and supplies it could muster.

It was imperative for the Confederacy to hold Vicksburg to prolong the war. Van Dorn had to anticipate Grant's sending a force from the north of the city to join Williams in an assault upon its rear. He diligently improved his defenses. "Let it be borne in mind by all," he warned the defenders, "that the army here is defending the place against occupation . . . even though this . . . city should be laid in ruins."[7] From the eastern part of the state at his request came supplies by rail. He replaced disabled guns with new ones. He strengthened his gun crews; his engineers constructed new fortifications. With the arrival of General Breckinridge's force of approximately 5,000 from southern Mississippi, he was able to establish a heavy line of pickets along the lower bank of the river and thus discourage any landing efforts from the river. He placed light artillery in position to guard all roads

5. Van Dorn's speech quoted from *De Bow's Review*, II, 189.
6. *Official Records Army*, XV, 14.
7. *Ibid.*, pp. 769–770.

leading into the city and reassigned his cavalry forces to guard the Confederate flanks toward the Yazoo River and below the city. The batteries of heavy guns already in position on the crest of the hills overlooking the river he kept active, and his gun crews constantly moved these guns to keep the enemy from determining their exact locations. They would run a gun forward on rails until it projected over the cliff, fire it, and then run it back out of sight of the river and reload for another shot.

Life was exciting around Vicksburg in the hot summer of 1862. General Van Dorn's aide-de-camp, Lieutenant Sulivane, later described some of the actions around the city at the height of the Federal attack:

> During the month of July, 1862 . . . my sole occupation was, as ordered by General Van Dorn, to make myself thoroughly familiar with the country around Vicksburg, its woods, hills, bayous, roads, etc. . . . and I spent the whole month in solitary rides of exploration. . . . Repeatedly General Van Dorn said to me, "They can never seriously menace Vicksburg, certainly can never take it, but by landing a heavy force to the south of the city, either above or below the Big Black. If above, I must meet them before they make good their footing—if below, I must meet them at the Big Black. . . ."[8]

To citizen and soldier alike, Vicksburg was "the last ditch, so far as the Mississippi was concerned, and here they were determined to make a final stand."[9] Peter Walker calls it a "temper," a spirit of resistence.[10] Civilians and soldiers alike performed the impossible. One brigade among the pickets forced its way through a swamp earlier deemed impassable and made a rush toward some Federal gunboats that had been moored to the shore to reconnoiter. This spirited activity forced the gunboats to withdraw from their scouting project and return to their main fleet. Farragut recognized the stubborn Southern defense on June 28 in a letter to his own Secretary of the Navy in which he despaired of his chances for victory. "I am satisfied that it is not possible for us to take Vicksburg without an army force of 12,000 or 15,000 men," he lamented.[11]

For the moment Van Dorn was again the hero of his native state. But at Vicksburg as elsewhere in his checkered military career, he

8. *A Soldier's Honor,* p. 93.
9. David D. Porter, *The Naval History of the Civil War,* p. 248.
10. *Vicksburg: A People at War,* p. 79.
11. *The War of the Rebellion: A Compilation of the Official Records of the Union and Confederate Navies,* Ser. 1, XVIII, 588.

found to his sorrow that defensive warfare has many other aspects besides bravely repelling an enemy attack against strong breastworks. A commander must keep discipline among his troops, and when fighting in and among the citizenry, he must maintain order over disparate elements that often frown on military authority. In the defense of Vicksburg he had to draw upon the population of the surrounding countryside for supplies, equipment, and manpower whether the populace wished to co-operate or not. Fighting an invading enemy required sacrifice from everyone. Associating Vicksburg's defense with the welfare of all those people in Mississippi and eastern Louisiana, Van Dorn took a momentous step in July during the very days that the Federal fleet rained shot and shell against his Vicksburg position. On July 4 he issued General Order Number 9 from Vicksburg. This order recognized the existence of total war around Vicksburg by declaring martial law in Mississippi and eastern Louisiana and promising swift disciplinary action to those civilians who violated any of its specifications. The offenses were the following: trading with or signaling to the enemy, refusing to receive Confederate money in payment of debts, charging exorbitant prices for "commodities of life," and "publication of any article in the newspaper in reference to movements of the troops."[12] The order also declared that no editorial article or copy should appear that was "calculated to impair confidence in any of the commanding officers."[13] Why Van Dorn issued this order at this particular time is difficult to perceive. It was certainly a violation of the principles of freedom of speech and press. Van Dorn's supporters, hard pressed to defend the general, recorded that the action of the commander was in pursuance of a policy of department commanders "to use the utmost vigilance to prevent the exportation of cotton" in hopes of eventually forcing England to come to the South's aid.[14] Despite this defense, the law was not popular, and many people criticized Van Dorn for taking such a step.

Van Dorn's proclamation of martial law, if not the first, was one of the best examples of similar desperate actions taken by Confederate commanders to control their military districts. President Davis had set a dangerous precedent early in the war when he asked for and received

12. Mobile *Advertiser and Register*, August 14, 1862, p. 1.
13. *Ibid.*, August 27, 1862, p. 1.
14. *A Soldier's Honor*, p. 100.

from Congress the power to suspend the writ of habeas corpus to better control the citizenry and prevent them from interfering in military affairs. Van Dorn's action came during the first of three different periods in which the President exercised this unusual power.

In late June Governor Thomas Overton Moore of Louisiana, recognizing the problems created by the presence of Federal troops in his state, had anticipated Van Dorn's proclamation with one of his own. He declared "a state of public war" which affected all citizens of Louisiana.[15] His regulations called for "absolute non-intercourse" with the enemy. In concluding his lengthy proclamation he included a list of regulations that greatly limited the freedom of the people of the state. Moore and other Southern leaders saw where they thought they needed controls, and they acted with what they considered to be a positive remedy. Before the summer of 1862 had passed, at least two other Confederate officers besides Van Dorn had followed this precedent of drastic action to curtail civilian interference in military operations—General Hindman in Arkansas and General Bragg in Tennessee.

Continued usurpation of powers by field commanders finally forced the Confederate Congress to inquire into a need for legislation to restrain the authority of military officers, and it was Van Dorn's example that provided the hottest topic of discussion among the Congressmen.[16] A representative from Louisiana stated that he was sure that Van Dorn had no intention of doing wrong but warned that he was setting a dangerous precedent. Another representative from Louisiana, a critic of the general, stated that he cared not who "promulged such atrocious sentiments," it was time for people to take a stand against this "tyranny."[17]

An admirer of Van Dorn among the Congressmen pointed out that the general was hard-pressed by the enemy from the north and the south and that desperate measures were necessary to defend Vicksburg. It was hardly possible, he said, for a man in such a predicament to see whether his course were sanctioned by law. Another representative defended Van Dorn, saying that these criticisms "did a gallant officer . . .

15. *Official Records Army*, XV, 505.

16. For Congressional reactions to martial law as it concerned the writ of habeas corpus, *see* Wilfred B. Yearns, *The Confederate Congress*, pp. 150–161. Professor Yearns does not deal with Van Dorn in any detail.

17. Proceedings of the First Confederate Congress, Second Session, p. 243.

and as pure a patriot as breathes, rank injustice by accusing him of power usurpation to satisfy his own personal egotism."[18]

Outside the Confederate Congress, the debates over Van Dorn's martial law decree ranged far and wide. Across the Mississippi River, an old foe was especially condemnatory of the seizure of power. With bitterness General Pike wrote:

> Neither generals nor their provost-marshals have any power to make, alter, or modify laws, either military or civil; nor can they declare what shall be crimes, either military or civil or establish any tribunal to punish what they may declare.[19]

In this letter Pike singled out his old enemy of the Arkansas campaign as the chief offender. Pike still recalled the frontier days when assumption of power by the military had resulted in tragedy and confusion in Indian negotiations.

Several newspapers, including the important Mobile papers, were outspoken in their denunciation of Van Dorn's seizure of power. This action by the department commander greatly curtailed their own activities in the war zones where they had special correspondents traveling with the armies in the field, and they lashed out against undue military authority. Even the Vicksburg *Whig*, though caught in the midst of the struggle for survival, was adamant in its opposition:

> We see several of our exchanges are pretty severe upon General Van Dorn for shackling the press of this department. Although severe, we cannot say they are unjustly so, for his order regarding the press is without parallel in the Confederacy, and will ever remain a blemish upon his escutcheon . . . his assumption [of power is in] violation of the Constitution of the land.[20]

Whether Van Dorn accomplished what he desired by his decree or not is difficult to ascertain, but he did jeopardize a reputation already under a shadow. Few spoke out for him at this time, though later one of his unknown admirers tried to express what he felt to be the general's feelings:

> We will not admit that in time of peace the above sentiments [See Vicksburg *Whig* statement above] are true, but in time of war or invasion, with the peril of losing all freedom, not only of the press but of personal liberty and property, [is not] martial law right? If [a general] is heedless of discipline

18. *Ibid.*, p. 247.
19. *Official Records Army*, XIII, 900–901.
20. Quoted in *A Soldier's Honor*, p. 344.

and careless he will lose the esteem of the people and have the scorn of the public.[21]

From his other actions at Vicksburg it seems plausible to think that when he issued his proclamation of July 4, Van Dorn had the best interests of his department at heart. But he still appears to have been tactless in his use of power and in his assumption that he could handle a difficult situation with martial law.[22] The South, with its emphasis upon states' rights, was especially sensitive to centralized authority, and it was not unusual for generals and statesmen alike to discover this peculiarity at some expense.

Van Dorn's action in regard to civilians was consistent with his earlier actions concerning his own troops, however, for on June 29 he had spoken out harshly in a general order against military destruction of private property. "Injuries done will be assessed, and the regimental officers will be required to pay for it in proportion to the amount of their pay," he had warned.[23] He had failed in Arkansas partly because of a lack of discipline among the citizens of the state. He wanted nothing in his way in Mississippi. His main concern was to hold back the Northern invaders, and he worried little about the sentiments of the people.

The debate over the powers of commanding generals raged for several months both inside and outside Congress. Finally, in September, the Confederate Secretary of War announced abruptly from Richmond that martial law could be declared only by the President and that such martial law had not been declared in Mississippi. Forced to rescind his special orders, Van Dorn did so with misgivings, contending that he had acted only in the best interests of his country. Meanwhile a war still raged at Vicksburg, and this occupied most of the general's time and thought during the months of July and August.

Few battles in the history of American warfare show the persistency of attack and the tenacity of defense that one sees in the long series of sieges of the port of Vicksburg. Families lived on in the town amidst rubble and exploding shells, keeping wits together well enough to help

21. *Ibid.*, p. 345.
22. Earlier Van Dorn had lost favor with the citizens of Louisiana and the lower part of Mississippi by seizing guns and supplies belonging to the state of Louisiana. Thomas E. Adams to Earl Van Dorn, June 23, 1862, Manuscript Collection of the Confederate States of America, Library of Congress.
23. *Official Records Army*, XV, 1121.

reconstruct part of the damage and occasionally hurl taunts at the attackers. Among the citizens within the city, a Mrs. Gamble showed
unusual bravery. Ordered from the besieged port with the rest of her
sex, she refused to leave; she remained to administer aid to the sick and
the wounded until she was killed by a Federal shell fragment.

The Union attackers, meanwhile, continued their steady shelling of
the city, always hoping for a break so they might land troops and occupy
this place of such fierce resistance. During June and July they pounded
away at the Confederate defenses. Van Dorn did little to modify his
general strategy during this time. His was a simple operation in a complicated framework—just hang on and hope. Always it was defensive
warfare, with undying hopes that "cotton diplomacy" would eventually
bring in some allies. From across the river a Northern newspaper man
gave this interesting description of the defending city in July:

> We ... go down every day to the point opposite Vicksburg and look across
> at the deserted city, in which we see no change, no sign of life, except the
> strengthening of the rebel positions above and below the town by the throw-
> ing up of a few earthworks. Even this seems to be done by unseen hands,
> for somehow we never catch the rebels at the work, and all that we have
> seen of [their] army ... are the sentinels that pace slowly up and down the
> ramparts.[24]

Meanwhile, Federal plans and operations underwent change after
change in attempts to dislodge the defenders. When their small naval
force first moved up the Mississippi River from New Orleans in mid-
May, it was the hope of the commander of the Department of the Gulf,
Major General Benjamin F. Butler, to attack and destroy Vicksburg
as soon as possible. General Williams was to "occupy or land and aid
in taking any point where resistance may be offered," and it seems
certain that Williams intended eventually to occupy the city.[25] Butler
saw that the fall of Vicksburg would probably open the river to the
Federals all the way from New Orleans to the Ohio. Certainly a combined army and navy attack from his own command would break the
city's defense.

Farragut shared this optimism at first, but arriving in sight of Vicks-

24. An article from the Chicago *Tribune* quoted in the Mobile *Advertiser and Register*, July 26, 1862, p. 1.
25. *Official Records Army*, XV, 423.

burg and noting the well-organized plan of defense, he modified his views. As early as May 22, 1862, he wrote that both he and General Williams believed that there was little to be gained in attacking the city solely from the river for the Confederate guns on the heights above were "so elevated" that they would be little affected by Federal fire. Farragut then determined to blockade the city and harass it with fire until the Federal army in central Mississippi could approach from the land side and join the attack. Farragut had the right idea, but it would take many months to bring into action all the forces necessary for such an operation.

Farragut's river siege accomplished little for the Northern forces in late May and early June except to tie up many of their gunboats. Meanwhile, in Washington, President Lincoln's Secretary of the Navy, Gideon Welles, looked at a map of Vicksburg and came up with an interesting new idea on how to conquer the city. Across the river from Vicksburg was a narrow peninsula that jutted out toward the city. Why not, reasoned Welles, divert the river across this neck of land by digging a ditch four or five feet deep across the peninsula? This just might change the course of the river, diverting it through the peninsula thus leaving Vicksburg high and dry five miles from the river. Northern vessels could then pass through the new channel, move freely up and down the Mississippi, and completely bypass an isolated Vicksburg.

A shortage of transports delayed General Williams on his return up the river, he did not arrive in Vicksburg until June 25. He then sent out armed parties to the neighboring plantations and gathered between eleven and twelve hundred Negro workers to do the digging. On June 27 his work crew broke ground. As work on the canal progressed during the first part of July, the Federal fleet contented itself with firing only a few shells a day at the defending garrison. This gave Van Dorn an important respite that he needed to put some finishing touches on his own defense position.

From the beginning of work on the canal, many people were skeptical over the possibilities of its success.[26] Confederate sources reported

26. Early in the history of this region a boundary dispute between Louisiana and Mississippi had produced the first attempt to dig such a canal across the peninsula. A boundary settlement had halted work on that canal attempt before its completion.

optimistically that a canal could not "be made effectual in changing the course of the river before fall," if at all.[27] A reporter from a Chicago paper feared failure for the project. "Let not too much be expected from it," he warned.[28]

This pessimism over the chances of success in this grandiose project soon proved to be well founded. Northern engineers admitted that they had not anticipated such a difficult situation. The soil was hard clay, and it was necessary to dig down ten feet to get to sand. Sand had to be reached if the canal were to be a success, for the river's current would not wash the clay. By July 12, the ditch was deep enough all across the peninsula so that a trickle of water ran through, but success quickly turned to failure when the Federal engineers realized that the river was dropping rather than rising as expected. Work continued for a short time longer with less enthusiasm than before. In the meantime, the Federals resumed their heavy bombardment of the city as if in disgust over their canal failure. The engineers finally abandoned the canal project when they decided that the ditch would have to be thirty-five to forty feet deep to be really effective. This depth would require two months or more of steady digging.

June 1862 ended, and July began to the roar of Federal guns. Vicksburg gave vivid testimony to the heavy bombardment and the enemy blockade. Toppled houses, crumbled chimneys, cracked roofs, broken trees, the ground torn by bursting shells—all were evidence of the increasing accuracy of the Federal gun crews. A remarkable people had defended their city well, though, and many writers took note of their courage. "Traverse its [Vicksburg's] deserted streets," wrote a man from Jackson, Mississippi,

enter the sacred precincts of its churches; roam, saddened and sick at heart through its lovely and neglected gardens; seek admittance for trade or curiosity to its closed hotels, stores, and court-rooms, and you will see of what a brave and virtuous people are capable when inspired by the noblest sentiment of humanity and true patriotism.[29]

But flesh and blood endure only so much. Days passed. Among the weary defenders hope was failing, and the city's worried commander

27. Vicksburg *Mississippian*, July 9, 1862, p. 1.
28. Chicago *Times*, quoted in Mobile *Advertiser and Register*, July 30, 1862, p. 2.
29. Quoted in Richmond *Dispatch*, July 16, 1862, p. 1.

realized that the siege must be broken soon or victory would elude his grasp. To whom could he turn for help? Bragg was still at Tupelo, but already he was making bigger plans. He would be unwilling to risk any of his force toward Vicksburg at this time. Bragg's eyes were toward Chattanooga and a possible move to Kentucky. Van Dorn would have to seek help elsewhere.

With no aid from the ground forces in the West in sight, Van Dorn turned to the Confederate Navy for assistance. Before arriving at Vicksburg, he had realized the need to counterattack the Federal fleet with vessels of his own. From President Davis he had requested such aid. The President's reply explained the paucity of available Southern ships, but he did promise the use on the Mississippi of an ironclad ram, the *Arkansas*, which was then at Yazoo City, Mississippi, undergoing a complete overhaul.

To the casual observer the *Arkansas* was no prize. She was actually an old river vessel that had been converted into an ironclad. She was big—eighty feet in length with a thirty-foot beam. Her power was furnished by two low-pressure, reconditioned engines with propellers seven feet in diameter which operated independently. She was protected by an armor of railroad iron, well greased and "set at an angle and backed by several feet of heavy timber."[30] Rumor had it that she also possessed a steam hose apparatus to repel boarders; but if this were true, it was a novelty first introduced into naval warfare by her captain. Construction on this strange-looking vessel had begun in the spring in Memphis; but before the finishing touches could be applied, she had been moved first to Greenwood, Mississippi, and finally to Yazoo City.

Despite her limitations, the *Arkansas* was a ray of hope to the imaginative commander of Vicksburg's beleaguered garrison. From the moment he heard of her presence at Yazoo City, he had been anxious to bring the vessel into active service in the Mississippi River near Vicksburg. On June 24 a messenger was dispatched from his headquarters to Lieutenant Isaac Brown, the ram's commander, suggesting that the vessel be brought out of her hiding place and driven past the Federal squadron north of Vicksburg. Van Dorn hoped that this single ironclad vessel would give him a weapon he needed to force the enemy to give up the siege.

30. S. B. Coleman, "A. July Morning with the Rebel Ram 'Arkansas,' " War Papers of the Michigan Commandry, p. 6.

Getting the *Arkansas* into action required more than just a message from a department commander, however. Early in June, Lieutenant Brown had described part of his predicament. "[W]ith all our efforts," he wrote, "we cannot yet raise steam or use the engines."[31] Two weeks later he was no more optimistic. The engines were working, sporadically, but the vessel's armament was not ready, and the lieutenant was having trouble finding a crew. When General Van Dorn expressed his disgust at the delay, Lieutenant Brown replied indignantly on June 25: "I regret to find that by implication it is thought I would prefer burning the *Arkansas* in Yazoo River to hurling the vessel against the enemy."[32] Brown then requested a delay.

When Lieutenant Brown again complained of difficulties in getting a crew, Van Dorn ordered 126 men from General Jeff Thompson's command to that vessel. Brown still delayed. Armament problems, wheezing old engines, and ill-disciplined troops combined to make his prospects for an early appearance into the Mississippi very dismal. So Brown worked on his ram in his isolated haven up the Yazoo, and Van Dorn's hopes for using the vessel against Farragut's fleet faded.

While men worked furiously to ready the ironclad for action, a new spirit seemed suddenly to possess the Vicksburg defenders. Confederate batteries on the bluffs above the river began to take heavy tolls among the Federals in savage artillery duels. Along the river banks patrols also showed their mettle by continually fighting off Union reconnaissance parties that landed in the swamps below the city. In this latter action, Van Dorn exhibited his own knowledge of guerrilla tactics by using small units to harass the enemy continually and thus allow his gun crews on the hills to move their big weapons from position to position.

Van Dorn seemed happy in the midst of constant danger at Vicksburg. In late July 1862, he wrote to his wife: "We are bombarded every day. Sometimes it is grand, we all take it coolly. . . . Have gotten used to it."[33]

It was all rather exhilarating to him. One day during one of the heavy attacks, he, General Lovell, and General Breckinridge ventured "to amuse themselves" by manning the guns at one post in a private duel

31. *Official Records Army*, XV, 751–752.
32. *Ibid.*, p. 765.
33. *A Soldier's Honor*, p. 309.

with an enemy gunboat. Shot and shell rained all about them when the enemy learned of "the presence of distinguished visitors," but fortunately none of the generals were injured in this foolhardy demonstration.[34]

July 15 was a red-letter day for the defending Confederate garrison at Vicksburg. Well before dawn the *Arkansas* finally began steaming down the Yazoo River toward the Mississippi. Thirty-seven Federal vessels of varied sorts, including some recent arrivals from Memphis, lay in the Mississippi within sight of Vicksburg as Lieutenant Brown guided his ram toward Farragut's fleet. Under orders from Van Dorn to attack and destroy as many of these vessels as possible, Brown planned to slip into the Mississippi River about daybreak and attack some of the vessels before their commanders could prepare a defense. With stronger and more reliable engines, Brown might have succeeded, but delays caused by faulty equipment slowed his progress long enough for Farragut to be warned of his presence while the ram was still struggling down the Yazoo.

Farragut, thinking the Confederates incapable of building a first-rate vessel, had rather foolishly allowed his own fleet to lie with low fires; so he had to send three small vessels up the Yazoo to meet the new threat. These vessels departed just at daybreak. They were the gunboat *Tyler*, the ironclad *Carondelet*, and the ram *Queen of the West*.

The crew of the *Tyler* spotted the *Arkansas* through the thick morning haze about six miles up the Yazoo. The *Arkansas* fired first, sending a shot from a light howitzer across the bow of the smaller vessel. The *Tyler* cleared for action and then responded to the challenge with heavy fire from her thirty-two and sixty-four pounders. The *Carondelet* and the *Queen* quickly got into the fight, but their firepower did little but bounce balls off the tough sides of the Rebel ram. Quickly the *Arkansas* took charge. The *Carondelet* ran ashore trying to escape and should have been forced to surrender except that the ironclad could not risk delay. The damaged *Queen of the West* escaped down the river. The *Tyler*, hardest hit of all, also retreated down the Yazoo River, hotly pursued by the victorious *Arkansas*. Unaware of the power of the *Arkansas*, some of the Federal officers aboard the other vessels above Vicksburg concluded from the closeness of the chase that the *Tyler* had actually captured the *Arkansas*.

34. Mobile *Advertiser and Register*, July 11, 1862, p. 1.

How mistaken these officers were! Brown's vessel was damaged, and her engines sputtered badly, but pushed by river tide and her faulty steam power, she proudly entered the Mississippi River. Seeing the fleet before him, Brown decided not to attack as originally planned but to seek the protective shelter of shore batteries. Of course this meant running through the entire Northern fleet stationed above the city. There was much excitement in the Federal vessels as he made his move. In a maze of smoke, shot, and shell, Brown pushed the battered ram into their midst. With their engine fires still too low to pursue, the Federal vessels fired as best they could and struggled to get up their steam. The *Brooklyn* and at least two other vessels did follow the ram, but the Confederates on shore opened fire from nine different batteries and discouraged further pursuit.

Meanwhile, the *Arkansas* steamed majestically toward Vicksburg harbor, and when her weird-looking profile limped into view of Vicksburg, she was a happy sight to the defenders looking down from the bluffs. The firing from the Federal fleet and the Confederate batteries blended their noise and the "earth rocked and trembled" from their explosions.[35] From the shore Van Dorn watched the ironclad come "gloriously through twelve or thirteen of the enemy's gunboats and sloops of war."[36] One of his men commented on the scene below: "We could see the monster in her grim and battered condition with numerous holes in her smokestack, made by shots from the enemy's guns. . . . Her crew was composed of the most daring despicable smoke-begrimed, looking set I ever beheld."[37] To Van Dorn it was "the most brilliant" achievement "ever recorded in naval annals."[38]

Damage to both the *Arkansas* and the Federal vessels was heavy. When the firing ceased, the ram lay stunned in a small cove under the cover of Confederate shore batteries. Van Dorn greeted the ram's arrival by taking a small boat out to the vessel. Upon boarding her, he witnessed the havoc and destruction the Federals had wrought upon her. Ten of her crew members were dead, and Lieutenant Brown was

35. Lieutenant L. D. Young, *Reminiscences of a Soldier of the Orphan Brigade*, p. 37.

36. Earl Van Dorn to Emily Miller, no date, found among the miscellaneous papers in the Van Dorn Collection, Montgomery, Alabama.

37. Young, *Reminiscences*, p. 38.

38. *Official Records Army*, XV, 16.

among the wounded. Van Dorn promptly ordered the vessel to remain nearby for the next few days until necessary repairs could be made.

The Mississippi fleet recovered rapidly from the confusion created by the sudden arrival of the enemy vessel. July 15 ended with a murderous barrage from the Federal gunboats upon both the city and the stranded *Arkansas*. The ram and the shore batteries both answered the attack, and firing continued all night. Much additional damage was recorded on both sides, but the *Arkansas* held on; her crude armor repelled the heaviest barrages the Federals could offer.

For more than a week the fighting was centered around the *Arkansas*. Time after time Farragut's gunboats attempted without success to eliminate their adversary by throwing a fifteen-inch shell onto her vulnerable deck. Despite her troublesome engines, the *Arkansas* continually shifted her position in the harbor; every move was covered by the mobile guns on the cliffs above. Infantry and Mississippi partisans waited anxiously in the marshes and woods below the city, poised for action if the Yankees attempted to board their ram.

By late July the affair at Vicksburg had definitely taken on the proportions of a stalemate with neither commander able to offer a sustained offensive. Attacker and defender alike felt the pressures of sustained battle, and both camps reported a shortage of ammunition. To Farragut it became obvious that Vicksburg could hold out much longer than he could. To break the siege he must have a co-operative land effort from the other side of the city. None appeared to be developing. Federal commanders at both New Orleans and Memphis refused to support him with such an attack. Meanwhile, overwork, scurvy, and malaria cut heavily into General Williams's force, incapacitating it for an invasion if an opening did appear. Even nature co-operated with the Confederates. The river was falling rapidly after a summer drought, and a vessel stranded in shallow water would serve as a perfect target for the sharpshooting Confederate shore batteries. Farragut decided to admit defeat and move away from the city.

At the suggestion of Lieutenant Colonel Alfred W. Ellet, commander of the *Queen of the West*, the Federal commanders decided to make one last desperate attempt to destroy the *Arkansas* in hopes that such a success would force the surrender of the Vicksburg garrison. The attempt was unco-ordinated, however, and a pitched battle at close quarters developed between the ironclad and two Northern vessels, the sturdy *Queen of the West* and the gunboat *Essex*. All participating vessels suffered severe damage; the *Arkansas* was hardest hit. A shot from the *Essex* killed seven of her crew and wounded six others, but the *Queen* dealt her the most telling blow of the engagement when her sharp prow collided into the broadside of the ram. The *Arkansas* never fully recovered from this blow though she continued to fight and successfully beat off her attackers.

Farragut decided it was futile to continue the siege. Orders were issued, and the Federal ships began to move. General Williams loaded his canal diggers aboard transports, and on July 24 the fleet under Farragut steamed back to New Orleans. On the same day the flotilla lying above the city departed for Memphis; the siege was lifted. Though Van Dorn had not defeated the enemy in a great battle, he had accomplished his first significant success in this war.

The fight at Vicksburg had been a long but courageous one by soldiers and civilians alike. Van Dorn's own evaluation of the victory is interesting, for he seemed to hit upon many of the ingredients that appeared so regularly for more than a year in the city as the Federals sought to break her domination of the Mississippi River. With a magnanimity not always apparent in the man, he wrote:

> The successful defense of Vicksburg is due to the unflinching valor of the cannoneers, who, unwearied by watchfulness, night and day stood by their guns . . . to the sleepless vigilance and undaunted courage of the troops, who lay at all hours in close supporting distance of every battery, ready to beat back the invader so soon as his footsteps should touch the shore; to the skillful location of scattered batteries, and last, but not least, to that great moral power—a high and patriotic resolve . . . that at every cost the enemy should be repelled.[39]

Van Dorn's personal courage had also been an important factor in the siege, and he must be commended for valiant and wise leadership. The Confederate Government took cognizance of this in a general order which stated that he deserved the thanks of his country for his gallant action. The men of Vicksburg, said the report, "have shown that bombardments of cities, if bravely resisted, achieve nothing for the enemy,

39. *Ibid.*

and only serve to unveil his malice and the hypocrisy of his pretended wish to restore the Union."[40]

Southern poet Paul H. Hayne also took note of Vicksburg's fortitudinous action by dedicating a poem "with respect and admiration to Major General Earl Van Dorn for the stand against the enemy."[41]

Though much of Van Dorn's success can be credited to the defensive position set up by General Smith before his arrival and by the lack of co-ordination in the Federal attack, the general did remove much of the stigma against his name by this defense. The departure of the Federal fleet also restored his own confidence, and he became his old flamboyant self. "I resolved to strike a blow before he had time to organize and mature a new scheme of assault," he wrote with a new enthusiasm after the Federal vessels had departed.[42] The question was where to strike? From Tangipahoa, Louisiana, General Daniel Ruggles reported that the enemy was entrenching at Baton Rouge and arming Negroes there. General Ruggles had been watching Baton Rouge before the departure of the Federals from Vicksburg, and he had earlier recommended a move against Baton Rouge and New Orleans. The last Federal vessel was hardly out of sight of Vicksburg when Van Dorn issued orders for an offensive toward Louisiana. "I want Baton Rouge and Port Hudson," he echoed General Ruggles, "giving me the mouth of the Red River."[43] On July 26 he selected General Breckinridge to take 5,000 men from the Vicksburg garrison and proceed by rail to Camp Moore just northeast of Baton Rouge.

Van Dorn should have contented himself with his successful stand at Vicksburg, for the Baton Rouge invasion went awry from its beginning. As he had done at Elkhorn, he considered only the military strategy and failed to give proper consideration to such vital factors as the weather, the terrain, the condition of his troops, and the inabilities of his subordinate commanders. By July 30 General Breckinridge was at Camp Moore, but with only 3,600 effective troops, including a brigade under

40. *Ibid.*, p. 19.

41. A copy of this dedication and the poem are found in the Van Dorn Collection, Montgomery, Alabama. The poem was written by Paul H. Hayne at Columbia, South Carolina, August 6, 1862.

42. *Official Records Army*, XV, 16.

43. *Ibid.*, LII, Pt. 2, 334.

General Ruggles that had been added to the original complement. In hospitals at camp hundreds of others lay too ill to be of service. These men had endured much at Vicksburg and had finally broken under increased pressures. They had suffered from the weather, from inadequate food, for lack of rest, and from polluted water. A long march and new exposure came too soon after the crises at Vicksburg.

When General Breckinridge discovered that his force was in such a deplorable state, he frantically wired to General Van Dorn asking the use of the *Arkansas* to support him in his attack. Actually the ram was in no condition to make such a move or fight a battle. Severely damaged in the last days of the Vicksburg fight and partially disabled from the *Queen of the West's* telling blow, the old ironclad was in need of major repairs. Captain (recently promoted) Brown was reluctant to allow her to leave the Vicksburg harbor in such a condition. It is said that Van Dorn himself ordered Brown to co-operate with Breckinridge and relieved the commander of the vessel when he refused. Brown, in his writings after the war, makes no mention of such an action, stating merely that he was forced from his command by illness. Whatever the reason, Brown relinquished the command to less-experienced Lieutenant Henry K. Stevens. With a new commander, an untrained crew, and engines in need of major repairs, the *Arkansas* departed from Vicksburg to assist in the attack on Baton Rouge.

With forces finally reduced to about 2,500 General Breckinridge made his attack against Baton Rouge on August 5. The garrison was under the command of General Williams, and many of the men had also served at Vicksburg. Both armies were unfit for battle though the men fought well under the circumstances. Losses were light on both sides; the major casualty was General Williams. The Southern army was forced from the field, and the spoils of victory belonged to the North. Van Dorn's abortive expedition had failed. Even the *Arkansas* could not save a deplorable situation. In fact, that vessel never arrived at Baton Rouge to participate in the battle. Before reaching her scheduled destination her starboard engine finally gave way. After a brief exchange of fire with the *Essex*, her crew destroyed the noble old craft to prevent capture.

Although the Baton Rouge expedition failed to occupy that city, the operation itself was not a complete failure for the Confederates. The Federal force was so reduced by battle casualties and sickness that

General Butler decided to evacuate the Baton Rouge area soon after the battle there. When he returned his force to New Orleans, General Breckinridge occupied nearby Port Hudson and closed the mouth of the Red River to the Federal fleet. Port Hudson remained in Confederate hands, a thorn in the side of the enemy, until its fall in the summer of 1863.

Summer 1862 had brought new challenges to Earl Van Dorn in a new type of command. He had responded with energy and enthusiasm, and he had shown some flashes of brilliance in his defense of a beleaguered city. He repeatedly demonstrated his rare courage before the enemy, and he offered counsel and encouragement that helped sustain the city's garrison. But always the dark star hovered overhead. Too often he acted without taking proper precautions, and his misuse of Breckinridge and the *Arkansas* at Baton Rouge is inexcusable. Even in the moments of his greatest achievements, there was frustration. As was so often the cause with Van Dorn, much of his frustration in command in 1862 related directly to his own personality. As the glory and praise he so diligently sought eluded him, he became morose and defensive. In moments of stress and change his pride and his temper showed, often bringing him into conflict with his fellow officers. Every change in assignment seemed to be a threat to his own position. Such was the case in the summer of 1862.

After the evacuation of Corinth, Van Dorn had willingly relinquished his command of the Army of the West for the independent Vicksburg assignment. In June, however, in a realistic reorganization, General Bragg realigned his Western command into one large department which included Mississippi, Alabama, and part of Georgia. In this shuffle Van Dorn was made commander of the newly created District of Mississippi, a district he felt was not commensurate to his rank. Again the threat was there. "This department [is] now reduced to [a] district," he complained directly to President Davis. "I have been ever thus trammeled and cannot help but feel it."[44]

President Davis soothed his ruffled feelings: "Your gallantry has fulfilled my expectations," he confided in reply. "Accept my thanks and congratulations for what has been achieved. . . . The junction of the departments arose from no want of confidence, but to render the

44. *Ibid.*, p. 328.

whole force most available to the paramount object—the defense of our country."[45] Van Dorn pursued the matter no further for new concerns confronted the generals in the West as plans for an offensive took shape. Suddenly all attention focused on General Braxton Bragg.

July 1862 found the Confederate force in Mississippi divided into four units and stationed in three strategic areas. At Tupelo were Hardee's Army of the Mississippi and Price's Army of the West— 68,000 troops; at Vicksburg Van Dorn had 14,000; and Brigadier General John H. Forney had 9,000 additional troops at Mobile, Alabama. There was also a force of 3,000 troops at Chattanooga under Major General John P. McCown. In a separate command in East Tennessee, General Kirby Smith had about 18,000 troops.

The largest Union army ever organized in the West had been broken up by its commander, General Halleck, and dispatched piecemeal to certain key areas in Tennessee and Mississippi to serve as defensive units until the Northern high command could plan a new offensive. It was the movement of one of these Federal units under General Don Carlos Buell that spurred Bragg into action. Aware of the Union sentiment in East Tennessee, President Lincoln had directed Halleck to send Buell into that region in hopes of relieving Northern sympathizers of the pressures created by Confederate occupation. Buell advanced slowly and deliberately toward Chattanooga with continual delays as the troops took time to repair the Memphis and Charleston Railroad. In mid-July this Federal force threatened Chattanooga.

General McCown brought news to General Bragg of this threat. Shocked into action, Bragg decided to move a large part of his own army to Chattanooga and intercept Buell. When a telegram from General Smith confirmed McCown's report, Bragg departed from Mississippi on July 24 leaving Van Dorn at Vicksburg and Price at Tupelo with a combined force of about 30,000. Before his departure Bragg ordered Van Dorn to "do all things deemed needful without awaiting instructions."[46] He and Price were to operate separately, but they were to "consult freely" and to co-operate when possible. Their prime mission was to defend the section of the Mississippi River still in Confederate hands and to prevent the Federal troops remaining in Mississippi from following General Bragg on his march across Tennessee.

45. *Ibid.*, XV, 778.
46. *Ibid.*, XVII, Pt. 2, 656.

From the beginning of this new action, General Bragg appears to have been a bit apprehensive of his general at Vicksburg. Bragg should have given the Mississippian complete authority in the state to make command assignments clear, but he may have split the authority between Price and Van Dorn deliberately to limit the latitude of Van Dorn. During his march through Tennessee and into Kentucky it was Price to whom Bragg continually turned, and it was always with less enthusiasm that he shared his plans with Van Dorn. Once he even warned Price not to "depend much on Van Dorn; he has his hands full."[47] Bragg was more of a realist than Van Dorn, and this fact may well have concerned Bragg. Well he might be concerned, for even as he moved against Buell, Van Dorn continued to have his dreams of grand strategy. At times it was New Orleans that was his objective—more often it was a march through western Tennessee into Kentucky and Ohio that occupied his mind.

So in Mississippi there was always the conflict in command with the higher-ranking Van Dorn having no clear-cut authority over Price. As long as Price received his orders directly from Bragg, Van Dorn was hamstrung. The situation was a trying one, and the cordiality and co-operation that had marked their earlier efforts disappeared in August and early September as each tried to persuade the other of the feasibility of his own plan. Price, holding hopes of disposing General Rosecrans's force at Corinth as a first step toward eventually joining Bragg, urged Van Dorn later in July to join with him in a concerted move toward Grand Junction "or some point on or near the Tennessee line."[48] Van Dorn, still occupied with his Baton Rouge fiasco, argued against the action. He preferred to march the "combined armies through western Tennessee toward Paducah [Kentucky], and thence wherever circumstances may dictate."[49]

Throughout August Van Dorn and Price went their separate ways. The telegraph lines joining the two commands carried numerous proposals for joint action, but to no avail. General Bragg did little to clear-up the discord between his two major generals in Mississippi. His own plans were just not firm enough to offer concrete suggestions to either officer. On August 10 he confided to Kirby Smith what he

47. *Ibid.*, p. 682.
48. *Ibid.*, p. 665.
49. *Ibid.*, p. 687.

hoped would be the ultimate action in the West: "Van Dorn and Price will advance simultaneously with us from Mississippi or West Tennessee, and I trust we may all unite in Ohio."[50]

But to Van Dorn, Bragg was less decisive:

I cannot give you specific instructions, as circumstances and military conditions in your front may vary materially from day to day. To move your available force to Holly Springs by railroad, thence into West Tennessee, co-operating with General Price . . . or to move to Tupelo by rail and join Price, are suggestions only. Positive instructions, except to strike at the most assailable point, cannot be given when so little is known and when circumstances may change daily.[51]

As though to complicate the picture even more, Bragg directed Van Dorn to act in conjunction with General Price. From this point on Bragg's interest centered more and more on his own front, and he left the two generals on their own. "Move as fast as practicable," was his vague order to Van Dorn on August 25.[52]

Meanwhile, in Mississippi Price and Van Dorn each pressed his own plan. "A brilliant field is before us yet," the Mississippian wrote on August 25.[53] Price received this sort of news with little enthusiasm always countering with the proposal that the combined forces should first attack Corinth. Van Dorn approved of the basic idea of Price's plans but quickly replied that he was not yet ready for such an offensive. Finally he did speak of the possibilities of such an action about the middle of September.

The Missourian was displeased at thoughts of waiting so long. Word from General Bragg on September 2 was that Buell was retreating full-scale toward Nashville. "Watch Rosecrans and prevent a junction," warned Bragg.[54] Price took this to mean he must delay no longer. Again he solicited Van Dorn's aid requesting a junction of their troops immediately. The reply was again disappointing. It would be September 12 at the earliest before the Mississippian could accommodate him.

Actually Van Dorn still was unconvinced of the need for an attack against Corinth. His main concern was to keep the large Federal forces in Tennessee and Mississippi apart. "Let us join between the forces of

50. *Ibid.*, XVI, Pt. 2, 749.
51. *Ibid.*, XVII, Pt. 2, 676.
52. *Ibid.*, p. 897.
53. *Ibid.*
54. *Ibid.*, p. 690.

the enemy," he proposed to Price, "somewhere between Grand Junction and Corinth; then bearing off toward his line of supplies we will compel him to fly . . . without being able to receive forces of Sherman and Grant."[55] Meanwhile, he was also in direct contact with Richmond over the question of rank. If he could order Price as he pleased, he could move as he pleased. "I ought to have command of the movements of Price," he informed the Secretary of War.[56] Since Bragg was out of reach, would the Secretary grant him such authority?

The Secretary hesitated: "I suppose these matters would be regulated by General Bragg," he wrote in an endorsement of Van Dorn's message to President Davis. "[I] . . . feel some hesitation in giving directions which might conflict with his plans."[57]

Davis was also unwilling to intervene. "The rank of Van Dorn secures to him the command of all the troops with whom he will be operating," he wrote evasively. But Van Dorn and Price were not operating together. Did this not leave Van Dorn where he started?

Two days later Davis tried to clarify his orders. He wrote to Van Dorn: "The troops must co-operate, and can only do so by having one head. Your rank makes you the commander." Then as an afterthought, he equivocated by adding: "and such I supposed were the instructions of General Bragg given in his orders to you."[58]

Van Dorn's continued reluctance to join him so disgusted Price that he decided to disregard the Mississippian's suggestions and move his own force as he was capable. "I was very anxious to place myself and my army under your command, so that we might together liberate West Tennessee, and regain control of the Mississippi," he wrote Van Dorn on September 9. "General Bragg has, however, just ordered me to 'move rapidly for Nashville,' " he added decisively.[59] With no further ado, Price moved alone.

Price's move was toward Iuka, Mississippi, a village recently occupied by a small part of General Rosecrans's army. Rosecrans was at Corinth with the rest of his force. Price occupied Iuka against little resistance on September 14. Three days later he received another dispatch from Bragg urging him to hasten his advance into Tennessee.

55. *Ibid.*, Pt. 2, 691–692.
56. *Ibid.*, p. 697.
57. *Ibid.*, pp. 697–698.
58. *Ibid.*, p. 700.
59. *Ibid.*, p. 698.

Realizing that the major force blocking such an advance was Rose-crans's army, he promptly sent another dispatch to Van Dorn again suggesting a co-operative attack upon Rosecrans at Corinth from a point north of the city. Van Dorn finally agreed to co-operate. He could not move alone; he must join Price. He would then be in command, and after Rosecrans's defeat he would decide the next move. He agreed to meet Price at Pocahontas, Tennessee, to prepare for the attack.

Price's preparations for a union with Van Dorn were nearly completed when General Grant, often the spoiler of schemes, suddenly intervened and changed the entire situation. From his headquarters at Bolivar, Grant decided that the time had come to attack the Confederates before Van Dorn and Price would effect a union against him. For the moment Bragg was out of the picture, and Grant watched Van Dorn's move with interest. Satisfied that the Confederate general would not reach Corinth for four days, he garrisoned that town with only a token force; and then he ordered Generals Rosecrans and E. O. C. Ord to move against Price at Iuka. On September 19 Rosecrans's advance force drove in Price's pickets on the outskirts of the village.

Joined by General Ord, who attacked Iuka from another direction, Rosecrans soon had Price's troops fighting desperately to hold their position. Finally after a bloody battle in the streets of the town, the Federals forced the Confederates out of the town into a retreat toward Baldwin. At Baldwin the Missourian reorganized his army and moved on to Ripley where he finally joined Van Dorn on September 28. General Grant had helped a "perplexed general ready a decision."[60] Price and Van Dorn could vacillate no longer.

During this battle Van Dorn had been unaware of Price's exact location and of Grant's attack. Advancing to Davis's Mill, a few miles from Grand Junction, Tennessee, he hoped to meet Price there. On September 20, pending the arrival of his supply trains, he marched his troops to within seven miles of Bolivar, driving several brigades of the enemy back into the city. Then he returned to Ripley to await Price.

As Van Dorn waited his mind was on Corinth, a fortress he knew well because of his recent service there. He also knew the Federal commander, General William S. Rosecrans, for the two men had been graduated from West Point in the same class.[61] Corinth had finally

60. Williams, *Lincoln Finds a General*, IV, 71.
61. General Rosecrans commanded the Third Division of Grant's District of Western Tennessee at this time.

become a reality to him, a place to conquer before he could make his larger move, a condition "precedent to the accomplishment of anything of importance in West Tennessee."[62] He could have captured Memphis with ease but with no important military result, for he could never have held it against naval forces on one side and land forces on the other. He could have attacked Bolivar, but that would expose his own lines to the Corinth garrison. Corinth had finally become the salient point.

The problem of command had also been cleared up. On September 25 Bragg finally made his communications a bit more precise: "We have driven and drawn the enemy clear back to the Ohio," he reported. "Push your columns to our support, and arouse the people to re-enforce us. . . . Trusting to your energy and zeal we shall confidently expect a diversion in our favor against the overwhelming force now concentrating in our front."[63] Even the War Department took a stand: "Assume forthwith the command of all the troops left in Mississippi, including General Price's column," the orders were late, but they were specific.[64]

Van Dorn had his mandate. The move was toward Corinth. He was on his own again with another large but better-disciplined army. He would have his second chance.

62. *Official Records Army*, XVII, Pt. 1, 453.
63. *Ibid.*, Pt. 2, 713.
64. *Ibid.*, p. 715.

CHAPTER TEN

Van Dorn Attacks Rosecrans

GENERAL Earl Van Dorn hastily surveyed his new army at Ripley. His mind was already made up. He must attack the Federals. His troop strength was about 22,000, the largest force he had ever commanded, and he may well have been a bit reckless in his hopes for its success. General William Rosecrans was at Corinth with about 15,000 Union troops, but this was misleading for the Federal general could quickly draw in 8,000 additional defenders from his nearby outposts. Federal forces at Bolivar and Jackson also represented potential reinforcements. Van Dorn could not delay. He would keep the Yankees off-balance by masking his own moves, but he must move. "The fact of junction [at Ripley] could not be long concealed from the enemy," he said later in defense of his action. His attention focused on Corinth.

Corinth's importance as a railroad center and the concentration of much of Rosecrans's army there were indeed grounds for more than casual Confederate interest. Here the Memphis and Charleston Railroad, running east and west, crossed the Mobile and Ohio railroad, running north and south. The Mississippi Central from Jackson, Tennessee, to Jackson, Mississippi, ran only a few miles to the west. Highways from Iuka, Jacinto, Tupelo, Ripley, Pocahontas, and Kossuth entered the town. With Rosecrans in control of Corinth, any movement of Van Dorn's army could be closely watched and impeded at will. To the Confederate commander it seemed clear that if he could successfully attack Corinth, he could drive the Federals deep into Mississippi. Then the Federals would have to surrender. With Corinth in Confederate hands and Rosecrans's army dispersed, Van Dorn could then attack Jackson. These conquests would help him regain Western

Tennessee and would force Grant to turn his attention away from Bragg's army.

Despite many factors that worked against his chances for success, Van Dorn had reasons for being optimistic. He was familiar with the town, having spent several weeks there with General Beauregard's army earlier in the year. While there he had acquainted himself with the surrounding countryside by personal reconnaissance, by studying maps, and by interrogating citizens who lived in the vicinity. The road by which part of his troops advanced for the attack upon the city had actually been laid out and cut earlier that year under his "personal superintendence."[1] In addition to this first-hand knowledge of the Federal stronghold, he also had a spy inside the city. Though she later proved ineffective, Van Dorn still thought of her as an added asset in September and October.[2] Van Dorn also had a good army, weak in discipline and training compared with the armies in the East, but much better than the force he led against General Curtis. Thus he decided to risk one of the most hazardous of military maneuvers, a frontal attack, against his old classmate. This time he would not flank the enemy as he had done at Pea Ridge. By sheer numbers and audacity he would attempt to overpower Rosecrans and the Corinth garrison. Most of his troops were veterans of actions at Pea Ridge, Shiloh, or earlier battles in the West, and they were expected to give good account of themselves under any circumstances.

Price joined Van Dorn on September 28 and confirmed the attack plans with the Missourian. On the same day Van Dorn directed his officers and men to prepare a three day supply of cooked rations and be ready to march at a moment's notice. At the same time he ordered his chief commissary to order "400,000 rations of breadstuffs and salt and 92,000 rations of salt meat" in addition to "1,000 head of beef cattle."[3] The Confederates would move immediately, feinting toward Tennessee until the last possible moment. Van Dorn would then cut back sharply toward Mississippi, finally striking Corinth from the north-

1. *Official Records Army*, XVII, Pt. 1, 435.
2. The information provided by a Burton woman proved to be a hindrance rather than a help, for most of her data was incorrect. Probably correct at the time she released the information to her Confederate colleagues, the data was outdated by constant Federal activity within the city.
3. *Official Records Army*, XVII Pt. 1, 443.

west. This would keep Grant guessing and prevent him from concentrating his forces.

On September 29, without informing his subordinate commanders of the exact nature of his plans, Van Dorn marched his troops from Ripley to Metamora, a little village just south of Pocahontas. "I have made union with General Price and am now before Corinth," he wrote eagerly. "Expect to take Corinth; [will] move division to [Chewalla] . . . in the morning to feel position and strength, and to cut, with cavalry, the road to Jackson, Tenn."[4]

Though Van Dorn was enthusiastic about his chances, there were some signs of dissension in his command. One of Price's colonels threatened to leave the Missourians if they were placed under the Mississippian. General Breckenridge was happy over a transfer to Chattanooga. But the sharpest indictment of his leadership came from his own commanding officer, General Bragg, who expressed his fears in a letter to the Confederate President in late September. Bragg was reacting to Van Dorn's vacillation in Mississippi when he wrote:

I regret to add that there has been a want of cordial co-operation on the part of Genl Van Dorn since his department was merged in mine. . . . The general is most true to our cause and gallant to a fault, but he is self willed, rather weak minded and totally deficient in organization and system. He never knows the state of his command, and wields it only in fragments.[5]

Others were not so critical. Even as Bragg poured out his feelings, South Carolina expressed her disappointment that he had not been transferred there to assume command of that state's defenses.

The dusty roads in northern Mississippi and southern Tennessee and the scarcity of water along their route of march brought much discomfort to the advancing Confederates. But having departed from Ripley in fine spirits, well-equipped, and well-fed, these men were still in fair condition when they arrived in Metamora. Here Van Dorn continued his attempt to mask his final objective from the enemy by dispatching cavalry units toward both Bolivar and Corinth. This maneuver evidently succeeded in deceiving both Generals Grant and Rosecrans. Grant refused to concentrate his troops in the face of this

---

4. *Ibid.*, Pt. 2, 717.

5. Original in the Braxton Bragg collection at West Point; quoted in Grady McWhiney, "Controversy in Kentucky: Braxton Bragg's Campaign of 1862," *Civil War History*, VI, 23.

uncertainty lest he invite an attack upon his outposts and his weaker units. It was not until Tuesday, September 30, that he suspected Van Dorn's objective, and then he so notified Rosecrans. Still he was not sure enough of the Confederate plans to commit himself. Instead of assembling a large defense force at Corinth, he waited.

At Corinth, Rosecrans also watched the Confederates and wondered at their destination. On September 21 he had written General Grant of the confidence he held in his own command to defend or attack if necessary:

If you can let me know that there is a good opportunity to cross the railroad and march on to Holly Springs to cut off the forces of Buck Van Dorn I will be in readiness to take everything. If we could get them across the Hatchie they would be clean up the spout.[6]

On October 1, he was not quite so cocksure of his army or of himself. Van Dorn's move seems to have confused him. In his report of the battle he wrote:

Rumors that the attack was to take the direction of Jackson or Bolivar via Bethel were so rife, and the fortifications of Corinth were so well known to the rebels, that I had hopes they would undertake to mask me, and, passing north, give me an opportunity to beat the masking force and cut off their retreat.[7]

As late as the early morning of the battle, the Federal commander at Corinth was still a bit confused as to Van Dorn's move. He reported that one of his sources of information had satisfied him that Van Dorn's forces intended "to make their main move on Bolivar."[8]

As the enemy sat undecided, awaiting a definite indication of Van Dorn's direction of attack, the Confederate commander suddenly turned his main force toward Corinth and moved rapidly in that direction. Though still fooled by the enemy maneuvering, Rosecrans, inside Corinth, gave evidence of the natural ability that had placed him near the top of his West Point class by adapting his position to the advance whatever course it might take. He reinforced his patrols near Chewalla and called in several of his troop units from villages near the town. Meanwhile, Van Dorn rode eagerly to battle without conducting a proper reconnaissance.

6. *Official Records Army*, XVII, Pt. 1, 71.
7. *Ibid.*, p. 166.
8. *Ibid.*, p. 160.

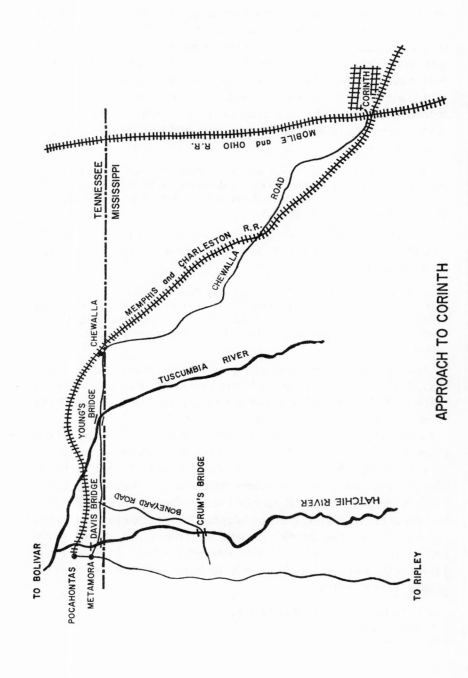

APPROACH TO CORINTH

The road between Pocahontas and Corinth is intersected at points about five miles apart by two rivers, the Hatchie and the Tuscumbia. Early Thursday morning at the Hatchie, Van Dorn discovered his poor reconnaissance. To deter him from Corinth and to delay his march, Federal patrols had torn up the bridge that had spanned the stream. Van Dorn fretted while General Mansfield Lovell's lead troops repaired the damage. The bridge was repaired without incident, but they had lost valuable time. The Confederates resumed their march in the heat of the day with much grumbling and complaining in the ranks.

Then came another delay. At the Tuscumbia River, the advance scouts discovered that Young's Bridge was also in a state of disrepair. Again the engineers and the advance troops went to work. A hot, tiring army was stretched out for several miles between the two rivers; its irritated commander was impatient with the efforts of his men and the delay. Thursday afternoon passed, and some of the troops near the Hatchie amused themselves by picking muscadines; others nearer the Tuscumbia were not so fortunate. As the bridge crew worked to repair the damage, Federal pickets came out and fired across the stream; a hot skirmish was initiated. Though the Confederates routed the enemy force, the skirmish temporarily halted work on the bridge and further upset Van Dorn's timetable of operations. There could be little hope for his two primary tactical obsessions, speed and surprise, as the final attack was made.

In Corinth, General Rosecrans listened to reports from his outposts, but still suspecting that the Butternuts would turn and move on Bolivar, he initiated no further offensive.

As repairmen worked feverishly to repair Young's Bridge, Van Dorn called a conference of his ranking officers. There for the first time he informed them of his plans for the Corinth attack. Earlier in the day he had consulted a citizen guide about road changes since the spring. From the information he received and from his own knowledge of the countryside, he sketched a map of the region in and around Corinth. He used this sketch to describe his plan of action to his officers.

Several of the officers were quite surprised when they learned that their chief planned a frontal attack against the enemy fortifications. One of the brigade commanders, General John Bowen, was especially resentful. He said that only the evening before Van Dorn had implied that he would not sacrifice his men against the Corinth position. "I endeavored to elicit from [Van Dorn and Price] . . . what was the point to be attacked. General Van Dorn replied in substance that he intended to maneuver the enemy out of Memphis, Jackson, Bolivar, and Corinth."[9] The impression left on the mind of some of the officers at the conference was that they would fight the Federals "in the open field."

Bowen was also critical of his chief's method of explaining the operation. He later described the sketch as a crude one on a piece of letter paper drawn to no particular scale, completely inadequate for the ordinary movements of an army. Generals Price and Dabney Maury said that Van Dorn had one of the best maps of Corinth available, but neither could explain his use of the drawing. Other officers were as critical of their chief as the division commanders. Just as at Pea Ridge Van Dorn would go into battle with his ranking officers uninformed and resentful. This was hardly the mood of command to bring success on the battlefield.

Late on Thursday, October 2, the Confederates moved across the repaired bridge and marched to Chewalla. There they bivouacked for the night only a short distance from Rosecrans's guns. As the men slept, their commanders met again to make final preparations for the attack. Meanwhile, behind the Union lines, Rosecrans learned definitely of the impending attack. At 1:30 A.M. on Friday, October 3, he issued an order that warned of "indications of a possible attack on Corinth immediately."[10] Too late for them to participate in the first day's action, he began calling in his reserves.

To successfully rout Rosecrans's army from Corinth, Van Dorn could expect to break three major lines of defense. The first line, the old Confederate earthworks, extended in a semicircle around the northern sector of the town about five miles out from the town's center. The second line covered only the line between the Mobile and Ohio Railroad and the Columbus Road about one and a half miles from the town and included 3 lettered redoubts. Clockwise from Columbus Road they were Batteries D, E, and F. The final line formed a circle immediately around Corinth and consisted of a series of formidable redoubts and artillery positions. They offered a last line of defense to

9. *Ibid.*, p. 422.
10. *Ibid.*, p. 167.

the town and were strategically located to cover most of the possible routes of attack. In a clockwise direction from the south they included Batteries Lothrop, Tannrath, Phillips, Williams, Robinette, Powell, and Madison.

Van Dorn's attack on Corinth was from the northwest, centering at first along the Chewalla road. He began his approach down the road toward the town at 4:00 A.M. on Friday with his divisions in a column, Lovell in the lead. To sever communications between Corinth and Jackson, Tennessee, he dispatched a squadron of General Frank Armstrong's cavalry to cut the railroad that joined the two towns.[11] Already Rosecrans was setting his defense and by 9:00 that morning he had formed a defensive position with his four divisions forming a long, curved line at the earthworks. From left to right these divisions were commanded by Generals David S. Stanley, Thomas J. McKean, Thomas A. Davies, and Charles S. Hamilton.

About 9:00 A.M. Lovell's lead troops began the first sharp fighting of the day against a brigade of General McKean's division. This brigade retreated cautiously toward Corinth until the men settled briefly at a good defensive position just north of the Memphis and Charleston Railroad. The lead Confederate brigade crossed Indian Creek with difficulty about three miles from the city where their advance was halted as they engaged in heavy skirmishing with the Federals. The other Confederate units crossed the stream under heavy Union artillery fire.

Van Dorn arrived at the battle line about 10:00 o'clock and promptly made his first major tactical error of the day. He placed his divisions in a line forming an arc facing the city, keeping in reserve only two brigades and detachments from two others. Kenneth W. Williams has criticized this maneuver; he says that Van Dorn needed a strong reserve for the type of attack he was using since he needed troops to attack the inner intrenchments once the first wave broke through.[12] It was the Mississippian's first thought to break the strong line before him, and he gave little attention to the inner defenses of the town. Spreading his divisions out across the irregular terrain forced him to

11. This effort came too late to be of much concern to the Federals, for on October 2 at Jackson, General Grant had anticipated such a move, and he had immediately ordered the return of the supply trains to Jackson.

12. *Lincoln Finds a General*, IV, 90.

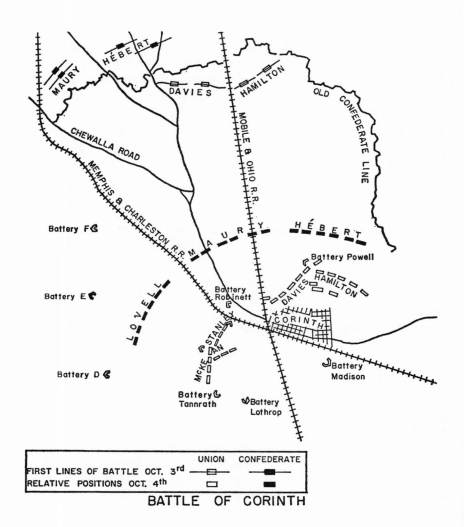

BATTLE OF CORINTH

attack in three basic sectors, however, and he never maintained the control over his troops that such an offensive demanded. What advantages he gained by his wide-spread tactical arrangement were lost in the confusion created by the difficulties of co-ordination and communication that resulted from the complex front. Because of this arrangement, the first day of battle was actually composed of three separate engagements.

The new Confederate alignment for the advance toward the city was with the three divisions in a semi-circle as follows: General Lovell was to operate as the Confederate right between the Columbus Road and the Memphis and Charleston Railroad; General Maury was to cover the distance between the two railroads; General Louis Hébert, replacing General Price as division commander, controlled the area east of the Mobile and Ohio line. In the new arrangement the Confederate commander also split his cavalry, placing Brigadier General William H. Jackson's force on the right side of his line and General Armstrong's men in a similar position on his left. He intended to open the attack from his right so that the enemy would deploy its strength to meet this assault. He would then make a show of force on his left with Maury and Hébert and move on into Corinth.

As Van Dorn dispersed his troops across their broader front, the fighting became general all along the line. As the tempo of battle increased he remained in close contact with General Lovell's division when they engaged the Federals on the right of his new line. Lovell's division advanced steadily two brigades in line, driving hard against the enemy's advance skirmishers, pushing them back behind hastily constructed breastworks. As Lovell forced the blue line back, the fighting became hotter. Checked momentarily, the Confederates regrouped and renewed their assault through an enfilading fire from the Federal position. Losses were heavy on both sides.

Leaving his right wing engaged, Van Dorn rode quickly toward his left wing where he ordered the advance of the divisions of Hébert and Maury to relieve the pressure against Lovell. Immediately these two units became engaged in desperate combat. "We raised and forwarded on them," wrote one of the attackers.[13] For a moment the earth trembled in the wake of the heavy artillery fire and the roar of

13. Payne, "The Test of the Missourians," *Confederate Veterans*, XXXVII, 464.

small arms. The Yanks gave their enemies such a barrage "that it left a line of gray where it struck."

The most determined Federal stand of the day took place in this area when the blue-clad veterans massed at the forks of a creek for a desperate struggle. Sweating, swearing Johnnie Rebs finally drove them out of their little stronghold with the bayonet. Then for a moment the hungry Southerners paused. The departing enemy had left their larder. Bread, butter, and cheese were hastily consumed and the attackers moved on.

On drove the gray line—over fallen trees, underbrush, vines, rocks and other obstacles—always under a murderous enemy fire. Rosecrans himself could hardly have planned the Confederate assault better. The Rebels moved precisely where the Federal artillery could concentrate its heaviest fire. Rebels charged on, stumbling over fallen trees and heavy earthworks. Ricocheting Federal bullets filled the air with flying splinters from dry timber. Dust mingled with smoke to choke Rebel lungs and burn their eyes. Their attack was relentless despite the hazards of the field, however, and the Federals gradually retreated before its fury. Monroe Cockrill, a student of this battle for many years, identified five different defensive stands taken by the Federals in their retreat as they gave ground reluctantly.[14]

But sometimes the Confederate pressures were just too great. On one occasion the Federals broke and "ran like hens running from a hawk," wrote Private Calkin. They hid "behind every log and in every place they could find," he continued.[15] This was unusual, however, and as the battling armies reached the inner ring of redoubts the men in blue were separated from their attackers only by thirty to fifty yards. Federal troops fought gallantly in the face of heavy odds, but Maury and Hébert were determined in their drive. It was evident by this time "that the enemy were in full strength and meant mischief," Rosecrans finally admitted early in the afternoon.[16]

By 1:30 P.M. the entire center works of the Union army's outer defense had been carried. Rosecrans, who had expressed his delight at the trap which the Confederates seemed to have entered, saw his forces begin to retreat. "The weight of the enemy on the center was

14. *The Lost Account*, p. 64.
15. "Elk Horn to Vicksburg," *Civil War History*, II, 34.
16. *Official Records Army*, XVII, Pt. 1, 168.

in evidence," Rosecrans admitted.[17] But the Federals fought on, contesting hotly every foot they gave up to the determined Confederates.

By 3:00 o'clock, the Confederate left had moved to within a mile of Corinth. General Price personally directed much of the action. "Here the fighting was of unparalleled fierceness along the whole extent of my line," he wrote.[18] Heavy enemy resistance behind fences, heavy timber, and thick underbrush blocked his path toward the town. For two more hours the two forces struggled in desperation with no final decision. The early evening shadows appeared, and tired, thirsty troops on both sides welcomed a respite in the action. Price's troops had taken possession of the Federal commander's headquarters and other parts of the enemy fortifications.

On the right flank of the Confederate line, General Lovell's and part of General Maury's divisions were also engaged as they penetrated a gap between two Northern divisions and also pushed the enemy troops in the area back toward Corinth. This, too, came from hard fighting, although action on the Confederate right seems to have been less severe than elsewhere. Lovell's troops advanced over equally hazardous terrain as others in the Confederate line, but they did not meet the murderous artillery barrage or the close infighting that took such a toll among Price's men.

At sundown on October 3, Corinth was threatened by Confederate troops from the north and the northwest just as Van Dorn had planned earlier in the day. Strong Confederate forces had reached points less than one-half mile from the town itself, and they seemed poised for the final drive. Van Dorn had to make an important decision at sunset. Originally he had had hopes of terminating the battle on the first day. Should he continue his successful attack on into the night and hope for complete victory, or should he hold up his advance until dawn? The little general knew the hazards of a night attack, but he also feared a reinforced enemy on the morrow. There was also the problem of human flesh and blood. He had no reserves left to storm the citadel, and his troops were exhausted from the day's action. The hot day, the hard fighting, the lack of supplies, and Van Dorn's poor tactical planning had taken their toll. There seemed to be but one answer. "I knew my antagonist—knew that he would avail himself of every resource in

17. *Ibid.*
18. *Ibid.*, p. 386.

his power, but I could not prudently hazard a night attack," he concluded.[19] There was nothing he could do but bivouac and await the dawn before continuing his attack. Firing continued until darkness fell, but the Southerners made no further attempt to occupy Corinth on Friday.

That night Earl Van Dorn received the congratulations of most of his officers on the left. There was pride of achievement within the ranks as the battered soldiers bivouacked in the very presence of their enemy. But among some of them there was consternation. Did the Missourians not recall another night like this at Elkhorn Tavern when an army directed by Van Dorn awaited a new dawn? Did the veterans of Shiloh not recall another victorious first day that ended in tragedy?

Among the commanders the old dissensions again appeared. Some of them criticized their commander severely for his failure to continue the attack. One general contended that his men were in first-rate battle condition when the attack halted. He believed that the Confederates could have taken the town, although that very morning he had spoken of the move against Corinth as "madness."[20] Another general believed that had the attack been continued, the enemy would have been routed by 8:00 P.M. General Lovell also felt that the attack should have been continued. Brigadier General Martin E. Green, who had fought with Price on the left, stated that he believed his brigade could have gone into the town that night. Even one Federal commander questioned the wisdom of halting the assault for the night; he stated that "had the enemy pushed his advantage . . . the result might have been disastrous [for the Federals]."[21]

Other officers did not share these sentiments. Which of the opinions was correct is not easy to determine. From the records it appears that Van Dorn was in the best position to make the final decision. The generals who were so critical had not been in the thick of the day's fighting. General Green had taken a severe beating, and from his own report of the battle it hardly seems likely that his troops were in condition to pursue the attack. Van Dorn had joined Price's command early in the day and had remained in the field with that unit during most of their bloody attack. Several times during the day he rode near the front lines and encouraged his faltering brigade commanders. He had

19. *Ibid.*, p. 457.
20. *Ibid.*, p. 417.
21. *Ibid.*, p. 205.

followed the hotly contested advance of Price through the heat of the day and of battle, and he knew from first-hand experience the condition of his men. Confronted with a similar decision at Elkhorn Tavern in March, he had also decided not to make a night attack. At Corinth on Friday evening, he must surely have realized that time was an extremely important factor, but he made the same decision. Therefore, when Van Dorn, whose daring had highlighted his career in three wars, risked a halt at darkness, he must have felt sincerely that there was little advantage in pouring troops into a situation that could easily become disastrous. He later expressed his sentiments:

> I saw with regret the sun sink behind the horizon as the last shot of our sharpshooters followed the retreating foe into their innermost lines. One hour more of daylight, and victory would have soothed our grief.[22]

Whether he could have completed the conquest in another hour is questionable. General Price, who had also been in the thick of the hottest part of the day's action, concurred with the Mississippian. He wrote that under the circumstances, "it was prudent to delay the attack . . . until the succeeding morning."[23]

At dusk the Confederates before Corinth prepared for a night of uneasiness and a day of uncertainty. Just as at Elkhorn, they slept on their arms among the dead and wounded of both armies, deep in the territory that earlier in the day an outnumbered Federal garrison had gallantly defended.

Van Dorn attempted to scout out the enemy position during the night, but he had little success. His troops were too tired and disorganized to penetrate the enemy lines. The Confederates would have to strike blindly against a Union position that might well be strengthened during the night. Van Dorn defended his failure to scout the enemy position by pointing up the fact that Federal sharpshooters were only 100 yards from his camp, and they spotted his every move. The Confederate commander slept little if any during that long night. The noise of moving wagons in the enemy camp worried him and his officers, but after a consultation with Price he concluded that the Federals were evacuating their supplies in anticipation of a successful Confederate dawn attack. At his headquarters the Confederate commander made his plans for attack without knowing the exact location of the

22. Quoted in Davis, *The Rise and Fall*, II, 389.
23. *Official Records Army*, XVII, Pt. 1, 433.

enemy within Corinth. In town Rosecrans also planned, optimistic over his prospects against the coming assault. "If they fight us tomorrow," he telegraphed General Grant at 11:30 P.M., "I think we shall whip them. If they go to attack you we shall advance upon them."[24] Rosecrans still had difficulty believing that Van Dorn would fight against his strong position.

To renew his attack Van Dorn ordered three batteries of artillery to take positions on the ridge overlooking the city from the northwest. Their instructions were to begin firing on the enemy about 4:00 A.M. General Hébert was to mask part of his division on the left, and with one of Maury's brigades and Armstrong's cavalry he was to begin the ground attack at daybreak. On the right flank Lovell was to await Hébert's attack and then move rapidly toward the town, forcing his way into the low section of the southwestern part of Corinth. In the center Maury was to move at the same time Lovell began his advance and assault the heavily defended center of the enemy line.

During the night there was plenty of activity behind the Federal lines. The actions of the Union commanders indicated that they concerned themselves not with the losses of the first day but more with preparations for continuing the battle on their own terms. Rosecrans held a staff meeting of his commanders and planned his new defense. Fresh troops from his outposts arrived during the night to add strength to undermanned positions.[25] Assignments for the veterans of the first day's battle were changed to meet the anticipated dawn assault. The troops in position slept on their arms awaiting a strange and unpredictable new day.

The cannonading by the Confederate artillery began at four o'clock as scheduled.[26] Brigadier General Napoleon B. Buford, commanding Hamilton's First Brigade on the Union right, described the fireworks:

At dawn the cannonading announced the beginning of another sharp contest. It was grand. The different calibers, metals, shapes, and distances

24. *Ibid.*, p. 161.

25. The exact number of reinforcements was not mentioned in any Federal report of the battle, but *Official Records* show that the Fifty-Sixth Illinois Infantry, the Fifth Minnesota Infantry, and the Forty-Third and Eightieth Ohio Infantry units were brought into the Federal garrison between dusk and dawn.

26. There is no concensus as to the exact time the artillery barrage began, but the heavy firing seems to have been underway about 4:00 A.M.

of the guns caused the sounds to resemble the chimes of old Rome when all her bells rang out. In one hour it was interspersed with one continuous roar of musketry.[27]

Van Dorn was tense as he watched the fireworks and awaited the action he expected from his left. Federal mortars repeatedly threw shells into his position from long range; they did little damage except to intensify the war of nerves. Daylight came, and there was no attack on the Confederate left as expected. The Mississippian waited impatiently and then dispatched a staff officer to that sector of his line to search out the trouble. Meanwhile, some of Moore's brigade moved out from their position near the center of the line and skirmished indecisively with Union pickets. They returned to their position about 9:30. Where was Hébert?[28] Why had he not attacked?

Sometime after seven o'clock when the attack should have been well under way, the missing Hébert finally made his appearance at Van Dorn's headquarters where he reported himself too ill to take part in the day's attack.[29] The mysterious ailment was a costly one. A frustrated commander quickly replaced Hébert with General Green. Was it too late? Hoping to recoup the precious lost minutes, Van Dorn directed Green to attack just as soon as he could. The word was passed down the long line to prepare to move out. Then while Green reshuffled some of his command, Maury moved out prematurely in the center. He attacked the Federal center down the Chewalla Road, and without support from his left he soon was taking a terrible beating from a reinforced enemy.

Chewalla road entered the outskirts of Corinth near a ridge sparsely cumbered with stumps and undergrowth. Upon the apex of the ridge was Battery Robinett, six Parrott guns centered on the road. Back of these guns across the railroad and overtopping the Robinett position

27. *Official Records Army*, XVII, Pt. 1, 217.

28. Hébert was a questionable choice for responsible command. His record was not that of a dependable officer. In Texas he had been "a superb example of the type of officer Texans despised." He appears to have been intelligent, but he was also arrogant and self-centered. Stephen B. Oates, "Texas Under the Secessionists," p. 194.

29. Louis Hébert was the cousin of Paul O. Hébert, who had replaced Van Dorn in Texas in 1861. Louis Hébert had been captured at Pea Ridge and was later exchanged and promoted to brigadier general. He fought at both Iuka and Corinth. He later fought with distinction in North Carolina.

was Battery Williams with nine guns. These gun positions were re-inforced with lunettes and well-constructed rifle pits. It was in the direction of these obstacles that Maury's troops made their move.

As brigade after brigade went into action all along the Confederate front, Van Dorn realized that the movements within the enemy camp during the previous night had not been sounds of evacuation. It had been movement of new troops that had created the confusion. But it was too late to halt his own attack. He probably would not have re-called it if he could. He must strike harder. In the field with his troops, near the center of his line where the fighting was most intense, Van Dorn threw men into the developing fray with almost frenzied madness. The whole of Corinth lay in sight just before him. In a paroxysm of fury he led his men to the very mouths of the enemy gunbarrels. There for a fleeting moment his big drive appeared to be a success.

As the Confederates emerged from their shelters, near panic seized many of the Yankee soldiers in General Davies's defending line. It was the slow, steady tramp of the thousands of advancing feet that unnerved even the battle-hardened veterans. A captain's voice was heard down the line in an attempt to bolster their courage. "[I]f the butternuts come close enough, remember you have good bayonets on your rifles and use them!"[30] The unevenness of the ground and the tangled trees screened the gray line from nervous eyes. Federal riflemen lay low, nervous but ready.

Slowly advancing Rebels captured some men and guns in a Wisconsin artillery unit, and the other Yankees ran quickly to the rear. Confed-erates turned the flank of the Ninth Illinois in the yard of a house and then opened an enfilading fire on the brigade of Colonel Thomas W. Sweeny. Colonel Sweeny and several other units retired as the gray-clad troops moved in.

Then it happened! Line officers leaped to their feet! "Boys, give them a volley," they yelled to their companies.[31] "We could see thousands of gray uniforms swarming from the woods and climbing over the fallen timber," wrote a private in the Fifteenth Iowa Infantry.[32] Federal riflemen raised themselves above their protective parapets and fired point blank at moving gray forms. "Their column appeared to reel like

30. Oscar L. Jackson, *The Colonel's Diary*, p. 71.
31. *Ibid.*, p. 72.
32. Quoted in Bettersworth, *Mississippi in the Confederacy*, p. 96.

a rope shaken at the end,"[33] wrote Captain Oscar L. Jackson whose company was in the thick of the action.

Orders were snapped in haste in the Confederate ranks. The men deployed and fought with desperation. General Maury moved one of his brigades around a Federal position and into the main part of the town where it occupied the Tishomingo Hotel and the buildings near the railroad depot. Hand-to-hand fighting in the streets accompanied this move, and even in the yard of General Rosecrans's headquarters bayonets flashed as the indomitable Southerners pressed on and on. Before Battery Robinett, a heroic colonel from Texas died at the edge of the Federal trenches after he had displayed a courage that was cheered by men in both armies. Colonel William P. Rogers, who had served with Colonel Jefferson Davis in Mexico and was Van Dorn's aide at Farmington, led his troops to the very center of the strongest part of the enemy line before he went down. A reporter described some of this action, one of the most dramatic of the day:

> At a given signal they [Colonel Rogers's men] moved forward rapidly under a heavy fire of grape and cannister from our artillery in front and the battery to the left, followed at supporting distances by their reserves . . . They crossed with difficulty the abattis of trees just outside the town, and gaining a position where there were no obstructions, they came gallantly forward at a charge, sweeping everything before them.[34]

But these were only temporary successes—the death throes of an agonized army. Maury's forces reeled under the pressure of the Federal reinforcements. The "Stars and Bars" flew briefly over Robinett, but then it went down. The Federal infantry struck back; their bayonets and rifle butts took a heavy toll in hand-to-hand action. The Confederates captured some Federal artillery and were just turning it to fire into Corinth "when a long *blue* line of uniforms could be seen rising out of the grass and bushes and with a *cheer* [the Federals] rushed on the victorious enemy."[35] The countercharge was a wild one. "The ranks of the rebels melted like snow," wrote an Iowa private, "and most of them stood their ground and died in and around the little fort."[36]

33. *The Colonel's Diary*, p. 72.
34. Memphis *Bulletin*, October 14, 1862, p. 1.
35. Quoted in Bettersworth, *Mississippi in the Confederacy*, p. 96.
36. *Ibid.*

"It reminded me of a man cutting heavy grain, striking at a thick place," wrote Captain Jackson.[37]

Lieutenant Labruzan of the Forty-Second Alabama Infantry viewed the scene as one of the attackers:

> I saw men running at full speed, stop suddenly and fall upon their faces, with their brains scattered all around; others, with legs and arms cut off, shrieking with agony. . . . The ground was literally strewn with mangled corpses. . . . I seemed to be moving right in the mouth of the cannon, for the air was filled with grape and canister. Ahead was one continuous blaze. I rushed to the ditch of the fort, right between some large cannon. I grappled into and half way up the sloping wall. The enemy was only three or four feet from me on the other side of the wall . . . we were butchered like dogs. . . . The men fell ten at a time . . . the survivors tried to save themselves as best they could. . . .[38]

All along the Corinth line Federal guns raked the Confederates with a galling fire. Over on the Confederate left the belated drive of General Green's troops also moved into the city but with extremely heavy losses. Green pushed his four brigades relentlessly until they occupied a position in the woods just north of the city. Then, rushing from the woods, two brigades attacked Battery Powell, another strong redoubt, while the other two brigades struck the Federal line to the east of the battery. The Federals responded with a steady fire which repulsed the two brigades on the east, but the first two brigades captured Battery Powell.

As with the center, Confederate success on the left was only temporary. Reinforced Federal units attacked their lost battery, and with great losses on both sides they pushed Green's troops from their recently won prize. General Price called for and received reinforcements from the Confederate right, but these troops were hardly in his line before the enemy's great reserve strength overwhelmed them. The batteries of Federal artillery opened "a most destructive fire at short range," and swept over the entire Confederate front.[39] The Rebels broke under the fire. Survivors turned and ran quickly toward the protective woods where they had so recently emerged with such fury.

On the Confederate right, General Lovell's division was also under heavy Federal fire. Delayed by Hébert's failure to advance, Lovell had

37. *The Colonel's Diary*, p. 74.
38. Quoted in *ibid.*, pp. 86–87.
39. *Official Records Army*, XVII, Pt. 1, 387.

attacked with two brigades leading and one in reserve. The Confederates proceeded toward a redoubt that they thought harbored three large guns, but they met such a vicious fire from that fortification and the two others flanking it that the brigade commanders realized they had made a serious miscalculation and halted the attack. The troops then took up a firing position and awaited new orders from General Lovell.

Lovell was in the process of reconnoitering his position for new assault possibilities when he received orders from Van Dorn to detach one of his brigades and send it to the support of Maury's battered division in the center of the Confederate lines. Too late! Maury's broken ranks streamed in disorder from the bloody field before Batteries Robinett and Williams. Lovell then braced himself to aid the battered division and poured his own troops into Maury's earlier position. It was at this point that new orders came from the commanding general. All units facing Corinth were to begin a full-scale retreat! The attack had ended; Corinth was lost!

Lovell received the order, surveyed his fresh troops and said to Colonel James Gordon. "I don't understand this, Colonel. I've got a position here, and I can whip anything that can come out of Corinth or hell and by G–d, I don't want to leave it."[40] Colonel Gordon reminded him that the troops in the other parts of the line had been cut to pieces and Lovell acquiesced.

The assault on Corinth on Saturday morning occurred in little more than an hour. In that time some of the most furious fighting of the entire war took place. From a position on the hotly contested Rebel left, Van Dorn watched his troops first gain their objective and then lose it. He had seen tired, courageous veterans dash with desperation into the fray in a frenzied effort to push the enemy from his stronghold. As the Confederate ranks thinned and the men fell before the murderous fire, he realized that he had failed again. In his own words he admitted his failure: "Exhausted from loss of sleep, wearied from hard marching and fighting, companies and regiments without officers, our troops—let no one censure them—gave way. The day was lost."[41]

The task was now to evacuate the beaten army. Again he must have

40. Colonel James Gordon, "Battle of Corinth and Subsequent Retreat," *Publications of the Mississippi State Historical Society*, IV, 69.
41. *Official Records Army*, XVII, Pt. 1, 380.

been reminded of Elkhorn. With Lovell's division in the center to support his broken lines, Van Dorn began his withdrawal. As Maury's center broke completely Lovell took over. His new line held briefly under the hot noonday sun while battered Confederates streamed down the road to Chewalla.

On the battlefield Rosecrans looked over the situation. Seeing his own force so fatigued and disseminated, he delayed his pursuit. With victory in his hands, he ordered his troops to rest, to replenish their ammunition, and to prepare for a pursuit on Sunday morning. General William T. Sherman criticized this delay in his *Memoirs*. Had he pursued relentlessly, Sherman contended, "Van Dorn's army would surely have been utterly ruined."[42] To Van Dorn's advantage, Rosecrans—lacking that quality of persistency that makes for great leadership—procrastinated.

During the afternoon and evening the Confederates managed to regroup at Chewalla where they formed a crude bivouac. Staff officers found it difficult to understand why Van Dorn halted so near the enemy line. "If retreating, and there seemed nothing else to do," said one of them, "we surely should have crossed the Tuscumbia River only four miles off, where our trains still reposed, if indeed, we did not continue over the Hatchie, requiring a march of only four miles more, while the bridges were yet in our possession."[43]

The Mississippian had his own reasons for remaining in Chewalla that night. He would admit a defeat on Saturday in his official reports, but Saturday night he still believed he could take Corinth. He wanted to make one last desperate effort to nullify the preceding day's humiliating defeat. During the night he spoke of his new attack plans to his staff officers. Then he directed General Price to prepare for an attack on Federal-occupied Rienzi on the next day. Van Dorn planned to occupy this town and then prepare for another attack upon Corinth from that direction.

This new order promptly shocked Price into action. He assembled three of his own staff members, discussed the matter with them, and

42. *Memoirs*, I, 290–291.

43. "Colonel Celsus Price on the Relations between Generals Van Dorn and Price," an undated newspaper clipping of a paper prepared and read by Colonel Celsus Price, the son of General Sterling Price, in 1866, found in the Van Dorn Collection, Montgomery, Alabama.

decided to confront his commander with the realities of the situation. Searching out Van Dorn, he found him asleep in an ambulance. Price awakened him and quickly explained that the condition of the troops just was not up to another fight. The Missourian then suggested that the Confederates should withdraw from Chewalla by the same route they had used on their approach to Corinth and fall back as rapidly as possible toward Ripley and Oxford. Price insisted that the army's wagon train which had been halted between the Hatchie and Tuscumbia rivers during the battle would be lost if they did not fall back and secure it. General Maury, who was with Price at this midnight conference, said that Price then looked at his chief and said: "Van Dorn, you are the only man I ever saw who loves danger for its own sake. When any daring enterprise is before you, you cannot adequately estimate the obstacle in your way."[44]

According to Maury, Van Dorn's answer came back as follows:

While I do not admit the correctness of your criticism I feel how wrong I shall be to imperil this army through my personal peculiarities, after what such a friend as you have told me they are, and I will countermand the orders and move at once on the road to Ripley.[45]

The Confederate commander immediately did as he promised. Before again retiring, he ordered his troops to construct a new bridge over the Tuscumbia as a prerequisite for crossing that stream on Sunday morning. He also countermanded an order directing most of his cavalry and a battery of his artillery to Rienzi and prepared to depart from Chewalla at dawn with all his force in the direction of Pocahontas. At daybreak he sent a dispatch to Colonel E. R. Hawkins, who was guarding the supply train which he had left at a point two miles east of the Hatchie, to join Colonel Wirt Adams, whose cavalry unit had been assigned to guard the Hatchie bridge on the west bank of the river, and oppose any Federal move across the stream.

It appears that at this point Van Dorn had not yet charted an exact escape route. He knew the countryside well, and he probably preferred to await the disposition of the Federal troops from Bolivar under General E. O. C. Ord before committing himself. His best route was to cross the Hatchie at Davis's Mill and then move over good roads to

---

44. "Van Dorn, the Hero of Mississippi," *Annals of the War*, p. 464.
45. *Ibid.*, pp. 464–465.

Holly Springs. He would have to beat Ord to the bridge to use this route. That he expected to do just this was revealed when he chose to burn a bridge over the Hatchie at Crum's Mill just six miles south of Davis's Mill. This closed an escape route over the Bone Yard Road, but it also prevented Rosecrans from sending troops from Corinth to molest his flanks after he had made the Davis's Mill crossing.

His beaten army resumed its march early Sunday morning, returning over the same road it had traveled with such great expectations only three days earlier. To hold the bridge at Davis's Mill, he hurried advance units to that area. En route he learned that enemy troops from Bolivar had already arrived there, but he continued to hope that he could engage them long enough to cover the movements of his supply train and artillery wagons.

Across the Hatchie River, Colonel Adams was having his troubles with Ord's advance troops. He had already engaged some of the Bolivar troops at Middleton the day before, but he had failed to check their advance. Adams met Colonel Hawkins east of the Hatchie about 8:30 Sunday morning, October 5, and ordered him across the river to help oppose the advance of the Bolivar troops. Hawkins moved his troops across the bridge into "a galling fire of grapeshot and shell."[46] The Federals had arrived in force.

When he was informed of the trouble at the Hatchie, Van Dorn dispatched a brigade to support Adams and Hawkins at the bridge. At the same time he directed General Lovell to leave one of his brigades to guard the Confederate rear at the Tuscumbia against the pursuit that he expected from Rosecrans. Lovell did this and then set his other two brigades toward the Hatchie.

Trapped for the moment between the two rivers, Van Dorn decided definitely on his escape route. He would follow the Bone Yard road to Crum's Mill, and he would take his chances on a safe crossing of the river although the bridge had been burned. His troops were in no condition for another prolonged engagement, and he had no desire to be attacked in his precarious position. The Bone Yard road was actually a trail that intersected the main road about two and a half miles from the Tuscumbia and then ran off toward the southeast between the two rivers toward Bone Yard and Kossuth. Its surface would bear the wagons. The big problem was to keep the Federals off the road.

46. *Official Records Army*, XVII, Pt. 1, 392–393.

To gain the necessary time to move his slow wagons and to keep General Ord's forces west of the Hatchie, Van Dorn ordered Moore to "push forward, cross the bridge, form a line of battle on the right of the road, and then advance, take, and hold the heights at Metamora . . ."[47] Moore followed these instructions as best he could. Arriving at the bridge, he found the enemy in force already occupying the Metamora hills; the batteries stationed there were aimed at the bridge and the Confederate troops of Adams and Hawkins. Confederate reinforcements crossed the bridge under heavy fire and obtained a position in a strip of woods on the west bank. Seeing the precariousness of his situation when the Federal guns hit him with such telling effect, their colonel dispatched a messenger back to Van Dorn with a request for support. He then tried to hold his position until the reinforcements arrived. The enemy fire was too heavy, though, and the colonel finally decided to withdraw back to the east side of the river. His troops crossed the river "at such points of the stream as they found most convenient," under a withering fire.[48] Troops from the battered commands of Adams and Hawkins also crossed the river under fire, some by the bridge, others any way they could. Many of the troops found swimming to be the "most convenient" mode of crossing.[49]

Casualties were numerous and nearly all the men lost their guns. General Ord later reported that his force took more than 200 Confederate prisoners in this action, including Van Dorn's aide and nephew, Lieutenant Sulivane.[50]

Across the bridge Confederate units supported by some heavy guns bought a delaying action. One of the most destructive Confederate barrages of the day hit Ord's troops as they advanced over the bridge. Ord himself went down, sorely wounded, and General Stephen A. Hurlbut replaced him in command even as the crossing was being made. The small Confederate force used "shell, canister, and grape" as they held their position.[51] Northern troops reeled under the heavy fire, and there was confusion in several of the advancing Federal regiments. They soon reformed, and the new blue line poured a galling fire back

47. *Ibid.*, p. 399.
48. *Ibid.*, p. 400.
49. S. B. Barron, *The Lone Star Defenders*, p. 121.
50. Sulivane was later exchanged and returned to his post as his uncle's aide-de-camp.
51. *Official Records Army*, XVII, Pt. 1, 312.

at the Confederates across the bridge. Just as these Confederates began to falter under the new barrage, fresh troops arrived. The Rebels under fire retreated in good order, and the fresh troops engaged the Federals furiously while Van Dorn's wagons rolled down the Bone Yard Road and away from the action.

As Hurlbut fought the desperate "caged animal" before him, Rosecrans finally got a pursuing force under Major General James B. McPherson up to the Tuscumbia River. As the battle ran its course at the Hatchie late that eventful Sunday, October 5, McPherson struck the rearguard of the Confederate army near Young's Bridge. This fight was short and hot; a Rebel brigade severely chastized McPherson's force in what proved to be the final major action of the day. While guns boomed at both ends of the Southern line, most of the Confederates were on the trail moving toward Crum's Mill, six miles distant.

Crossing the Hatchie at the mill was achieved without interference because of the initiative of General Price. "Old Pap" directed the construction of a temporary bridge by "pulling down the gable end" of the mill over the stream.[52] While the wagons and soldiers crossed this curious bridge, he sat on his horse nearby and directed the traffic. "Drive up! Drive up!" he shouted through the darkness until all the troops and wagons were west of the river again.[53]

Crossing the river took up most of the night of October 5. As each unit arrived safely on the opposite banks, it marched briskly toward Ripley by a full moon over dusty roads. At Ripley a battleline was made to meet an expected attack, but when no attack materialized Van Dorn continued on his way to Holly Springs. It was October 10 before all the units arrived there. Generals Rosecrans and Hurlbut had been slow in getting their pursuits started and had only followed as far as Ripley. Here General Grant halted them because they were not prepared for an extended field operation.

For the numbers engaged, Corinth was a bloody affair. Van Dorn called it the bloodiest battle of the fourteen in which he had personally participated up to that time.[54] Figures concerning losses vary widely within the official reports of the battle commanders, but the figures

52. Barron, *op. cit.*, pp. 122–123.
53. *Ibid.*
54. Van Dorn to his wife, October 14, 1862, Van Dorn Collection, Montgomery, Alabama.

that Thomas L. Livermore gives in his *Numbers and Losses in the Civil War in America*, whether accurate or not, do suggest the intensity of the struggle. Northern losses were given as 355 killed, 1841 wounded, and 324 missing.[55] This meant that a little more than ten percent of all the Federal troops engaged were killed, wounded, or captured.

Losses to the attackers are more difficult to gauge. Livermore's figure reveal 473 killed, 1997 wounded, and 1763 missing. Van Dorn's figures were higher. One man in every five Confederates engaged had been a casualty.

General Van Dorn was severely criticized for his loss of the Corinth campaign. Major General T. H. Holmes, writing from Little Rock, expressed the feelings of many when he said that he "was too much out of temper to write about the defeat" or he could give an account "of mismanagement and stupidity that would make you grieve for the cause intrusted to such heads."[56] Though Holmes's criticism probably represents the sentiments of a disgruntled officer, others also noted concern for Van Dorn's abilities as a commander. Josiah Gorgas noted in his diary that the Mississippian "was evidently out-generaled, allowing himself to be drawn into a trap, and getting his forces very much cut up."[57] Gorgas also contended that the entire risk at Corinth was without worthwhile objective.

One of the bitterest reactions to the campaign is recorded by one of the noncommissioned officers. Sergeant Edwin H. Fay was a chronic complainer, but earlier he had commented that though he thought Van Dorn was basically a poor general he still was "better to his men than almost any Genl in service." His reaction to the Corinth attack was not so generous:

Our retreat was conducted with the greatest confusion and Van Dorn was drunk all the time and Villipigue too and I expect Price too. Everybody was commander and Price did the fighting. We lost half of Price's army killed and *straggling*. Such demoralization was never seen in an army before . . . Price, I never considered a General, and I do not think now Van Dorn and Lovell are for we were led into a trap. I could see the want of Generalship but could never fight again under Van Dorn or Lovell . . .[58]

55. p. 94.
56. *Official Records Army*, XIII, Pt. 1, 888.
57. Frank E. Vandiver (ed.), *The Civil War Diary of General Josiah Gorgas*, p. 22.
58. Bell I. Wiley (ed.), *"The Infernal War" Letters*, pp. 85, 165.

The charges of drunkenness and inefficiency even penetrated the Union line. Private Boyd of the Iowa troops reported that "the prisoners tell us Van Dorn commanded and that he was *drunk* and ordered his men to drink whiskey and *gun powder* and then ordered them to take the works at any cost *however great.*"[59] Of course these were idle charges, but they do indicate some of the general disposition of the men who served under a discredited commander.

Official criticism of the attack on Corinth came quickly in the form of official charges which were preferred against Van Dorn by General Bowen. Though there were personal feelings involved, Bowen was not just a disgruntled critic. He was a well-respected officer in the Confederate army. Born in Georgia, he had entered the United States Military Academy from Missouri. He finished fifth in the class of 1853 and was appointed a second lieutenant in the engineer corps. After serving two years in Texas, he resigned his commission and became an architect and contractor in St. Louis. At the first signs of discord between North and South, he secured a commission as major in the Missouri State Guard but later resigned and reported to Richmond. Appointed a colonel of infantry in the Confederate Army, he was assigned to General A. S. Johnston's army in Tennessee. He showed courage and ability at the battle of Shiloh, where he was wounded and had two horses shot from under him.

General Bowen first came under Van Dorn's command at Vicksburg. After serving with Van Dorn at the siege during the summer of 1862, he was assigned to General John Breckinridge's force that attacked Baton Rouge. It was probably in this connection that he shared the former Vice President's dislike for Van Dorn. After the Confederate defeat at Baton Rouge, he joined General Lovell, under whose immediate command he fought at Corinth.[60] General Bowen formally charged his commander with attacking without due consideration or forethought and with general failure and neglect of duty.

To protect his reputation and his service record, Van Dorn applied to President Davis for a trial to investigate the allegations made by

59. Quoted in Bettersworth, *Mississippi in the Confederacy*, p. 97.
60. After the battle of Corinth, General Bowen remained in Mississippi with General Pemberton. He was one of those later captured at the fall of Vicksburg in July 1863. A short official biography of General Bowen is found in the Service Jacket of Major General John S. Bowen, Collection of Confederate Records, General Services Administration, National Archives.

Bowen. The President, though disappointed in his friend, continued to defend his fellow Mississippian, and instead of a trial he ordered an inquiry to test the force of Bowen's accusations. President Davis's reflections on the matter are worth noting. Writing to Van Dorn on November 4, he said:

> While I was reflecting on your case with a view to meet both your interest and your wish, a telegram was brought to me to announce that you were under charges and that you desired a trial. It was consistent with your character to meet promptly any proposition for investigation. It did not appear to me, however, proper to accept your waiver as to the consultation of a court to sit upon your commission, and therefore I directed that instead of a trial there should be an inquiry to test the force of the allegations made.
>
> I need not say to you that the occasion is one which has given me much pain, and hope that your vindication may be as complete as I am sure your motives were patriotic. As the event of which you wrote is to be submitted to inquiry, I will say nothing on the subject.[61]

Davis did add an important reprimand in the letter when he commented that Van Dorn had injured himself "by attempting to give to officers position and command to which you could not properly assign them, for which you were sufficiently warned . . . by the War Department."

The court of inquiry convened at Abbeville, Mississippi, on November 15, 1862. It consisted of Generals Sterling Price, Dabney Maury, and Lloyd Tilghman; it was obviously weighted in favor of the Mississippian. At Van Dorn's request the accusation of drunkenness, which was being publicly bruited against him, was embodied in another charge to be added to those under consideration by the court.

General Bowen seemed bitter as he presented his case to the court. He accused his commander of failing to provide his officers with proper maps, eschewing engineer services, negligent reconnoitering, marching with insufficient supplies, marching in a hasty and disorderly manner, and disastrously delaying an attack on the evening of the first day of the battle. General Albert Rust and sometimes General Green sided with Bowen in criticizing Van Dorn's actions. Generals Price, Maury, and even Lovell defended his actions.

After several days of testimony and cross-examination, the defendant took the stand. He reminded the officers of the court of his twenty-five

61. *A Soldier's Honor*, p. 324.

years service in the army, emphasizing that he had devoted his "whole time and energies" to the services of his country. He then asked the court to make a complete investigation of the charges against him. He said emphatically that he was not guilty of any of the charges.

"If these accusations are well founded," he said with determination, "they must deeply touch my character as a soldier and a man. If they be true I am neither fit for society nor command."[62]

He then took some of the major charges against him one by one and presented his defense or explanation of the actions involved in each case. He defended his decision to attack Corinth as a legitimate military target. He explained in some detail his preparations for the battle, demonstrating that his actions had taken a natural course and were perfectly acceptable to the military protocol that governed that particular situation. He justified halting the attack on Friday evening when he seemed to be just on the verge of achieving a great victory.

As to the charges dealing with his treatment of his men and the criticisms offered against him concerning his handling of supplies and the wounded, he simply stated: "It would be inexcusable in me before this tribunal to notice the remaining accusations made against me." He did, however, consider the accuser, particularly in terms of the relationship between the commander and his lieutenants. Of Bowen as a brigade commander Van Dorn said:

> I thought his duty was to obey orders and I did not call him to counsel with me . . . I do not doubt the gallantry of my accuser, but his criticisms as a brigade commander, confined in his knowledge to what appears before him, ignorant of the operations going on in two-thirds of the line of battle, and unapprised of the plan of operations of the general in command, reminds me of Cowper's fly on the dome at St. Paul's, who, with a vision that extended only a few inches around him, was found discoursing on the architecture of the entire building.[63]

The defendant then spoke briefly of his own career as a soldier and of his personal loyalty to his state. "I struck for her as I would for wife or child," he said somewhat ironically. Finally he brought his impassioned remarks to an end with what might be called his own personal philosophy of life and history:

> Gentlemen of the court, these extended remarks are not meant alone for your ears. In this tribunal I know my character is safe; but the accusations

62. Van Dorn's testimony is found in *Official Records Army*, XVII, Pt. 1, 452–459.
63. *Ibid.*, pp. 456–457.

against me will take an enduring form by becoming part of the archives of the nation, and the jealousy with which a soldier guards his reputation prompts me to place by their side an antidote to the poison they contain.[64]

The court then closed for deliberation. After a careful consideration of all the evidence presented, they exonerated Van Dorn completely of the charges, unanimously reporting their disapproval of "every allegation contained in the said charges."[65]

As to the special consideration concerning drunkenness, the court also cleared his name. This decision was made in light of the extensive testimony given in the general's behalf. Since the charge of drunkenness was so often publicly spoken against him during his military career, it is interesting to note the testimonies in his behalf at this time.

"General Van Dorn was entirely free from any perceptible influence of liquor during the whole of the 3d, 4th, and 5th," said Dabney Maury, always Van Dorn's defender. "I feel sure that he is not unduly addicted to the use of liquor," he continued.[66]

Major Manning M. Kimmel, Van Dorn's adjutant general; Colonel J. T. Ward, volunteer aide to the general during the three-day fight; and Lieutenant Colonel James P. Major, who had known Van Dorn since the days of his first Texas service—all agreed that Van Dorn was not drunk during any part of the campaign.[67] Colonel Ward said that he had known the general for five years, and during that time he had seen Van Dorn take only "one or two drinks" but never saw him under the influence of strong drink.

General Green confirmed these opinions and even General Bowen, who had initiated the other charges, agreed that Van Dorn was completely sober on the battlefield. "I saw Van Dorn repeatedly on the march to Corinth and two or three times on the retreat," he said. "He was perfectly sober, and was, as far as I could judge, active and energetic in discharging his duties as a commanding officer."[68]

Whatever his guilt concerning all the charges brought against him, Van Dorn lost much with the Corinth defeat. Never again was he entrusted with the command of an army, and from then on his name was mentioned in the West with considerably less enthusiasm. John Pemberton was promoted to lieutenant general despite the fact that Van Dorn was the ranking major general in the Confederate Army.

64. *Ibid.*, p. 458.
65. *Ibid.*, p. 459.
66. *Ibid.*, p. 436.

67. *Ibid.*, pp. 448–449.
68. *Ibid.*, p. 430.

Though exonerated by a court of inquiry and defended by some individuals, Van Dorn's actions at the battle of Corinth leave him subject to criticism. As at Pea Ridge he did not take proper precautions to find out all he could about the battlefield area. By relying too much on his earlier knowledge of the town and its fortifications, he jeopardized the lives of thousands of men in his command by attacking positions whose strength he could only guess. When the enemy positions proved too strong for his army, he pressed his troops against the Federal positions until the battlefield was littered with the bodies of his own army. One is reminded of the actions of General Ambrose Burnside at Fredericksburg. These officers and others seemed to possess such a rigidity of mind and purpose that once a course of action was set, it had to be acted upon whatever the odds or the opposition. In his Corinth defeat, Van Dorn proved once and for all that he did not have that special temperament for handling large commands in battle.

Thus the question remains: was Corinth the right objective? Van Dorn successfully defended this attack to a biased court of inquiry. Even with hindsight, it is still difficult to determine a clear answer to this question. In Van Dorn's defense, this was a terrible decision to have to make, one fraught with risk and uncertainty. By early October he may have had no choice. General Leonidas Polk later said that General Bragg left his Mississippi commanders in an impossible position. They had orders to advance and join Bragg, but they also faced Grant's large force which blocked their path. General Polk's son said that Van Dorn suffered defeat because he tried to obey Bragg's instructions. "History must search elsewhere for General Bragg's discomfiture," he wrote tartly.[69]

But Corinth was also Van Dorn's decision! "Corinth, so hurtful to us while in the possession of the enemy, so advantageous to us if in our own," he wrote, "ought to have been attacked by me unless my repulse was an inevitable event."[70] Generals Price, Lovell, and Maury, the division commanders, all seemed to concur with him. Said Price at the court of inquiry: "I think it warranted more than the usual hazard of battle."[71] General Lovell said on the eve of the battle that if the army

69. Polk, Leonidas Polk, II, 132–133.
70. Ibid., p. 453.
71. Ibid., p. 441.

could not take Corinth they "had better lay down [their] . . . arms and go home."[72]

Other officers in the command were not so enthusiastic. One of them called it an "impetuous attack."[73] Another spoke of the heavy odds against routing an entrenched Federal army. But Van Dorn concerned himself little with his critics. He made the decision alone. "Subsequent reflection and additional information" did little to change his decision.[74] A sympathetic journalist from the *Mobile Advertiser and Register* gave him credit for acting against the enemy if for nothing else:

So far as General Van Dorn is concerned, I will simply state that he acted as any other officer holding the same position would have acted; he thought that with the force he commanded a dash upon Corinth would result in its capture. He tried—and failed. He is just as good an officer now as he was when held up for general glorification at Vicksburg by the papers who now herald his incompetency; and is as much entitled to the public confidence.[75]

The defeat and the subsequent change in public opinion grieved the sensitive little general very much. It was not until October 14 that he spoke of the battle to his wife. Then almost apologetically he wrote: "Do not blush that I have lost a battle, for the enemy themselves say that we fought as valiantly as men ever fought before."[76] Then defending himself against the sudden reversal of public opinion, he continued:

Many falsehoods are told of me by the cowards who fled from the field. . . . Do not believe them. . . . Had I been successful I would have been lifted on their vile breath as high as the heavens. Yet I am the same man today I was yesterday. The first day of the battle we carried everything before us and I received the congratulations and applause of the army. The next day the Army failed and the people damned me. . . . Do not be mortified at what they say. We cannot expect impossibilities.[77]

Before the results of the court of inquiry were made known, Van Dorn felt so "well-abused" that he thought he had no friends. The verdict of the court restored his spirits. Soon after the trial he wrote his

72. *Ibid.*, p. 417.
73. *Ibid.*, p. 441.
74. *Ibid.*, p. 455.
75. November 5, 1862, p. 1.
76. Van Dorn Collection, Montgomery, Alabama.
77. *Ibid.*

sister that he had been grossly mistreated, but that he still lived, "and until it pleases God to take me from the vile race I shall continue to do so unharmed."[78]

Though he was able to eat all his meals "with a very good appetite," Van Dorn was no longer one of the great prospects for command that he had been earlier in the war. Like Beauregard, Polk, Hardee, and others from whom so much had been expected, he had failed. Corinth had been his great opportunity for redeeming the Elkhorn defeat. He made the same mistakes. Again fate and his own deficiencies denied him the glory he coveted so much.

78. Van Dorn to Emily Miller, October 30, 1862, Van Dorn Collection, Montgomery, Alabama.

CHAPTER ELEVEN

A Cavalry Raid

*T*HERE was much discouragement in Richmond in the early fall of 1862. Lee's repulse at Sharpsburg, Bragg's retreat from Kentucky, and Van Dorn's defeat at Corinth struck staggering blows at the Confederacy. Coming so soon after a summer of hope, the Confederate Government reeled under these punches. President Davis, active in military affairs as was his custom, was especially concerned about the affairs in the West. Both Tennessee and Mississippi defenses threatened complete collapse. Much of the fault could be attributed to two commanders, both Davis's favorites. Van Dorn and Bragg had both failed to live up to expectations. Both had failed in crucial situations. What was wrong?

General Bragg reported to Richmond and explained to the President the circumstances surrounding his fiasco in Kentucky. Davis seemed impressed and retained Bragg in command despite much criticism from the general's own officers.

The case of Van Dorn was not so easy to settle. The little Mississippian had already been relieved of his department just before Corinth. It was hoped that he would conquer himself a new department by advancing into West Tennessee. Major General John Pemberton had relieved him of his responsibilities in Louisiana and Mississippi, so his return to Mississippi after his defeat further confused matters. Pemberton commanded a department in which two officers, Van Dorn and Lovell, outranked him. Van Dorn was only in charge of "an isolated body in the field in Mississippi" with no real command.[1] The solution came when the War Department promoted Pemberton and left Van

---

1. *Official Records Army*, XVII, Pt. 2, 727.

Dorn to serve as his field commander operating against Grant's invading forces. Van Dorn's headquarters were at Holly Springs.

The days immediately following the defeat at Corinth weighed heavily upon sensitive Earl. Not only did Confederate military leaders criticize him, but citizens of his own state attacked his character also. Again certain aspects of his private life were associated with the Southern dilemma in Mississippi. Robert H. Read expressed one severe indictment of the general:

> I would say that General Van Dorn has sadly lost caste in this State by a course of life in private that gives no promise of a successfully conducted campaign against our enemies in this department . . . his name is sadly handled for intemperance and other vices. I do hope these charges are unfounded, but from all the light before me I fear they are too true.[2]

Even after the court of inquiry cleared his name, criticism came at him from every angle. Southern journalists penned sharp criticism against the hero of Vicksburg. A prominent Mississippi politician, Senator James Phelan, wrote to President Davis that the atmosphere in Mississippi was "dense with horrid narratives of his negligence, whoring, and drunkenness."[3] Phelan said that these stories of Van Dorn were so fastened in the public mind that "an acquittal by a court-martial of angels would not relieve him of the charge." The Senator then suggested that Davis remove Van Dorn from the state since its citizens regarded him as the source of all their woe.

Van Dorn's spirits sagged under the weight of defeat and invective. "I am weary, weary," he wrote to his wife.

> I sigh for rest of mind and body. If I could retire from the army and join you and my dear children I should be happy. . . . Command is worse than a subordinate position. Indeed, if my death would give pain to no one I should court it. I have seen enough of life and feel its emptiness and its vanity. I am not ambitious and yet I have laboured and have won position. Position has brought misfortune, criticism, falsehood, slander, and all the vile things belonging to the human heart upon me. I have struggled for others and they abuse me.[4]

Had his great thirst for glory finally been satiated? His motivating ambition temporarily dulled, he staggered under the responsibilities of

2. *Ibid.*, LII, Pt. 2, 371.
3. *Ibid.*, XVII, Pt. 2, 789.
4. November 1862, Van Dorn Collection, Montgomery, Alabama.

command. To a friend he wrote that he had seen no editorial statements in any newspaper regarding his conduct at Corinth that were correct. Displeased with his new assignment he insisted upon a transfer, but President Davis felt it an inopportune time for him to withdraw from Mississippi. Against his will he served in his native state under constant attack from the citizens. His feelings for his fellow Mississippians finally exploded in a letter he wrote to a Confederate colonel; it revealed his bitterness over his rejection by the very people whose favor he had so long sought.

The occasion for the letter came in November when a group of school girls from his home town, Port Gibson, sent him a hundred pairs of fine woolen socks for his men. With these socks came instructions to have them distributed among the Texans of his command. Van Dorn turned them over to Colonel T. N. Waul's Texans with the following note to the colonel:

You will observe that these little angels identify me with Texas. They are right. I am a Texan. A Mississippian no longer except in my love for the pure hearted children of her evil who have not yet learned to make the name and fame of one of her sons the butt of malignant archery.[5]

Despite his melancholy, there was something stronger in the man that finally rallied his flagging spirits. Though condemned by many in Mississippi and often moved by self-pity, Van Dorn never slackened his efforts to rebuild his shattered command. He was indefatigable as he struggled to put a strong force in the field. He retained the respect and support of many of his fellow officers who watched his actions with enthusiasm. While some defamed him, Generals Price and Maury continued to defend him. Colonel Albert F. Brown expressed deep admiration for his commander. Colonel Waul, the Texan, testified to a personal pride in serving with him. "Time and conduct have confirmed our appreciation of your merits as a soldier and a gentleman," he wrote.[6]

Solace came to Van Dorn at this time from another source, an unusual one. General William T. Sherman in his *Memoirs* tells of an interesting incident that took place while Van Dorn was still at Holly Springs. Sherman learned of the hardships of the Southerners in that region, and in particular he heard that Van Dorn, his former friend of West

5. November 29, 1862, Van Dorn Collection, Montgomery, Alabama.
6. December 12, 1862, Van Dorn Collection, Montgomery, Alabama.

Point days, was "suffering for the comforts of life." To relieve his friend's discomfort, Sherman dispatched cigars, liquor, boots, and gloves through the lines for the Confederate general's use.[7]

By late October the veterans of Elkhorn, Shiloh, and Corinth again began to take on the appearance of an army. Returned prisoners replaced some of the battlefield losses, and some new equipment and supplies appeared to refurbish their quartermaster supplies. But it was never enough! The Federals increased their troops strength faster and accumulated more equipment and supplies. Despite the improved condition of his own army, Van Dorn could not hold Holly Springs long against such a force as Grant's. With troops scattered into neighboring towns and farmhouses for shelter and sustenance, the Confederates offered a poor defense against a well-organized enemy.

From Jackson, Tennessee, General Grant watched his enemy constantly while his own forces increased in strength. In late October his command consisted of 23,000 troops in and around Corinth, 20,0000 at Jackson, 56,000 at Memphis, and 6,000 at Columbus, Mississippi. Well aware of Van Dorn weaknesses, he felt free to take the offensive early in November. On November 1, he ordered General Charles S. Hamilton to prepare for an advance towards Holly Springs with three divisions of his troops from the Corinth garrison. General Grant had his eye on Vicksburg, but he felt that he must first remove all obstacles in his path before he made another attempt to conquer it. Grant's purpose for an inland advance against the Confederates probably came out of his desire to draw out all of General Pemberton's command for a showdown. Grant knew his own strength was greater than Pemberton's; once the large Southern army was out of his way, the Federals could easily take Vicksburg on the land side. Grant's advance against Van Dorn's army also seems in line with this general strategy.

Van Dorn correctly assessed Grant's move toward his position, but he was in no position to contest it. His field command numbered only about 24,000 troops, still poorly armed and in ill-health. Winter had struck early that year with snow in October, a most unusual occurrence for Mississippi. Weakened men too easily fell victim to the rigors of intense cold. When Van Dorn requested more troops from Pemberton to hold his position, there were none available; the new department commander

7. Sherman, *Memoirs*, I, 284.

could only advise him to take a position south of the Tallahatchie River if the enemy advanced in force against him.

On November 4, General Hamilton's cavalry drove in Van Dorn's pickets at La Grange and Grand Junction, Tennessee. The Confederate commander promptly ordered workers to prepare the bridge across the Tallahatchie River, and on the fifth he began to deploy his supply trains over it toward Abbeville, Mississippi. On November 7, General Pemberton met Van Dorn at Holly Springs and after a conference with the leading officers of his command, he ordered Van Dorn to evacuate the town. On the night of November 9, Van Dorn quietly moved all his troops except his cavalry to Abbeville. The cavalry joined the main body three days later, and at 12:30 P.M. on November 13, Northern cavalry commanded by Colonel Albert L. Lee occupied Holly Springs.

Van Dorn remained at Abbeville during November while Grant reorganized his force. The Northern general was mounting a massive offensive toward Vicksburg that he hoped would break the back of the Confederates in the Mississippi valley. This was the first major campaign that Grant had planned on his own, and he was anxious to dispel the doubts that persisted in the North about his generalship. Second in command to Henry W. Halleck, Grant was promoted with Halleck's transfer to Washington. But in November 1862 another shadow threatened Grant's position, General John A. McClernand, one of President Lincoln's political appointments, also assigned the task of opening the Mississippi River. Grant also watched him with consternation and pushed his campaign harder. In November he may have pushed just a bit too hard. From his new headquarters at La Grange, Tennessee, Grant wrote to General Sherman at Memphis to suggest that he bring three of his divisions, if possible, to Holly Springs to co-operate in a new offensive. Grant then moved to Holly Springs to await these reinforcements. General Sherman arrived near the end of the month but with only two divisions, all that he could spare from the Memphis defense. This force had just arrived at Holly Springs when Grant received orders from Washington approving his new offensive. He began the advance at once.

Van Dorn watched intently. Grant soon threatened Abbeville, and the Confederates withdrew to Oxford. As Grant continued to advance his well-fed army, Van Dorn retreated toward Coffeeville, skirmishing with the lead elements of the Union forces as both commands pushed deeper and deeper into Southern territory. Van Dorn's troops engaged elements of the advancing army at the bridge at Spring Dale and battled them until dark on December 3 when the Federals crossed the stream on logs and drove the Rebels to cover. Colonel Edward Hatch reported the capture of 92 of Van Dorn's command.

Early the next morning the skirmishing continued as the Confederates retreated into Water Valley. Just outside the town Colonel Hatch charged directly into Van Dorn's rear units. Undaunted by his loss Van Dorn attacked part of Colonel Hatch's command, overwhelmed the Union pickets, and forced the colonel to take up a defensive position. Van Dorn's counterattack was quickly repelled by the stronger Federal army, however, again with some loss to the Confederates. This time Colonel Hatch reported the capture of 183 of the Rebel force.

At Coffeeville another skirmish between Van Dorn's and Grant's commands resulted when elements of the Northern army arrived at the outskirts of the town before the complete withdrawal of the Confederate troops. According to General Tilghman the fighting began about a mile from Coffeeville on December 5 at 2:30 P.M. The advancing elements of the Federal army—units under Colonels T. Lyle Dickey, Edward Hatch, and Albert L. Lee—tried to move a Confederate unit under General Tilghman, but they found a much stronger foe than they had anticipated. After a brief skirmish Tilghman ordered a charge into the Federal position. With the Ninth Arkansas and the Eighth Kentucky Infantry Regiments leading the way, the Confederates dealt severely with the enemy in a short struggle. The Federal units were forced back nearly two miles over narrow, muddy roads, through a dense growth of oak trees and underbrush. According to Colonel Dickey it was often "impossible to see the enemy's position or note his strength."[8]

The short skirmish gave Van Dorn necessary time to move his own troops into Grenada, and it also showed Grant that he may have been pushing his own troops too hard and too long. Grant would have to consolidate his command and strengthen his ever-lengthening supply and communications lines. The Coffeeville skirmish was indecisive for the Confederates, however; it slowed the Federal advance only for the moment despite Van Dorn's optimistic observation to Pemberton that the enemy "will be careful how he comes up again."[9]

8. *Official Records Army*, XVII, Pt. 1, 496.
9. *Ibid.*, p. 503.

Some reports indicated that Van Dorn himself had a narrow escape during the skirmishes in Water Valley. Only prompt action on the part of his bodyguard and a small cavalry unit saved him from being captured after he and his staff were discovered by the enemy at a small hotel in the town.

Van Dorn pulled his forces back to Grenada and watched Grant occupy Coffeeville and Oxford. The Confederate army was in deep trouble, and its officers knew it. Dabney Maury's words gave expression to many men's thoughts: "In my opinion," he wrote, "we should all be concentrated about Grenada with our 'staves in our hands and our loins girt about,' and ready for a quick exodus."[10]

The situation in Mississippi was as serious as the Confederate authorities feared. Reports that the Federal army could go as far in the state as Grant wished were true. "How far south would you like me to go?" Grant telegraphed General Halleck on December 4. "We . . . can go as far as supplies can be taken."[11] It was General Grant, however, and not the Confederate army that finally halted the advance of the Federals just short of Grenada. "With my present force," Grant wrote, "it would not be safe to go beyond Grenada and attempt to hold present lines of communications."[12] With his supply line a single long thread from Bolivar to Oxford, he felt that for the moment Oxford was his southern limit.

Grant began to consolidate his position. To divert attention from his supply line, he decided to make a strong move against Vicksburg, his real objective. He ordered General Sherman back to Memphis to organize another land force that would work in conjunction with him in making the attack. He also ordered the Union commander at Helena, Arkansas, to prepare to launch an attack from across the river at the same time his and Sherman's forces made their move. Meanwhile he repaired the railroad back to Corinth and across to Memphis and established a depot at Grenada to supply his planned Vicksburg move.

While Van Dorn fretted and fussed with an army inadequate for the challenge before it, Richmond was also having its problems. The War Department, so often in the spotlight because of President Davis's involvement in so much of Confederate military policy, underwent a

10. *Ibid.*, Pt. 2, 903.
11. *Ibid.*, p. 472.
12. *Ibid.*

startling change when Secretary of War George W. Randolph resigned. The War Department in a search for new designs for victory had decided tentatively to send General Joseph E. Johnston to the West to assume command of all the forces of Bragg and Pemberton. Randolph's resignation delayed Johnston's appointment until November 24. Johnston's new command consisted of all the territory between the Alleghenies and the Mississippi River; unfortunately, his own role in the new arrangement was somewhat ill-defined. Bragg kept his own command, and General Pemberton remained at Vicksburg as commander of the Department of Mississippi and East Louisiana. In a reorganization within the latter command, Van Dorn and Price became commanders of the First and Second corps, respectively, of the department.

Johnston entered Tennessee just after Grant had begun his two-pronged advance toward Vicksburg. Sherman was moving toward the hills north of the city, and Grant was hoping to attack from the east to break Vicksburg's land defenses. Somehow, Johnston must stop them.

Johnston was just getting his bearings in unfamiliar surroundings when he received word that President Davis was also coming to Tennessee "to settle military questions and to improve civilian morale by his presence."[13] After a high-level conference at Chattanooga in which Davis, Bragg, and Johnston were the principals, Davis telegraphed the following back to newly appointed Secretary of War James A. Seddon: "Enemy is kept close in to Nashville and indicates only defensive purposes. Cavalry expeditions are projected to break up railroad communications between Louisville and Nashville and between Memphis and Grant's army."[14]

Grant's weak link was his supply line. Cutting this line was the one hope of saving Mississippi. Success in such an operation could be achieved only by a force possessing speed and mobility. Why not use cavalry? Even as Davis was informing his Secretary of War of the extended use of cavalry in new tactical operations in the West, one of the most important of these cavalry expeditions was already assembling in Mississippi. Its actions in the field would be associated with the continuing career of the much-maligned but ever active Buck Van Dorn.

The operation which Van Dorn was to supervise began at a remote

13. Quoted in Archer Jones, *Confederate Strategy from Shiloh to Vicksburg,* p. 117.
14. Quoted in Hudson Stroud, *Jefferson Davis: Confederate President,* p. 348.

base near Grenada, Mississippi, in early December. According to Victor M. Rose, one of the cavalrymen, the plan for this particular expedition grew out of a letter written by Lieutenant Colonel John S. Griffith which suggested "the propriety of a cavalry expedition into the enemy's rear."[15] Griffith's suggestion also related to the choice of a large number of officers for the new unit's commander. He wrote:

[I]f you will fit up a cavalry expedition, comprising three or four thousand men, and give us Major-General Earl Van Dorn, than whom no braver man lives, to command us, we will penetrate to the rear of the enemy, capture Holly Springs, Memphis, and other points, and perhaps, force him to retreat to Coffeeville; if not, we can certainly force more of the enemy to remain in their rear, to protect their supplies, than the cavalry could whip if we remained at the front.[16]

According to Rose, Pemberton immediately called Griffith into a private conference to discuss the details of such an arrangement. After considerable discussion, Pemberton agreed to give it a try. He notified Van Dorn of the new arrangement and assigned him three brigades of cavalry troops for his force.

The new command began to assemble at Grenada about December 12. Its complement was about 3,500 men made up of Colonel Griffith's Texas Brigade, Colonel William H. Jackson's Tennessee Brigade, and Colonel Robert M. McCullough's Missouri and Mississippi brigade. Most of these men had no idea of their specific assignment, they were just to report to Grenada under their respective commanders.

On December 15, these brigades withdrew from Grenada and moved quietly across the Yalabusha River. They encamped for the night on the river's bank and awaited the arrival of the officer who would direct some exciting but as yet unidentified action. About nine o'clock that evening they received orders to be ready for a lengthy march to begin at daybreak. As they moved out the next morning, their new commander suddenly made his dramatic appearance. The men cheered lustily when Buck Van Dorn joined them. The Mississippian at last had received a command for which he seemed fitted. He had excelled in cavalry tactics at West Point and on the frontier, and finally the Confederate leaders had seen fit to return him to command of the military unit he knew best.

The men with whom he rode were either unaware of his recent repu-

15. Rose, *Texas Brigade*, p. 131.
16. Quoted in *ibid*.

tation of failure or else they were unconcerned about it for they seemed
eager to ride under his leadership. This proved to be proper tonic for a
man beridden with defeat. As the expedition moved out from Grenada,
the dapper little general rode at the head of the departing column
"straight as an Indian, sitting his horse like a knight, and looking every
inch a soldier."[17] "[S]eeing Gen. Van Dorn on a little rise, seated on his
fine black mare," wrote one of the raiders, "I thought him as fine a general as I had ever seen."[18]

Van Dorn's unannounced objective was Holly Springs, Grant's chief
base of supplies for his prong of the operations toward Vicksburg. The
importance of Holly Springs as a military and supply base is readily
apparent by the abundant amount of equipment and supplies which
were stored there. Mrs. Carrington Mason, a Southern lady living in
Holly Springs at the time of the raid, later wrote that all the buildings in
the town had been crammed to capacity with whiskey, canned goods,
clothing, and other products needed by a large army. On the railroad
tracks were enough filled cars to make three normal-sized trains. Hundreds of sutlers, small dealers, and cotton buyers had entered the town
with the Union army, and many officers and their wives were quartered
in the town's better homes.

Van Dorn's mounted men, unaware of their exact mission, were ready
for whatever action awaited them. Each was well mounted and supplied
with three days' rations, a bottle of turpentine, a box of matches, and
sixty rounds of ammunition. A Mobile correspondent who accompanied
the expedition predicted its success: "Van Dorn," he wrote, ". . . has
been placed in a position where he will assuredly wipe out the stigmas
upon his military character and give him a fame equal to that of Stuart
and Morgan." Then he made an interesting prediction:

Van Dorn is undoubtedly the right man in the right place, and if he be
permitted to retain command of our cavalry force he will make what so far
has been one of the poorest arms of the body one of the most efficient and
famous.[19]

These must have been sweet words to a man more often maligned by
the press than praised. For a man who continually sought glory and so

17. A. F. Brown, "Van Dorn's Operations in Northern Mississippi," *Southern
Historical Association Papers*, VI, 155.
18. *A Soldier's Honor*, p. 237.
19. Mobile *Register and Advertiser*, December 27, 1862, p. 1.

seldom found it in the lean months of 1862, Van Dorn accepted this new responsibility with an enthusiasm that is commendable despite the fact that he may have seen in the assignment a new pathway to personal fame and honor.

The new commander wasted no time in beginning his new advance. During the entire day of December 16 and throughout most of the night, the men moved steadily in the direction of Houston, Mississippi. After a short bivouac they reached Houston about noon on Wednesday, the seventeenth. Their movement had been slow and rough because rain and storms had continually impeded their progress.

The troopers spent Wednesday night about fifteen miles north of Houston where they fed their horses from an adjacent corn field. Next day they were in the saddle early and arrived at Pontotoc by midmorning. "Passing through the beautiful town of Pontotoc," later wrote Victor Rose, "the hungry troopers were enthusiastically welcomed by the . . . citizens of the place; and trays, dishes, and baskets of the choicest edibles were offered on all sides, and pitchers of wine and milk as well."[20] But, Van Dorn allowed no respite, and the troops left the town munching the welcomed food and vocally praising the citizenry for their efforts.

At Pontotoc a strange episode took place that nearly put an end to the expedition. In mid-December General William T. Sherman, working out his plans to attack Vicksburg, had dispatched Colonel T. Lyle Dickey with 800 cavalry troops to cut the Mobile and Ohio Railroad, which ran north and south just eighteen miles east of Pontotoc. Their journey to and from the railroad carried them through Pontotoc. Sylvanus Cadwallader, who accompanied Dickey's force, said that the Federals successfully destroyed the railroad at several points and were returning to their home base when they discovered Van Dorn's troops.[21]

Dickey's troops had halted for lunch about six miles east of Pontotoc when the colonel received word that a large Confederate cavalry force had been seen moving through the town all that morning. Dickey figured that this was enemy cavalry sent after him, so he ordered his troops into Pontotoc where he planned a defensive stand. Arriving at the little town he saw the last units of Van Dorn's force leaving the town, moving northward. Dickey fully expected the larger enemy force to turn and

20. *Texas Brigade*, p. 84.
21. Cadwallader, *Three Years with Grant*, p. 34.

attack him at this point, and he made plans to retreat before the Confederate onrush.

Van Dorn could hardly afford to risk an encounter with such a force, so he calmly disdained the Union force. Others in his command were not so unruffled with the Federals behind them. One colonel who commanded part of the Confederate rearguard hurriedly dispatched a messenger to his chief. The messenger arrived at the head of the long column and saluted the little general: "General, Colonel ——— sent me to inform you that the Yankees have fired on his rear!" he reported.

"Are they in the rear?" asked Van Dorn.

"Yes Sir," replied the courier.

"Well," said the general, "you go back and tell Col ——— that that is exactly where I want them."[22]

Colonel Dickey, seeing that Van Dorn was not going to attack him, demonstrated briefly before moving on. Unable to reach Oxford before nightfall, he bivouacked for the night after dispatching word to General Grant of his encounter with the large Confederate force. Unfortunately for the Federals, his couriers got lost during the night and did not get the news of Van Dorn's movement to Grant until the morning of December 20 after Dickey had already conveyed the news to Grant in person. Too late, Grant dispatched Colonel John K. Mizner from Water Valley to pursue the Southern cavalry. Too late, also, he notified his garrison at Holly Springs to be on the lookout for a hostile enemy force.

Van Dorn continued his advance toward Holly Springs. Never once did he give any clue as to his objective. He deliberately crossed all the roads leading to Holly Springs to deceive citizens and Yankee patrols into believing that he was moving toward Bolivar.

He arrived at New Albany on the evening of December 18, crossed the Tallahatchie River, and encamped on the west banks of that stream for the night. "We were jaded," wrote cavalryman J. G. Deupree after his many hours in the saddle.[23] The men were bedded down and asleep when suddenly "a fearful storm" struck them, drenching men and equipment. Moving to higher ground in the darkness, the troops slept through the rest of the night in a drier area.

In motion again on December 19, Van Dorn continued his march northward on the prominent Ripley road. The day was very cold, but

22. Barron, *The Lone Star Defenders*, p. 133.
23. "The Capture of Holly Springs," p. 53.

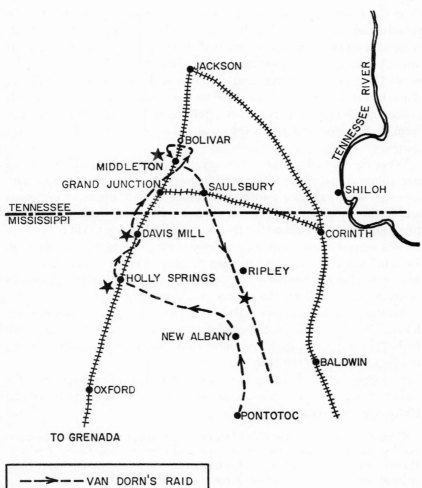

VAN DORN'S RAID ON HOLLY SPRINGS

Legend:
- ➤ – – – VAN DORN'S RAID
- ★ SKIRMISH

Map labels: JACKSON, BOLIVAR, MIDDLETON, GRAND JUNCTION, SAULSBURY, SHILOH, TENNESSEE MISSISSIPPI, DAVIS MILL, CORINTH, RIPLEY, HOLLY SPRINGS, NEW ALBANY, BALDWIN, OXFORD, PONTOTOC, TO GRENADA, TENNESSEE RIVER

his troops rode with marked enthusiasm. About noon several of them began complaining of hunger. To assuage their "stomach gnawings," their chief promised them "rations in abundance" on the morrow, a promise the men received with good cheer.[24] Later in the day they arrived at an unused trail that forked off from the Ripley road and went directly crosscountry to Holly Springs about twenty-five miles to the west. The trail was rugged and swampy, and the going was difficult. Since it was important not to come into contact with the enemy's outposts, Van Dorn halted his men at a point some twelve to fourteen miles from his objective and sent a spy on ahead to size up the Holly Springs garrison.

While he awaited word from his spy, Van Dorn divided his troops into two columns and readied men and horses for an attack. The spy soon returned with valuable information about the arrangement of troops within the town, and the general made his final plans. About dusk the two columns moved out on the final lap of their journey to Holly Springs.

"We moved slowly and very quietly during the night," wrote S. B. Barron, "and while we were moving directly towards the town, guards were placed at the houses we passed lest some citizen might be treacherous enough to inform the enemy of our movements."[25]

Arriving inside the town's picket lines, just a few miles from the courthouse, Van Dorn halted and rested his men. It was now well after midnight. The night was dark and bitter cold. No fires were built, and the troopers suffered in the early morning air.

Sometime before dawn on December 20, General Grant received the following report from Colonel Robert C. Murphy, commander of the Holly Springs garrison:

Contraband just in reports Van Dorn only 14 miles from here [with] 5,000 cavalry, intending to destroy stores here, and then dash on Grand Junction. He is on the Ripley road and [is] expected to reach here by daylight. Have ordered out my cavalry, but my force is only a handful.[26]

With fewer than 500 troops at his immediate disposal in and around Holly Springs, Colonel Murphy was concerned. But though he feared the advance of what he believed to be an enemy force of 12,000, he failed to give information of the impending attack to the infantry camp just north of the town or to Major John J. Mudd, commanding the Sec-

24. *Ibid.*, pp. 53–54.
25. *The Lone Star Defenders*, p. 134.
26. *Official Records Army*, XVII, Pt. 2, 444.

ond Illinois Cavalry stationed near the town's fairgrounds. In his official report of the battle Major Mudd complained of drunkenness and inefficiency on the part of the garrison's commanding officers; he accused them of inadequate preparation for defense and of sleeping at the homes of rebels instead of being with their troops. Colonel Murphy was later court-martialed for his incompetency.

Early Saturday morning, December 20, the Federal garrison at Holly Springs was distributed in three major areas of concentration. Part of the infantry occupied quarters in the courthouse and other buildings in the center of the town; other infantrymen camped near the railway depot; and six companies of cavalry billeted on the fairgrounds just outside the town limits. These three units were one half to three quarters of a mile apart. Van Dorn knew that to attack all three of these positions simultaneously would have called for a flanking movement of great dimensions. Since enemy pickets would have quickly detected such an attack, he decided not to split his force. A staff officer later described his attack:

> The first or head of the column was to dash into and capture the infantry camped in front of us; the second, following immediately after the first, was to sweep by the encampment, move straight into the town until it reached the street leading north to the fair grounds, then wheel to the right and charge the cavalry camp; the third, following immediately after the second, was to dash through the town, disregarding everything until it struck the infantry occupying the public square.[27]

The Mississippi troops were to enter the town from the northeast, charge through the infantry, and attack the cavalry. The Missourians were to dismount and follow the Mississippians and engage the aroused infantry. The Texans were to approach Holly Springs from the east, attacking positions in their path and preventing reinforcements from the east and south. The Tennesseans were to guard the north of the town against an attack from Bolivar. Official reports of the Northern officers at the various points of the attack seem to verify the fact that this is generally the pattern of battle that developed.

Lying in bed in town, Mrs. Mason heard what sounded to her like the "singing of a wood fire."[28] As the noise came closer, she recognized the rebel yell. Riding at a full gallop the Mississippians entered the city;

27. Brown, "Van Dorn's Operations," p. 156.
28. Mrs. Mason, "Raid on Holly Springs," clipping found in Van Dorn Collection, Montgomery, Alabama.

each column dashed for its own particular objective, and caught the enemy completely unprepared for the attack. According to Colonel Brown, who was in the thick of the action, the Confederates literally rode over the enemy infantry before they could fully awaken. How the Rebels got past Colonel Murphy's pickets is still a matter of conjecture. Reports from some of the Confederates, written years after the war, speak of a detachment under an officer which silenced the pickets before the attack. A Northern newspaper account said that no warning came from the pickets because they were not strategically placed, and the Confederates probably entered between outposts. The latter explanation seems in line with the circumstances of the attack. Van Dorn knew where Murphy had his outposts, and he meticulously avoided them as he and his troops descended upon the town.

As the Confederates entered Holly Springs, many of the Yankees rushed from their tents to make some effort at defense only to find themselves blocked by the charging, yelling horsemen. Many of the men laid down their arms and surrendered on the spot. In the center of the advancing party, General Van Dorn directed the assault. He rode into the town with three or four other horsemen and when his troops recognized him, they sent up a great cheer for their commanding officer. "Old Buck" acknowledged the cheer and dramatically pointed his sword toward the enemy. The effect of this action was "electrical." The Confederate charge then struck the enemy camp like a "thunderbolt." Citizens emerged from their houses and their cheers rang through the air: "Hurrah for Van Dorn! Hurrah for the Confederacy!! Hurrah for Jeff Davis!!!"[29]

The correspondent accompanying the raiders later wrote a colorful description of the community's reaction to the attack:

The rapidity with which the tents of the enemy were vacated was marvellous; and impelled by burning torches and rapid discharges of sidearms, the Yankees took no time to prepare for their toilets, but rushed out into the cool atmosphere of a December morning clothed very similarly to Joseph when the lady Potiphar attempted to detain him. The scene was wild, exciting, tumultuous. Yankees running, tents burning, torches flaming, Confederates shouting, guns popping, sabres clanking; Abolitionists begging for mercy, "rebels" shouting exultingly, women en dishabille clapping their hands, frantic with joy, crying "kill them, kill them"—a heterogeneous mass

29. Brown, "Van Dorn's Operations," p. 157.

of excited, frantic, frightened human beings presenting an indescribable picture, more adapted for the pencil of Hogarth than the pen of a newspaper correspondent.[30]

Several Federal officers, including Major Mudd, rallied their troops for a defensive stand against the invaders, and though completely surrounded by the Confederates they fought gallantly for some time. Sabers swished the air, horsemen rode pell mell at one another, and the air filled with shouts, cheers, and pistol shots. Confederate strength soon forced most of the defenders to throw down their arms, but Major Mudd and six companies of his men refused to surrender. With their swords, about 130 of them cut their way through Van Dorn's men and escaped.

The struggle near the fairgrounds ended the fighting for the day, and by 8:00 A.M. Van Dorn was in complete possession of Holly Springs. It was then that pandemonium broke loose. Women dashed from nearby houses robed in night clothes to greet the Rebel cavalry. Officers shouted commands in a desperate attempt to restore some semblance of order. The Confederates had been hungry, thirsty, and in need of clothing too long to miss an opportunity to sack the abundant supplies that filled most of the buildings in the town. Boots and hats were the items most in demand other than whiskey. Cigars were also a popular item. Confederate officers let barrels of whiskey overflow to keep their men from becoming incapacitated for further action, but they hardly made a dent in the large supply of liquor in the town. Victor Rose said that the streets were literally flooded with whiskey. "We had stepped from privation to plenty," he wrote, "and many were disposed to inaugurate a jubilee, inspired by the spirit of John Barleycorn, Esq."[31]

Many Negroes who had been brought into Holly Springs by Grant's invading army also went berserk and began to loot and pillage as never before. They concentrated their efforts upon the post office and the liquor warehouses. While many of them spent the day drinking whiskey, others opened letters in which they hoped to find money.

In spite of all the turmoil, Van Dorn managed to reorganize his command, and some sort of order was finally restored. Houses were searched for Federal officers, and all prisoners were assembled in the town square. The Confederates then began a systematic destruction of the Federal supplies in the town. Van Dorn first ordered that the warehouses and

30. Mobile *Advertiser and Register,* January 7, 1863, p. 2.
31. *Texas Brigade,* pp. 88–89.

the supply depots be burned. The railway depot met a similar fate. Explosion of ammunition dumps helped spread the fire to other buildings. Surgeon Horace R. Wirtz of the town's garrison appeared before Van Dorn to plead for the town's hospital, a former six-unit Confederate arsenal, but his efforts were in vain. Federal medical officers protested the destruction of this building; they accused the invaders of riddling the hospital with flying balls and shells before the interns could remove the inmates. No record of Van Dorn's defense of this action remains, but it can only be suggested that in the haste to destroy the important Union base, the men took little notice of the contents of any particular building. "For about ten hours," wrote a member of the Third Texas cavalry, "we labored destroying, burning. . . ."[32]

According to some sources, Mrs. Grant was at the Harvey W. Walker house within the town during the raid. When they discovered her identity, the troops treated her with great respect.

The destruction wrought by the Confederates at Holly Springs was heavy. Van Dorn estimated the Northern losses to be valued at $1,500,000. General Grant admitted losses of goods amounting to $400,000. Colonel Murphy, already under censure for misconduct at the battle of Iuka, was saddled with full responsibility for the losses. "My fate is most mortifying," he wrote later. "I have wished a hundred times today that I had been killed."[33]

General Grant, disgusted at the heavy losses, also reflected on what he considered the disgrace of the Holly Springs's affair:

With all the cotton, public stores, and substantial buildings about the depot it would have been perfectly practicable to have made in a few hours defenses sufficient to resist with a small garrison all the cavalry force brought against them until the re-enforcements which the commanding officer was notified were marching to his relief could have reached him.[34]

Once the Confederates had destroyed the major part of Grant's supplies, Van Dorn made no effort to consolidate his position or to maintain control of Holly Springs. Obviously his raid was only to destroy. By 4:00 P.M. his troops were remounted, many on captured horses, and

32. Barron, *The Lone Star Defenders*, p. 135.

33. *Official Records Army*, XXVII, Pt. 1, 508–509. The reporter from the Mobile paper later wrote that Murphy was pulled from under his bed by captors and presented in his night clothes to the Confederate commander. Mobile *Register and Advertiser*, January 7, 1863.

34. *Ibid.*, p. 515.

were ready to move away from his greatest triumph, "the best equipped body of cavalry in the Confederate service."[35] Their route of departure was toward Davis's Mill.

Late Saturday Van Dorn made his only report of the attack. It was short and to the point, overstated in all probability, but void of much of the conceit and superfluous language that marked so much of his correspondence: "I surprised the enemy at this place at daylight this morning," he wrote, "burned up all the quartermaster's stores, cotton . . . an immense amount; burned up many trains; took a great many arms and about 1,500 prisoners. I presume the value of stores would amount to $1,500,000."[36]

As usual, reports of undesirable personal conduct followed Van Dorn from Holly Springs. The Memphis *Bulletin* described at length the drunkenness among the Confederate troops after their successful raid, and one article stated that Van Dorn himself was "as drunk as a Lord" upon his departure from Holly Springs.[37] Undoubtedly this is enemy newspaper talk, but true or false, the Northern troops in the Holly Springs area were left in utter confusion, and important supplies for Grant's Vicksburg project were completely destroyed.

The Federals should have initiated their pursuit of the wily Rebel at once if they desired to eliminate this menace behind their lines. Because of a mix-up in orders, however, it was not until the afternoon of December 22 that Colonel Benjamin H. Grierson of the Sixth Illinois Cavalry headed north from Holly Springs having been ordered to that post earlier by Grant. Van Dorn took advantage of this lapse and on December 21, he rode boldly up to Davis's Mill to repeat his success of the previous day.

Davis's Mill was a sleepy little Mississippi hamlet lying eighteen miles north of Holly Springs. Only a small garrison of about 250 men defended it, and the Southerners felt confident of another quick success. This time Van Dorn reckoned without knowledge of the merits of the town's commanding officer, Colonel H. Morgan. This proud officer was a startling contrast to the humiliated Murphy. Warned by Grant of Van Dorn's advance, Morgan had prepared his small garrison for the best possible defense.

35. Deupree, "The Capture of Holly Springs," p. 58.
36. *Official Records Army*, XVII, Pt. 2, 463.
37. Memphis *Bulletin*, December 23, 1862, p. 2.

Van Dorn looked over Morgan's position across the narrow but treacherous Wolf River and decided to attack on foot instead of on horseback as he had done at Holly Springs. He decided to crush him by sheer power of numbers before the Federals could bring in reinforcements. Just before noon he launched a furious but confused assault across the little river. The gray dragoons pushed in the enemy pickets with little difficulty, but they hit the fury of the enemy defense when they arrived before Morgan's well-defended fortifications. Morgan had converted an old sawmill into a blockhouse with railroad ties and cotton bales and had thus prepared an almost impregnable position. He hit the advancing Confederates with such galling fire that Van Dorn halted his charge far short of his objective.

The first charge was repulsed. Van Dorn, still confident of his superiority of numbers, ordered a second and then a third assault to dislodge the stubborn Morgan. A few Confederates crossed the river successfully only to be pinned down under a bridge by Federal fire. Repulsed the third time, Van Dorn called off his attacking party and prepared to move out. Several of his men were killed as they tried to recross the stream. Colonel Morgan reported later that the unsuccessful attack cost Van Dorn twenty-two dead, thirty wounded, and twenty prisoners. The impetuous little general had misjudged his opponent's position. With time running out for him, there was little he could do but to pull his small force away from Morgan's fortress and ride north. Time was rapidly becoming their major consideration. There would certainly be a Federal pursuit, and they must strike quickly and move to new objectives.

For the next two days Van Dorn's wearying dragoons rode north and northeast, cutting telegraph lines and railroads as they went. Federal reports indicate that Grant's commanders in northern Mississippi and southern Tennessee were never quite sure of Van Dorn's exact whereabouts. Federals "saw" the Confederate commander in the vicinity of Brownsville, Tennessee, at Memphis, and at other prominent Federal outposts. Actually on these two days he and his men were riding toward Bolivar, where he finally feinted an attack. Instead of attacking the Tennessee town, however, he daringly dashed south of it, cut off and captured the pickets, and then rode toward the south, pursued by Colonel Grierson who had finally found his trail.

Arriving at Middleton, Tennessee, seven miles south of Bolivar on December 24, Van Dorn demanded the surrender of the town's garrison of 115 men. Colonel William H. Graves, the town's commander, acted in accordance with Grant's suggestion and refused to surrender. Again the Confederates failed to dislodge a strongly entrenched Federal position. Van Dorn continued the assault for nearly two hours, and then seeing that success was not possible without artillery, he finally pulled back and retreated southward through Van Buren and on to Saulsbury. This retreat followed the exact route that Grierson's cavalry had taken as they had pursued the Confederate horsemen toward Bolivar several days earlier. Grant now had his sights on Van Dorn, and Van Dorn had no further need to break the Federal line of supply.

After the little fray at Middleton, Van Dorn began his retreat in earnest. The alarm was out and Colonels Grierson, Edward Hatch, Mizner, and James B. McPherson were alerted to his presence near the Mississippi-Tennessee border. The weary Confederates spent Christmas day in the saddle with Grierson's troops breathing down their necks. Outracing the pursuing Federals seemed out of the question, so the wily Van Dorn decided upon another scheme. Arriving at Ripley late on Christmas day, he abruptly divided his small force. Leaving one unit of his rear guard and a few scouts at Ripley, he continued his retreat with his main force. Instead of following the Pontotoc road to the southwest, the route which he had traveled on his way to Holly Springs, he turned his force down a small road heading toward the southwest.

Meanwhile Colonel Grierson encountered what must have been Van Dorn's rearguard near Ripley. Hoping to delay the Federal cavalry, the Confederates fired at Grierson's troops and then quickly retreated. They repeated this operation until they lost a lieutenant and ten men. Then they hurried southward out of Grierson's reach. Grierson reported, probably in error, that Van Dorn himself commanded the unit he met at Ripley. Evidence seems to place the Confederate captain with the main body retreating toward Grenada. Though Grierson was again at Van Dorn's rear before the main body of the Confederates reached Grenada, the Federals were never able to gain the advantage they held outside Ripley. When Van Dorn finally crossed the Tallahatchie River and entered camp on December 28, the pursuing cavalry halted and returned to its own headquarters near Holly Springs.

Van Dorn and his riders had traveled more than 500 miles during the two-week period, and in that time they gave the invading Union army one of its most humiliating if not severest defeats in Mississippi. The raid had not only been an immediate military success, but it also had helped prove that cavalry raids behind enemy lines could be effective in combating larger, better-equipped commands. Surprise and speed coupled with good horsemanship and daring leaders were indeed key factors for their success. Where the enemy was well prepared for an attack, there was little chance of doing much damage; but a swift, well-organized cavalry band could swoop down upon a poorly defended supply base and deal the enemy a severe blow. This success at Holly Springs and similar attacks set the pattern for later Confederate cavalry action in the West. Van Dorn, Forrest, Morgan, and Wheeler—all achieved fame as commanders of units operating behind enemy lines.

Even as Van Dorn's troops were in the field, similar tactics were being employed in West Tennessee by Bedford Forrest. Leaving Columbia on December 11, Forrest had proceeded into West Tennessee, where on December 17 he struck at Lexington, about eighty miles northeast of Holly Springs. Then while Van Dorn moved in on Colonel Murphy's unsuspecting garrison, Forrest attacked—in quick succession—Trenton, Humboldt, and Union City, Tennessee. In and around these communities he did more damage than Van Dorn was doing on his raid. On December 20 while Van Dorn was attacking Grant's leading supply base, Forrest was beginning the destruction of the Mobile and Ohio Railroad some seventy miles to the north. As the Mississippian returned to his base at Grenada, Forrest also returned to his base in central Tennessee. In the two weeks these officers had operated behind Union lines, they had caused Grant more concern than during any single period of equal length during the winter season. Van Dorn broke up a prime supply base. Forrest temporarily destroyed the usefulness of the Mobile and Ohio Railroad and captured 2,500 Federal troops and destroyed much equipment and many supplies.

Van Dorn and Forrest had brought a double calamity upon General Grant. Their raids into West Tennessee did not restore Confederate supremacy in that region, nor did they make it possible for Generals Johnston or Bragg to drastically revise offensive or defensive strategy, but these raids had an important over-all effect upon the war in the West at the end of its second year. The destruction wrought placed Grant in a very difficult position. Equipment and food required by a large advancing army were not available in quantity in desolate Mississippi. Unlike Sherman in Georgia two years later, Grant was not yet ready to live off the countryside. He was forced to halt his offensive and to protect his remaining supply bases. When he moved his troops from Oxford back to Holly Springs, he was delaying a land attack against Vicksburg which he felt was imperative for a Union victory in the West. The Northern army had lost only a few hundred troops to the Confederate raiders, a negligible number for the large force then in Mississippi. More important, it had lost stores of great value, and with Van Dorn and Forrest still active, the Northern army was threatened with still greater losses. Further Union penetration of Mississippi was impossible before spring. Sherman attacked Chickasaw Bluffs with no help from Grant, and the Confederates contained this advance and others until the spring and summer of 1863.

The victory at Holly Springs was one of the most important Confederate triumphs of the year, a fine Christmas gift for a despondent President who was then visiting west of the Alleghenies. It raised the morale of all mounted troops, especially those in Mississippi who had been retreating before Grant's relentless drive. A splendid cavalry force was then formed to harass the Union army in Tennessee for many months. From different ends of the enemy supply line, Forrest and Van Dorn joined their forces for what the War Department figured would be a more effective operation.

More important for Earl Van Dorn than the victory over Murphy and the destruction of the valuable supplies was the new prestige that he gained by the bold raid. It was really an amazing raid—cutting through numerous Federal outposts, avoiding Union pursuit, destroying an important supply depot. Confederate leaders finally realized that although he was no leader of armies, there was a place for Van Dorn in the Confederate command system. Van Dorn was a cavalry officer or more appropriately a commander of mounted infantry; he understood the significance of cavalry's maneuverability. On the Holly Springs raid he proved that he could effectively handle this type of troop unit. One of the men who participated in this raid summarized his capabilities: "At the head of an infantry column," wrote S. B. Barron, "he moved too rapidly, too many of his over-marched men failed to get into his battles; but place him in front of good men well mounted, and he stood at the head of the class of fine cavalry commanders."[38]

38. *The Lone Star Defenders*, p. 132.

Van Dorn and his troops returned to Grenada tired and worn from their long excursion into Tennessee. Shortly after his return, the general applied for and received one of his infrequent leaves of absence. Late in December he departed from Grenada to visit his family. His wife and children were then living in Mt. Vernon, Alabama, at the new home of Mrs. Van Dorn's parents, and Earl spent several pleasant days in their company. Earl's sister later said that the general seemed to enjoy himself thoroughly on this visit for at this time he became acquainted with his little daughter. While the general worked in the big yard of the Godbold estate, laying off flower gardens and planning walks and driveways, Livy followed him everywhere. There appears to have been a real bond between them.[39]

Mrs. Van Dorn was also happy over her husband's visit. "Were you not surprised that Earl had paid me a visit?" she later wrote to his sister. "It was a delightful surprise, I assure you," she continued in one of the few bits of her correspondence that remains.[40]

The community received the Mississippian with an enthusiasm which belied the mutterings against him that still circulated so freely in Alabama. His wife later expressed her feelings in the matter shortly after his return to duty. "I have read the proceedings of that Court of Inquiry," she said, "and everything was disproved, and all the slanders by the people of his state had circulated were repudiated, and by those who were with him and knew him best. . . . He has passed through a severe ordeal, but I knew all the time that *my* general was all right."[41]

It was the last time that Van Dorn saw his family.

39. *A Soldier's Honor*, p. 244.
40. Mrs. Van Dorn to Emily Miller, *ibid.*, p. 345.
41. *Ibid.*

CHAPTER TWELVE

Victory in Tennessee

*I*N the hills and valleys of Tennessee and northern Mississippi in 1863 a strange quiet settled like an ominous fog. The echoes of Stone's River's heavy guns and the cries of agony from that battlefield died down, but men waited almost with impatience for continued action. Quietness contrasted to the earlier sounds of violence, so much so that one observer suggested the possibility that "evil powers" were raising the stillness so that they might "pause to gather fresh strength" for "a fiercer and deadlier blast."[1]

Just below Nashville, Confederate General Braxton Bragg's army blocked the southward advance of Federal General William Rosecrans's Army of the Cumberland. Bragg's line of defense extended from Shelbyville to Wartrace. His men offered the last line of resistance toward Chattanooga after their withdrawal from Kentucky and the defeat at Stone's River. Bragg's cavalrymen patrolled the countryside from Columbia to McMinnville outside his main line. Their missions were ill defined, their ranks were rent by chronic absenteeism and desertion, and yet they were always on the alert to the waning possibilities of raiding a supply depot or attacking an isolated Federal unit. These mounted troops with more courage than manpower continually harassed the blue-clad army settled so firmly before them. They were commanded by some of the finest cavalry officers of the war—Joseph Wheeler, Nathan Bedford Forrest, and Earl Van Dorn—soon household words to Tennesseans who looked to horse and dragoon for their delivery from Yankee aggression. The cavalry so impressed General Joseph E. Johnston during these months that he later credited them with holding the destiny of the Confederacy in their hands in early 1863.

1. Thomas C. DeLeon, *Four Years in Rebel Capitals*, p. 250.

The Southern cavalry in Tennessee also impressed the Federals. At his Murfreesboro headquarters, General Rosecrans observed his enemy with consternation.[2] Because of his dependence upon a single railroad line to Louisville for his supplies, the Ohio commander viewed as premature any showdown action against Bragg's Army of Tennessee. Winter rains and floods threatening vital roads and waterways convinced Rosecrans that it would be unwise to undertake a campaign until he was thoroughly prepared. Criticism from Washington little influenced his tactical decisions as he delayed the momentous task of invasion. He called for reinforcements.

It was not a lack of courage that prevented the rival commanders in Tennessee from initiating the offensive operations urged upon them by their respective War Departments. Often both Bragg and Rosecrans had demonstrated courage, resourcefulness, and initiative when these qualities were sorely needed in both armies. Like many others thrown too quickly into war, these men lacked certain intangible qualities of leadership, best described by Karl von Clausewitz as "inner light" and "resolution," or perceiving the true meaning in any given situation and having the courage to follow it up.[3] In too many cases during the Civil War the "inner light" flickered and resolution waned as the size of the command increased. Officers who had been effective with small troop units lost their effectiveness overnight under the demands of heavier responsibilities. While troops chafed in camps and garrisons, telegraph wires were heated with requests for more troops, more supplies, and more time. Too rapid promotion thus affected Bragg and Rosecrans, and it is not unusual that the late winter and spring of 1863 became seasons of reconnaissances, raids, and skirmishes. In both armies in Tennessee the cavalry most often engaged the enemy at major times of indecision.

Van Dorn became an actor in this new drama as a result of a decision made by General Johnston in January 1863. To his War Department he reported: "I am preparing to send 6000 cavalry under Van Dorn to Bragg's aid to operate upon the enemy's communication."[4]

Van Dorn viewed this new arrangement with mixed emotions. The presence of General Pemberton at Vicksburg was a constant reminder

2. General Rosecrans replaced General Buell in Tennessee early in 1863. Rosecrans made his headquarters at Murfreesboro.

3. Karl von Clausewitz, *War Politics and Power*, p. 118.

4. *Official Records Army*, XVII, Pt. 2, 838.

to him of his own failure, the Corinth defeat, where victory could certainly have brought to his own shoulders instead of to Pemberton's the much-coveted stars of lieutenant-general. But in Tennessee the enemy was in force, and where the enemy was there was also opportunity for glory and advancement. Since the Holly Springs raid and the Confederate victory at Chickasaw Bluffs in late December, the most pressing challenge had shifted, at least for the moment, from Mississippi to central Tennessee where Bragg held a tenuous position just south of Nashville.

Whether the transfer of Van Dorn's command from Pemberton to Bragg was a wise move is still debatable. Pemberton always contended that the loss of this cavalry cost him heavily in the summer engagement with Grant in and around Vicksburg. This is probably true, but in reality both Confederate armies were understrength. Rapid transfer of troops seemed the only possible solution to their manpower problems. When Grant halted his Vicksburg offensive, if only temporarily, Johnston had little choice but to meet the greatest threat with the largest possible number, still maintaining a line of defense before Grant's Vicksburg force.

On January 11, 1863, General Johnston expressed to Pemberton his desire to combine the cavalry units in Mississippi and Tennessee under Van Dorn. On the same day Johnston justified this new arrangement to Bragg: "One of Van Dorn's greatest objects will be to cover your left by preventing Federal troops from going from West to Middle Tennessee," he wrote.[5] Two days later, as requested, Pemberton assigned Van Dorn to command most of the cavalry in his district with orders to report to General Johnston for further instructions.

Van Dorn assumed his new command in midwinter. He set to work making the necessary arrangements to prepare troops for the difficult trip to Tennessee. He called in cavalry units scattered from southern Mississippi to eastern Louisiana and united them at Tupelo in early February. Here he made final preparations for the long ride. Victor Rose, one of the riders, later remembered these preparations with some feeling:

Before commencing the long and fatiguing march, Van Dorn issued his celebrated "Order No. 5," in which he prescribed the minutest rules for the

5. *Ibid.*, p. 832.

government of his *corps*, whether in camp or on the march. Proper distances were prescribed to be observed on the march between companies, regiments, brigades, and divisions; a regular system of bugle calls was formulated; challenges and replies of videttes, etc. . . . the whole concluding with the impetuous declaration: "Cavalry knows no danger—knows no failure; *what it is ordered to do, it must do.*[6]

The troops seemed to be in the best physical condition of the year, and they shared their commander's enthusiasm. One of the men gave a somewhat strange evaluation of his own health at this time. Wrote Private Barron: "The severe horseback service we had had since the battle of Corinth, and our diet, principally sweet potatoes, had restored my health completely . . . and I was in good condition to do cavalry service."[7]

It was a dreary day when the Confederates finally departed from Tupelo. Approximately 7,500 troops organized into two divisions rode behind their commander. The height of the winter season was at hand, and wet, disagreeable weather dogged their path from the beginning. They plodded over broken roads, they waded river swamps, and they forded swollen streams. Their bodies ached for rest, and the occasional sunshine lacked the warmth needed to dry out clothing and supplies. Men and animals suffered alike. Some grumbled but never when the commanding general rode in their midst.

If Van Dorn suffered, no one knew about it. Always the youthful-looking general rode ahead of his troops; his eyes toward Tennessee glittered in anticipation even in the worst of conditions. As was his custom he pushed his men hard, but he spoke to no one of his plans or his route of march. At the evening campfire he made small talk with some of his officers, but brigadier generals and colonels learned their orders only as Van Dorn was ready to divulge them. High-ranking officers were as surprised as accompanying journalists as the exact route of their march unfolded before them.

Van Dorn directed his cavalry first to Florence, Alabama. Here they spent a day crossing the turbulent Tennessee River. Many a young man looked back toward warm Alabama before he reluctantly moved northward again.

From Florence travel conditions became worse. Struggling horses

6. *Texas Brigade*, p. 92.
7. *The Lone Star Defenders*, p. 144.

and weary riders followed ragged, imperceptible trails for endless hours. Sometimes the road terminated abruptly. Flooding streams blocked their paths. "[W]e had a great time pulling through the mud, and in some places we found it almost impassable," wrote Private Barron.[8]

Outnumbered Federal cavalry in outposts, whose officers were alerted to the unusual activity before them, reacted as best they could before the large force. They burned important bridges and threw roadblocks into expected pathways of the invading troops. This forced wearisome and time-consuming delays. To make matters worse, bushwackers offered a constant threat to lead units and stragglers. Enthusiasm so prominent at Tupelo faded as horses struggled in mud to their haunches, and men sat in their saddles—cold, wet, and disgusted.

Van Dorn watched his men anxiously, but still he continued his relentless pace. He instituted prompt disciplinary action for any violation of regimen that threatened to delay his progress. The February sun remained half-hidden in winter's haze, and the troops pushed on. Before him, in Bragg's command, there was yet another chance for Buck Van Dorn; it might be his last one!

February 20 was a frosty cold morning in central Tennessee. Confederate troops in camp near Columbia rose slowly and left their tents reluctantly. Suddenly these early risers were greeted with shouts by happy men on tired horses. To Van Dorn and his fatigued marchers, the outline of the city in the frost-covered dawn was a glorious sight. When they saw Columbia, they could not contain their enthusiasm. A wild cheer rang through their ranks as the horsemen rode into a Confederate camp; the men in camp soon took up the cheer.

Columbia also looked good to Van Dorn, but it was only a first step. From the moment he accepted his new assignment, the old dreams of Kentucky and Ohio had returned—dreams of himself as a victorious general leading a slashing, hard-charging army into the heart of the enemy territory. Just before his arrival at Columbia, General Leonidas Polk, also commanding in Tennessee, had inadvertently encouraged him in his unrealistic thoughts. On February 8, while the Mississippi cavalry struggled through southern Tennessee, Polk wrote Van Dorn that he had hopes for a concerted action by the Mississippian in conjunction with General Wheeler against a Federal force then threatening Wheeler's operations against Northern supply lines. Such an operation would take

8. *Ibid.*

VAN DORN'S THEATER OF OPERATIONS; LATE 1862 AND EARLY 1863

Van Dorn toward Kentucky and give him a start on his anticipated objective. Though he arrived in Columbia too late to participate in Polk's scheme, the proposal whetted his appetite. An incurable optimist, he never seemed to realize the problems at hand in his grandiose schemes; instead he seemed always to have his heart set on what he always termed "cutting loose."

Van Dorn probably accepted the Tennessee assignment with the understanding that he would operate unfettered against the enemy. This pattern of command already had been well established in central Tennessee by Generals Forrest, Wheeler, and John Morgan. All these officers operated in the field with great leeway in decisionmaking and in selecting objectives. Morgan, in particular, impressed Van Dorn. Here was the man of action. He liked Morgan's sudden, devastating blows behind enemy lines. This type of action not only wrecked enemy communications and supply lines, but it also brought distinction to the bold commander who conducted the raids.

The excitement of the intimacy of battle rang in his words when Van Dorn reported his arrival to General Johnston. "I am now here with my whole command," he announced, "and will be ready to make any movement you may desire."[9]

Then as if afraid that Johnston might not place him close enough to the front he suggested an attack on Franklin. After routing the Franklin garrison he would cross the Cumberland River and operate on its north bank and on to the banks of the Ohio, "unless General Bragg is threatened by General Rosecrans soon." It was action he sought, and there was a near pathos in his plea at the conclusion of his letter to Johnston: "[L]et me beg you not to make me and my command a part of the picket of any army. I can do you better service, I am sure. We are proud of being cavalry, and desire to win distinction under the title."[10]

General Johnston's reply was diplomatic but firm:

9. *Official Records Army*, LII, Pt. 2, 425.
10. "N'Importe," an anonymous reporter who accompanied Van Dorn from Mississippi, wrote that the general's new assignment was actually to contain Federal General Franz Sigel's force near Columbia and that this was a duty "very disagreeable and unpleasant to Van Dorn." N'Importe further stated that Van Dorn had entered Tennessee to render heavy blows against the enemy "by rapid and brilliant cavalry demonstrations" much as General Morgan had been doing. Mobile *Advertiser and Register*, March 8, 1863.

My first object in bringing you into Middle Tennessee was to enable you to take part in a battle, in the event of the advance of the Federal army; the second, that you might operate upon his lines of communications, previous to his moving from Murfreesborough, and up to the time of engagement, or, if it should appear to be expedient, battle being unlikely, that you might move into Kentucky or farther.[11]

For the moment there would be no attack on Franklin. Van Dorn must await the decisions of his commanding officer before engaging in unusual maneuvers. For the time being the orthodox actions were defense and reconnaissance. Van Dorn was not as free as he had hoped.

General Bragg did not keep his new cavalry commander in the wings for very long. On February 25 he placed the Mississippian and General Wheeler in command of five thousand troops. His division commanders were Brigadier Generals William T. Martin and William H. Jackson, two fine cavalry officers. Brigade commanders included Brigadier Generals Frank G. Armstrong and George B. Cosby and Colonel John W. Whitfield. General Forrest also joined this command, and his brigade brought the effective strength to about 6,500. These troops were to serve as the eyes and ears of the left wing of the Confederate line of defense. Their area of operation extended from Columbia to Spring Hill. Before them Federal cavalry commanded by two of Van Dorn's Elkhorn opponents of a year earlier, Generals Franz Sigel and Jefferson C. Davis, offered them formidable opposition. Van Dorn temporarily shelved his Kentucky invasion plans, because new excitement loomed for him as it became his responsibility to prevent the Union force before him from moving against the center of Bragg's line.

For his sector of the Confederate defense line Van Dorn looked to the north toward Franklin, one of the most active spots in the Northern line. As early as February 18, General Forrest had reported the danger of an attack from Franklin, and Bragg had hurriedly investigated the situation. Confederate pickets increased their vigil. Almost every day some new report circulated giving warning of unusual restlessness near the city.

General Rosecrans's plans did not include an advance but only a strengthening of his front, but each rumor of movement increased Southern apprehensions. Fearful of being caught off-balance Confederate cavalry crowded Franklin precariously during the last week of

11. *Official Records Army*, XXIII, Pt. 2, 646.

February and the first days of March. To Rosecrans this action seemed too much like an offensive, and his response was to treat those Confederate moves as such. On March 3 he issued an order through his chief of staff, Brigadier General James A. Garfield, directing Brigadier General Charles C. Gilbert to send a sufficient cavalry force down the Spring Hill road to investigate Confederate activity in that vicinity.

The Federals made two important mistakes in planning and carrying out this mission. First they underestimated the strength of the opponents before them. A reinforced brigade was ample as a task force against outposts and over-extended enemy lines; it was not adequate against cavalry divisions with mobile artillery. A second mistake was a result of the first. "Take a forage train along," Garfield directed.[12] Expecting only token resistance in the Spring Hill area, he ordered his troops to serve as a convoy for a wagon train which he hoped would gather forage from the countryside for the Franklin garrison. Thus encumbered, the reconnaissance force was at great disadvantage in any large-scale skirmish.

The Union commander who led the foray toward Spring Hill was Colonel John Coburn, "a brave and determined commander."[13] Gilbert later justified his actions as follows: "As my own troops were scattered through the town, or engaged in work which was of importance, I deemed it most expeditious to send Colonel Coburn, whose command was compact and ready to move."[14]

Though Coburn possessed wide leeway of decisionmaking for his expedition, he, like Garfield, knew little of the details of the situation before him. He proceeded on an uncertain mission with more courage than understanding of what problems he might encounter.

Colonel Coburn, the commander of the Third Brigade of the First Division of the Reserve Corps of the Army of the Cumberland, left Franklin on March 4 at 9:00 A.M. with 2837 troops:[15] the Thirty-third and Eighty-fifth Indiana Infantry Regiments, the Twenty-second Wisconsin Infantry Regiment, and the Nineteenth Michigan Infantry Regiment from his own brigade; six hundred cavalry detached from the

12. *Ibid.*, Pt. 1, 75.
13. Robert S. Henry, *"First with the Most" Forrest*, p. 129.
14. *Official Records Army*, XXIII, Pt. 1, 76–77.
15. This is Colonel Coburn's figure. General Rosecrans and General Absalom Baird reported the number as 1845.

Fourth Kentucky and the Second Michigan Cavalry Regiments; and
the Eighteenth Ohio Battery. His line of march was toward Spring Hill,
thirteen miles distant, where he hoped to camp on his first night out.
He marched with four wagons for each of his regiments in addition to
the wagon train of eighty vehicles that strung out behind his troops in
a long line. "Wait for the wagons, boys, and we'll all take a ride," Van
Dorn remarked caustically when he heard of the train.[16]

The weather was "cool and favorable," and Coburn's troops marched
with a light step. This was just another reconnaissance to them, and
most of the men were happy to get away from routine garrison life for
a few days. Coburn himself harbored no thoughts of any large engagement. He planned to divide his command on his second day out. Then,
in conjunction with troops under Phil Sheridan from Murfreesboro that
he expected to meet near Spring Hill, he intended to search out and
report the enemy's position and his activities to his own headquarters.

On the same day that Coburn began his move, Earl Van Dorn initiated what he later described as a "forced reconnaissance" toward
Franklin also over the Spring Hill road. Brigadier General Jackson,
with three brigades (about 1200 mounted men) preceding his main
force, was on the road early in the day. Jackson's troops rode easily over
the hard-packed road, unaware of the Federal activity before them. By
midmorning they arrived at Thompson's Station, a small village about
nine miles south of Franklin. Their arrival on the south side of the
village coincided almost exactly with the arrival of Coburn's force on
the northern edge of the town.

Both commanders were surprised by the presence of the other force,
and for some minutes there was confusion in the two commands. Jackson recovered his composure first and drew his small force into a road-
block. He extended his line to the left and the right of the turnpike until
it was about five hundred feet in length. Behind this position, Captain
Houston King, commanding the Second Missouri Battery, quickly un-
limbered two artillery pieces and began pumping shots into "the large
body of enemy with [the] long baggage train."[17] In spite of the heavy
fire Coburn deployed his small force effectively; he sent Captain Charles

16. Mobile *Advertiser and Register,* May 14, 1863, p. 1.
17. *Official Records Army,* XXIII, Pt. 1, 116. Colonel Thomas J. Jordan, commanding the Ninth Pennsylvania, reported that the Federal artillery fired first.
Coburn and others say King's battery began the engagement.

C. Aleshire's Eighteenth Ohio Battery to an excellent defensive position on a knoll just to the left of the pike. From this position Aleshire returned the Confederate fire with telling effects. For more than an hour the two units continued a brisk artillery fire across a field just east of the village with indecisive results. All about the troops the ground was broken and irregular, "in many places steep and precipitous," except for the open field in front of them, and it was difficult for either commander to gain an immediate terrain advantage.

With shells falling in front of his position, Coburn watched for an opening. About noon he decided that he could wait no longer. Seizing the initiative, he impulsively lashed out against the Confederate position with his cavalry.

Jackson instinctively retreated before the new thrust. Surprise did not develop into rout, however. Jackson's troops crossed a hill in orderly formation, and Coburn's lead troops lost sight of them. Jackson then set up a longer line of defense in the hills south of Thompson's Station.[18] When the Confederates suddenly emerged from the woods in their long line in front of the two advancing Federal units, the charging bluecoats ceased their wild shouting and beat a hasty retreat back to their original position. If Jackson had any ideas of a counterattack, he shelved them in the face of well-aimed grape and canister fire from the Union position. General Van Dorn found the two forces thus when he arrived at the edge of Thompson's Station with the main body of his command. Casualties from the first skirmish had been light. Reports seem to agree that the Confederates suffered the greater losses with about fifteen killed and several others wounded as against only two or three Federals wounded.

Deceived by the Federal show of force into suspecting a larger army, Van Dorn decided that a counterattack for the moment was out of the question. He held his own line and gave a display of his strength from behind the protective covering of the irregular hills for several hours. Both armies settled in their positions and again conducted a sporadic artillery and small arms duel until near the end of the day.

Again it was the brave and energetic Coburn who moved. This time the troublesome wagon train brought on the action. The wagons had become a liability once the Federals were under fire, so when things settled

18. Lieutenant Colonel Edward Bloodgood of the Twenty-Second Wisconsin Infantry reported the line as "over a mile in length."

down a bit, Coburn requested and received permission to return them to Franklin. To divert Van Dorn's attention while the wagons were being put on the road, Coburn initiated what appeared to be an all-out offensive. Van Dorn was caught off guard by this action, and his artillery responded to the new threat with its heaviest fire of the afternoon. Thirty-nine of the wagons escaped, but heavy Confederate fire forced Coburn to halt this operation short of returning all the vehicles. Coburn terminated his offensive, realizing that any further advance would undoubtedly have brought on a full-scale engagement for which he knew his small force was inadequate. He withdrew his troops to a line of hills north of Thompson's Station. Action ceased for the day. During the night the two armies bivouacked in hills along the Columbia-Franklin pike about four miles apart.

The night was quiet except for occasional picket firing. During the night Van Dorn made an important discovery. Confederate scouts, entering the Union lines after dark, found Coburn's force to be much smaller than they had thought. The Confederate planning changed for the coming day as Van Dorn now "determined to give them battle."[19] But first he would allow Coburn to make his move.

Coburn's night was less productive of good news. He, too, gained information of his enemy, but his news was all bad. Negroes informed him that the Confederates possessed infantry, cavalry, and artillery in depth. Then just after dawn two Negro boys, who contended that they were refugees from the Confederate "army," informed Coburn that Van Dorn and an army of 15,000 were set to take Franklin.

Coburn was in a difficult situation. He knew that Van Dorn did not have 15,000 men, but he realized that the Confederates did greatly outnumber his small force. What should he do? He received a small ammunition resupply from Franklin just before dawn, but there was no word as to what he should do against the superior force before him. Reasoning to his own sorrow that his original orders meant he must push on, Coburn decided to move forward even if Van Dorn resisted his move. Certainly Sheridan's force, expected from another direction, would arrive in time to flank the Confederates and prevent them from continuing toward Franklin.

Coburn reflected on these matters as long as he felt time allowed. Then he quietly announced his decision to his young assistant adjutant-

19. *Official Records Army*, XXIII, Pt. 1, 116.

general, Lieutenant H. B. Adams: "I am going ahead," he said, "I have no option in the matter."[20] To his other officers he was a little more emphatic: "My orders are imperative," he informed them about seven o'clock. "I must go on or show cowardice." This last statement seems to reveal the key to what otherwise appears as a rash action.[21]

The hills south of Nashville dominate the landscape for miles around. In any season their quiet beauty impresses visitor and native alike. Some are rounded and barren. More often they have pointed peaks and are covered with trees. Cedars often predominate. To the casual observer there is little pattern in their arrangement; they seem to have just been spattered over the countryside.

To a military commander facing a determined enemy on the terrain between Columbia and Franklin, these Tennessee hills revealed less of beauty and more of tactical maneuvering. In a campaign, the hills could serve either as excellent defensive positions or as obstacles to an advance. An artillery piece properly placed on the rim of a hill could command a wide stretch of the valley before it. On the other hand, a costly attack would be required to remove an enemy in a line of hills.

Thompson's Station, a whistle stop on the Nashville and Decatur Railroad in 1863, is almost completely surrounded by these small irregular hills. On the morning of March 5, the Confederate position was set in a prominent line of hills just south of the village. This range traversed the Columbia pike at right angles. Van Dorn had placed troops on high knobs on either side of the road. After passing through the range of hills, the road descended into a large open valley, then an open field, actually the eastern limits of the village. East of the road the field extended about three-quarters of a mile, and then the irregular hills again appeared. West of the road the field narrowed slightly as the range occupied by the Confederates angled slightly to the north and then faded off to the northwest. At the base of the hills on the west side of the pike was the village of Thompson's Station, little more than a station house, a school, and several undistinguished buildings. These buildings were on the railroad about three hundred yards from the turnpike.

Just south of the village near the foot of one of the highest hills ran a gully, about one hundred yards in length. Paralleling the gully was a stone fence of about the same length. Behind these obstacles Con-

20. *Ibid.*, p. 94.
21. *Ibid.*, p. 98.

federate dismounted troops faced the village, awaiting whatever action might develop within the Union lines on the north side of town. Confederate skirmishers and sharpshooters also occupied the station house and several of the buildings to warn the main line of Confederates of any attack in the direction of the village. Across the southern range of hills, the Confederates lined up as follows: To the east on the extreme right facing toward Franklin, across the turnpike, General Forrest was on the second of two prominent knolls; just west of Forrest, General Armstrong also was part of the Confederate right; across the road Jackson's troops extended westward to the railroad; and Whitfield's brigade was stationed behind the stone fence. Since the railroad veered off toward the southwest away from the turnpike after leaving the station, the Confederate line must have extended for more than a mile.

To the north of Thompson's Station the hills are not so impressive until across the West Harpeth River, about two and one-half miles north. Despite the absence of dominating hills, there are several prominent knolls and all through the region the ground is irregular and broken as it is near the southern position. Just beyond the West Harpeth River, about three and a half miles north of the village, the turnpike again bisects a range of high hills. From their shelter Coburn began his offensive on the morning of March 5.

Coburn carefully surveyed his map of the countryside. His first concern was for two small roads that paralleled the turnpike; they were perfect for an enemy flanking movement. How could he prevent this possibility? Turning abruptly to his cavalry commander, Colonel Thomas J. Jordan, he asked him "to send a sufficient force of cavalry on each of these roads" and keep him informed of any Confederate moves on them. "I will delay my forces a sufficient length of time for them to give said information," he promised Jordan.[22]

True to his word Coburn delayed his attack until eight o'clock. He then moved slowly toward the Confederate position with his remaining cavalry in the lead. Skirmishing with advance Confederate pickets began almost as soon as the Federals began their march, but it was not until ten o'clock that the real engagement began about a half mile north of the village.

"Here," wrote Colonel William L. Utley, commanding the Twenty-Second Wisconsin Regiment, "the booming of cannon and the howling

22. *Ibid.*

of a shell . . . admonished us that there was work ahead."[23] Here, indeed, was work for the Federals. The first shell from Captain King's battery atop a knoll just east of the turnpike fell in the midst of the advancing Federal cavalry and did not explode. Not so the other shells. As King shot into the advancing troops, Coburn's cavalry fell off to the side of the road. Coburn quickly ordered his infantry units to take up a line of attack—the Thirty-third and the Eighty-fifth Indiana Regiments on the west side of the turnpike, the Twenty-second Wisconsin and the Nineteenth Michigan Regiments on the east. Captain Aleshire's artillery was moved to the hill to the left of the pike behind the infantry units where it attempted to dislodge the Confederates from their strong position.

The Federals were not easily dissuaded from their attack. Even as Coburn organized his new line, Confederate artillery punished the Federals with 6, 12, and 18 pounders as well as intense small-arms fire. As the artillery barrage increased its tempo, Coburn decided quickly that removal of this obstacle was of first order. Turning to Colonel John P. Baird, commanding the Eighty-fifth Indiana Regiment, he asked if he could displace the artillery barrier in the hills before them. "I'll try," replied the colonel with all the confidence he could muster.

"I will send the 33d with you," replied Coburn. Then he added, "and if you take the battery on the right, take the other close by on the left also."[24]

The attack of the Indiana troops, first against the station house and then toward the stone fence, took much of the late morning and early afternoon. These troops attacked the depot area about 11:30 A.M. and pushed the Confederates there back to their main positions with little difficulty. With Coburn in command, they then made one of the most dramatic moves of the day. With grape and canister falling all about them, they crossed an open field toward the stone fence.

The sun shone brightly on the blue uniforms as the riflemen pushed across the five hundred yards of open field. "Never on drill or parade have I seen them move with more precision," wrote the commander of the Thirty-third Indiana Regiment, Lieutenant Colonel James M. Henderson.[25] The going was rough. Some of the Yanks stumbled over obstacles; others dropped from the ranks, victims of sporadic Confed-

23. *Ibid.*, p. 106.
24. *Ibid.*, p. 99.
25. *Ibid.*, p. 101.

erate gunfire from behind the fence. With his position threatened by the large force behind the fence, Jackson quickly reinforced this gray line with Colonel Samuel G. Earle's Third Arkansas Cavalry from Armstrong's position. The reinforced line watched the advancing Federals with muted admiration; they held their main fire until the blue line was just in front of their position.

Suddenly sharp commands from behind the fence started the Confederate line's fire. The blue line melted in front of them; the survivors retreated rapidly under the heavy fire. Well-masked by the fence and gully, the Arkansans and Texans continued to fire with unabated energy. Dusty, perspiring boys from Indiana fought on as though possessed of demons while retreating. They sought shelter anywhere—among scrubby cedars, along the embankment of the railroad, in the buildings near the depot—and persistently fired back at their antagonists. Still, the Confederate fire seemed to search them out of their hiding places; they retreated again under pressure.

Confederate commanders had been waiting for this time. They yelled down the line for a counterattack, and the gray line moved across the stone wall. "With a shout, men and officers all rushed to the encounter, and in a moment the foe was driven from . . . shelter, and compelled in the wildest confusion to seek refuge behind a hill a mile to his rear . . ."[26]

From across the turnpike the Nineteenth Michigan Regiment moved hastily to join the Indianians on the hill. The reinforced Federals took up an excellent position. It was up to the Confederates now to displace them. Since courage was hardly lacking in either army, some of the bloodiest fighting of the day took place before the new Federal position.

The Confederates delayed only momentarily before assaulting the new Federal position. Captain King's artillery prepared the way for them. From a nearby hill the Missourians poured a heavy barrage toward their Union objective. The artillery was still firing when shouting Rebels leaped from the valley floor east of the railroad and attacked the hill in great fury. Rocks and foliage blocked their paths, but on they charged up the slope. Over the dead and wounded of both armies they slowly made their way until they arrived within twenty yards of the Federal line. Here they met the full force of Federal small-arms fire. Before this murderous onslaught they halted their own attack and turned reluctantly to their earlier position near the railroad.

26. *Ibid.*, p. 124.

The sun was hot, the troops were short of water, the wounded needed medical attention, but swearing officers quickly formed their ranks again. Signals echoed down the line, and the Confederates doggedly charged up the hill again. Once more they gained the summit at a severe cost, only to be stopped once more by the determined defenders. This charge was even more costly to both armies than the first one. Confederate Colonel Earle died at the head of his regiment; he was leading his men across the rim of the hill when the fatal bullet struck him down. It was on this charge that seventeen-year old Alice Thompson ran from her residence in the village, "raised the fallen flag and rallied the wavering regiment" of Confederate troops.[27]

At the foot of the hill after the second repulse, Confederate officers faced the prospects of a third charge with some misgivings. Surely they could dislodge the small enemy force. But where was Forrest?

East of and across the turnpike Forrest had not been inactive; he too had been seriously engaged since the early morning. Using his mobile artillery to great effect, he had battled the left wing of the Union force in the hills east of the pike from the very first moments of the battle. His persistent efforts, coupled with Coburn's transfer of the Nineteenth Michigan Regiment finally broke the Federal defenders before him. The Twenty-Second Wisconsin Regiment and the cavalry detachments with them scurried toward the West Harpeth River just as the second Confederate charge failed on the other side of the road.

Van Dorn was elated. Forrest was free now to engage the center of the line. Sensing a new opportunity, Van Dorn ordered Forrest to Jackson's aid. "If possible," he instructed, "get in rear of the enemy."[28]

Forrest executed the last part of this order with dexterity; he moved his army as far as possible around the Federal left to avoid other troop units that might be in the area. It was no easy matter for him to cross the valleys and cedar-covered hills; his troops moved as quickly as possible. With Forrest advancing north to Coburn's rear, Van Dorn delayed further activity near the railroad until General George B. Cosby's regiment had joined the Texans and Arkansans from Armstrong's brigade. Then he ordered the third charge.

General William Jackson began Van Dorn's new attack in front of the Union position. Again shouting, firing, swearing Confederates mounted

27. Henry, *"First with the Most" Forrest,* p. 130.
28. *Official Records Army,* XXIII, Pt. 1, 120.

the hill toward the flaming Federal guns. Again firepower from the hill halted the impetuous Confederates short of their objective.

Suddenly there was a roar in the Federal rear. Through the trees near the base of Coburn's hill charged Forrest and two reinforced regiments of dismounted cavalry. Forrest's troopers had fought hard to arrive behind the lines, and they were now set to turn the tide of battle. Forrest was on foot because his giant charger, Roderick, had just been shot from under him. Warning shouts alerted the battered Federals on the hill to the fresh attack. There was some confusion among the grim defenders, but raw courage caused many of them to turn and fire into the midst of the new threat. Lieutenant Colonel E. B. Trezevant and Captain Montgomery Little, two of Forrest's bravest officers, fell mortally wounded in front of the new Union line; the charge continued unabated. The surging Confederates rushed to a point within twenty feet of the exhausted defenders where a young Confederate captain, dashing from his ranks, seized the colors of a Michigan regiment.

Colonel Coburn ordered his men to fix their bayonets and prepare for a fight to the finish. Then the Federal commander discovered that Forrest had yet another unit in reserve, and his mood of desperation changed to one of futility. He surveyed his position quickly. His ammunition was nearly gone; his cavalry and artillery had mysteriously "disappeared"; Confederates beset his position from every side; his paths of escape were blocked. Coburn was not prepared to sacrifice more brave men to a hopeless cause. White flags suddenly appeared from within the Union lines. Van Dorn halted his advance. It was all over—the flags told the story. Coburn and his garrison had surrendered.

The afternoon sun was low on the horizon when the Confederates took over the field, but there was time for looting and pillaging by the victorious troops as was usual in such situations. "It was a sad and revolting sight," remarked a Federal officer, "to witness the barbarity of the inhuman demons stripping our noble dead."[29] But Yankee shoes, guns, belts, knives, and other small articles were prizes too valuable for destitute Confederates to resist. The battlefield became their informal quartermaster.

Records of battle casualties vary in the different reports of the com-

29. *Ibid.*, p. 109.

manders involved. Van Dorn's report shows 357 killed, wounded, and missing among his own troops in the two-day battle. Coburn gives the Northern losses as 378 killed, wounded, and missing in addition to 1221 who were captured in the final moments of the action. A few of the Northern soldiers had escaped down the Franklin pike with the last of the wagon train. But most of Coburn's original command surrendered with their colonel. (After a short internment in Southern prisons, Coburn and most of his officers were exchanged and returned to duty. The enlisted men were also soon exchanged, and Coburn was able to again command the Third Brigade in late June.)

Thompson's Station was not an important battle in deciding the fate of central Tennessee. It began no great Southern offensive; it stymied no important Federal move. The Thompson's Station battle was another of the many clashes between cavalry units that was typical of a new mode of combat that dominated action in the West until the close of the war.

Although both commanders showed courage and initiative in the fighting in those Tennessee hills, they were also guilty of certain tactical errors that were costly to their own troops and to their reputations as commanders. Coburn probably made the biggest mistake when he engaged the large enemy force, but part of this blame can also be laid to his own commanders. General Rosecrans took note of this when he wrote that the "unnecessary" loss at the station was caused by Coburn's "want of proper caution" plus General Gilbert's "indecision."[30] But Coburn fought a good fight. Outnumbered, surrounded, and continually charged by the Confederates he "fought with a valor worthy of a better issue."[31]

Van Dorn was fast proving himself a skillful tactician with mounted infantry, but he too made important errors. He did select a fine defensive position in which to meet the enemy, but when the enemy struck his position he was both premature in striking back and slow in flanking the outnumbered force. His original strategy backfired when the Arkansas and Missouri troops attacked too soon and Coburn was able to fight from a good defensive position. But Van Dorn rallied his men well, continued the fight until the enemy was beaten, and ad-

30. *Ibid.*, p. 74.
31. Rose, *Texas Brigade*, p. 93.

justed well to a changing battle situation. To his own credit, he
stayed with his men at the front, as did Coburn, and personally led
them to victory.

Dr. John A. Wyeth has offered one of the most interesting criticisms
of Van Dorn's actions at Thompson's Station. Though Wyeth is writing
to defend General Forrest, his arguments are still worth considering.
"General Van Dorn knew almost exactly the strength of his adversary
the night before the engagement," wrote the doctor, "and he had troops
in abundance to have interposed in Coburn's rear enough cavalry to
have prevented this retreat and insured the capture of all the enemy's
wagons, artillery, and practically all his force."[32]

The Confederates won the field at Thompson's Station, but it was
somewhat of a hollow victory. The village was untenable for future
operations, and the Confederates departed its bounds before the day
ended. Federal prisoners were hustled southward quickly to Tullahoma and on to Southern prisons, and the Confederate cavalry returned to Columbia. The victory was an important delaying action
for the Confederates, however. If Colonel Coburn had succeeded at
Thompson's Station, he would probably have joined General Philip
Sheridan's force that had marched from Murfreesboro. The two forces
might well have conducted a combined attack against Columbia.
After Coburn's defeat, Sheridan's command returned to Triune.

Again there was joy in the ranks of the Confederate cavalry. Those
who loved Van Dorn applauded his latest success with enthusiasm.
The Mobile reporter recorded the general's triumphant return to his
headquarters:

As Van Dorn rode along the column after the strife had ceased, cheer upon
cheer greeted him from the enthusiastic soldiery, who under his daring direction had achieved the victory, and he is undoubtedly held high at the present
moment in the estimation of his forces, and this confidence is well deserved.[33]

There was still some hope that the War Department might recon-
sider that long-coveted promotion. "I *am* a soldier," he wrote his sister
soon after he returned to Columbia, "and my soul swells up and tells
me that I *am* worthy to lead the armies of my country."[34]

32. *Life of General Nathan Bedford Forrest*, pp. 162–163.
33. Mobile *Advertiser and Register*, March 20, 1863, p. 1.
34. Earl Van Dorn to Emily Miller, April 1, 1863, Van Dorn Collection, Montgomery, Alabama.

CHAPTER THIRTEEN

Cavalry Action in Tennessee

*I*T was "hard times" for the Confederate soldiers in Tennessee in the early months of 1863. Sickness was prevalent in every camp; men were saddlesore from long hours of patrolling the extensive defense line; forage for horses was scarce. Shortages from rations to ammunition were prevalent in every command, but it was the lack of plain food that drew the most considerable complaint from the ranks. "We get occasionally a box of luxuries . . . but no one as yet sent us a mess of turnip greens, which is nearly as much prayed for as the recognition of our independence," lamented one soldier from the Thirty-Second Tennessee Regiment.[1]

All along the Confederate Tennessee front troops pilfered food, stole horses, and bickered with their fellow soldiers. Many took absence without leave. Others deserted outright. Constant and aggressive conscription was necessary to keep troop units even at minimum strength.

There was an air of unreality in both armies in Tennessee as Generals Bragg and Rosecrans settled, almost comfortably, in their respective camps. It was almost as though they expected the war to be fought elsewhere, and they were merely awaiting the results. In the ranks the men grumbled, wrote unexciting letters home, and wished for the end of the conflict. Only the cavalry seemed to be interested in engaging the enemy. Between reviews and parades they roved through the countryside—reconnoitering enemy positions, attacking supply trains, clashing with pickets. Tennessee was in the full bloom of spring, and the cavalry in Bragg's army was in its finest hour. Northern cavalry was also developing, however, and these months would be the South's last period of cavalry domination.

1. Quoted in Fayetteville (Tennessee) *Observer*, March 19, 1863, p. 1.

This was the time of Morgan, Forrest, Wheeler, and Van Dorn in the West—an amazing combination of cavalry leadership, brought into focus by the peculiar type of warfare in Tennessee. Each of these generals made his own mark in the Confederate army, and each contributed to the misery inflicted upon Northern armies during the hard days of 1863. None was more active or energetic than Van Dorn. Though he accomplished nothing of dramatic importance, he and his men were constantly in the saddle, harrying supply and communication lines, always threatening to instigate the big fight.

After the battle at Thompson's Station, Van Dorn retired to a bivouac area at College Grove. Knowing that General Philip Sheridan was in the vicinity, he sent out numerous pickets to learn of any new enemy approach. His reconnaissance patrols covered all roads leading toward Murfreesboro and Shelbyville, and his cavalry kept alert for the possibilities of a Federal counterattack. His next brush with the enemy came as a result of an order by General Polk to Van Dorn which directed the Mississippian to co-operate with a Confederate force from Shelbyville to push Generals Sheridan and James B. Steedman away from the Spring Hill–Columbia area.

According to General Steedman, a Confederate force that was the same one that had defeated Coburn approached his own troop unit with a display of force on Sunday morning, March 8, on the Harpeth River near Triune. The Confederates commanded by Buck Van Dorn tried to draw the Federals across the river. The Shelbyville force never arrived, so after pouring twenty-five or thirty rounds of artillery into Steedman's troops, Van Dorn's troops attempted a river crossing at a ford about a mile away. After a sharp, indecisive skirmish at the ford, the Confederates, possibly fearing that they were facing a superior force, rode off to Spring Hill about two o'clock in the afternoon.

On Monday the Union cavalry again pressed Van Dorn, this time near Columbia. Late Monday afternoon, Colonel Robert Minty pushed the Confederate pickets from Thompson's Station, and on March 10, he threatened the general's headquarters at Spring Hill. When Minty's force was joined by another Federal unit, Van Dorn realized that his own detachment was too small to combat the advancing enemy, so he gave ground before the advance. His only escape was across the Duck River into Columbia; he began building a pontoon bridge across that stream. As the enemy was rapidly advancing, Van Dorn attempted to move his wagons and guns across the swollen river. This proved to be a near impossibility, and when the pontoons gave way he had to use other methods to escape the clutches of the advancing blue-coated cavalrymen. He made a quick attack in force toward Minty's right hoping to divert the enemy into reinforcing this position from the Federal left. This ruse worked, and the besieged Confederates had their path to freedom.

With Forrest's command serving as a rear guard, the Confederate command rode rapidly beside the Duck River past the tricked enemy; they eventually crossed the turbulent waters on a ferry near a prospective bridge site. Their horses swam alongside the ferry. Forrest finally escaped by riding twenty-five miles along the river bank to a bridge. The Federal force refused to cross the Duck River and soon returned from Spring Hill to Franklin. Van Dorn had saved his jeopardized force.

"On this occasion," pridefully wrote Victor Rose, "he unquestionably showed those qualities of quick perception, rapid decision, and indomitable pluck, that characterizes the captain of genius.[2]

An Ohio enlisted man was not so complimentary of Van Dorn's action. "Our cannon soon began to roar and drive Vandorn [sic] and his forces threw [sic] duck river rather faster than they wanted to go I guess," William M. Johnson of an Ohio Volunteer Infantry Regiment wrote his father. "[T]he report is that their [sic] was a good many of them got drownded while wading the river."[3]

In Columbia Van Dorn and his troops and horses rested after nearly two weeks constantly in the saddle or in battle. As the cavalry recouped its strength, engineers built a new pontoon bridge across Duck River. On March 15 Van Dorn's force recrossed the stream and reoccupied his old headquarters at Spring Hill. Here he received orders to watch the enemy closely and attack him when success was most probable. Bragg's orders at this point were simple: [F]eel the enemy closely and pursue vigorously if . . . [you] find him in retreat."[4]

The front was quiet for a week after Van Dorn's return to Spring Hill. If ever the cavalry needed a respite, this was the time. The

2. *Texas Brigade*, p. 93.
3. Correspondence of William M. Johnson, letter of March 14, 1863, private collection.
4. *Official Records Army*, XXIII, Pt. 2, 707.

roads had been muddy; the wind had cut their faces; their animals were suffering from the elements. The rest period ended abruptly on March 20 when Van Dorn received news that the enemy was advancing toward Spring Hill. He responded with his usual enthusiasm. "Am ready to fight, and will do so," he informed General Bragg. To Major K. Falconer he was more specific. He would get behind the enemy if possible "and strike at Franklin, Brentwood, and other points in the vicinity." He would, however, prefer to rest his horses a while longer before engaging the enemy.[5]

Van Dorn sent a brigade of cavalry and a section of his artillery toward Franklin and Brentwood the following day to test this new report of an enemy advance and to make demonstrations before the enemy. This foray caused the Federals to think that the Confederate general was planning an attack against their strong Franklin position, and so they brought in their outlying pickets to help strengthen the town's defense. This was the signal for a Confederate attack, but not upon Franklin and not by Van Dorn.

After his brilliant efforts at Thompson's Station and Spring Hill, Forrest had assumed a divisional command and had begun operating as an independent outpost unit under Van Dorn's supervision.[6] He established a picket line from Thompson's Station to College Grove, and from his scouts he was able to follow very closely the movements of the Union troops in the vicinity of Franklin. Noting the concentration of the Union force at Franklin, he suddenly moved his cavalry upon Brentwood, nine miles away. Federals were caught completely off balance, and Forrest had little difficulty in subduing the small Brentwood garrison. He took 800 prisoners and a good deal of booty and shocked the Union army in Tennessee with his audacity. Certain now that the Confederates were planning to assault Franklin, the Federal commanders took every precaution to prevent such an attack. Meanwhile Van Dorn fell back to Spring Hill, occasionally skirmishing near the town, scouting only a very limited area.

Again Van Dorn and his men welcomed a short period of relative inactivity. Inactivity did not mean quiescence though. When not in the field the troops were continually preparing for action. Daily drills

---

5. *Ibid.*, p. 715.
6. Van Dorn's command had become a cavalry corps although it consisted of less men than a standard infantry division.

were common in the garrison, for Van Dorn and his officers never ceased carefully disciplining their men for battle. The cavalry required special training to handle their delicate assignments, and additional drill and parade were always in order. Even General Forrest, who once had opposed formal drill, saw profitable results from this training and took an active part in it. A typical drill parade in early April in which Van Dorn was involved has been described by an onlooker who spent half a day in the hot sun and dust awaiting the final formation of the troops.

The review began with a flourish. Van Dorn waited in the wings, astride his beautiful gray horse, while the troops gathered. Suddenly a smartly dressed officer astride an immaculately groomed horse rode up to him, saluted, and reported everything in readiness for the big event. "What a sight is now presented to the eye," wrote the observer.

Thousands of horses formed in line extend as far as the observer can take in. . . . Everything is ready for inspection—the high-spirited boys, the dancing horses, the gleaming guns and glittering sabres. From the center in front dashes Van Dorn, the general commanding, and his staff. Off they go in a gallop to meet the senior commander, Forrest, and then, accompanied by him and his staff, away the whole party dash at a running gallop to the end of the column.[7]

Drilling did not prevent the troops from keeping a close watch on the enemy. When General Granger was sharply criticized for not rounding up the Confederate cavalry in middle Tennessee, he understandably reported:

You do not seem to understand why it is so difficult to surprise and crush Van Dorn. In the first place, he keeps every road and lane and hill-top for miles picketed; the country people are his friends and are always ready to give information. His policy is to fight when he is sure to win, and always run when his success is doubtful. The nature of his troops being mounted, without baggage or transportation, enables him to do this with great facility.[8]

In many ways it appeared that the cavalry commander in Tennessee was a much subdued Earl Van Dorn as compared with the officer in his earlier roles, subdued in his military actions if not in his personal life. As a cavalry commander he seemed to resign himself, for the moment at least, to the job before him, and he set about doing what he could to make the most of his situation. In Tennessee he appeared

7. "Personne," *Marginalia or Gleanings from an Army Notebook*, p. 168.
8. *Official Records Army*, XXIII, Pt. 2, 233.

to be a better officer, a bit more mature, a little less intent upon the grand sweep, concerned over the problems of his part of the Confederate line.

He was not happy though as he faced an uncertain, sometimes unpromising future. On April 1 he wrote one of his most revealing letters of his feelings to Emily, and in it we see a melancholy that reminds us of the feelings of a young cadet in his dismal days of West Point confinement.

This war is a terrible calamity upon us all, especially upon those who live on the paths where the contending armies must pass, worse than the crawl of the viper over the sweet sensitive mimosa. Pray God it may soon end and that peace may be restored to our distracted country. I presume it is the fate of all who rise above the general level he earn trouble of mind [,] anxiety and all the train that follow after position. I am not yet gray, however, nor have I a gray hair in my head, and my spirits are as buoyant as a boy.

He then thanked her for contacting a Mr. Ellit to intervene for his promotion to lieutenant general but suggested pessimistically that such efforts would also be in vain. He felt that the stigma of Corinth was still just too much. Then with a touch of bitterness he added:

I unhesitatingly say that the attack on Corinth was the best thing I ever did in my life—if it had been successful I would have been pronounced by the onion mouthed "Oi Polloi" and military men *too*! the most brilliant General of the war. . . . Few there are who take the trouble to think for themselves—few there are who *can* do so, or who are able by education to be critics of a General's movements or his strategy—I was not wounded in spirit by the powerful "vox populi" at all—only when falsehood assailed my private character, and made me the butt of malignant archery in my own native state—expelling me after weary watchfulness and long mental pain for them from his soil. Then I felt bitterness in my heart and covered my face with my hands and desired to depart.

Emphatically he continued, as if inflamed by personal anguish:

I would have flung the sword she gave me back at her feet and told her to place it in hands more worthy of their praise, but then it would have been seemingly a display of temper, or want of greatness of Soul to yield to such storms.[9]

Despite these glorious outbursts, there is still something less than grandiose about him. But he was becoming an effective cavalry com-

9. Van Dorn Collection, Montgomery, Alabama.

mander although his leadership still revealed basic weaknesses. Other departments recognized his effectiveness and requested his services. From Mississippi, General Pemberton contended that he must have Van Dorn and his cavalry back with him if he expected to thwart a new attempt by General Grant against Vicksburg. General Johnston's answer to this request by Pemberton was prompt and emphatic. "Van Dorn's cavalry is much more needed in this department than in that of Mississippi and Eastern Louisiana," he wrote. In fact, he continued, the cavalry was "absolutely necessary to enable General Bragg to hold the best part of the country from which he draws supplies."[10]

In Spring Hill, while nearly everybody pronounced judgment upon him, Van Dorn continued to look toward Franklin. Short of supplies and forage and aware that Franklin was an enemy stronghold, he at first refrained from making any move toward the town. Then early in April, possibly believing that the enemy had removed the major part of the town's garrison for service in another part of the theater, he decided to have a closer look at his long-coveted target. On April 10 he advanced his command of between 3000 and 4000 troops down the Columbia-Franklin road for a large-scale reconnaissance or possibly to draw Federal troops from Tullahoma where Rosecrans was concentrating a part of his army against Bragg. Whatever the plans, General Granger at Franklin anticipated the move and prepared for it. Instead of diminishing his garrison, he had kept his strength intact.

Van Dorn never wrote an official report of the engagement at Franklin that followed, but from the few sources of information available it appears that his plans did not call for a full-scale attack on that town. Though he had made desperate charges at Corinth, Elkhorn, and Thompson's Station, he had always directed his troops against what he considered an outnumbered enemy. It hardly seems possible that he would have planned to risk his small command against the strong Federal position at Franklin. A fort nearly forty feet high rose above the general surface of the country and commanded the entrance of the town. Other fortifications protected the city from attackers from almost any direction. Granger also had more troops, better equipment, and superior weapons. Van Dorn may not have known all this, but he must have suspected that his chances for a successful frontal attack were not good.

10. *Official Records Army*, XXIV, Pt. 3, 686.

When first warned of the approach of the brash Confederate force, Granger began preparations for defense against what he considered to be a full-scale attack. In his official report of the battle he explained his feelings:

Judging from the configuration of the country on both sides of the Harpeth, and from the fact that nearly the whole of Van Dorn's force was mounted and from the strength of that force, I did not think the attack would be made directly in our front, but that it would be made by falling upon our rear and flanks after the enemy would cross the river above and below Franklin.[11]

General Granger distributed his units to meet an assault at almost any vulnerable point. He concentrated the main body of his infantry within the fortress on the opposite side of the river from the Confederate approach. He sent Major General David S. Stanley's mounted troops to watch the ford at Hughes Mill on the north side of the river. He directed Brigadier General Absalom Baird's infantry division to watch the fords below Franklin. General Green Clay Smith's cavalry, he held in reserve just north of the city.

"I am extremely anxious to whip Van Dorn," Granger wrote, "and settle up accounts with him contracted at Thompson's Station and Brentwood."[12]

The tenth of April had begun bright and shiny, but by midmorning it was dark and cloudy. The wind came up and dust was thick in the faces of the troops riding toward Franklin. About three miles from Franklin, Van Dorn split his command. His own group continued on toward Franklin on the Columbia road. The other force, under Forrest, cut across country to the Lewisburg road and approached Franklin from another direction. Both of these units advanced rapidly until about 10:30 A.M. when they came upon the enemy pickets guarding the town. On the Columbia pike Van Dorn delayed briefly and then attacked the pickets about noon with such little vigor that Granger began to suspect that this movement was only a feint at Franklin. The darkness of the day prevented the Federals from discerning just exactly what Van Dorn was up to, but Granger had suspicions that the Confederate objective was again toward Brentwood. When word reached him from Brentwood that the Confederates under Forrest had driven in their pickets, Granger acted quickly and impulsively. Without proper

11. *Ibid.*, XXIII, Pt. 1, 224.
12. *Ibid.*, Pt. 2, 233.

investigation he dispatched General Smith's reserve cavalry unit to the relief of what he suspected to be a besieged garrison. The attack report from Brentwood proved to be a false alarm, however, for the Confederates made no serious move toward that little town at anytime during the day. General Granger's hasty action cost him an important cavalry force that he might well have used to destroy an enterprising enemy. Fortunately for Granger, General Stanley's force was within marching distance of Franklin, and it was a simple matter to rush it to the support of the town's garrison against what developed into the major attack.

On the Columbia pike the Fortieth Ohio Infantry Regiment guarded the town of Franklin from the south side of the Harpeth River. As Van Dorn's force approached the town, General Jackson, commanding one of his own units, had little trouble pushing this Union regiment all the way back into Franklin. With Generals Forrest and Armstrong also riding to another entrance to the town, Granger sent word to his fort to open all heavy guns at the first sign of an attack. Colonel Brown of Van Dorn's command later contended that the Federals invited an attack by the Columbia pike force when they moved a column of their infantry "out on a piece of open ground."

"This was too much for a man of Van Dorn's temperament," wrote Brown. "Without a moment's hesitation, he ordered a charge."[13]

For a few moments the action was heavy. Van Dorn's horse was shot from under him as he led the first wave, but he signaled for the attack to continue. The charging rebels pushed the Federals back. For a moment it appeared that they had broken the line. Then heavy guns and reinforcements swung the balance, and the attack faded. Blazing firepower finally halted the Confederate assault that was taking on all the earmarks of a full-scale attack.

Having halted this threat, Granger then made plans to crush the entire Confederate force. At this point, he missed his cavalry. Unperturbed, however, he ordered two regiments of infantry to move as quickly as possible to Hughes Mill to reinforce General Stanley. Granger's plan was for Stanley's unit to flank the Confederate force on the Lewisburg road as soon as it had passed the point of intersection with the Hughes Mill road. Then when Stanley's force was striking at Forrest's rear guard, General Baird was to cross the Harpeth River

13. Brown, "Van Dorn's Operations," p. 161.

and attack the head of Forrest's column. With Union troops outnumbering the Confederates nearly three to one, they might well have executed this maneuver and disastrously defeated the Confederates. Fortunately for Van Dorn this maneuver never materialized because of the slow advance of the infantry moving to reinforce General Stanley. Had General Smith's cavalry been available, Van Dorn might well have witnessed the destruction of his entire command.

Impetuous action by General Stanley also contributed to the Confederate escape. Across the river from the main attack, Stanley heard the firing outside of Franklin and longed to engage in the battle. Seeing what he thought was a chance to turn the enemy's rear, he acted on his own initiative before the arrival of the infantry reinforcements with Granger's new orders. He decided to move down the Hughes Mill Road and flank the Confederates before they became aware of his presence in the area. This was similar to Granger's proposed strategy, but Stanley's launching of the attack proved to be illtimed and poorly executed. Without informing his commanding officer, Stanley moved rapidly across the Harpeth River toward the Lewisburg road. Here he ran head on into General Forrest's brigade commanded by Colonel James W. Starnes.

Stanley's first contact was with the artillery unit of Captain S. L. Freeman, Forrest's artillery chief. This artillery unit was easily routed, and Stanley took about thirty-six prisoners. His attack had been so sudden that Freeman's men were unable to fire a single shot. Freeman had turned to face his attackers with four loaded pieces, but Stanley's cavalry quickly overwhelmed the position.

Hearing gunfire in the rear of his unit, Colonel Starnes turned his command abruptly and dashed back toward his artillery support. Leading an attack on Stanley's force, he recaptured all his guns and most of his men. When other elements of Forrest's division also attacked Stanley, the Union force was routed and their maneuver failed. Captain Freeman was one of the battle casualties.

Van Dorn allowed the battle to terminate with this success against Stanley. Nearly caught by Granger's alertness, he was fortunate to escape in the wake of the Northern commander's mistakes. Thus while Stanley's forces were still retreating in confusion, Van Dorn ordered his command from the field, and they retreated back toward Spring Hill. Although Granger's cavalry pursued the Rebels until after dark, they were never able to overtake them and force another showdown. At Spring Hill the pursuers halted. Granger was unwilling to attack Van Dorn "in his chosen position."[14]

Casualties were light in both armies; the Confederates suffered more from the deadly artillery fire from Franklin early in the battle. Why Van Dorn attacked such a position in the first place is still a mystery. He probably underestimated the size and firepower of the garrison, and he certainly succumbed to his own impetuosity once he had made contact with the enemy. "This officer is the bravest of the brave," ran one brief account of Van Dorn's conduct before the enemy, ". . . but [he] has not the prudence, the self-control nor ability to hold an independent command."[15] The attack accomplished little except to reveal the Union strength in the area and discourage any contemplated attack by the Confederates against a very well-armed position.

Two days after his encounter with the Confederates before Franklin, General Granger suggested to Rosecrans that he be allowed to pursue Van Dorn to his lair. Granger said that all he needed was a force large enough to put pressure on the slippery little officer. Rosecrans turned down the request promptly; he stressed that his former classmate was a clever officer and could anticipate enemy movements when they were made in piecemeal fashion.

At Spring Hill Van Dorn's army rested; it was safe for the moment from an enemy attack. But within the command, all was not well. There had been too much tension, and high-strung officers could not relax even in the quiet of the garrison. Good officers are usually sensitive men. In Tennessee in early 1863, Forrest, Morgan, Van Dorn, and Wheeler—all excelled as cavalry commanders. They were able to anticipate the actions of the enemy and prevent his success. But all were individualists, eager for the acclaim of the moment; each was set in his own pattern of action. Too often they disagreed, and it was not unusual for tempers to flare and words to fly. At Spring Hill there occurred another of these personal altercations that make up such an interesting and tragic aspect of the Civil War.

Relations between Generals Van Dorn and Forrest must have been somewhat strained at best during most of the period they worked together in early 1863. Van Dorn was a professional soldier, West

14. *Official Records Army*, XXIII, Pt. 1, 226; Pt. 2, 228.
15. Mobile *Advertiser and Register*, April 15, 1863, p. 1.

Point–trained, one of the most distinguished officers in the old army and an unusually high-strung individual. Forrest was a direct contrast—a practical soldier, "the son of the people," unpolished but brilliant, a better soldier than Van Dorn but forced by circumstance to serve under the dapper little general. Forrest was a businessman with few thoughts of a professional career, but he was proud and desirous of fighting the war in his own particular way. Forrest had already clashed with another West Pointer, General Wheeler, and many of Van Dorn's personal characteristics must have irritated him.[16] Van Dorn, on the other hand, surely burned under the popular acclaim that seemed to follow Forrest from one assignment to the next. Under the circumstances and with the independence of command in the Confederate Army, a clash between these two might have been inevitable.

Such a clash did occur, probably in mid-April, although one version of the affair places the date late in March or in early April. At least three accounts of the clash have been handed down, each differing somewhat in detail from the others. All the accounts agree that the affair occurred in Spring Hill, and that it stemmed from happenings at the engagements at Thompson's Station and Brentwood. After these battles General Forrest had confiscated much of the property seized from the Federals for his own command. Van Dorn, concerned with the welfare of the entire army and probably smarting over the publicity given to Forrest by the local press, resented this usurpation of authority. To complicate matters General Bragg also heard of Forrest's activities and ordered Van Dorn to recover the goods and send them to Confederate headquarters in Tennessee for proper distribution.

Van Dorn promptly called Forrest to his own headquarters in Spring Hill to discuss the matter. One account says that Van Dorn began by accusing Forrest of having had articles published in the Chattanooga *Rebel*, which claimed honors at Thompson's Station and Brentwood for Forrest's command. Another account says that Van Dorn accused Forrest of misrepresenting certain military information to Confederate headquarters. Whatever was said, it led to more words until both men lost their tempers. They were just on the verge of settling the argument

16. Forrest had declared that he would never again serve under Wheeler because of what he considered poor leadership by the West Pointer in an earlier attack. Wheeler allowed Forrest to transfer to Van Dorn's command at the time.

with their swords when one of them suddenly regained his composure. One account says it was Forrest who recovered himself. He was then supposed to have said to his equally agitated comrade:

General Van Dorn, you know I'm not afraid of you—but I will not fight you—and leave you to reconcile with yourself the gross wrongs you have done me. It would never do for two officers of our rank to set such an example to the troops and I remember, if you forget, what we both owe to the cause.[17]

The same source continued: Van Dorn was taken aback by this outburst: "I never felt so ashamed of myself in my life," he recounted later. "I immediately replied that he was right, and apologized for having used such expressions to him. And so we parted to be somewhat better friends, I believe, then we have been before. What else he may be, the man certainly is no coward."

Dr. Wyeth's account is not so detailed. Though it is slightly different from the first account, there is a ring of authenticity about it. His account is supposed to be from Major J. Minnick Williams of Van Dorn's staff, supposedly the only person actually to witness the scene. According to Wyeth, Williams said that Van Dorn opened the door for disagreement by storming out at Forrest:

"I am informed that several articles published in the Chattanooga *Rebel*, in which the honors of Thompson's Station and Brentwood were claimed for yourself, were written by one of your staff."

"I know nothing of the articles you refer to," answered Forrest angrily, "and I demand from you your authority for this assertion. I shall hold him responsible and make him eat his words, or run my sabre through him; and I say to you as well, that I will hold you personally responsible if you do not produce the author."

Van Dorn was taken aback by this outburst and asked Major Williams if he knew the identity of the author of the publications. Williams's reply was: "I do not; and I think, general, that you have done General Forrest an injustice in the suspicion that the articles originated from his headquarters."

This seemed to satisfy Van Dorn and he replied quickly: "I do not assert, nor do I believe, that General Forrest inspired those articles, or had any knowledge of them."

17. *A Soldier's Honor*, p. 279.

The tension lifted on this note, and Forrest concluded the argument by saying: "General Van Dorn and I have enough to fighting the enemies of our country without fighting each other."[18]

A third account of the affair is more colorful and little melodramatic. The author wrote it in 1877 and admits that he cannot vouch for the accuracy of his details. It is interesting to note even here in an account by a man sympathetic to Van Dorn that Forrest made the first gesture for reconciliation. According to Colonel Edward Dillon, who rode with Van Dorn for some months during the war, the conversation between the two angry generals went as follows:

Van Dorn: "Either your report to me was incorrect or your command is in possession of the property, and you must produce and deliver it up."

Forrest replied indignantly that he wasn't used to being talked to like that, and that time would come when he would demand satisfaction.

Van Dorn (quietly): "My rank shall be no barrier; you can have satisfaction at any time you desire."

Forrest (passes his hand thoughtfully across his brow): "I have been hasty, General, and am sorry for it. I do not fear that anybody will misunderstand me, but the truth is you and I have enough Yankees to fight without fighting each other, and I hope this matter will be forgotten."

Van Dorn: "You are right General, and I am sure nobody will ever suspect you of not being ready for any kind of a fight at any time; I certainly am willing to drop the matter, and can assure you that I have no feeling about it; but I must insist that my orders shall be obeyed as long as I am your commander; let us drop the subject, however, as I have work for you to do."[19]

This was probably the last confrontation between the two generals. The "work" Van Dorn had for Forrest was a cavalry mission into Alabama and Georgia after Yankee Colonel Abel D. Streight of Rosecrans's command. The two officers probably respected the abilities of each other, but they were operating too close and in too confused a department to work in harmony for long. As Forrest rode south, he saluted his commander for the last time.

Van Dorn remained at Spring Hill after General Forrest's departure and kept on the alert for activity from the Union camps. Every day his troops were in the saddle, reconnoitering enemy positions and constantly annoying Rosecrans by raiding his isolated outposts. When a Confederate spy reported that the Federals were transferring all their

18. John A. Wyeth, *Life of General Nathan Bedford Forrest*, p. 176.
19. "General Van Dorn's Operations between Columbia and Nashville," *Southern Historical Society Papers*, XIX, 199.

gunboats on the Cumberland River to the Tennessee River, Van Dorn posted scouting parties below Fort Donelson and Fort Henry to observe these actions and impede them as best he could. Meanwhile he reported that he was conditioning his horses and drilling his men for any movement that the commanding general might direct against Rosecrans's position. His "present for duty" roster seldom exceeded 4,000 healthy troopers, "poorly clothed" and hard pressed for proper food and forage for their mounts; but somehow Van Dorn kept his men in the field and constantly threatened the enemy units around him. His greatest success was in keeping these units off balance and unaware of his next move.

A few days after the Franklin raid, rumors in Rosecrans's command were that Van Dorn and Wheeler were planning an important combined offensive against some Federal position yet unknown. They drew this conclusion when they learned that both generals had dispatched all their sick and convalescents to Alabama.[20] Confederate actions or correspondence fail to confirm such plans, but the Northern army set itself to act against such a move. Actually neither Wheeler nor Van Dorn had the wherewithal necessary for such an undertaking. It was more important that each use his limited forces to harass the enemy with a minimum of risk to his own command. Of course each officer had great leeway in deciding his own course of action, and sometimes these impulsive officers took undue advantage of this fact. Sometimes their forays were successful. On other occasions they miscalculated.

One of Van Dorn's most costly ventures was on April 27 when he pushed his outposts too far toward enemy lines. In a spectacular early morning raid, General Granger captured 125 men and 300 horses from his Texas Legion. But there was always a resilience about Van Dorn no matter what his defeat. Undaunted by this loss, he quickly countered by moving toward Florence, Alabama, where he forced the Union commander, General Dodge, to fall back to his fortifications. Van Dorn then moved his own force toward Eastport.

The Spring days of 1863 continued to be busy and dangerous ones for the Confederates near Nashville. Two days after his cavalry action against General Dodge, General Bragg ordered Van Dorn to move toward Florence again and observe the activities of Union troops that had recently entered Alabama. "Resist any attempt . . . to cross the river," Bragg warned his impetuous officer. Van Dorn carried out these

20. *Official Records Army*, XXIII, Pt. 2, p. 803.

orders and returned to his headquarters at Spring Hill. The Federals were now pressing against this position as they were pressing all along the Confederate line. The Confederates felt these new pressures daily. It was apparent that the giant army before them would soon shake itself from its lethargy and again become a mobile force. Day by day the Confederates found it increasingly difficult to cut enemy supply and communications lines and to hold their own against strengthened Federal cavalry. Van Dorn reveals the pressures against his own position in an official message to General Polk on May 2: "Enemy have been reenforced at Franklin. Will attempt to drive me away, I think. Came out yesterday with all cavalry and two brigades of infantry, but went back. Can you send me an engineer officer and some intrenching tools?"[21]

Despite the build-up in the Federal army, May began quietly at Spring Hill. Dancing, card-playing, and drinking commanded as much attention as the enemy. Meanwhile, a prominent Spring Hill doctor made plans that related directly to Buck Van Dorn.

21. *Ibid.*, p. 807.

CHAPTER FOURTEEN

An Assassination at Spring Hill

SPRING Hill is a sleepy little village "set in the idyllic rolling hills of blue-grass pasture land" about thirty miles south of Nashville. Riding into Spring Hill from Columbia in 1863, the visitor was struck with the loveliness of the little agrarian community. Among its great and majestic trees stood square mansions—their Greek columns lordly in the surroundings, their size and beauty testifying to the wealth accumulated over the years by a few of the village's leading citizens. In the center of town the red brick, four-column home of William McKissack seemed to dominate the scene. McKissack built his house in 1845, and he and his family had achieved a prominence in social circles throughout the area.

Today Spring Hill remains much as it was in the nineteenth century. Its citizens seem little affected by the passing parade, and many appear unconcerned with their town's generally quiet past. But for a few moments in the spring of 1863, the currents of history ran as fitfully there as in other more prominent centers of the war-torn Confederacy. In one of the square brick mansions, the home of Martin Cheairs, death came abruptly to an ill-fated Confederate general by the hand of a prominent doctor, and it left a mystery that has yet to be resolved.

Assassinations, as we know so well in our own day, always smack of mystery and intrigue. Too often the facts of the case are blurred in secrecy and confusion. In the assassination of General Earl Van Dorn, the true facts will probably never be known since so much of the evidence has been destroyed either deliberately or by the passing of time and persons involved. "New light" will be cast upon the events that led up to the fatal shooting, but much that took place on that fateful day will forever remain in the shadows. With records destroyed or colored by years of reinterpretation, one can only present the evidence and speculate on the real conclusions.

For months before the tragedy, Earl Van Dorn's name had been associated with gay living and improprieties hardly becoming the honor of a husband and father. Under serious popular indictment for military reverses, he also felt the sharp barbs of public and private criticism against his personal conduct. The often-critical press took the lead in circulating tales of his vice and corruption. On May 3 the Chattanooga *Rebel* charged him with corruption, drunkenness, and licentiousness. It further stated that the people in Tennessee were fast losing confidence in him as one of their military leaders.

A story appeared earlier in a Mobile paper that stressed Van Dorn's weakness in a different way. The correspondent who followed the general from the middle of the summer of 1862 to his death told of a conversation which he said took place between Van Dorn and a buxom young widow of twenty-four at Spring Hill. She had just congratulated him on his successes in battle, then she added:

"General, you are older than I am, but let me give you a little advice —let the women alone until the war is over."

"My God, Madam!" exclaimed Van Dorn, "I cannot do that, for it is all I am fighting for. I hate all men, and were it not for the women, I should not fight at all; besides, if I accepted your generous advice, I would not now be speaking to you."[1]

This same reporter also contended that Van Dorn was "much of a flirt." "[I]t is publicly stated that he is the terror of ugly husbands and serious papas." The newsman also recalled a charcoal sketch in a hotel room in Spring Hill of a man on horseback "with a sabre hanging by his side, his cloak thrown negligently over his shoulders, the broad brimmed hat turned up on one side and down on the other, with an immence gold lace bow knot at the back . . . recognizable at first glance." Beneath the picture in large black letters was the title: "Ye gay Dragoon on ye black mare."

Others besides the press also concerned themselves with the Mississippian's conduct. Robert G. H. Kean recorded in his diary that Van Dorn had the "reputation of being horrible rake."[2] Lieutenant William L. Nugent of the Twenty-eighth Mississippi Cavalry wrote also of his

1. Mobile *Advertiser and Register*, March 22, 1863, p. 1.
2. Edward Younger (ed.), *Inside the Confederate Government*, p. 58.

concern for the general's unusual interest in women: "[Y]ou can see at times some fine looking *ladies* driving about in his splendid four-horse Ambulance."[3]

Stories of this sort harassed the general throughout so much of his military career that one has to decide whether such rumors were based on fact or were just idle talk compounded by critical public opinion about a person whose limitations as a man and officer made him a fit subject for such scurrilous remarks. Captain G. A. Hanson of Van Dorn's command said that during their free time in Tennessee, "the officers, from the General down, found time for sport and amusement amongst the generally wealthy and hospitable citizens. . . . " "Of course," he added defensively, "gossip soon began to connect these festival occasions with matters not very creditable to some of the participants."[4]

Whether these observations about his personal life were fact or fiction, Earl Van Dorn established a reputation that he was indeed a "horrible rake" both within the ranks and among the citizens of Mississippi and Tennessee. There is little in his personal association with his wife and family or in his correspondence that disproves this.

Though no one witnessed the actual murder, it is obvious that a Tennessee doctor, George B. Peters, shot and killed the little general. Van Dorn's murderer was no ordinary man. Dr. Peters was born in North Carolina, probably in 1815. He came to Hardeman County, Tennessee, in the 1830s and was a prominent physician there for many years. While serving as a small-town doctor, he took a great interest in real estate, and the land records of Hardeman County show that he bought several tracts of land before 1860. After the war he owned land across the river from Memphis in Arkansas, and one account of the doctor's career reveals that he may have purchased this property before the war. Besides a real-estate speculator, the doctor was also a prominent slave dealer.

Distinguished in the field of medicine, Dr. Peters was elected vice president of the Hardeman County Medical Society in 1857. At a meeting of the society that year, the chairman assigned him the task of preparing an important report on ulceration, a subject in which he was well versed. He was an active member of the Board of the Female

3. Lieutenant William L. Nugent to his wife from near Vicksburg, Mississippi, March 24, 1863.
4. *Minor Incidents of the Late War*, p. 32.

Academy of Bolivar, a member of the Bolivar Episcopal Church, and a prominent Mason. Dr. Peters also served as a state senator from Tennessee in the decade before the war.

Tragedy struck often in the life of this Southern doctor. His first marriage in 1839 ended a year later with the death of his wife in childbirth. His second wife bore him seven children before she died in 1855. In 1858 the forty-six-year-old physician took his third mate, twenty-year-old Jessie Helen McKissack, of the Spring Hill McKissacks, described at the time as "gay and fashionable."[5] When the war came, the doctor took an oath of allegiance to the Union, and he seems to have neglected his family while he engaged in some unknown business behind Federal lines. According to a newspaper report, he had a brother who was an officer in Polk's command, a son in the Confederate Army, and another son in the Confederate Navy.

Jessie Peters, described as a beautiful brunette, must have been a vivacious and popular young lady. About a year after the tragedy, troops passing through Spring Hill commented that they found this young matron to be "a very handsome woman."[6] In the spring of 1863 she was one of a coterie of young ladies in Spring Hill who made the acquaintance of the dashing Confederate officers using some of the homes in the little village for their headquarters. Rumors have it that Earl Van Dorn, the garrison's commander, cast his expert eye toward Jessie; and it is possible, under such circumstances, that their acquaintance was more than casual.[7] At least common gossip in the community related this view of their relationship. A Montgomery journalist even wrote that the general and Mrs. Peters were often seen riding together in her carriage.

Edward Caffery, a kinsman of the late general, has recently suggested that it may well have been Mrs. Peters rather than the general who encouraged their friendship. Caffery remembers seeing copies of letters that passed between the two, and most of these were merely expressions of gratitude from the general to the lady for her kindness to his troops either as an individual or through some committee. Caffery also recalled a note written by Van Dorn's adjutant begging his chief not to attend

5. *Ibid.*, p. 32.

6. Alderson, "The Civil War Reminiscences of John Johnson," p. 73.

7. This fact has not been established to the complete satisfaction of this writer, but many of the old-timers in and around the area concur with the many rumors of such that were handed down through the generations.

a party that was to be given in his honor by Mrs. Peters, possibly a suggestion that the general was getting himself too involved.[8]

Several officers in Van Dorn's immediate Tennessee command would probably have shared this viewpoint. They later contended that though there had been friendly visits between Mrs. Peters and the general, there was certainly no "improper intimacy" between them.[9] They also condemned the writings of newspapers "that have given publicity to the false rumors" surrounding the assassination.

In his own account of the killing, possibly an apocryphal one, the doctor said he had heard that Van Dorn had paid undue attention to his wife, but that he was unaware of the extent of the general's attentions until he made a surprise visit to Spring Hill on April 12.[10] Alarmed at the many rumors in the little town that associated his wife too intimately with the Confederate officer, he determined to find out what was really happening.

Nearly three weeks went by and during this time, the doctor became convinced of the truth of the rumors of Van Dorn's improprieties with Mrs. Peters. He decided to take desperate measures against his rival. When he caught a servant delivering a note from Van Dorn to Mrs. Peters, the enraged husband confronted the unfortunate man with an ultimatum: "I distinctly told him," he wrote, "I would blow his brains out if he ever entered the premise again." As for Van Dorn, he would suffer the same fate, as would any member of his staff, if he so much as ever even set foot inside the Peters's yard.

This incident, the doctor said, preceded his own visit to Nashville where he remained for several days on business. When he returned through the lines to Spring Hill, he learned that Van Dorn had visited his wife every night during his absence. After this discovery the doctor set a trap for his wife's alleged paramour. Feigning a trip to Shelbyville, he hid out to watch the general's actions. Two days passed, and then at 2:30 on the morning of May 6, he finally caught Van Dorn "where I expected to find him." Peters said he confronted the intruder with a

8. Edward Caffery to John R. Peacock, June 7, 1954. Copy in possession of author.

9. Letter recorded in the Mobile *Advertiser and Register* by the following members of Van Dorn's staff on May 16, 1863: M. M. Kimmel, Assistant Adjutant General; W. C. Schaunburg, Assistant Adjutant General; Clement Sulivane, Aide-de-camp; and R. Shoemaker, Aide-de-camp.

10. Voluntary Statement of Dr. George B. Peters in Fitch, *Annals of the Army of the Cumberland*, p. 618.

weapon, and the general acknowledged his right to shoot on the spot. Concerned about his wife's honor, the doctor offered Van Dorn a chance to sign a statement exonerating his wife of any guilt in exchange for his freedom. Van Dorn agreed to sign the statement. After all, he supposedly told the doctor, what had he to lose! He cared very little about his own wife anyway.

The doctor continued his statement of the assassination by stating that early on Thursday morning, May 7, he called at Van Dorn's headquarters office to pick up the promised statement. When the general could not produce the statement, Peters gave him thirty minutes to prepare one. The angry physician then went into the village while Van Dorn was writing. Returning on schedule the doctor read what had been written. Dissatisfied with the general's statement, Peters denounced him for bad faith. Van Dorn answered that he had changed his mind about the statement because it would hurt the "cause" and his own reputation at that time. Peters replied indignantly: "You did not think so thirty hours ago, when your life was in my hands: you were then ready to promise anything . . . now . . . if you don't comply with my demands, I will instantly blow your brains out."

"You d——d cowardly dog," Van Dorn was purported to have answered, "take that door, or I will kick you out of it."

This was too much, said the doctor. He immediately drew his pistol, "aiming to shoot him in the forehead," he said, but when Van Dorn made a "convulsive movement of his head," Peters's shot struck "in the left side of his head just above the ear, killing him instantly."

Then, said Peters, he picked up Van Dorn's written statement, dashed from the room, jumped astride his horse, and headed toward Shelbyville, where he planned to surrender to authorities. But these plans were changed, he said, when he learned that General Polk had ordered his arrest. He then disguised himself and proceeded through Winchester and Gallatin into Nashville, where he arrived on May 11.

Much of this report is strange. It is difficult to imagine a man like Earl Van Dorn submitting to the doctor's treatment. Why did the general not make some preparation to defend himself during the half-hour leave the doctor took of him on the morning of the shooting? These two visits are not confirmed by any of the other reports of the murder. How and why was the doctor able to move so freely in and out of headquarters?

This account, though questionable in part, does have a remarkable similarity to an account in the Nashville *Dispatch* on May 13, 1863, which was supposedly written by a reporter after a visit with the doctor soon after the assassination.[11] One can only surmise from these two reports that the doctor was telling a fairly consistent story and that he left out much that would have given insight into the real meaning of this strange episode.

In a book by one of Van Dorn's cavalrymen, Victor Rose, is another statement of the murder. This is a statement of A. W. Sparks, another cavalryman, who was camped only 300 yards from the murder house when Peters fired his fatal shot.[12]

Sparks spoke of a murder that occurred at the home of "Major Cheairs."[13] The shooting actually took place at the Martin Cheairs home, a house located very near to Dr. Peters's own residence. According to Sparks, Van Dorn went to his office early that fateful morning. There he found the doctor waiting for him, supposedly to sign a pass through the lines to Franklin. Passing through the lines was a fairly common practice, so Van Dorn sat down at his desk to sign a pass. It was Sparks's opinion that Peters waited until the signature was on the paper before acting. He then "drew a Smith and Wesson revolver and fired, the ball entering the back of [Van Dorn's] . . . head, and lodging just under the surface of the right eye."

After shooting the general, Dr. Peters escaped through the Union lines with his pass. He later made his way to Mississippi where he was apprehended and tried by a Confederate court and acquitted. Sparks quotes an account of the arrest and interrogation of the murderer by his captor, Lieutenant Dan C. Alley of Company G, the Third Texas Cavalry. Alley wrote that Dr. Peters was very much incensed at his capture. The doctor feared that Lieutenant Alley, a Texan, would kill him in revenge for Van Dorn's murder. After receiving assurance that this would not be the case, the assassin talked freely to his captors; he abused both his wife and General Van Dorn. Peters said that he had parted from his wife once for a similar offense with a man other than Van Dorn, and he was not surprised at her conduct. He then stated that he only condoned her fall from virtue because of their children.

11. May 18, 1863, p. 2.
12. *History of the Ross Brigade,* pp. 99–100.
13. Van Dorn had recently moved from the Aaron White home to the Cheairs residence.

According to Alley's report, Peters said that he caught Van Dorn in the doctor's house on May 5. Van Dorn ran out of the front door and hid under the house. The doctor pursued him and finally caught him; he threatened him with a gun. Peters said that Van Dorn, intoxicated at the time, sobered up enough to beg for his life. The offended husband then gained a promise of a note confessing intimacy between the general and Mrs. Peters. Alley reported the doctor's saying that he went to Van Dorn's office early on the morning of May 7 for the signed confession "and that Van Dorn exclaimed indignantly: 'Take the door, you —— puppy!' [W]hereupon he [Dr. Peters] drew his pistol and fired."[14]

Again it is difficult to imagine a man as courageous as Earl Van Dorn being dragged from under the house by the irate doctor. The doctor's story, though, is fairly consistent with the ones published earlier except that in this account he takes a more critical attitude toward his wife. Possibly this is because he was in the hands of the enemy at the time and under the circumstances felt it wiser not to put all the blame on Van Dorn.

As to the fate of Dr. Peters, Lieutenant Alley said that he learned later "that he was tried and acquitted, and then he returned home, and took to his bosom the twice-discarded wife." The Peters were indeed remarried soon after the war.

Captain G. A. Hanson, also of the Spring Hill garrison, later claimed that he heard the fatal shot and took part in the pursuit of the assassin. Hanson said he knew Peters well; the doctor had served as his family's physician for many years. He said that the doctor came to Spring Hill from the Union lines when news reached him that connected "in a disreputable way" the name of his wife with General Van Dorn. Dr. Peters seems to have decided to use this knowledge against the general by demanding the privilege "of coming and going at will through the lines," a privilege he had been accorded earlier by the Federals. Van Dorn refused to accept such a proposition, so Hanson said the doctor took matters into his own hands.[15]

Early on May 7, Captain Hanson was on his way from his boarding house to Van Dorn's headquarters nearby when he heard "a clear, sharp, and very loud report of a pistol." The sound of the shot came from the direction of his chief's office, and it was followed by shouts

14. Rose, *op. cit.*
15. Hanson, *Minor Incidents of the Late War*, pp. 32–33.

and commands and hasty mounting of troops. Hanson entered Van Dorn's office and found that the general had been shot "in the back of the head with a Derringer pistol of the largest calibre." "The general was already dead," he reported.

Hanson then rode out, following the tracks of Peters's horse, and found that the doctor had deliberately planned his escape route by earlier removing parts of fences to clear a path into a canebrake. Thus it was impossible to track him. The murder, concluded the captain, "was one of the coolest and boldest ever attempted, and could scarcely have succeeded without aid and assistance from friends."

The thought that others might have been involved or that the murder was part of a greater plot against the Confederacy has been a popular one among those who have defended the reputation of the Mississippian. The four staff members who presented their defense of Van Dorn in the Mobile press first made this accusation in their suggestion that there were "darker motives" than an illicit love affair behind the shooting. Dr. Peters had remarked earlier, said their statement, "that he had lost his land and Negroes in Arkansas, but he thought he would shortly do something which would get them back."[16] They believed that the doctor premeditated the murder and merely used the intimacy with his wife as an excuse. Another defender agreed. "The fact that his property, which had been confiscated by the Federals, was later returned to him was probably responsible for the report that he had been hired to do the deed," ran his account.[17]

Emily Van Dorn Miller, defending her brother years after his death, recorded a letter written to her by an unnamed officer of Van Dorn's command who was very close to the scene of the crime when it happened and who also suspected sinister motives on the part of the assassin. Though there is little to authenticate either the letter or its author, the account is another one that must be added to an already garbled mystery. This officer said that on the morning of May 7, just before breakfast, he was standing within twenty feet of the Cheairs's house when he saw the doctor (he does not call him by name), a well-known figure in Spring Hill, enter the building. Within ten minutes the doctor made his exit and rode away. The writer does not mention hearing a

16. A *Soldier's Honor*, p. 350; also recorded in Mobile *Advertiser and Register*, May 16, 1863, p. 1.
17. "Justice to Van Dorn," Washington *Post*, January 27, 1902.

shot, but he says that the doctor was hardly out of sight when a shout came from within the house that the general had been wounded. He and the other officers in the area then rushed into the building and there they found the general "seated in his chair, his head leaning against the window pane . . . and his right arm resting on his writing table. . . . His left arm was on his lap, blood was flowing from the back of his head against the glass, and he was convulsively shuddering. . . ."[18]

This officer then went on to say that he tried to initiate a pursuit of the doctor, but he was greatly delayed by the absence at that early hour of Van Dorn's personal bodyguard. He then returned to the general's room and examined the prostrate form of the murdered man. "There had evidently been no struggle of any kind," he said. His report does indicate that the general had just written something, though, for "a piece of writing paper, and a pen still wet with ink, and the inkstand, were on the table near the General's hand." His report continues:

The pistol ball had entered the center of the back of his head and lodged under the forehead, the right eye soon becoming swollen and dark from the effects of it. [This description is similar to some of those given of Lincoln's fatal wound two years later.] There was a *very* small round hole in the head, evidently made by a ball from a parlor pistol, which makes no noise louder than the snapping of a cap, and hence it was not heard.[19]

It was the opinion of this officer that the doctor, supposedly a friend of the general, had entered the room to pick up a pass to go through the enemy lines; he had followed this procedure several times before. While Van Dorn was writing the pass, the assassin stood a few paces behind him. Just as the general finished, the doctor inflicted the fatal wound either for the reward involved or for the personal recognition which he hoped to receive.

Writing recently, Edward Caffery also suggests the interesting possibility of intrigue. Could the doctor *and* his wife have been Federal agents with the set goal of eliminating an enemy commander in Tennessee? In a war where spying, espionage, and secret dealings with the enemy were employed in both armies in a most haphazard fashion rather than as an organized endeavor, this is a distinct possibility. If this were the case, "the affair," if such existed between Mrs. Peters and the general, could have been staged for the final act of the drama, the

18. *A Soldier's Honor*, p. 351.
19. *Ibid.*

murder.[20] The main evidence for such observation seems to be in the remarriage of the Peters and the return of his property by the Federals, possibly in payment for something the doctor did.

Whatever the case, reports of intrigue in the shooting reached the Confederate President, and in due time he ordered an investigation of the murder. One of the first reports he received was from Colonel P. B. Starke, a regimental commander in the Spring Hill area. Starke seems to have been a personal friend of the Davis family as well as a close associate to General Van Dorn. He had been with the general on their wild charge into Franklin just a few weeks before the assassination. On May 11 he made the following report about the death of his commanding officer:

After conversing with one of the late Genl's staff officers I find that Dr Peters was moved to kill the Genl. in consequence of his familiarity with Mrs. Peters in visiting her and remaining at her house until late hours of the night and that in the absence of the Doct. *The impropriety of this conduct was freely discussed and condemned in and out of the army.* That he "was a gallant soldier and pure (?) patriot" is conceded by all.[21]

Colonel Starke questioned the manner of the shooting. "The Doct went into his room and found him alone," Starke continued. "The firing of a pistol caused his staff to go in to the room. They met the Doct coming out who mounted his horse and rode rappidly [*sic*] off." Starke said that he did not see the body, but someone told him that Van Dorn was shot from behind as he sat at his table.

There was no attempt made by Colonel Starke to whitewash the "illicit affair" aspect of the murder. In fact Starke contributes to the support of the idea that the general and Mrs. Peters may indeed have been intimate. *"That the Genl. had great weaknesses in such matters must be admitted,"* he said emphatically.

Despite the pall of intrigue that lingered over the Spring Hill murder, some Southern newspapers continued to accept the idea of self-induced tragedy. One of the most furious indictments was in the Atlanta *Confederacy* in late May. Whether the statements in this article were compounded from public gossip or from actual knowledge is impos-

20. Edward Caffery to John R. Peacock, July 6, 1954. Copy in possession of author.

21. Colonel P. B. Starke to Jefferson Davis, May 11, 1863. The original is in the "Jefferson Davis Papers" at Duke University.

sible to say, but they probably reveal much of the thinking in the public mind. The article lambasted the statements made by Van Dorn's staff in his defense as "a lame effort to whitewash" their chief and "relieve him of some of the odium which attaches to his name in connection with his death." Then the journalist issued a most blistering indictment, one of the strongest on record, against the Confederate commander:

Van Dorn has been recognized for years as a rake, a most wicked libertine —and most especially of late. If he had led a virtuous life, he would not have died—unwept, unhonored and unsung. Think of the universal respect paid to the lamented Jackson. The whole country is filled with mourning and tears at his death, while no man expresses even a *regret* at the fate of Van Dorn. Here is a striking difference between sin and righteousness—between the devotion of a man's life to the most infamous and debasing of all human vices and the most commendable and elevating Christian virtues. The country has sustained no loss in the death of Van Dorn. It is a happy riddance. He was unfit to live, let alone having charge of such important trusts as he had.[22]

Two other newspapers offered critical statements concerning the assassinated general. In the Montgomery *Weekly Advertiser* was the following:

The impression around Spring Hill is that Van Dorn was rightly killed. He had been quite intimate with Mrs. Peters for sometime prior to his death, had rode in her carriage to Columbia, and frequently had passed half a day at her house in the absence of her husband. It is conjectured that Dr. Peters absented himself from home, but returned and observed his wife from a secure hiding place. When informed of the death of Van Dorn and the flight of her husband, Mrs. Peters is reported to have remarked that "she was a widow indeed, as her husband had fled and her sweetheart was dead." To a minister who had advised her to become pious and to lead a secluded life, she merely replied that she was too young, showing an eager love for gay society.[23]

And in the Nashville *Dispatch* in late May, a Richmond correspondent offered some sharp criticisms:

My informant tells me that he [Van Dorn] had degraded the cause, and disgusted every one by his inattention to his duties and his constant devotion to the ladies . . . wine and women ruined him as they have ruined many others. . . . He was never at his post when he ought to be. He was either tied to a woman's apron strings or heated with wine.[24]

22. Quoted in Fayetteville *Observer*, June 4, 1863, p. 1.
23. June 17, 1863, p. 1.
24. May 24, 1863, p. 3.

These statements may or may not have validity, but they certainly offer a specific point of view. Did the newspapers applaud Van Dorn's death because he had stifled the press in his own military operations? Or was there some other flaw in his personality that antagonized them?

And so the controversy continued as to why and how the doctor shot and killed the egregious little general. Van Dorn's sister, Emily, later compiled an entire book of the writings of friends, admirers, and members of his command, which defended the honor and reputation of her brother. A personal friend of the family, I. F. H. Claiborne of Mississippi, who planned at one time to be the general's first biographer, said of his friend: "I have not yet had a particular and detailed account of the murder of the general. . . . I always believed that the Nashville authority had some connivance and concern with it."[25] A memorial by Mary Emily Donelson, the daughter of Andrew Donelson of Andrew Jackson's staff, wrote that Dr. Peters's wife later testified that Van Dorn had never approached her save in a respectful manner. Despite these efforts, however, many of the soldiers in the ranks were unconvinced of their commander's innocence. Young Robert Partin, writing from one of the military units near Spring Hill, told his wife that he was not inclined to be "gossipy," but there was one piece of news he wanted to share. "Gen Van Dorn was killed yesterday," he wrote, "for tampering with a fellow's wife; if that be the case he was served right."[26]

Because of all these conflicting viewpoints, the shadows of uncertainty and confusion yet hang over Van Dorn's death. Plagued by defeat and malicious criticism during the last fourteen months of his life, he was not exonerated by death. Dr. Peters also remains a man of mystery. Many reports of the doctor circulated on both sides of the lines after he had escaped through the Confederate outposts. He was in Nashville for some time after the shooting, but for what purpose there seems to be no answer. On July 12 a Nashville newspaper reported that someone had made an attempt on his life in his hotel room, but there were no details on the circumstances of this action. Finally on November 3, 1863, General Joseph E. Johnston dispatched a message to the Secretary of War from Mississippi that seems to match the

25. I. F. H. Claiborne to Clement Sulivane, November 5, 1866. Van Dorn Collection, Montgomery, Alabama.
26. Robert Partin, "A Confederate Sergeant's Report to His Wife," *Tennessee Historical Quarterly*, XII, 301.

report of Lieutenant Dan H. Alley, mentioned previously. "Our cavalry has arrested and sent in the murderer of Maj Gen Van Dorn, a citizen. What course can be taken? There are no courts for us in Tennessee."[27] Johnston made no mention of the name of the captured man, and there is not further reference to him in the *Official Records*.

The capture of the doctor was also reported in the Nashville newspapers as well as in others throughout the South. The *Dispatch* reported that Dr. Peters expressed relief at being captured; he said that it had been his intention for some time to return to the South and stand trial.[28] Evidently he was brought to trial and released. The Richmond *Whig* reported that he was brought before a judge at Okalona, Mississippi, and after a hearing he was discharged because there was nothing to justify detention.[29]

That the doctor did divorce his wife is true but not until after the war, and they remarried some time later. In the divorce proceedings, the doctor was the complainant. He stated that he and Mrs. Peters had been separated since May 1, 1863, a week before Van Dorn's death. By 1870 the Peters were well established in Memphis and western Arkansas, where he owned land in Phillips County. The doctor was very popular in Arkansas and served one term there in the state senate. He died in Tennessee in 1889 at the age of 74 and was buried at the side of his second wife. At the time of his death, though, he was living with Jessie, the shadowy figure in the Van Dorn mystery. One interesting story, probably with no other substance but hearsay, is that Jessie dutifully wore a black veil to her husband's funeral but was heard to remark afterward; "Well, I never cared for George, but I guess I owe him this much."[30]

Jessie Peters lived on at the residence in a prominent part of Memphis which she had shared with her husband until her death at the age of 83 in 1921. She is also buried in Elmwood Cemetery in Memphis by the side of Dr. Peters. Her stepson, George B. Peters, Jr., became a prominent lawyer in Memphis in the late nineteenth century; he rose in political circles to the lower house of the General Assembly and to Attorney General of Shelby County.

27. *Official Records Army*, XXXI, Pt. 3, 689.
28. December 3, 1863, p. 1.
29. December 4, 1863, p. 1.
30. Hugh Walker, "The Day the Doctor Shot the General," Nashville *Tennessee Magazine*, July 14, 1863.

In the maelstrom of activity that colored the summer of 1863, the press took little notice of the death of Earl Van Dorn. The loss of Stonewall Jackson hit the South too hard for her citizens to be concerned over a lesser officer in an obscure part of the country. Tucked into a secluded spot on page three, the *Daily Mississippian* gave a brief report of the murder. Other papers gave even less coverage.[31]

Van Dorn's funeral was impressive but solemn. A contemporary account describes the proceedings:

> The command was mounted, and drawn up on either side of the street. The body, in a metallic casket, was laid in the hearse; on the head of the coffin reposed his Mexican Sombrero, bearing a gold Texas star; along the breast reposed his gold-hilted sword, a present from the State of Mississippi; at the foot of the coffin stood his military boots. Following the hearse was his horse, bridled and saddled. As the hearse passed down the lines, the officers and men saluted their dead chieftain with the saber; and though extremest silence reigned, many an eye was moist.[32]

That all eyes were not moist was revealed in a statement two days after the funeral by one of the noncommissioned officers in the command. Sergeant Edwin H. Fay also described some of the feelings in the commands when he wrote: "Yesterday Van Dorn was buried in Columbia having been shot by a Dr. Peters whose wife he had been too intimate with. . . . It may be a great gain to the Confederacy. I do not think it was a great loss."[33] Whether this was just Fay's personal feeling or a more widespread one is difficult to ascertain since the sergeant's judgment was certainly colored by the fact that he was still bitter at his commander because of the general's refusal to sign discharge papers for him only three weeks earlier. But Howard Swiggart also commented in the same vein about his own feelings toward his commander. Swiggart said that Van Dorn had been killed because he had been "slipping into Spring Hill for the seduction of Mrs. Peters." "I found him where I expected to find him," he said upon receiving news of the shooting.[34]

31. A later issue of the Jackson *Daily Mississippian* showed some concern over the assassination. "Whatever the cause," the article continued, "the fact of an army officer of General Van Dorn's high position, and at the time doing service in the field, being killed by a citizen, shows that there must have been something more than an ordinary quarrel or insult to have caused such a lamentable result."

32. Rose, *Ross' Texas Brigade*, p. 101.

33. Wiley, *"The Infernal War,"* p. 261–262.

34. Howard Swiggart, *Rebel Raiders*, p. 119.

Even one of the Confederate generals stationed in central Tennessee echoed the sentiments of these two enlisted men. St. John R. Liddell, hardly an admirer of the officer who had rebuffed him so noticeably at Corinth, criticized Van Dorn's character. "The common opinion," he wrote after the war, "was clearly expressive of condemnation, mingled with little or no regret for a man whose willful violation of social rights led him to such an inglorious end." Liddell contended that Van Dorn had failed in every assignment he had undertaken until "in utter recklessness at his fallen state, [he] gave way to passions that soon ruined him."[35]

Even though these opinions may have been colored by personal feelings and Swiggart may have just been repeating idle camp gossip, it is nevertheless obvious that there was no expression for Van Dorn like the surge of madness that followed Jackson's death. In the South and particularly in Virginia there was deep mourning over the death of Lee's great lieutenant, but in the West little praise attended the death of Earl Van Dorn. There were statements in his favor by the usually critical press, but the highest praise for his achievements came from military men who had known him intimately. From Spring Hill, General William H. Jackson signed a general order to his memory:

Upon the battlefield he was the personification of courage and chivalry. No knight of the olden times ever advanced to the contest more eagerly, and after the fury of the conflict had passed away none was ever more generous and human to the sufferers than he. As a commander he was warmly beloved and highly respected; as a gentleman his social qualities were of the rarest order. . . . His deeds have rendered his name worthy to be enrolled by the side of the proudest in the Capitol of the Confederacy, and long will be sacredly and proudly cherished in the hearts of his command.[36]

After lying in state in Columbia, Tennessee, Van Dorn's body was removed to Mount Vernon, Alabama, to the home of his father-in-law, Colonel Godbold, where the last rites were performed. The family buried the general on the Godbold estate since the Van Dorn burial grounds at Port Gibson were then within enemy lines. Thirty-six years

35. Unpublished Memoirs of General St. John R. Liddell, p. 146.
36. General Orders Number 3 of Headquarters, First Cavalry Corps, Spring Hill, Tennessee, May 7, 1863, recorded in Mobile *Advertiser and Register,* May 8, 1863.

later his body was removed to the city cemetery in Port Gibson, where it now lies, marked by a simple stone with only the words "Earl Van Dorn" written thereon.

Caroline Van Dorn evidently grieved over her husband's death for the rest of her days. She never remarried and lived the rest of her short and sheltered life in the seclusion of her father's home. In 1865 when an army unit camped near the Godbold residence—a plain, white, two-story frame house—one of the soldiers wrote that Mrs. Van Dorn "was living in the quiet lonely region, retired from the world with no companion save her mother."[37]

Though the haze of self-induced tragedy hangs over the murder of the Confederate commander from Mississippi, several achievements of importance stand out in his action-filled, if not spectacular, career. The Comte de Paris said that at one time Van Dorn was the only general of mounted infantry in the South.[38] Though this is an exaggeration, the officer's success with this type of combat unit is noteworthy. His success with large infantry commands was limited, and he was often accused of inability in handling commands commensurate with his rank. But no one knew as well as he, Forrest, and Philip Sheridan how to maneuver the complex and difficult instrument of mounted infantry. Had it not been for his assassination, he might possibly have further improved his position in the military history of his country for just prior to his death he had finally been given commands that befitted his leadership capabilities—small, mounted infantry units. His early death possibly prevented his sharing in Tennessee the brilliant reputation of his one-time subordinate, General Forrest, who succeeded him in command. Van Dorn possessed many of Forest's attributes, and he also had the advantages of a sound military education and a background of professional military experience. He did not, however, possess Forrest's understanding of men, nor did he have that sound military intuition that carried Forrest to such heights.

Attention has also been called to Van Dorn for his program of secrecy in handling military information and for his censorship of the press. James G. Randall has written that the Civil War was noted as "a period of remarkably keen journalistic enterprise coincided with a . . . laxity

37. Charles B. Johnson, *Muskets and Medicine*, p. 227.
38. Comte de Paris, *History of the Civil War in America*, I, 252.

in the matter of press control."[39] Modern warfare has proved that if certain safeguards are not used against newspapers, there is a serious weakening of military effectiveness. Van Dorn, realizing this fact as early as March 1862, became one of the first of the military commanders of his day to shackle the press for the good of the troops, or at least what he considered their good, but his doing so was often criticized by the newspapers. Much of the criticism directed toward him by the Vicksburg, Jackson, Mobile, and Atlanta papers in other matters can probably be associated with their resentment of his enforced martial law, which greatly restricted their journalistic activities in the war theaters.

One of the most neglected achievements of Earl Van Dorn was his successful defense of Vicksburg in the summer of 1862. An attack and lengthy bombardment of the city by the Federal naval vessels and several invasion attempts of more than 3000 Northern troops that accompanied the navy on transports failed to capture the city. Van Dorn certainly rates some of the credit for this successful defense because of his diligent service as the city's commander and for the defensive patterns he helped to employ.

On the other hand, there is also much to criticize in a general who often made mistakes that led to hardships and disaster for his troops. Although trained in the Indian wars of the frontier where scouting was of the essence, he neglected this important phase of military activity. Had there been better reconnoitering at Elkhorn, Corinth, and Thompson's Station, the results of these battles might well have helped swing the balance of unsuccessful campaigns. At Corinth he made the mistake of depending upon outdated information. He considered the fortifications at that town as they had been when he had helped construct them earlier that year, and he made little allowance for Federal innovations. A thorough reconnaissance and consultation with his staff officers might well have discouraged the sanguinary frontal attacks that he used in a vain attempt to break these defenses. His reckless handling of his men at this battle can hardly be defended. His regard for their safety seemed to be lost in his lust for victory. Corinth alone cost Van Dorn the glory for which he so diligently sought and placed him in this category of commanders like Ambrose Burnside who

39. "The Newspaper Problem in its Bearing upon Military Secrecy during the Civil War," *American Historical Review*, XXIII, p. 303.

frantically sacrificed men in futile efforts to rectify personal errors of judgment.

Clement Sulivane, his nephew and one of his staff officers, said that his uncle was "a born child of War"—Earl Van Dorn *was* almost child-like in his enthusiasm for battle. Tactics and strategy he left to others if he could lead his forces against the enemy. From West Point days, he spent the years from 1838 to 1863 in military uniform. His happiest moments were those when he could straddle a fine cavalry mount and dash with his troops into the thick of a raging battle, be his foe Mexican, Indian, or Yankee.

Van Dorn was an attractive officer—both to the ladies and to his fellow officers. His voice could be soft and gentle in song or speech, but in battle it grew deep and harsh as he entered the melee. He was an omnivorous reader and was thoroughly familiar with the classics as well as the literature of his own times. Quotations from famous works are often found in his personal letters. One of his female admirers described him as "an inimitable raconteur, with an inexhaustible fund of apropos quotations."[40] Friends said that he was a delightful fireside and table companion, and they welcomed him into social gatherings in both community and camp.

Among his own troops there was mixed feeling about the general. Generals Sterling Price, Fitzhugh Lee, and Dabney Maury recorded praise of his leadership. Generals Albert Pike, John S. Bowen, John C. Breckinridge, and T. H. Holmes were his critics. But it was from among the enlisted men that the sharpest attacks came. Even today one man still recalls his grandfather's account of the troops in his command cheering when informed of Van Dorn's death. The incomparable Watson called Van Dorn a "careless fellow . . . a good poker player . . . not fit to enter a ten-acre field with [General James] McIntosh."[41] Sergeant Edwin Fay suggested that the Confederate soldiers were "disgracefully treated" by being subjected to commanders like Van Dorn.[42]

Who then was Earl Van Dorn? A symbol of a now long-dead South, a South that may never have existed, he well represented the glorious traditions of militancy and chivalry that have so often characterized

40. *A Soldier's Honor*, p. 270.
41. Watson, *Life*, p. 281.
42. Wiley, *"The Infernal War,"* p. 184.

that region. He was of her aristocracy, an aristocracy which, when shaken free of Jeffersonian liberalism, followed Calhoun, Yancey, and Davis to states' rights and secession. Always Van Dorn was a Southerner in this tradition. His great courage, his flowery rhetoric, his flamboyant zeal for action, his dramatic presentations of even the most obscure incidents, his passionate belief in the rightness of "the cause"— these and other traits make him more representative of the strengths and weaknesses of a section which was fighting not just for slavery and states' rights but for the survival of its way of life. Van Dorn and others like him were more numerous and more influential in the long run on the course of the South's destiny in the war than many others whose names recall fonder hopes. Their failures, their weaknesses, their inconsistencies, their excesses were traditional in the Confederacy; these limitations had to be countenanced for there were but few better leaders to replace them. When the Lees, Jacksons, Johnstons, and Forrests had been screened, there was nothing the South could do but to turn to men like Van Dorn. Then the Confederate War Department gave them important assignments because they had proved themselves on other if lesser battlefields. Even when they failed in their leadership roles, they were usually given additional trusts for they were still part of the select group.

Many of these men, like Earl Van Dorn, soon found places for themselves and served their troops capably but usually not until tragedy had stalked their footsteps as they filled roles for which they were unsuited. Men like Van Dorn, Braxton Bragg, John Hood, Leonidas Polk, and A. P. Hill, to name only a few, represent more consistently the strengths and weaknesses of an archaic region and in many ways are more symbolic of its leadership than more popular and brilliant commanders such as Lee, Jackson, and Joe Johnston.

As with many of the other Confederate leaders personal glory seemed to be Van Dorn's great motivating force, and his interests in family, home, and friends were usually subordinated to this one great passion. Eternally adolescent in his search for fame and honor, he was highly pleased when glory came his way—when a wandering Frenchman composed a hymn to his achievements, or a poet dedicated a poem to him with respect and admiration, or admiring Mississippians presented him with a sword, or the North placed a high reward on his head. These were the things that counted for so much to him and to many like him in both the Southern and the Northern armies during those dismal days of 1861 to 1865. The cost for such leadership was often heavy in human sacrifice as are the costs of war. War itself is irrational, and irrational men too often dominate its day-to-day proceedings. Earl Van Dorn was one such irrational being, one who tried to lead to a victory he probably never would have completely understood. Certainly he is enshrined in the history of this bloody war only because of the greatness of the conflict.

Afterword
to the Paperback Edition

A S historian James Robertson wrote in his review of the original edition of this book, "Van Dorn will forever remain an enigma." Upon completing the research for this study a century after the war's end, I had come to the same conclusion. Now nearly thirty years later, I have not changed my view. So much about Van Dorn's life and death remains the subject of controversy. Was his murder an assassination, or was it the result of a personal vendetta? Was the general the rake depicted by so many, or was he the victim of a press offended by his highhanded methods? Did he neglect his wife for the company of other women, and was such behavior responsible for bringing him down? Was his wife the cause for their peculiar relationship? Even the gun that killed the general remains part of the mystery: some claim that in 1963 the murder weapon was found in a closet of the Martin Cheairs home, others that the pistol disappeared with Van Dorn's murderer, Dr. George Peters. And what of his leadership of the Second Cavalry against frontier Indians? Muddled by two conflicting governmental orders, Van Dorn's attack on a village including women and children draws the type of censure later more widely accorded Wounded Knee.

This book helped initiate new studies of a largely neglected theater of operations. In the years since its first publication, other books, representing a variety of scholarly perspectives, have carefully examined the war in the West. High on this list are the two volumes by the late Thomas Connelly, *Army of the Heartland: The Army of Tennessee, 1861–1863* (Louisiana State Univ. Press, 1967) and *Autumn of Glory: The Army of Tennessee, 1862–1865* (Louisiana State Univ. Press, 1971), worthy companions of the many good studies of the Eastern Theater. Connelly contends that Van Dorn was particularly ineffective in the last two months before his death because of having received no specific orders as to his duties.

Grady McWhiney's *Braxton Bragg and Confederate Defeat*, vol. 1 (Univ. of Alabama Press, 1991) explores the life and career of one of Van

Dorn's commanders in the Army of Tennessee. According to McWhiney, Bragg was especially critical of Van Dorn. During his campaigns against Grant, he wrote that he was "dissatisfied with many of his subordinates" and none more so than Van Dorn. After Van Dorn held General Breckinridge in Mississippi much to Bragg's consternation, Bragg wrote critically to President Davis: "I regret to add, that there has been a want of cordial cooperation on the part of General Van Dorn since his department was merged in mine. The general is most true to our cause and gallant to a fault, but he is self-willed, rather weak minded & totally deficient in organization and system. He never knows the state of his command, and wields it only in fragments." This seems to confirm other evaluations of Van Dorn, but it also raises doubts about Bragg's own limitations as a leader of the Army of Tennessee. According to McWhiney, Bragg never made it clear to Price and Van Dorn just what their specific assignments were.

Albert Castel has written a fine biography of Sterling Price, Van Dorn's fellow commander at the disasters at Pea Ridge and Corinth (*General Sterling Price and the Civil War in the West* [Louisiana State Univ. Press, 1968]). Castel provides a good account of these battles, especially developing the relationship between the two commanders somewhat to Van Dorn's advantage.

Craig L. Symonds, in his excellent biography *Joseph E. Johnston: A Civil War Biography* (Norton, 1992) is not centrally concerned with Van Dorn, but his book and Byron Farwell's *Stonewall: A Biography of General Thomas J. Jackson* (Norton, 1992) are excellent models for the military biographer who wishes to include criticisms as well as praise.

In *Under Two Flags: The American Navy in the Civil War* (Norton, 1990; Avon, 1991), William M. Fowler, Jr., adds some observations to the *Arkansas* incident, as does Tom Z. Parrish in *The Saga of the Confederate Ram* Arkansas (Hill College Press, 1987). Parrish is particularly critical of Van Dorn in his handling of the ironclad in its forays around Vicksburg, saying that more trained personnel were needed for the tasks Van Dorn assigned to the vessel's commander. Raw courage was not enough, writes Parrish, who places the blame on Van Dorn for the loss of the vessel. In Van Dorn's defense, it did seem that the enemy was indeed threatening and that some immediate response was imperative. After all, the *Arkansas* had been inactive for several months, and Van Dorn "expected her actions would make up" for lost time.

Van Dorn's cavalry operations appear in Northern perspective among the eighteen volumes of *The Papers of Ulysses S. Grant, 1822–1885* (Southern Illinois Univ. Press, 1967–) in which Grant confirms the fact that the raid brought great discomfort to him and delayed his advance southward.

John W. Rowell uses Northern general Thomas Jefferson Jordan's account of Van Dorn's death in *Yankee Cavalrymen: Through the Civil War with the Ninth Pennsylvania Cavalry* (Univ. of Tennessee Press, 1975) to show what he considered to be the Northern contempt for the Mississippian: "Thus perished General Earl Van Dorn, a graduate of West Point, before the war a major in the old Second Cavalry, who deserted his regiment, took office in the Confederate army, and died the death due to a rebel to the flag of the country that had educated him and given him position, a serpent in a virtuous family, and a profligate who knew not what it was to have an honorable sentiment or exalted feeling. With all his talents, he groveled in the slime of licentiousness and met the fate due to his crimes."

To understand Van Dorn fully, it still seems necessary to consider closely his Southern heritage. Bertram Wyatt-Brown, in *Southern Honor: Ethics and Behavior in the Old South* (Oxford Univ. Press, 1982), offers some help in this search for understanding Van Dorn's deficiencies. In a society nurtured by the duel, the feud, and the militant slave system, honor was of the greatest importance, and Van Dorn put honor and glory before all else. Beyond that, however, war seemed to him to be "ennobling," the fulfillment of life.

The real Van Dorn appears, somewhat poignantly, in his own report of the battle of Corinth: "In my zeal for my country I may have ventured too far without adequate means. . . . Yet I feel that if the spirits of the gallant dead, who now lie beneath the batteries of Corinth, see and judge the motives of men, they do not rebuke me, for there is no sting in my conscience, nor does retrospection admonish me of error or of a reckless disregard of their valued lives." Nevertheless, the enigma and the controversy remain.

To the gallant but rash soldier, it was the Cause that counted. But like brave Colonel William P. Rogers, Van Dorn was sometimes foolish in seeking conclusions with gallantry as his chief weapon and was too often caught up in his own desires for glory. Ultimately, these are the character traits that color posterity's judgment of Earl Van Dorn.

R. H.
December 1993

Bibliography

A Soldier's Honor: With Reminiscences of Major-General Earl Van Dorn. By his comrades. New York: Abbey Press, 1902.

Abel, Annie H. *The American Indian as Participant in the Civil War.* Cleveland: The Arthur H. Clark Company, 1919.

———. *The American Indian as Slaveholder and Secessionist.* Cleveland: The Arthur H. Clark Company, 1915.

Alderson, William T. (ed.). "The Civil War Reminiscences of John Johnson, 1861–1865," *Tennessee Historical Quarterly,* XIII (June 1954), 156–178.

Alexander, E. P. *Military Memoirs of a Confederate.* New York, Charles Scribner's Sons, 1907.

Anderson, Robert. *An Artillery Officer in the Mexican War 1846–47.* New York: G. P. Putnam's Sons, 1911.

Arkansas *Gazette* (Little Rock), 1887.

Badeau, Adam. *Military History of Ulysses S. Grant.* 3 vols. New York: D. Appleton and Company, 1881.

Bancroft, Hubert H. *History of Mexico.* San Francisco: A. L. Bancroft and Company, 1883–1888.

[Lucius W. Barber]. *Army Memoirs of Lucius W. Barber.* Chicago: J. M. W. Jones Stationery and Printing Company, 1894.

Barrett, Arrie. "Western Frontier Forts of Texas 1845–1861," *West Texas Historical Association Yearbook,* VII (June 1931), 115–140.

Barron, Samuel B. *The Lone Star Defenders; a chronicle of the Third Texas Cavalry, Ross' brigade.* New York and Washington: The Neale Publishing Company, 1908.

Barry, Louise. "With the First U.S. Cavalry in Indian Country, 1859–1861," *Kansas Historical Quarterly,* XXIV (Autumn 1958), 257–285.

Basso, Hamilton. *Beauregard the Great Creole.* New York: Charles Scribner's Sons, 1933.

Baumer, William H., Jr. *West Point: Moulder of Men.* New York: D. Appleton-Century Company, 1942.

Baxter, William. *Pea Ridge and Prairie Grove*. Cincinnati: Poe and Hitchcock, 1864.

Baylies, Francis. *A Narrative of Major General Wool's Campaign in Mexico*. Albany, New York: Little and Company, 1851.

Bearss, Edwin C. "The Battle of Pea Ridge," *Arkansas Historical Quarterly*, XX (Spring 1961), 74–95.

———. "The First Day at Pea Ridge, March 7, 1862," *Arkansas Historical Quarterly*, XVII (Summer 1958), 134–154.

Bejach, Wilena Roberts. "Civil War Letters of a Mother and Son," *West Tennessee Historical Society Papers*, IV (1950), 50–72.

Bettersworth, John K. (ed.). *Mississippi in the Confederacy as They Saw It*. Baton Rouge: Louisiana State University Press, 1961.

Billenstein, J. T. "Journalized Cruise of the U.S. Sloop of War 'Brooklyn,' " in John K. Bettersworth (ed.). *Mississippi in the Confederacy as They Saw It*. Baton Rouge: Louisiana State University Press, 1961.

Bishop, Albert W. *Loyalty on the Frontier: or Sketches of Union Men of the South-West*. St. Louis: R. P. Studley and Company Printers, 1863.

Blackford, William W. *War Years with Jeb Stuart*. New York: Charles Scribner's Sons, 1945.

Blodgett, Edward A. "The Army of the Southwest and The Battle of Pea Ridge," in *Military Essays and Recollections*, by the Committee of the Illinois Commandry, Chicago: McClurg and Company, 1894, pp. 289–313.

Brackett, Albert G. *History of the United States Cavalry*. New York: Harper and Brothers, 1865.

Brackett, William S. "Fitzhugh Lee and Bumble Bee," *Journal of the U.S. Cavalry*, XII (June 1899), 215.

Britton, Wiley. *The Civil War on the Border*. 2 vols. New York: G. P. Putnam's Sons, 1891–1904.

———. *The Union Indian Brigade in the Civil War*. Kansas City, Missouri: Franklin Hudson Publishing Company, 1922.

Brown, A. F. "Van Dorn's Operations in Northern Mississippi—Recollections of a Cavalryman," *Southern Historical Society Papers*, V (October, 1878), 151–161.

Brown, Walter L. Life of Albert Pike. Austin: Unpublished Ph.D. Dissertation, University of Texas, 1955.

———. "Pea Ridge: Gettysburg of the West," *Arkansas Historical Quarterly*, XV (Spring 1956).

Burton, Harley T. "A History of the JA Ranch," *Southwestern Historical Quarterly*, XXXI (October 1927), 89–116.

Cadwallader, Sylvanus. *Three Years with Grant, As Recalled by War Correspondent Sylvanus Cadwallader*. Edited and with an Introduction and Notes by Benjamin P. Thomas. New York: Alfred A. Knopf, 1955.

Caffery, Edward, to John R. Peacock, June 7 and July 9, 1954. Photostats in the possession of the author.

Calkin, Homer L. "Elk Horn to Vicksburg," *Civil War History*, II (March 1956), 7–44.

Catton, Bruce. *Grant Moves South*. Boston: Little, Brown and Company, 1960.

Chattanooga *Rebel*, 1863.

Chesnut, Mary B. *A Diary from Dixie*. Boston: Houghton-Mifflin Company, 1949.

Clark, Fannie M. "A Chapter in the History of Young Territory," *Texas Historical Quarterly*, XI (July 1905), 51–65.

Clayton, W. Woodford. *History of Davidson County, Tennessee*. Philadelphia: J. W. Lewis and Company, 1880.

Cleaves, Freeman. *Rock of Chickamauga*. Norman: University of Oklahoma Press, 1948.

Cockrell, Monroe F. (ed.). *The Lost Account of the Battle of Corinth and the Court Martial of Gen. Van Dorn*. Jackson, Tennessee: McCowat-Mercer Press, 1955.

Coleman, S. B. "A July Morning with the Rebel Ram 'Arkansas,' " *War Paper Number 16* of the Military Order of the Loyal Legion of the United States. Detroit: The Michigan Commandery, 1890.

"Colonel Celsus Price on the Relations between Generals Van Dorn and Price." An unsigned paper in the Van Dorn Collection, Alabama State Department of Archives and History, Montgomery, Alabama.

Comte de Paris. *History of the Civil War in America*. 4 vols. Philadelphia: Porter and Coats, 1875.

Coppée, Henry. *Grant and His Comrades*. New York: Charles B. Richardson, 1866.

Correspondence of William M. Johnson. Original letters in private hands. Photostat copies in the files of the author.

Coulter, E. Merton. *The Confederate States of America, 1861–1865*. Vol. VII of *A History of the South*. Baton Rouge: Louisiana State University Press, 1950.

Crane, John, and James F. Kieley. *West Point: "The Key to America"*. New York: McGraw-Hill, 1947.

Crane, R. C. "Robert E. Lee's Expedition in Upper Brazos and Colorado Country," *West Texas Historical Association Yearbook*, XIII (October 1937), 53–64.

Crimmins, Colonel M. L. "Camp Cooper and Fort Griffin, Texas," *West Texas Historical Association Yearbook*, XVII (October 1941), 32–44.

———. "First Sergeant John W. Spangler, Co. H., Second United States Cavalry," *West Texas Historical Association Yearbook*, XXVI (October 1950), 68–76.

———. " 'Jack' Hayes Story of Fitzhugh Lee's Indian Fight," *West Texas Historical Association Yearbook*, XIII (October 1937), 40–49.

———. "Major Earl Van Dorn in Texas," *West Texas Historical Association Yearbook*, XVI (October 1940), 121–130.

——. "Robert E. Lee in Texas: Letters and Diaries," *West Texas Historical Association Yearbook*, VIII (June 1932), 3–25.

——. "The Military History of Camp Colorado," *West Texas Historical Association Yearbook*, XXVIII (October 1952) 71–81.

Cullum, George W. *Biographical Register of the Officers and Graduates of the United States Military Academy from 1802 to 1867*. 2 vols. and supplement. New York: James Miller, 1879.

Davis, Jefferson. *The Rise and Fall of the Confederate Government*. 2 vols. New York: D. Appleton and Company, 1881.

Davis, Louise. "Last Supper Setting," Nashville *Tennessean Magazine*, November 27, 1949, pp. 6–7.

Dawson, Sarah Morgan. *A Confederate Girl's Diary*. New York: Houghton-Mifflin Company, 1913.

De Bow's Review, Vol. II, After the War Series (August 1866), 189–201.

DeLeon, T. C. *Four Years in Rebel Capitals*. Mobile: The Gossip Publishing Company, 1890.

Deupree, J. G. "The Capture of Holly Springs, Mississippi, December 20, 1862," *Publications of the Mississippi Historical Society*, IV (1901), 49–61.

Dietzler, John P. "Major General Samuel Ryan Curtis, City Engineer," *Missouri Historical Review*, LI (July 1957), 354–362.

Dillon, Edward. "General Van Dorn's Operations between Columbia and Nashville in 1863," *Southern Historical Society Papers*, XIX (January 1891), 198–201.

Dodd, William E. *Jefferson Davis*. Philadelphia: G. W. Jacobs and Company, 1907.

Donald, David. *Lincoln Reconsidered*. New York: Alfred A. Knopf, 1956.

——. (ed.). *Why the North Won the Civil War*. Baton Rouge: Louisiana State University Press, 1960.

Dorsey, Sarah A. *Recollections of Henry Watkins Allen*. New York: M. Doolady, 1866.

Doubleday, Rhoda Tanner. (ed.). *Journals of the Late Brevet Major Philip Norbourne Barbour and his Wife Martha Isabella Hopkins Barbour*. New York: G. P. Putnam's Sons, 1936.

Duncan, Robert L. *Reluctant General*. New York: Duttons, 1961.

Dupuy, Colonel R. Ernest. *The Story of West Point*. Washington: The Infantry Journal, 1943.

—— and Trevor N. Dupuy. *Military Heritage of America*. New York: McGraw-Hill, 1956.

"Earl Van Dorn," *Encyclopedia of Mississippi History*. Dunbar Rowland, editor. 2 vols. Madison, Wisconsin: S. A. Brant, 1907.

Early, Jubal A. *Autobiographical Sketch and Narrative of the War Between the States*. Philadelphia: J. B. Lippincott Company, 1912.

Eaton, Clement. *A History of the Southern Confederacy*. New York: The Macmillan Company, 1954.

Eckenrode, Hamilton J. *Jefferson Davis: President of the South.* New York: The Macmillan Company, 1923.

Eliot, Ellsworth, Jr. *West Point in the Confederacy.* New York: G. A. Baker and Company, 1941.

Eno, Clara B. *History of Crawford County, Arkansas.* Van Buren, Arkansas: The Press-Argus, 1951.

Estep, Raymond, "William E. Burnett: Removal of Indians from Texas," *Chronicles of Oklahoma,* XXXVIII (Autumn 1960), 15–41.

Evans, Clement A. (ed.). *Confederate Military History.* 12 vols. Atlanta: Confederate Publishing Company, 1899.

Fayetteville *Observer* (Tennessee), 1862–1863.

Fiske, John. *The Mississippi Valley in the Civil War.* Boston: Houghton, Mifflin and Company, 1900.

Fitch, John. *Annals of the Army of the Cumberland.* Philadelphia: J. B. Lippincott and Company, 1864.

Fitzhugh, Lester V. "Saluria, Fort Esperanza, and Military Operations on the Texas Coast, 1861–64," *Southwestern Historical Quarterly,* LXI (July 1957), 66–101.

Florida *Sentinel* (Tallahassee), 1863.

Force, M. F. *From Fort Henry to Corinth.* Vol. II of *Campaigns of the Civil War.* 10 vols. New York: Charles Scribner's Sons, 1881.

Ford, Harvey S. "Van Dorn and the Pea Ridge Campaign," *Journal of the American Military Institute,* III (Winter 1939), 220–235.

Foreman, Grant. *Advancing the Frontier 1830–1860.* Norman: University of Oklahoma Press, 1933.

———. "Early Trails through Oklahoma," *Chronicles of Oklahoma,* III (June 1925), 99–119.

———. "Historical Background of the Kiowa-Comanche Reservations," *Chronicles of Oklahoma,* XIX (June 1941), 129–141.

———. (ed.). "Survey of a Wagon Road from Fort Smith to the Colorado River," *Chronicles of Oklahoma,* XII (March 1934), 74–79.

"Fort Belknap, Indian Reservation," (by a correspondent of the Gazette) *West Texas Historical Association Yearbook,* I (June 1925), 78.

Freeman, Douglas S. *Lee's Lieutenants.* 3 vols. New York: Charles Scribner's Sons, 1944–1945.

———. *R. E. Lee.* 4 vols. New York: Charles Scribner's Sons, 1935.

Furber, George C. *The Twelve Months Volunteer.* Cincinnati: J. A. and U. P. James, 1850.

Gage, Larry J. "The Texas Road to Secession and War," *Southwest Historical Quarterly,* LXII (October 1958), 191–227.

Galveston *News* (Texas), 1861.

Gammage, W. L. *The Camp, the Bivouac and the Battle Field.* Little Rock: Arkansas Southern Press, 1958.

Ganoe, William A. *The History of the United States Army.* New York: D. Appleton-Century Company, 1942.

"General Harney," *Journal of the United States Cavalry Association,* III (March 1890), 1–9.

Gorden, James. "Battle of Corinth and Subsequent Retreat," *Publications of the Mississippi Historical Society,* IV (1907), 63–73.

Gosnell, Harpur A. *Guns of the Western Waters.* Baton Rouge: Louisiana State University Press, 1949.

Govan, Gilbert E., and James W. Livingood. *A Different Valor.* New York: Bobbs-Merrill, 1956.

Grant, Ben O. "Explorers and Early Settlers of Shackelford County," *West Texas Historical Association Yearbook,* XI (November 1935), 17–38.

Grant, Ulysses S. *Personal Memoirs of U. S. Grant.* Edited by E. B. Long. New York: World Publishing Company, 1952.

"Grasshoppers and Indian Raids," *West Texas Historical Association Yearbook,* I (June 1925).

Greene, Francis V. *The Mississippi.* Vol. VIII of *Campaigns of the Civil War.* 10 vols. New York: Charles Scribner's Sons, 1881.

Hanson, G. A. *Minor Incidents of the Late War.* Bartow, Florida: Sessions, Baker and Kilpatrick, 1887.

Harrison, Mrs. Burton. *Recollections Grave and Gay.* New York: Charles Scribner's Sons, 1912.

Hartje, Robert. "A Confederate Dilemma Across the Mississippi," *Arkansas Historical Quarterly,* XVII (Summer 1958), 110–131.

———. "The Gray Dragoon Wins His Final Victory," *Tennessee Historical Quarterly,* XXIII (March 1964), 38–59.

Hawkins, H. G. "History of Port Gibson, Mississippi," *Publications of the Mississippi Historical Society,* X (1909), 279–301.

Hay, Thomas R. "Confederate Leadership at Vicksburg," *Mississippi Valley Historical Review,* XI (1924–1925), 543–560.

Henry, Robert Selph. *"First with the Most" Forrest.* New York: Bobbs-Merrill, 1944.

———. *The Story of the Mexican War.* Indianapolis: Bobbs-Merrill, 1950; New York: F. Ungar Publishing Company, 1961.

Hoffman, Wickham. *Camp, Court and Siege.* New York: Harper and Brothers, 1877.

Holden, W. C. "Frontier Defense in Texas During the Civil War," *West Texas Historical Association Yearbook,* IV (June 1928), 16–31.

Honeyman, A. Van Doren. *The Van Doorn Family in Holland and America, 1088–1908.* Plainfield, New Jersey: Honeyman's Publishing House, 1909.

Hood, John B. *Advance and Retreat: Personal Experiences in the United States and Confederate State Armies.* New Orleans: G. T. Beauregard, 1880.

Horn, Stanley F. *The Army of Tennessee.* New York: Bobbs-Merrill Company, 1941.

House Executive Document No. 5, 31st Congress, 1st Session. Vol I. Washington, D.C.: Government Printing Office (Serial 569), 1852.

House Executive Document No. 5, 31st Congress, 1st Session. Vol. I, Pt. II. Washington, D.C.: Government Printing Office (Serial 570), 1852.

House Executive Document No. 2, 35th Congress, 2nd Session. Vol. II, Pt. II. Washington, D.C.: Government Printing Office (Serial 998), 1858.

House Executive Document No. 2, 35th Congress, 2nd Session. Vol. II, Pt. III. Washington, D.C.: Government Printing Office (Serial 999), 1858.

Hubbard, John M. *Notes of a Private.* Memphis: E. H. Clarke and Brother, 1909.

Hughes, W. J. *Rebellious Ranger.* Norman: University of Oklahoma Press, 1954.

Hunter, Robert (collector). *Sketches of War History 1861–1865—Papers Read Before the Ohio Commandery of the Military Order of the Loyal Legion of the United States.* Cincinnati: Robert Clark Company, 1888.

Irvine, Dallas D. "The French Discovery of Clausewitz and Napoleon," *Studies on War.* Fort Benning, Georgia: The Infantry School, 1943.

[Jackson, Oscar Lawrence.] *The Colonel's Diary: Journals Kept before and during The Civil War by The Late Colonel Oscar L. Jackson.* Sharon, Pennsylvania: (No publisher listed) 1922.

James, J. B. "Life at West Point One Hundred Years Ago," *Mississippi Valley Historical Review,* XXXI (1944–1945), 21–40.

Johnson, Charles B. *Muskets and Medicine: or Army Life in The Sixties.* Philadelphia: F. A. Davis Company, 1917.

Johnson, John. "Story of the Confederate Armored Ram *Arkansas,*" *Southern Historical Society Papers,* XXXIII (January-December 1905), 1–16.

Johnson, Richard W. *A Soldier's Reminiscences in Peace and War.* Philadelphia: J. B. Lippincott Company, 1886.

———. *Memoirs of Major General George H. Thomas.* Philadelphia: J. B. Lippincott Company, 1881.

Johnson, Robert U., and Clarence C. Buel (eds.). *Battles and Leaders of the Civil War.* 4 vols. New York: Century Company, 1884–1888.

Johnston, Joseph E. *Narrative of Military Operations Directed During the Late War Between the States.* New York: D. Appleton and Company, 1874.

Johnston, William P. *The Life of Albert Sidney Johnston.* New York: D. Appleton and Company, 1879.

Jones, Archer. *Confederate Strategy from Shiloh to Vicksburg.* Baton Rouge: Louisiana State University Press, 1961.

Jones, J. B. *A Rebel War Clerk's Diary at the Confederate States Capital.* 2 vols. Philadelphia: J. B. Lippincott Company, 1866.

Jones, Katherine M. *The Plantation South.* New York: Bobbs-Merrill Company, 1957.

Jones, Virgil C. *The Civil War at Sea.* 2 vols. New York: Holt, Rinehart and Winston, 1961.

Jones, William J. *Life and Letters of Robert Edward Lee.* New York and Washington, D.C., 1906.

Jordan, Thomas, and Roger Pryor. *The Campaigns of Lieut. General N. B. Forrest and of Forrest's Cavalry.* New York: Blelock and Company, 1868.

"Justice to Van Dorn," Washington *Post,* January 27, 1902. Copy in the Van Dorn Collection, Alabama State Department of Archives and History, Montgomery, Alabama.

Kenly, John R. *Memoirs of a Maryland Volunteer.* Philadelphia: J. B. Lippincott and Company, 1873.

Kimbrough, W. C. "The Frontier Background of Clay County," *West Texas Historical Association Yearbook,* XVIII (October 1942), 116–132.

Koch, Clara Lena. "The Federal Indian Policy in Texas, 1845–1860," *Southwestern Historical Quarterly,* XXIX (July 1925), 98–128.

Lasswell, Mary (ed.). *Rags and Hope.* New York: (No publisher listed), 1961.

Lauterbach, Albert T. "The German Idea of Military Society," *Studies on War.* Fort Benning, Georgia: The Infantry School, 1943.

Lawton, Eba Anderson (compiler). *An Artillery Officer in the Mexican War.* New York: G. P. Putnam's Sons, 1911.

Lebold, Foreman M. Manuscript Collection. Chicago, Illinois.

Lee, Fitzhugh. *General Lee.* New York: D. Appleton and Company, 1894.

Lemke, W. J. "The Paths of Glory," *Arkansas Historical Quarterly,* XV (Winter 1956), 344–360.

Lewis, Lloyd. *Captain Sam Grant.* Boston: Little, Brown and Company, 1950.

———. *Sherman: Fighting Prophet.* New York: Harcourt, Brace and Company, 1932.

Liddell, General St. John R. Unpublished Memoirs (1866), with a biographical sketch by Francis D. Richardson (1887). In the possession of N. C. Hughes, Jr.

Liddell, St. John R. "Liddell's Record of the Civil War," *Southern Bivouac,* I, NS (December 1885), 411–420; (February 1886), 529–535.

Little Rock *True Democrat* (Arkansas), 1861–1862.

Livermore, Thomas L. *Numbers and Losses in the Civil War in America 1861–65.* New York: Houghton, Mifflin and Company, 1900.

Livermore, William R. "The Vicksburg Campaign," in *Papers of the Military Historical Society of Massachusetts,* IX. Boston: The Military Historical Society of Massachusetts, Cadet Armory, Ferdinand Street, 1912, pp. 541–571.

Long, Armistead L. *Memoirs of Robert E. Lee.* New York: J. M. Stoddart and Company, 1886.

Longstreet, James. *From Manassas to Appomattox.* Philadelphia: J. B. Lippincott Company, 1896.

Loon, Ella. *Foreigners in the Confederacy.* Chapel Hill: University of North Carolina Press, 1940.

Lord, Walter (ed.). *The Fremantle Diary.* Boston: Little, Brown and Company, 1954.

Lossing, Benson J. *Pictorial History of the Civil War.* 3 vols. Philadelphia: David McKay, 1866.

Luvaas, Jay. *The Military Legacy of the Civil War.* Chicago: University of Chicago Press, 1959.

Lytle, Andrew N. *Bedford Forrest and His Critter Company.* New York: Minton, Balch and Company, 1931.

MacArtney, Charles E. *Highways and Byways of the Civil War.* New York: Dorrance and Company, 1926.

McCall, George A. *Letters from the Frontiers.* Philadelphia: Lippincott and Company, 1886.

McElroy, John. *The Struggle for Missouri.* Washington, D.C.: The National Tribune Company, 1909.

McWhiney, Grady. "Controversy in Kentucky: Braxton Bragg's Campaign of 1862," *Civil War History,* VI (March 1960), 5–43.

Mahan, Dennis H. *A Treatise on Field Fortifications.* New York: J. Wiley, 1836.

Mason, Mrs. Carrington. "Raid on Holly Springs," Memphis *Commercial Appeal,* May 30, 1901.

Mathes, J. H. "Battles in Trans-Mississippi Department," *Confederate Veteran,* II (February 1894), 79.

———. *General Forrest.* New York: O. Appleton and Company, 1902.

Matthews, W. M. "Dr. George Boddie Peters," Bolivar (Tennessee) *Bulletin and Hardeman County Times,* October 27, 1949.

Maury, Dabney H. *Recollections of a Virginian in the Mexican, Indian, and Civil Wars.* New York: Charles Scribner's Sons, 1894.

———. "Recollections of Campaigns against Grant in North Mississippi in 1862-63," *Southern Historical Society Papers,* XIII (1885), 285–311.

———. "Recollections of the Elkhorn Campaign," *Southern Historical Society Papers,* II (September 1876), 180–192.

———. "Recollections of General Earl Van Dorn," *Southern Historical Society Papers,* XIX (January 1891), 191–198.

———. "Van Dorn, the Hero of Mississippi," in *Annals of the War,* written by leading participants. Philadelphia: Times Publishing Company, 1879.

Meade, George G. *The Life and Letters of G. G. Meade.* 2 vols. New York: Scribner's, 1913.

Memphis *Bulletin* (Tennessee), 1862.

Military Record of Major-General Earl Van Dorn, Adjutant-General's office, Records Section, Washington, D.C.

Millis, Walter. *Arms and Men.* New York: The New American Library, 1958.

Miscellaneous Letters, Division of Manuscripts, Duke University Library, Durham, North Carolina.

Miscellaneous Letters, Division of Manuscripts, Library of Congress, Washington, D.C.

Mississippi, A Guide to the Magnolia State. American Guide Series, Compiled and Written by the Federal Writers' Project of the WPA. New York: Hastings House, 1949.

Mobile *Advertiser and Register* [sometimes *Register and Advertiser*] (Alabama), 1861–1863.

Mobile *Daily Herald* (Alabama), 1899.

Monaghan, Jay. *Civil War on the Western Border*. Boston: Little, Brown and Company, 1955.

Montgomery *Weekly Advertiser* (Alabama), 1863.

Moody, Claire N. *Battle of Pea Ridge: or, Elkhorn Tavern*. Little Rock: Arkansas Valley Print Company, 1956.

Moore, Frank. *The Civil War in Song and Story*. New York: P. F. Collier, Publishers, 1889.

——. *The Rebellion Record*. 11 vols. and supplement. New York: D. Van Nostrand, 1867.

Morrison, William B. "Fort Arbuckle," *Chronicles of Oklahoma*, VI (March 1928), 26–35.

——. *Military Posts and Camps in Oklahoma*. Oklahoma City: Harlow Publishing Corporation, 1936.

Morton, John W. *The Artillery of Nathan Bedford Forrest's Cavalry*. Nashville: Publishing House of the Methodist Episcopal Church, South, 1909.

Myers, William S. (ed.). *The Mexican War Diary of George B. McClellan*. Princeton: Princeton University Press, 1917.

Nashville *Dispatch* (Tennessee), 1863.

Nevins, Allan. *The Emergence of Lincoln*. 2 vols. New York: Scribners 1950.

New York *Tribune*, 1861.

Noble, John W. "Battle of Pea Ridge or Elk Horn Tavern," in *Commandry of Missouri, War Papers, and Personal Reminiscences 1861-1865*. St. Louis: (No Publisher listed), 1892, pp. 211–243.

Nugent, Lientenant William L., to his wife from camp near Vicksburg, Mississippi, March 24, 1863. Typescript of this letter in possession of Lucy Somerville Howarth, Washington, D.C.

Nye, William S. "Battle of Wichita Village," *Chronicles of Oklahoma*, XV (June 1937), 226–227.

——. *Carbine and Lance*. Norman: University of Oklahoma Press, 1937.

Oates, Stephen B. *Confederate Cavalry West of the River*. Austin: University of Texas Press, 1961.

——. "Recruiting Cavalry in Texas," *Southwestern Historical Quarterly*, LXIV (April 1961), 461–477.

——. "Texas Under the Secessionists," *Southwestern Historical Quarterly*, LXVII (October 1963), 167–177.

O'Connor, Richard. *Hood: Cavalier General*. New York: Prentice-Hall, 1949.

——. *Thomas: Rock of Chickamauga*. New York: Prentice-Hall, 1948.

Official Register of the Officers and Cadets of the U.S. Military Academy at West Point, 1819-1843. New York: The United States Military Academy, 1819–1843.

O'Flaherty, Daniel. *General Jo Shelby: Undefeated Rebel.* Chapel Hill: University of North Carolina Press, 1954.

Pace, Eleanor Damon (ed.). "The Diary and Letters of William P. Rogers, 1846-1862," *Southwestern Historical Quarterly,* XXXII (April 1929), 257–300.

Papers of the Confederate States of America, Division of Manuscripts, Library of Congress, Washington, D.C.

Papers of Jefferson Davis, Division of Manuscripts, Library of Congress, Washington, D.C.

Papers of Jefferson Davis, Duke University Library, Durham, North Carolina.

Papers of Robert E. Lee, Division of Manuscripts, Library of Congress, Washington, D. C.

Parks, Joseph H. *General Edmund Kirby Smith, C.S.A.* Baton Rouge: Louisiana State University Press, 1954.

Partin, Robert. "A Confederate Sergeant's Report to His Wife during the Campaign from Tullahoma to Dalton," *Tennessee Historical Quarterly,* XII (December 1953), 291–309.

Payne, James E. "The Test of the Missourians," *Confederate Veteran,* XXXVII (February 1929), 64–65; XXXVII (March 1929), 101–103.

Pemberton, John C. *Pemberton Defender of Vicksburg.* Chapel Hill: University of North Carolina Press, 1942.

"Personne". *Marginalia or Gleanings from an Army Notebook.* Charleston: Steam Power of F. G. DeFontaine and Company, 1864.

"Peter Van Dorn," *Encyclopedia of Mississippi History.* Dunbar Rowland, editor. 2 vols. Madison, Wisconsin: S. A. Brant, 1907.

Peters, George B., v. Jessie B. Peters, in the Phillips County, Arkansas Circuit Court: Chancery Division: V. No. 88 (Chancery Court Record "I", p. 95 and "G", p. 109), May term, 1866.

Pirtle, John B. "Defense of Vicksburg in 1862—The Battle of Baton Rouge," *Southern Historical Society Papers,* VIII (January 1880), 324–332.

Platt, Donn. *General George H. Thomas.* Cincinnati: Robert Clark and Company, 1893.

Polk, William M. *Leonidas Polk: Bishop and General.* 2 vols. New York: Longmans, Green and Company, 1915.

Porter, David D. *The Naval History of the Civil War.* New York: The Sherman Publishing Company, 1889.

Posey, Mrs. Samuel. "Capture of the 'Star of the West,'" *Confederate Veteran,* XXXII (May 1924), 174.

Price, George F. *Across the Continent with the Fifth Cavalry.* New York: D. Van Nostrand, 1883.

"Proceedings of the First Confederate Congress, Second Session," in *Southern Historical Society Papers,* New Series, VII (May 1925), 225.

Radzyminski. "Charles Radsiminski," *Chronicles of Oklahoma,* XXXVIII (Winter 1960), 354–369.

Ramsey, Albert C. (trans. and ed.). *The Other Side: or Notes from the History of the War Between the United States and Mexico.* New York: Privately Printed, 1850.

Randall, James G. "The Newspaper Problem in its Bearing upon Military Secrecy During the Civil War," *American Historical Review,* XXIII (January 1918), 303–323.

Reavis, L. U. *The Life and Military Services of General William Selby Harney.* St. Louis: Bryan, Brand and Company, Publishers, 1878.

Recollections of Thomas A. Duncan: A Confederate Soldier. Nashville: McQuiddy Printing Company, 1922.

Reed, Sam Rockwell. *The Vicksburg Campaign.* Cincinnati: Robert Clark and Company, 1882.

Reid, Samuel C., Jr. *The Scouting Expeditions of McCulloch's Texas Rangers.* Austin: University of Texas Press, 1935.

Richardson, Rupert N. *The Comanche Barrier to South Plains Settlement.* Glendale, California: Arthur H. Clark Company, 1933.

———. "The Comanche Reservation in Texas," *West Texas Historical Association Yearbook,* V (June 1929), 43–65.

Richmond *Dispatch* (Virginia), 1861–1863.

Richmond *Whig* (Virginia), 1863.

Ridley, Bromfield L. *Battles and Sketches of the Army of Tennessee.* Mexico, Missouri: Missouri Printing and Publishing Company, 1906.

Ripley, Robert S. *The War with Mexico.* 2 vols. New York: Harper and Brothers, 1848.

Rister, Carl C. *Robert E. Lee in Texas.* Norman: University of Oklahoma Press, 1946.

Rives, George L. *The United States and Mexico, 1821-1848.* 2 vols. New York: Charles Scribner's Sons, 1913.

[Rizpah], "Cavalry Fights with the Comanches," *Magazine of American History,* XI (February 1884), 170–173.

Robinson, William M., Jr. *The Confederate Privateers.* New Haven: Yale University Press, 1928.

Rodenbough, Theodore F., and William L. Haskin. *The Army of the United States.* New York: Maynard, Merrill and Company, 1896.

Roland, Charles P. "Albert Sidney Johnston and the Loss of Forts Henry and Donelson," *Journal of Southern History,* XXIII (February 1957), 45–69.

———. *Albert Sidney Johnston: Soldier of Three Republics.* Austin: University of Texas Press, 1964.

——— and Richard Robbins (eds.). "The Diary of Eliza (Mrs. Albert Sidney) Johnston: The Second Cavalry Comes to Texas," *Southwest Historical Quarterly,* LX (April 1957), 463–500.

Rose, Victor M. *Ross' Texas Brigade.* Louisville: Courier-Journal, 1881.

———. *The Life and Services of General Ben McCulloch.* Philadelphia: Pictorial Bureau of the Press, 1888.

Rowland, Dunbar. *History of Mississippi: The Heart of the South.* 2 vols. Chicago: The S. J. Clarke Publishing Company, 1925.

—— (ed.). *Jefferson Davis, Constitutionalist: His Letters, Papers and Speeches.* 10 vols. New York: J. J. Little and Ives Company, 1923.

——. *The Official and Statistical Register of the State of Mississippi.* New York: J. J. Little and Company, 1928.

Schaff, Morris. *The Spirit of Old West Point, 1858-1862.* New York: Houghton Mifflin, 1909.

Schalk, Emil, *Campaigns of 1862 and 1863.* New York: J. B. Lippincott and Company, 1863.

[Sedgwick, John]. *Correspondence of John Sedgwick.* 2 vols. Printed for Carl and Ellen Battelle Stoeckel, the De Vinne Press, 1902.

Seitz, Don C. *Braxton Bragg: General of the Confederacy.* Columbia, South Carolina: The State Company, 1924.

Semmes, Raphael. *The Campaign of General Scott in the Valley of Mexico.* Cincinnati: Moore and Anderson, 1852.

Senate Document No. 388, 29th Congress, 1st Session. Washington, D.C.: Government Printing Office (Serial 477),1846.

Senate Document No. 1, 29th Congress, 2nd Session. Washington, D.C.: Government Printing Office (Serial 493), 1846.

Senate Executive Document No. 1 and Appendix, 30th Congress, 1st Session. Washington, D.C.: Government Printing Office (Serial 503), 1847.

Senate Executive Documents Number 52 and 60, 30th Congress, 1st Session. Vol. VII. Washington, D.C.: Government Printing Office (Serial 509), 1847.

Senate Executive Document No. 60, 30th Congress, 1st Session. Washington, D.C.: Government Printing Office (Serial 520), 1847.

Senate Executive Document No. 49, 31st Congress, 1st Session. Vol. XIII. Washington, D.C.: Government Printing Office (Serial 561), 1849.

Senate Executive Document No. 27, 32nd Congress, 1st Session. Vol. IV. Washington, D.C.: Government Printing Office (Serial 614), 1850.

Senate Executive Document No. 1, 34th Congress, 1st Session. Vol. II. Pt. 2. Washington, D.C.: Government Printing Office (Serial 811), 1852.

Senate Executive Document No. 5, 34th Congress, 3rd Session. Vol. IV. Washington, D.C.: Government Printing Office (Serial 877), 1852.

Senate Executive Document No. 1, 35th Congress, 1st Session, Vol. II. Washington, D.C.: Government Printing Office (Serial 920), 1856.

Senate Executive Document No. 1, 35th Congress, 2nd Session. Vol. II. Washington, D.C.: Government Printing Office (Serial 975), 1858.

Senate Executive Document No. 2, 36th Congress, 1st Session. Vol. II. Washington, D.C.: Government Printing Office (Serial 1024), 1859.

Service Jacket of General Earl Van Dorn, Collection of Confederate Records, General Services Administration, National Archives, Washington, D.C.

Service Jacket of Major General John S. Bowen, Collection of Confederate Records, General Services Administration, National Archives, Washington, D.C.

Sheppard, Eric W. *Bedford Forrest: The Confederacy's Greatest Cavalry-man.* Toronto: Longmans, Green and Company, 1930.

Sherman, William T. *Memoirs of General William T. Sherman.* 2 vols. New York: D. Appleton and Company, 1875.

Shipp, W. E. "Mounted Infantry," *Journal of the U.S. Cavalry Association,* V (March 1892), 76–81.

Shirk, George H. "Mail Call at Fort Washita," *Chronicles of Oklahoma,* XXXIII (Spring 1955), 14–36.

Singletary, Otis A. *The Mexican War.* Chicago: University of Chicago Press, 1960.

Smith, Edward C. *The Borderland in the Civil War.* New York: The Macmillan Company, 1927.

Smith, Gustavus W. *Confederate War Papers.* New York: Atlantic Publishing and Engraving Company, 1884.

Smith, Justin H. *The War with Mexico.* 2 vols. New York: The Macmillan Company, 1919.

Snead, Thomas L. *The Fight for Missouri from The Election of Lincoln to The Death of Lyon.* New York: Charles Scribner's Sons, 1886.

Snelling, Lois. "Leetown," Arkansas *Gazette Magazine,* July 9, 1861.

Sorrel, G. Moxley. *Recollections of a Confederate Staff Officer.* New York: The Neale Publishing Company, 1905.

Stanley, D. S. "The Battle of Corinth," in *Personal Recollections of the War of the Rebellion.* [Privately Printed], New York: 1897, 268–278.

Stewart, Fay L. "Battle of Pea Ridge," *Missouri Historical Review,* XXII (January 1928), 187–193.

Stillwell, Leander. *The Story of a Common Soldier.* (Place not listed): Franklin Hudson Publishing Company, 1920.

Strode, Hudson. *Jefferson Davis: Confederate President.* New York: Harcourt, Brace and Company, 1959.

Stuart, Edwin R. "The Federal Cavalry with the Armies in the West, 1861-1865," *Journal of the United States Cavalry Association,* XVII (October 1906), 195–259.

Sulivane, Clement. "The *Arkansas* at Vicksburg in 1862," *Confederate Veteran,* XXV (November 1917), 490–491.

Swiggett, Howard. *The Rebel Raiders.* Indianapolis: Bobbs-Merrill Company, 1934.

Taylor, Richard. *Destruction and Reconstruction.* Edited by Richard B. Harwell. New York: Longmans, Green and Company, 1955.

Taylor, Waltern N. (supervising ed.) and George H. Ethridge (ed. and author). *Mississippi: A History.* Jackson: Historical Records Association (no date).

Texas *State Gazette,* 1861.

The Centennial of the United States Military Academy at West Point, New York, 1802-1902. 2 vols. Washington, D.C.: Government Printing Office, 1904.

"The Operations Against Vicksburg," *Confederate Veteran*, XXV (October 1917), 442–444.
The Southern Historical Publication Society. *The South in the Building of the Nation*. 12 vols. Richmond: 1909.
Thoburn, Joseph B. "Indian Fight in Ford County in 1859," *Collections of the Kansas State Historical Society*, XII (1912), 312–329.
Thorpe, T. B. *Our Army at Monterrey*. Philadelphia: Carey and Hart, 1847.
To Mexico With Scott: Letters of Captain E. Kirby Smith to His Wife. Cambridge: Harvard University Press, 1917.
Trickett, Dean. "The Civil War in Indian Territory," *Chronicles of Oklahoma*, XIX (December 1941), 381–397.
Truesdale, John. *The Blue Coats and How They lived, Fought and Died for The Union*. Philadelphia: Jones Brothers and Company, 1867.
Truman, W. I. "The Battle of Elk Horn [sic.], or Pea Ridge, Arkansas," *Confederate Veteran*, XXXVI (May 1928), 168–171.
United States Navy Department. *The War of the Rebellion: A Compilation of the Official Records of the Union and Confederate Navies*. 30 vols. Washington, D.C.: Government Printing Office, 1894–1922.
United States War Department. *The War of the Rebellion: A Compilation of the Official Records of the Union and Confederate Armies*. 70 vols. in 218 parts and index. Washington, D.C.: Government Printing Office, 1880–1901.
Vandiver, Frank E. *Mighty Stonewall*. New York: McGraw-Hill, 1957.
———. (ed.). *The Civil War Diary of General Josiah Gorgas*. Tuscaloosa: University of Alabama Press, 1947.
Earl Van Dorn Collection, Alabama State Department of Archives and History, Montgomery, Alabama.
Earl Van Dorn Papers, Mississippi State Department of Archives and History, Jackson, Mississippi.
Vicksburg *Daily Mississippian*, 1862–1863.
Vicksburg *Whig*, 1862–1863.
von Clausewitz, Karl. *War, Politics and Power*. Chicago: Henry Regnery Company, Gateway edition, 1962.
Walker, Hugh. "The Day the Doctor Shot the General," Nashville *Tennessean Magazine*, July 14, 1863.
Walker, Peter. *Vicksburg: A People at War*. Chapel Hill: University of North Carolina Press, 1960.
Wallace, Edward S. *General William Jenkins Worth, Monterrey's Forgotten Hero*. Dallas: Southern Methodist University Press, 1953.
Washington *Post* (D.C.), 1902.
Washington *Telegraph* (Arkansas), 1862.
Watson, William. *Life in the Confederate Army*. London: Chapman and Hall, 1887.
Webb, Walter P. *The Texas Rangers*. New York: Houghton-Mifflin, 1935.
Wheeling *Daily Intelligencer* (Virginia), 1862–1863.

Wiley, Bell I. *"The Infernal War"*: *The Confederate Letters of Sgt. Edwin Fay*. Austin: University of Texas Press, 1958.

———. *The Life of Johnny Reb*. New York: Bobbs-Merrill Company, 1943.

Will of Peter A. Van Dorn, signed April 29, 1831, recorded March 1, 1837, Claiborne County Will Record, Port Gibson Court House, Port Gibson, Mississippi, Record B, p. 118.

Williams, J. W. "Military Roads of the 1850's in Central West Texas," *West Texas Historical Association Yearbook*, XVIII (October 1942), 77–92.

———. "Van Dorn Trails," *Southwestern Historical Quarterly*, XLIV (January 1941), 321–343.

Williams, Kenneth P. *Lincoln Finds a General*. 5 vols. New York: The Macmillan Company, 1949–1959.

Williams, T. Harry. *Lincoln and His Generals*. New York: Alfred A. Knopf, 1952.

———. *Military Leadership: North and South*. Harmon Memorial Lectures, Number 2, United States Air Force Academy, Colorado, 1960.

———. *P. G. T. Beauregard: Napoleon in Gray*. Baton Rouge: Louisiana State University Press, 1955.

———. "The Attack upon West Point During the Civil War," *Mississippi Valley Historical Review*, XXV (March 1939), 491–504.

——— (ed.). "The Civil War Letters of William L. Cage," *The Louisiana Historical Quarterly*, XXXIX (1956), 113–143.

———. "The Military Leadership of North and South," in *Why the North Won the Civil War*. Edited by David Donald. Baton Rouge: Louisiana State University Press, 1960.

——— (ed.). *With Beauregard in Mexico*. Baton Rouge: Louisiana State University Press, 1956.

Wingfield, Marshall, to John R. Peacock, May 24 and June 18, 1954. Dr. Wingfield furnished this information as president of the West Tennessee Historical Society. Photostats in the files of the author.

Wright, Mrs. D. Girard. *A Southern Girl in '61*. New York: Doubleday, Page and Company, 1905.

Wyeth, John A. *Life of General Nathan Bedford Forrest*. New York: Harper and Brothers, 1899.

Yearns, Wilfred B. *The Confederate Congress*. Athens: University of Georgia Press, 1960.

Young, Lieutenant L. D. *Reminiscences of a Soldier of the Orphan Brigade*. Paris, Kentucky: Privately printed by the author (no date).

Younger, Edward (ed.). *Inside the Confederate Government: The Diary of Robert Garlic Hill Kean*. New York: Oxford University Press, 1957.

Index